LANDSCAPE AND SUSTAINABILITY

This unique book is about landscape, sustainability and the practices of the professions which plan, design and manage landscapes at many scales and in many locations; urban, surburban and rural. Despite the ubiquity of 'sustainability' as a concept, this is the first book to address the relationship between landscape architecture and sustainability in a comprehensive way.

Much in the book is underpinned by landscape ecology, in contrast to the idea of landscape as only appealing to the eye or aspiring cerebrally to be fine art. As this book argues, landscape is and must be much more than this; landscape architecture is about making places which are biologically wholesome, socially just and spiritually rewarding.

The book argues that the sustainability agenda needs a new mindset among professionals. They need to stop asking first, is it affordable? Is it beautiful? Is it what the client wants? Is it art? Will my colleagues approve? And instead start asking, first and foremost, is it sustainable?

The chapters in the book move progressively from theory to practice, from the global to the local scale, and from issues of policy and planning through to detailed design and implementation and on to long-term maintenance and management. The contributors raise a complex array of research, policy and professional issues and agendas to contribute to the necessary ongoing debate about the future of both landscape and sustainability.

John Benson is Senior Lecturer and Director of Landscape Programmes at the University of Newcastle. He is Editor of the *Journal of Environmental Planning and Management*.

Maggie Roe is Lecturer in Landscape Architecture at the University of Newcastle.

LANDSCAPE AND SUSTAINABILITY

Edited by

John F. Benson and Maggie H. Roe

SPON PRESS
Taylor & Francis Group

London and New York

First published 2000
by Spon Press
11 New Fetter Lane, London EC4P 4EE

Simultaneously published in the USA and Canada
by Spon Press
29 West 35th Street, New York, NY 10001

Spon Press is an imprint of the Taylor & Francis Group

Typeset in Garamond by Florence Production Ltd,
Stoodleigh, Devon
Printed and bound in Great Britain by
St Edmundsbury Press, Bury St Edmunds, Suffolk

British Library Cataloguing in Publication Data
A catalogue record for this book is available from the British Library

Library of Congress Cataloging in Publication Data
A catalog record for this book has been requested

ISBN 0–419–25080–8

CONTENTS

PREFACE

Are you reading this in a bookshop, wondering whether to buy the book – or have you already made a purchase? Are you browsing among library shelves wondering whether it is worth investing the time and effort needed to get the most from a complex and challenging tome? Did you arrive here entirely by chance or because your lecturer or a professional colleague pointed the way? Whichever, we urge you to buy or borrow this book and explore a fascinating and stimulating subject. This is a complex book which integrates two topics – landscape and sustainability – each of which is vast and elusive, contentious and challenging, but ultimately important to you emotionally, environmentally, economically and socially. The contents are potentially 'difficult' in that they draw on a range of disciplines – including ecology, economics, philosophy – and professional areas – including land-use planning, landscape planning, design and management, horticulture, agriculture, forestry, politics and policy – which, depending on your disciplinary naïveté or illiteracy, may mean careful reading is needed in places to follow sometimes complex and challenging ideas, analyses and proposals. If your first interest is in landscape or landscape architecture, the 'territory' here will be familiar, even if the scale and scope of our conception of landscape are broader than you previously imagined, or if your previous contact with sustainability has been cursory or frustrating. If it is in sustainability from a quite different disciplinary perspective, the contents of the book will offer you new insights into a contested and some say overworked topic, and may change the way you think about what sustainability is or what it could become. If it is primarily neither of these, we still believe the subjects are in themselves important, and the treatment here accessible with effort, to be of interest to a wide range of students, academics, policy-makers and practitioners.

The advantage of a book written by a single author is that he or she has the space to produce a cogent and coherent volume with clear, integrated themes, a clear and perhaps personal message, and in a consistent style. The alternative – as here – has advantages and potential disadvantages. The potential disadvantages, or at least the dangers, are that the whole is not greater than the sum of the parts and, worse still, that the contributions are so disparate that they irritate everyone and satisfy no one. We hope and believe that this is not the case here. The advantages, however, are considerable. The span of these vast and mercurial subjects is beyond almost all but a prodigious polymath but entirely within the compass of the collective thinking of the talented commentators, thinkers, researchers and practitioners whom we persuaded to join us in this ambitious project. The reader gains, instead of perhaps 20–40 years of insight, knowledge and experience, an order of magnitude more – in this case approaching 400 years of experience.

We naturally have to thank all the contributors for their imaginative and eloquent chapters, sometimes written under considerable pressure and to tight deadlines which we imposed and, on their behalf, their colleagues, friends, partners and families for their support and tolerance. We obviously did not invite contributors whom we thought would not share our enthusiasm for the subjects but the remarkable thing is the way in which the contributions – which are often a personal view of the state of the subject and its future direction – merge, interrelate, coalesce and then separate when necessary to produce a coherent 'set'. This involved relatively little effort by us as editors to get a complex and diverse set of soloists playing from the same score. Whether we have created a symphony is for you to judge.

Caroline Mallinder and Rebecca Casey at Spon Press were enthusiasts from the start, never wavered in their support, never (or hardly ever) badgered or pressured us and saw the project through with patience and skill. Our thanks also to Emma Reynolds here in the School of Architecture, Planning and Landscape at the University of Newcastle, which remains a stimulating and enjoyable place in which to pursue an academic and professional career – teaching quality assessment, research assessment exercises, budget cuts and bureaucratic interference notwithstanding. Anne and Alistair tolerated our distraction with fortitude. In the end, the book is for Sarah, Andrew and Iona, even if they don't all realise it (yet).

John Benson and Maggie Roe
Newcastle upon Tyne
February 2000

NOTES ON CONTRIBUTORS

Helen Armstrong is an architect and has qualifications in landscape architecture. She has worked as an architect in private, local government and community practice. She is currently teaching part-time as a design tutor at the University of Greenwich and working part-time as a research student working on landscape planning for sustainable surface water management.

John F. Benson is a Chartered Biologist, a Chartered Landscape Architect (Science) and a Member of the Institute of Ecology and Environmental Management. He is currently senior lecturer and Director of Landscape Programmes at the University of Newcastle, Editor-in-Chief of the *Journal of Environmental Planning and Management* and has research interests in impact assessment, environmental economics and landscape restoration.

Helen Brown is a Chartered Landscape Architect (Design) who worked as a constructed textile designer before qualifying in landscape architecture at the University of Greenwich, where she is now an associate lecturer. She also works in private practice and her previous experience includes work with Wandsworth Borough Council in London and Medway Council in Kent.

Andy Clayden is a lecturer in the Department of Landscape at the University of Sheffield. He trained as a landscape architect after a period working in the landscape construction industry. His research interests include environmentally sustainable approaches to material selection and design detailing with particular reference to Scandinavia and Northern Europe.

Nigel Dunnett is a botanist and ecologist by training who applies ecological principles to the design and management of landscape plantings. He has published widely in both scientific, professional and popular journals and has experience of landscape research and practice in both North America and Europe. He is lecturer in the Department of Landscape at the University of Sheffield.

Michael Herrmann has worked as a landscape architect on a wide range of scales and types of projects. He now brings experience of ecological and participatory design to the fields of product, furniture and ecodesign, working with students at Leeds Metropolitan University, Goldsmiths and the Surrey Institute. His aim is to demystify sustainable design, enabling it to enter mainstream practice.

Kristina Hill was born in the Boston inner-city neighbourhood fondly known as 'Dot' and raised in Worcester, Massachusetts. She was educated in natural science and landscape architecture at Tufts and Harvard Universities. She began teaching urban design at the Massachusetts Institute of Technology and now teaches the design of ecological infrastructure at the University of Washington in Seattle.

Tony Kendle is lecturer in landscape management in the Department of Horticulture and Landscape at the University of Reading. He holds a PhD in restoration ecology from the University of Liverpool and a BSc in Horticulture from the University of Bath. He is a Member of the Institute of Ecology and Environmental Management and of the Research Sub-Committee of the Landscape Institute. His research interests include restoration of conservation value on degraded land and urban nature conservation.

Sue Kidd is a lecturer in the Department of Civic Design at the University of Liverpool and a professional town planner with a range of strategic planning experience at county and unitary authority levels. She has specialized in environmental planning and has combined her research activities with involvement in a range of practical planning commissions including the development of the Mersey Estuary Management Plan and the North West Regional Landscape Strategy. Most recently, she has been the leader of a study team advising the DETR on Integrated Coastal Planning in the North West Region.

Robert MacFarlane is a senior lecturer in GIS and Environmental Management at the University of Northumbria, Newcastle upon Tyne, where he runs the Centre for Environmental and Spatial Analysis. His current research interests are in agri-environmental policy, wilderness areas and urban landscape genesis among ethnic minority groups.

Andy Millard lectures in ecology and landscape science at Leeds Metropolitan University. After gaining a PhD at Durham University he taught in schools and adult education before taking up his current position. His research interests include urban ecology, the evaluation of urban green space and the wildlife of arable farmland.

Junko Oikawa has a BSc in Biology and an MSc and Kew Diploma in Horticulture. She is currently a research student in the Department of Horticulture and Landscape at the University of Reading, researching the application of sustainable development principles to site-based environmental education, with a focus on Botanic Gardens.

Adrian Phillips trained as a geographer and planner and has worked for UNEP in Kenya and IUCN in Geneva. He was Director General of the Countryside Commission for eleven years until 1992. He now holds a part-time chair at the University of Wales, Cardiff. Since 1994 he has been chair of IUCN's World Commission on Protected Areas (WCPA).

Colin Price graduated in forestry from Oxford University and subsequently took his doctorate in land use economics there. After brief periods of teaching urban and agricultural economics, he moved to the University of Wales Bangor, where he is now Professor of Environmental and Forestry Economics. His special interests are valuation of the environment and of the long-term future.

Maggie H. Roe is a Chartered Landscape Architect (Design) and is currently a lecturer in landscape architecture at the University of Newcastle. Her research interests have evolved from work in professional practice and study undertaken at the Graduate School of Design, Harvard University. These concentrate on sustainable landscape planning and design with a particular interest in landscape ecology, large-scale landscape planning and public participation in landscape projects.

Juliet E. Rose is a research student in the Department of Horticulture and Landscape at the University of Reading. She holds an MSc in Horticulture from Reading and a BSc in Biological Sciences from King's College London. Her areas of research address the restoration of degraded and desertified land on islands and the response to changing environments and land use capabilities.

Maisie Rowe completed an art foundation course at Chelsea School of Art and a degree in social geography before training as a landscape architect at the

University of Newcastle. She is a Chartered Landscape Architect (Design) and has worked with Groundwork Hackney for three years, sharing the lessons of that experience in a good practice guide, *Changing Estates: A Facilitator's Guide to Making Community Projects Work*.

Chris Royffe is Assistant Dean and Head of the School of Art, Architecture and Design at Leeds Metropolitan University. As an experienced landscape architect, urban designer and lecturer, he has contributed to the planning and design of a wide range of projects, with particular interests in garden art and designing with plants.

Paul Selman is Professor of Environmental Planning at Cheltenham and Gloucester College of Higher Education. With a background in environmental science and town planning, his research has focused on the sustainable development of rural land. His books include *Local Sustainability* (Paul Chapman)

and *Environmental Planning* (Sage) and he is editor of the journal *Landscape Research*.

Ian H. Thompson is a lecturer in landscape architecture in the School of Architecture, Planning and Landscape at the University of Newcastle upon Tyne. He studied philosophy before commencing his postgraduate studies in landscape architecture at Newcastle in 1977. He worked as a landscape architect, mostly for local government on Clydeside and Tyneside, for thirteen years before returning to Newcastle University as a teacher and researcher.

Tom Turner is the landscape group leader at the University of Greenwich. He is a landscape architect, a town planner and the author of books on *Landscape Planning and Environmental Design* (1998), *Cities as Landscape* (1996) and *English Garden Design Since 1650* (1986). In 1991 he wrote a report on *Towards a Green Strategy for London* for the London Advisory Committee.

FIGURES

TABLES

1

THE SCALE AND SCOPE OF LANDSCAPE AND SUSTAINABILITY

John F. Benson and Maggie H. Roe

INTRODUCTION

This book is about landscape, sustainability and the practices of the professions which plan, design and manage landscapes on many scales and in many locations, urban, suburban and rural. These professions are defined collectively in the United Kingdom, through the Royal Charter of the Landscape Institute, as 'landscape architects'. This is a broader compass than the term often implies, it often being associated only with professionals who design landscapes on relatively small scales. However, landscape planning, design and management are practised directly or indirectly by many others and in many sectors, including land use planning, agriculture, forestry, nature conservation, amenity land management, and so on, and we include all these in our approach. The term 'landscape' used here is also broad and includes much more than 'the appearance of the area of land which the eye can see at once' (Chambers, 1993). Landscape is an evolving cross-disciplinary area, which draws contributions from art, literature, ecology, geography and much more. We therefore use the term landscape in a broad and inclusive way because we believe it is the holistic and integrated focus on landscape which is the unique and distinctive feature of landscape architects, broadly defined.

Landscape architects cannot save the world (at least by themselves), but they do, we believe, regard themselves as important players or potential players in the local, regional, national and even international efforts to protect the environment, to promote sound development and to improve the quality of life for people now and in the future – commonly known as sustainable development. However, when we thought about the apparent interest in sustainability among landscape architects in the UK, at least based on published material, conferences and professional meetings, it brought to mind a famous Roman emperor, a capital city and music-making! In the 60-page report on the Landscape Institute Awards in 1997 (Landscape Design Trust, 1997), the word sustainable appears just four times and sustainable development and sustainability once each (the latter dismissively). So far as we can see, sustainability was not a criterion for judgement in any category, nor was it uttered (so far as we remember) at the awards ceremony. By 1999, the position had hardly changed (Landscape Design Trust, 1999). The word does appear once in the Royal Charter granted to the Landscape Institute in 1997 (Landscape Institute, 1997) but if you log-on to the Landscape Institute's web pages it is hard to find the word, except among the advertising puff by some professional practices. Also, in a recent review of the *Future for Landscape Research*, the academic journal of the Landscape Research Group (Burgess, 1996), the word is used but twice. More encouragingly the American Society of Landscape Architects includes commitments to the concept in their Code of Professional Practice and several policy declarations, but even then a search of two major North American-based web resources for education and practice in town planning, architecture and landscape fails to deliver any information on the search combination of '+landscape+sustainable/sustainability'. With two notable exceptions (Lyle, 1994; Thayer, 1994), there is relatively little written about sustainability or sustainable development by or for landscape architects.

In sharp contrast, the sustainability/sustainable development word-set is used so much elsewhere throughout academic, professional, political and social circles that complaints of over-use and disutility abound. A search of the world-wide web for 'sustainability' and 'sustainable' and 'sustainable development' produces almost 1 million pages using the Alta Vista search-engine, fewer than a search for 'sex' which produces more than 10 million pages, but impressive nonetheless. Searches of academic databases show a similar epidemic. However, it has become common to hear people complain that 'sustainability is meaningless' (and can therefore be ignored) or 'I wish someone would define it' (and I'll ignore it until they do) or 'not another conference (book, meeting) about sustainability'. There are arguments that 'sustainable development' (SD) is an oxymoron, like 'political science', 'business ethics', 'government organisation' and 'military intelligence' (and one of our contributors, Tom Turner, has also claimed another oxymoron in 'landscape architecture' but we'll let that pass). Kristina Hill points out in Chapter 14 that Gro Harlem Bruntland has claimed that SD was an intentional juxtaposition of two irreconcilable notions in order to bring opposing camps to the same conference table. It is therefore becoming something of a cliché to remark that sustainability is a cliché, a stereotypical, hackneyed term used to justify such a bundle of dislocated, contradictory and ill-defined notions that the term has lost all value and should be confined to the dustbin by all right-minded people.

What can we read into these observations? Have the discipline of 'landscape' and the landscape architecture profession no interest in sustainability and no contribution to make? Or is the profession so

content that it has been practising it all along that there is little more to be said? Or is it still looking for someone to bring light where there is heat, confusion and darkness? In fact, our view, and that of the contributors to this book, is that there is much to be said about landscape and sustainability, that 'landscape' is a concept *par excellence* for thinking about sustainability and that the landscape architecture profession does have a significant contribution to make. The aim of this book is therefore to shed light and to address some of these questions, perhaps even to try to begin to answer the bigger questions and weave together the interlocking parts of the grand puzzle which is landscape and sustainability. Landscape architects can think globally and act locally to make a difference. The real question is how to do it. Despite the 'sustainability' epidemic, there is no text which addresses the issues from the point of view of landscape architecture in a comprehensive way. Sustainability has been around long enough for several things to occur. The field is over-worked and over-populated to the point of confusion and a developing cynicism – it needs interpretation for landscape architecture. The time is ripe for the epidemic to be digested, to take stock, to set new agendas for landscape research and practice, and to look forward. We try to do these things in an introductory way in this chapter, setting the scene for what follows.

LANDSCAPE AND THE SCOPE OF LANDSCAPE ARCHITECTURE

The word landscape has entered our vocabulary as a noun, adjective and verb. Laurie Olin, a well-know American landscape architect, has described it as that 'vast, difficult, slippery and mercurial subject'. The *Oxford English Dictionary* cites its first use in its major modern sense – 'a tract of land with its distinguishing characteristics and features, esp. considered as a product of shaping processes and agents (usually natural)' (Burchfield, 1976) – in a book of 1886 by Geikie, a geologist. Before that it had been used in an evaluative sense to mean 'an ideal place', the use prevalent in the art, landscape painting and landscape design of earlier centuries. We have come to realise, of course, that human agency has shaped the landscape too and not just in the patently man-made rural, urban and industrial landscapes of a place like the UK, but also the allegedly natural landscapes or wildernesses of the American great plains or the Australian outback. The term is now used in a wider sense to mean a tract of land shaped over time by geological and biological processes and by human occupation and agency *and* by human imagination, for the essence and unifying value of the concept is the way in which it signifies and captures both natural and cultural features and values, with a special emphasis on the relationships between these. It is, we believe, different from 'environment' which is either, unhelpfully, the world minus oneself or more usually the physical, chemical or biological components and processes which comprise the planet.

However, the apparently unbreakable, dominating link between landscape and visual matters – 'scenery' and 'art' and 'aesthetics' – with an emphasis on how we see landscapes and treat them, by the act of 'landscaping', as a wholly or mainly visual act concerned with beauty and art (to the exclusion of our other senses and values) is an unfortunate throwback to an earlier time. It is perpetuated by the landscape professions themselves, by their institutions, by their competitions and their prizes, and by a sectoral policy focus on these things. Small wonder then that other, larger, more powerful and influential professions ignore landscape and landscape architects (a perpetual navel-gazing *cri de cœur* in the professional press) or think that what they do, professionally, is add the plants between the buildings and not much else. But as this book argues, through its wide ambit, landscape is and must be much more than this. As a noun its original use as a term of geologists and geographers is still used to refer to a tract of the earth's surface but expanded to include natural–cultural relationships. It is used as a theoretical concept and social construct around which an array of disciplines including geography, art, literature and science coalesce to explore these nature–human interrelationships. It is used as an adjective to qualify the shape or scene of almost anything, but there is a political landscape of sustainability explored in Chapter 6. It is also used as a verb ('to landscape') – much deplored and abhorred by many in the landscape professions – to signify the practice of designing, making, using and managing landscapes and places. However, Turner (1998) has offered an intelligent, spirited and imaginative critique of this narrow, conventional and rather restrictive notion of landscape architecture, offering instead at least twelve avenues of practice through which landscape architecture can truly be the science and art of making spaces (and ultimately places) which are biologically wholesome, socially just and spiritually rewarding.

As Ian Thompson explores partly in Chapter 2 and more fully in Thompson (2000), landscape architecture draws its theoretical foundations and approaches from many sources and this book is similarly eclectic. However, there is a strong underpinning to much in this book by landscape ecology, a relatively new and emerging disciplinary area developed further by various contributors, especially in Chapters 6–8. In a sense, this captures the view offered here of landscape and sustainability, in contrast to landscape as appealing mainly to the eye or aspiring cerebrally to be fine art. More succinctly, landscape architecture is about making fit places which fit. Perhaps this is why the profession might be inclined to feel that it has been practising sustainability for decades, although Ian Thompson challenges this complacency in Chapter 2. We believe that the sustainability agenda needs a new mind-set among professionals, landscape architects included. We need to stop – or postpone – asking, first, Is it affordable? Is it beautiful? Is it what the client wants? Is it art? Will my professional colleagues approve? – and instead start asking, first and foremost, is it sustainable? Or at least, is it less unsustainable? We try to bring some semblance of order to definitions and terms in the next section, but because sustainability is such a multi-faceted concept, and there are few (no?) absolutes, we hope readers will tolerate the use throughout this book of the terms sustainability, sustainable and sustainable development when, by any strict definition, the authors sometimes mean 'less unsustainable' and sometimes they mean an integrated and coherent approach which is different from 'business as usual'. In many ways the diagnoses and lessons for the landscape profession in this book are familiar, and many will undoubtedly say, fine, we know that, we do all these things already – we've been pursuing integration, a sense of place, local distinctiveness, protecting the environment, aiding economic and social regeneration for decades – so what's the problem? Our reply is that even if this were true, and we only acknowledge that it is partly true, previous and much current policy and practice is only very weakly sustainable and its impact has been modest. Creating new or restoring damaged landscapes need not always involve sustainable practices and the tyranny of small decisions applies in landscape just as in every other sphere of human endeavour. As the sustainability debate shows, and as our contributors develop the various dimensions of landscape and sustainability in more detail, the issues are complex and challenging. The scale of thinking and action needed is large and this distinguishes landscape architecture from many other professions. In a way that is both the strength and the weakness of both the concept and the profession.

SUSTAINABILITY AND THE SCOPE OF SUSTAINABLE DEVELOPMENT

It has often been remarked that Prime Minister Gro Harlem Bruntland and her United Nations Commission performed a remarkable feat in offering a definition of sustainable development (SD) – 'development which meets the needs of the present without compromising the ability of future generations to meet their own needs' – which must be the most oft-quoted definition in the whole debate (we've just done it again) and which has (apparently and at least superficially) gathered world-wide political consensus on the need for a new approach in almost every sphere of human activity. But many have argued that that consensus has only emerged because the definition offered, and its many progeny (e.g. Pearce *et al.*, 1989), is an oxymoron and can

mean anything one wishes. The harshest critics will argue that SD is an idea and label so over-used, manipulated and debased as to be worthless without some definition and precision, from which has developed a large industry on sustainability indicators designed to provide the measurable criteria needed to allow individuals and groups with widely differing ethics and values to find common ground. The focus on indicators is based on the quite reasonable notion that if judgements are to be made on whether we've achieved sustainable development, or whether this or that policy or project is moving us in the right direction, then we need to make measurements to give us the answer. Indicators have of course been used for years in many fields – biologists measure species diversity or species richness (the trendy term is now 'biodiversity'), hydrologists measure flow rates or pollution concentrations, foresters count trees or measure growth rates or seek to estimate maximum sustainable yield – while in the social sciences and in the economy generally we measure jobs created, houses built, roads widened or Gross National Product, inflation and interest rates, and so on. All of these indicators are used routinely in policy evaluation and formulation, so it's no surprise that SD has attracted much work on the use of indicators as a means of operationalising the issue. But even here analysts argue that this is trying to measure the immeasurable (Bell and Morse, 1999).

So the landscape of sustainability is just as vast, difficult, slippery and mercurial as landscape itself. An important starting point is to realize that the term SD has ideological and political content as well as a more familiar ecological, economic and social content. We do not explore the complex ideological and political dimensions in detail here or in this book because other books and reviews abound (e.g. Pezzoli, 1997a, 1997b; Baker *et al.*, 1997), but Chapter 2 does deal with aspects of philosophy and ethics related to landscape. We would, however, commend the view that SD is a social and political construct, like 'democracy', 'liberty' and 'social justice' and that society – and landscape professionals – need to move forward beyond a sterile search for a single, precise definition, or single measuring rod, into the interpretation and application of SD in practice.

To sustain means 'to hold up, to bear, to support, to keep going, to support the life of and to prolong' and sustainability, as a noun, means 'that which is capable of being sustained' (Chambers, 1993). Time is therefore crucially important because sustainability focuses on long, inter-generational timescales, in contrast to the alleged short-termism and intra-generational emphasis of contemporary societies (of course Bruntland's definition captures both but our neo-classical economic systems, discussed by Colin Price in Chapter 3, reflect the fact that presently-living humans do have time preferences and they discount the future in myriad ways). SD requires us to look to the long term while our present systems and behaviour are designed for the short term. However, strictly nothing is sustainable forever, socially, politically, ecologically, geologically or cosmologically, and so sustainability cannot, technically, be infinite; most commentators would probably settle for 'to all intents and purposes forever', that is, far beyond a future which is conceivable by the present.

Commentators (e.g. Kidd, 1992) have traced the roots of contemporary sustainability into several conceptual areas, including 'ecological carrying capacity', 'resource–environment links', 'the biosphere', 'the critique of technology', 'no/low growth' and 'eco-development', all of which have a primary focus on concerns for the environment, especially the global resource base, humankind's place within it and the social and physical environments. A series of seminal reports and developments starting in the 1960s and 1970s (e.g. the Club of Rome report *The Limits to Growth* in 1972) pointed out the long pedigree and the diversity of environmental concern but called for zero-growth strategies. The term 'sustainable development' was invented to describe a notion that rather than zero-growth, what was required and was feasible was a strategy which developed a mutual compatibility between environmental protection and continuing economic growth (a common but inadequate metric for 'development'). These multiple histories and debates are endlessly described and discussed elsewhere and will be familiar to most readers.

The debate has now developed to the point where three key components of SD are defined – economic sustainability, social sustainability and environmental sustainability, each with a strong focus on equity and futurity. The strongest roots derive from biological or environmental debates, especially discussions about harvesting and managing renewable resources such as crop plants, forests and fisheries. Such biologically renewable resources can, theoretically, be maintained in perpetuity, while harvesting a maximum sustainable yield and of course while protecting the integrity and resilience of the resource and the biophysical components on which each depends. Sadly the history of human exploitation of such resources (exploit is now used mainly in a pejorative sense) is not a happy one, whether one focuses on the exploitation and exhaustion of common resources such as fish stocks, or the contamination, pollution and degradation of water and soils by both the internal and external impacts of human sectoral activity including agriculture and of course industrial development. The diversity of the biological resource, beyond the monocultural crop, timber or fish stocks which have direct utility for humans, are now also a major focus of attention; extinction, as they say, is forever (but then those accursed genetic engineers weaken the conservation imperative by holding out the prospect of resurrecting species from DNA fragments).

The second so-called renewable resources identified are the energy flow resources of the great geophysical cycles – sun, tides, wind and water flow – which are strictly not renewable but rather inexhaustible and perpetual on human timescales, with the important caveat that these characteristics are not inviolate or problem-free (as global warming, climate change and ozone depletion demonstrate). Two other important groups of resources complete the 'environmental' shopping list; the fossil fuel (carbon) minerals and other minerals (the stock resources). The 'other' minerals have the characteristic that they are kept intact (notwithstanding some chemical transmogrification) by human use and so are, theoretically, recyclable, technically if not economically. As other authors in the book point out, imposing a very strong sustainability constraint on such minerals

– leaving them for future generations to leave for future generations to leave for future generations – is a sterile and empty notion. Many commentators have pointed out that much mineral scarcity is economic, not physical, and that many (especially bulk) minerals such as aggregates cannot realistically be conceived as ever running out. It is more often the damage caused to ecologically renewable or cultural resources during the winning of the mineral, or the physical and chemical side effects and impacts (such as noise, dust and visual degradation), which are contestable rather than 'consumption' of the mineral itself. The fourth resource group – the carbon minerals – is perhaps, with biological resources, the most debated. Exploitation of these fossil fuels for energy generation is a truly one-way street, for they are both exhaustible and exhausted by our use of them. In addition, of course, their use generates many impacts, locally, regionally, nationally and globally. These are therefore strictly one-way flow resources and because they were created over geological timescales and in conditions quite different from today, they are effectively irreplaceable.

All this is very familiar, and the prescription is apparently straightforward – don't damage biological resources or renewable energy sources, use stock resources slowly and recycle, and use carbon resources slowly and develop renewable substitutes. The first point to make is that 'landscape' allows us to conceptualize and embrace all of these resources, and their impacts and the interactions between them, in an holistic way. The second point is that SD attempts to change the human mind-set away from thinking that the human experiment, which has so far caused damage and depletion of these resources, can somehow solve these problems by ingenuity and innovation and towards a realisation that this is optimistic and unrealistic. The human experiment is critically dependent on these resources and the environmental services they provide, for which there are no substitutes. The environmental perspective just mentioned focuses crucially not just on the stock of resources, or even their energy flows and the uses we make of them, but rather the 'services' they provide and on which all human and other life depends. These include the moderation of climate, protection from radiation, the air we breathe, the processing of wastes, and so on, captured in systems, ecosystemic or landscape ecological thinking.

For some, the sustainability 'problem' is an economic one and economists have not been slow to capture the debate and make important conceptual and practical contributions to it. Much of the framing of the natural resource issue, summarized above, uses the language of economics, including terms such as capital and yield. Colin Price elaborates in Chapter 3, focusing on the special issues which surround an economic approach to landscape. However, two key points can be made here. First, it is pointed out that our economic systems do not value many of these resources and services and this is offered as one explanation of the problem. While many biological and stock resources derived from the land are owned by someone, and exploited, traded and sold, giving them a price or value which should mean that damage or scarcity is 'corrected' by the market (Chapter 3), there are many resources derived from the global commons (fish and other marine resources being the most obvious examples) which are owned by no one and everyone. There are also many other resources and almost all environmental services which have the same status, and our use of resources produces many impacts (externalities in the language of economics), each of which is largely outside the economic system and therefore none are valued, priced or properly 'accounted'. The fact that capital spending on landscape reclamation or pollution clean-up appears in the national accounts as a positive contribution to economic growth is an obvious and perverse example of the critique of 'business as usual'. These issues have generated a wealth of theoretical and practical work, ranging from techniques of accounting at national and enterprise scales, through proposals for environmental taxation, to methods to evaluate and value (in monetary terms) these resources.

Second, only an absurdly strong stance on sustainability would argue that there should be no trading or substitution between natural and human resources, so the problem becomes one of defining limits or carrying capacities. In the language of economics, how can we define critical natural capital (which must be protected, conserved and sustained in perpetuity) and how can we distinguish this from other capital which might be consumed or transformed in favour of development for human use and enjoyment? This is a profound, complex and intractable problem, exacerbated in the case of 'landscape resources' by the fact that they combine both natural and human elements.

The social (and then political) strand in sustainability comes about from many directions. One is that Bruntland's concerns included a focus on the current North–South divide, the needs of people and issues of equity and justice. Another is the continuing debate about civil society, democracy and power in modern societies (Pezzoli, 1997a). Others include the strong anthropocentric ethic that the focus of SD is on humans – their quality of life – and that of their children and their children, and so on. Achieving SD therefore requires profound changes in human societies – in values, attitudes, behaviour and lifestyles – and protecting and building human capital is just as important as protecting environmental and economic capital. Maggie Roe says more on this in Chapter 4.

Sustainability and SD therefore enjoin us to deal with these complex issues in an holistic and integrated way. SD is highly contested theoretically, philosophically and in practice. Ian Thompson says a little more about these contests in Chapter 2 and Colin Price uses one spectrum of conceptions to frame Chapter 3. Here we want to sketch out the breadth of SD notions along the familiar 'weak to absurdly strong' spectrum. Baker *et al.* (1997, chapter 1), call it a 'ladder' implying a movement upwards towards an idealised or 'ideal model' of SD. The current or unsustainable approach has been called the 'treadmill approach' or 'business as usual', where attitudes are extremely egocentric, economic growth and profit at the expense of the environment are the key goals and indicators, and solutions to problems (should they be acknowledged as problems at all) will be solved, it is believed, by human ingenuity, innovation and markets.

Weak SD is but a number of small steps up from here, where the environment is 'accounted' to some degree in the economic growth calculus, but the aim of SD is mainly to build capital. Environmental, economic and human capital is infinitely substitutable, one for another, so long as aggregate capital is increasing. Here the environment is now valued as a resource (rather than being treated as a free good, outwith the economic system in a conventional or 'business as usual' approach) and two aims are set: SD proper, taken to mean growth of per capita real incomes over time (the treadmill objective) *plus* sustainable uses of resources and the environment, whose capital values (as stock resources or in terms of assimilative capacities) are not depleted. Although there are variations and nuances of interpretation, this weak position might be said to characterize the main way in which SD has been embraced by industrialized societies, governments, businesses, professions and many international agencies. A host of technical, fiscal and other environmental management tools has been developed under this 'weak' confection of SD – environmental impact assessment (EIA), carbon and other taxes, tradable pollution permits, and so on. Some have been embraced with enthusiasm (for example, EIA, which is but a process, leaving the evaluative decisions to be resolved in the conventional way) while others are being used experimentally or locally, often in the face of considerable controversy. Whichever, weak SD requires that we value the environment but neither environmental nor economic nor social capital has any prior or over-riding claim on our attention.

Critics point out many difficulties with this approach. In general, the environment is valued mainly in accounting or monetary terms and not in cultural or spiritual terms. It leaves the neo-classical paradigm essentially intact, and reduces or conceptualizes environmental problems as technical or management problems, solvable within existing political, economic and social frameworks. The main focus is on present people and not future generations, and while critical natural capital might be defined (with difficulty), not much is likely to be so labelled because most human societies operate on principles of negotiation and compromise with very little being agreed as absolute and not negotiable in practice.

Whereas weak SD might assert that economic development is a precondition of environmental protection, strong SD (sometimes called 'ecological modernization') will assert the reverse position. In other words, 'developed' status is not a precondition for environmental protection, but rather what is required is a different kind of economic development where 'growth' might be qualitative as well as or instead of quantitative and where policies are first geared to sustaining the productive capacity of the environment and sustaining assets as a priority. Critical natural capital is a major constraint and much less (but still some) substitutability and trading across environmental–human capital is permitted.

Baker *et al.* (1997) place an 'ideal model' of SD above the 'strong' category, where the emphasis is placed firmly on profound structural changes in society and a strong ecocentric position adopted with regard to non-human life on earth (a very strong position on sustainability), but other authors have referred to 'absurdly strong' SD which has parallels with the ecocentric–biocentric ethical position described in Chapter 2. 'Absurdly' strong SD requires such radical changes in the ways of the world that we will say little more here because it is unlikely to impinge directly and for the foreseeable future on the operational policies and practices of landscape planning, design and management in industrialized countries, although it is for some an important ethical and philosophical position which influences debates and so cannot be ignored in holistic thinking about landscape or SD (Holland, 1997).

This spectrum or ladder of approaches is a useful device for understanding the philosophical and policy implications associated with different approaches to SD, but these categories are not discrete, rather, they try to capture broad schools of thought from the superficial to the radical. Policies or actions in different sectors of the economy or in landscape practices might be drawn from anywhere along the spectrum, and a detailed analysis of, say, current government or agency rhetoric or policies in forestry in the UK (Chapter 8) would reveal weak, strong, very strong and even 'absurdly' strong elements. Within the broad spectrum of landscape architecture practice in the last decade one can

identify similar diversity. This brief sketch confirms a number of key features of sustainability and SD, some of which are the source of frustration felt in many quarters. There are no absolutes, there are no clear distinctions between weak, strong and other conceptions and there are controversies and contests about concepts, definitions, indicators, and so on. There is philosophical and political debate, radical suggestions, accommodating suggestions, faith, visions, optimism and pessimism. Is this really such a surprise when the agenda is the future of the earth and human occupation of it? Most of the contributors to the book resist the temptation to define what they understand by SD in a restrictive way, nor do they declare a particular stance – weak, strong, absurdly strong – as underpinning their contribution. Those whose contribution is more theoretical (Chapters 2–4) expose the spectrum of definitions to their scrutiny, but the choice is yours, not theirs. Those who concentrate on policy and regional or strategic issues (Chapters 5–9) place their analysis and discussion firmly in contemporary policy debates and developments driven by sustainability considerations. Those who mainly focus on technical and detailed design and management issues (Chapters 10–13) are particularly practical and pragmatic in their exposition, but within their treatments there is a wide span of practical action possible. Finally, and uniquely, Chapter 14 is both visionary and personal, and from another part of the world, although we believe that Kristina Hill's vision resonates with the other contributions and that her thoughts and speculations are a fitting way to conclude a complex agenda.

THE END OF THE BEGINNING

There is an endless array of ways to address and structure this complex area. The main perspective here is, in the end, a view from a small but diverse (in terms of landscape) developed nation where the industrial revolution began and where it might yet end, if sustainable development proves as oxymoronic and intractable as its critics and cynics fear. However, this geographical restriction need not limit the widespread applicability of the debates and ideas which follow. Readers in other places and from other disciplines will recognize the parallels in their own countries and should be able to identify the local influences of international debates in philosophy and ethics, in international policies and programmes, in supra-national (especially European and similar federalist) programmes and in regional and local landscape planning, design and management practices. There is a logic to the structure of the book which we hope will be clear, with chapters moving progressively from theory to practice, from the global to the local scale, and from issues of policy and planning through to detailed design and implementation and on to long-term maintenance and management. However, this structure (indeed, any structure) is not entirely satisfactory and a topic which is complex in scale and scope, as well as inherently holistic and integrative, cannot work in a linear way, even with copious feedback and cross-referencing. A circular structure might be preferred and this is exemplified by a start at Chapter 2 and an end at Chapter 14 with two contributions which are strongly philosophical and ethical – visionary if you prefer – in their content, so closing the loop but not the argument. Be prepared then, to navigate through the material which follows by circuitous routes, varying your starting point and retracing your steps as you explore a complex array of interconnected issues.

This is what we have devised. We wanted each chapter to be comprehensible and intelligible on its own, but we also wanted a coherent 'set' which would share a common concern even if each contributor would not subscribe to everything in every chapter. We have therefore cross-referenced in a number of places, but sparingly, mainly where a significant exposition and development of a particular topic is treated extensively in another chapter. We have not been unremitting in trying to delete every case of overlap or repetition or even contradiction, because these make the links and cross-references for us, and demonstrate just how vast, mercurial and slippery landscape and sustainability can be. Also, the first and, for some, the fundamental leg of the sustainability stool – the environment and its resources and

services– does not receive its own chapter, because it underpins and pervades every chapter.

Ian Thompson begins by tackling the ethical basis of sustainability in Chapter 2 and also delves into the cultural shaping of both landscape and landscape architecture. As he argues, sustainable development is essentially a homocentric or anthropocentric ethical position on the spectrum of nature–human relationships, just one position on a broader spectrum of environmental ethics. He shows how landscape concerns with design, art, aesthetics and social issues interlink with shallow and deep ecological standpoints. In Chapter 3 Colin Price approaches landscape as an economist and explores the language of sustainability interpreted in economic terms and applied to landscape. The neo-classical economy–environment paradigm, including notions of man-made and critical natural capital, cost-benefit analysis, and human values for and the monetary valuation of 'landscapes' are all subjected to his incisive dissection and wry humour. Maggie Roe then treats social aspects in Chapter 4, where she sketches out two important dimensions of social sustainability, social structures and social learning. Although not overly theoretical, these chapters are the foundation on which the rest is built.

Chapters 5 and 6 move on to the international and national policy arenas. In Chapter 5 Adrian Phillips takes a global look at international conceptions, conventions and designations for natural and cultural landscape conservation and management, the agencies involved, and their policies and strategies, making links with European and national policies and designations. Much is changing in this field in the face of the developing debates on sustainability. In Chapter 6 Paul Selman then reviews the background to the political and policy 'landscape' of sustainability in the UK, and its continuing evolution, touching on key global issues and agendas and leading on to sustainability as expressed through European Union and government policy (national and local), statutory agencies (the Countryside Agency, the Environment Agency and English Nature), NGOs and others, with a focus on the contradictions, imperatives and lessons for landscapes (and landscape architecture). His main message, which is persuasive, is one of scale, pervasiveness and opportunity – the way in which landscape offers an important integrating framework for sustainable development – and how it needs to move beyond a purely sectoral activity into the mainstream.

Large-scale landscape planning policy is often approached in one of two complementary but sometimes contradictory and overlapping ways. Sue Kidd uses Chapter 7 to look at landscape planning on the regional scale, drawing on a pioneering case study from North West England which was embedded within the command-and-control approach to planning and the control of development. She then links this to the new forms of regional governance in the UK and the evolution of the statutory land use planning system. Chapter 8 then gives Rob MacFarlane the space to approach large-scale landscape planning and management – of agricultural and forest landscapes – via the second approach which is based on market-mechanisms, and in particular the Common Agricultural Policy (CAP) of the European Union. What he shows and analyses, of course, is the inherent unsustainability of the CAP, and the tentative moves towards a more sustainable development and management path using a combination of command-and-control, market-based and voluntary mechanisms. Helen Armstrong, Helen Brown and Tom Turner then move down a scale in Chapter 9 to examine Landscape Planning and City Form where they review how sustainability affects planning, management and regeneration of existing urban landscapes and townscapes designed on non-sustainable principles, touching on urban space and form, buildings, landform, vegetation, water and land use planning.

Chapters 10–13 move beyond the policy and planning scales towards the industry and practice of landscape architecture – the act of making and managing landscapes which are biologically wholesome, socially just and spiritually rewarding. Aldo Leopold offered the dictum that the first rule of intelligent tampering is to save all the pieces, and in Chapter 10 – Resources: The Raw Materials of Landscape – Nigel Dunnett and Andy Clayden dissect out the ways in which sustainability forces us

to rethink the ways in which raw materials are used in landscape work. Plant materials and planting design, embodied energy, construction materials, recycling and Life Cycle Analysis are all treated here. In Chapter 11 – Sustainable Landscape Design in Practice – Michael Herrmann, Andy Millard and Chris Royffe take on a review of how to design and build sustainable landscapes, using case studies to examine the design process and design practice. Their examples include the Earth Centre near Doncaster, the Center Parcs leisure developments, the Meanwhile Gardens project in London and the large-scale Oostvaardersplassen project in Holland. Their analyses reveal just how complex, difficult and intractable the practice of sustainable landscape design can be, but they also offer hope and thoughtful reflection on the way forward.

Michael Herrmann and his colleagues begin to challenge the narrow and conventional, 'business as usual' approach to landscape architecture – built on capital expenditure, a client, a brief, a design, a contract and implementation – in a number of ways, including their description of the Meanwhile Gardens in London, and this theme is developed further in Chapter 12 – The Community and the Landscape Professional – by Maggie Roe and Maisie Rowe who examine a widespread but little remarked way of working professionally and which has an important bearing on social aspects of sustainability – quality of life and lifestyles, engaging people, participation, empowerment and Local Agenda 21, linking back to Chapter 4. Chapter 13 – Sustainable Landscape Management – allows Tony Kendle, Juliet Rose and Junko Oikawa to offer a critical but constructive take on different approaches to managing landscapes in sustainable ways and on how to manage sustainable landscapes. As they point out, these are not necessarily the same thing. Their focus is mainly an urban and amenity one, but it links to Rob MacFarlane's earlier Chapter 8 on agricultural and forest landscape management.

It would have been possible to stop at that point, but this would risk giving the impression that landscape and sustainability is mainly or solely about a search for policy, technical, design or management 'fixes'. We believe, however, that it involves much more than this and Kristina Hill gives free rein in Chapter 14 – Visions of Sustainability – to her fertile imagination and offers a challenging view from another continent.

Assuming that you have read thus far, it is tempting for us to say 'follow that', for if this book does one thing it is probably to amaze and overwhelm you with the scale and scope of landscape and sustainability, and the potential role which is claimed for those who practise landscape architecture. Our contributors raise a complex array of research, policy and professional issues and agendas in what we hope will be an ongoing debate, because both agendas – landscape and sustainability – are uncertain and in a state of flux and both require fortitude, a light touch and lateral thinking. So to paraphrase a famous British Prime Minister, we don't regard this book as the end, nor even the beginning of the end, but rather the end of the beginning. We began, many months and many pages ago, with two convictions: that the landscape community, at least in the UK, has so far had very little to say about sustainability which is conspicuous, but that there is actually much to be said and an important contribution to be made. We haven't deviated from that position and the rich contents of the book convince us that our ambitious quest was fully justified. Whether your interest is mainly in landscape, or mainly in sustainability, whether it is mainly as a landscape theoretician or practitioner, or even in another disciplinary area, we believe there are rich seams here waiting to be exploited – sustainably, of course.

REFERENCES

Baker, S., Kousis, M., Richardson, D. and Young, S. (eds) (1997) *The Politics of Sustainable Development* (London, Routledge).

Bell, S. and Morse, S. (1999) *Sustainability Indicators: Measuring the Immeasurable* (London, Earthscan).

Burchfield, R. W. (ed.) (1976) Entry for 'Landscape', in *A Supplement to the Oxford English Dictionary* (Oxford, Oxford University Press).

Burgess, J. (1996) The future for landscape research, *Landscape Research*, 21(1), 5–12.

Chambers (1993) *The Chambers Dictionary* (Edinburgh, Larousse plc.).

Holland, A. (1997) Substitutability: or, why strong sustainability is weak and absurdly strong sustainability is not absurd, in J. Foster (ed.) *Valuing Nature? Economics, Ethics and Environment*, (London, Routledge) pp. 119–134.

Kidd, C. V. (1992) The evolution of sustainability, *Journal of Agricultural and Environmental Ethics*, 5(1), 1–26.

Landscape Design Trust (1997) *Landscape Institute Awards 1997* (Surrey, Reigate).

Landscape Design Trust (1999) Landscape Institute Awards 1999, *Landscape Design*, 285, November.

Landscape Institute (1997) Royal Charter (London, Landscape Institute).

Lyle, J. T. (1994) *Regenerative Design for Sustainable Development* (New York, John Wiley).

Meadows, D. H., Meadows, D. L., Randers, J. and Behrens, W. (1972) *The Limits to Growth* (London, Earth Island).

Pearce, D. W., Markandya, A. and Barbier, E. B. (1989) *Blueprint for a Green Economy: A Report for the UK Department of the Environment* (London, Earthscan).

Pezzey, J. (1989) *Definitions of Sustainability*, Working Paper 9, (UK Centre for Economic and Environmental Development).

Pezzoli, K. (1997a) Sustainable development: a transdisciplinary overview of the literature, *Journal of Environmental Planning and Management*, 40(5), 549–574.

Pezzoli, K. (1997b) Sustainable development literature: a transdisciplinary bibliography, *Journal of Environmental Planning and Management*, 40(5), 575–601.

Thayer, R. L. Jr., (1994) *Gray World, Green Heart: Technology, Nature, and the Sustainable Landscape* (New York, John Wiley).

Thompson, I. H. (2000) *Ecology, Community and Delight* (London, E & F N Spon).

Turner, T. (1998) Twelve alternatives, *Landscape Design*, 267, 42–45, February.

2

THE ETHICS OF SUSTAINABILITY

Ian H. Thompson

SUMMARY

This chapter argues that while 'sustainable development' is just one approach among many to ethical concerns about the environment, it seems to offer landscape architects a tangible way of relating their aesthetic, social and ecological values. 'Sustainable development', by virtue of its concern for human well-being, justice within and between generations, and for the integrity of supporting environmental systems, seems to offer a system of values which can, with some thought, be assimilated by environmental design professionals.

The extent to which the profession has already absorbed ideas of sustainability is then considered. On one hand, landscape architects may be open to the accusation that they have been complicit in the promotion of unsustainable development. On the other, they have demonstrated both a concern for the conservation, enhancement and creation of biodiverse habitats and a commitment to working with communities in ways which foster communal values. These are both valuable contributions towards sustainability. The chapter concludes by suggesting some of the directions landscape architecture must take if it is to place sustainable development at the heart of its concerns.

ENVIRONMENTAL ETHICS

In this chapter we will consider how the concept of 'sustainability' relates to the moral discourses within the profession of landscape architecture. As we shall see, 'sustainability' is a portmanteau expression which can be used to describe a variety of approaches to environmental questions, but it is most often used as shorthand for 'sustainable development', which is essentially an ethical idea involving notions of equity and justice which extend beyond the present totality of human beings to include generations yet to be born. Unless otherwise stated, 'sustainability' will be used in this sense in this chapter; thus the main focus of the chapter will be upon 'sustainable development', although the second section (Sustainability, p.17) will consider some other contexts in which the word 'sustainable' is used. Although widely adopted by governments and international organizations, 'sustainable development' is itself a problematic term. If 'development' is regarded as the continued expansion of human activity and the unceasing pursuit of economic growth, 'sustainable development' begins to seem like an oxymoron. However, there are other ways to think about 'development', some of which will be explored in the course of the third section (The role of the profession, p. 21).

The first step will be to weigh 'sustainable development' in the context of the broader field of environmental ethics. The second will be to assess the degree to which the profession of landscape architecture has incorporated environmental values and the extent to which these are consonant with notions of sustainability. The ultimate aim will be to suggest ways in which the activities and objectives of landscape professionals might change if sustainable ideas are to be fully absorbed.

The profession of landscape architecture, which is often strongly vocational, can be said to have three main agendas. The first is aesthetic – landscape architects have traditionally sought to conserve, enhance or create attractive landscapes. The second is social – broadly speaking, landscape architects think that their activities can improve the quality of people's lives. The third agenda is concerned with environmental issues, but it is more recent and there is much discussion within the profession about its relationship to earlier concerns (Thompson, 2000). Sustainable development, as this chapter will show, is not the whole of environmental ethics, and it may be that landscape architectural theory can draw upon other ethical arguments. At the same time, sustainable development does seem to present landscape architecture with the hope that its aesthetic, social and environmental goals might be synthesized. This is the promise which we will attempt to evaluate in this chapter, but first we need to map out the general ethical territory we will be entering.

'Sustainable development' has become a pervasive phrase, which at times seems to dominate debates on environmental policy to the exclusion of other ethical ideas. Our first task is to see where the notion of 'sustainable development' sits in relation to the sub-branch of moral philosophy known as environmental ethics. As a distinct subject area, the latter can be said to have developed after the publication, in 1949, of Aldo Leopold's *A Sand County Almanac*, the final chapter of which suggested that, in addition to the duties we might owe to our fellow human beings, we might owe duties towards the land itself. Leopold's 'land ethic' was a radical suggestion which incorporated the following ethical touchstone: 'A thing is right when it tends to preserve the integrity, beauty and stability of the biotic community. It is wrong when it tends otherwise.' (Leopold, 1949, p. 240). Under the impetus provided by mounting environmental concern, there has been a rapid proliferation of theories within this relatively recent field. We need to comprehend this prolixity.

HOMOCENTRIC ETHICS

Within environmental ethics there is a broad division between theories which place the human species at the centre of the moral universe, which are labelled 'anthropocentric' and theories which suggest that all living things – and in some cases non-living things like islands or mountains – have intrinsic moral value and therefore we owe duties towards them. Such theories are labelled 'non-anthropocentric' (see Table 2.1).

Anthropocentric theories can be subdivided into egocentric and homocentric categories. Egocentric ethics are generally associated with *laissez-faire* liberalism, capitalism and free markets, and see nature as a storehouse of resources to be exploited for human benefit. New Right thinkers see competition between individuals as natural and inevitable, but argue that it works in the best interests of society as a whole.

Egocentric thinking often pays scant regard to environmental concerns, but if it recognizes the reality of ecological harm, it may make an appeal to individuals on the grounds of enlightened self-interest. Garrett Hardin's *Tragedy of the Commons* (1968), for example, recognizes the evils of resource depletion and pollution. His remedy is a Hobbesian contract, whereby individuals mutually agree to governmental coercion to counter the adverse effects of unfettered competition. Thomas Hobbes (1588–1679), the English philosopher, held a fundamentally pessimistic view of human nature. Most people, he argued, cared only for themselves or for their immediate families. He did not deny that kindness and concern for others existed, just that they were not sufficiently widespread to form the basis for civil society. Only by giving up their individual rights to decide what was in their own best interests, could people rationally enter into a contract with government (in Hobbes's case the sovereign) as the best way to ensure their long-term survival. Having lived through the English Civil War, the threats which troubled Hobbes most were those of war and revolution, but his argument can be

Table 2.1 A typology of theories/positions within environmental ethics

Anthropocentric		Non-anthropocentric	
Egocentric	Homocentric	Biocentric	Ecocentric
Self-interest	Greatest good of the greatest number	Members of the biotic community have moral standing	Ecosystems and/or the biosphere have moral standing
Laissez-faire			
	Stewardship of nature (for human use and enjoyment)		Duty to the whole environment
Mutual coercion (mutually agreed)			
			Holism
Classical economics	Utilitarianism	Moral extensionism	Deep ecology
Capitalism	Marxism	Animal rights	Land ethic
New Right	Left Greens	Bio-egalitarianism	Gaianism
	Eco-socialism		Buddhism
	'Shallow' ecology		American Indian
Thomas Hobbes	J. S. Mill	Albert Schweitzer	Aldo Leopold
John Locke	Jeremy Bentham	Peter Singer	J. Baird Callicott
Adam Smith	Barry Commoner	Tom Regan	
Thomas Malthus	Murray Bookchin	Paul Taylor	
Garrett Hardin			
	Most landscape architects?		

Source: A modified version of Carolyn Merchant's 'Grounds for Environmental Ethics', 1992, pp. 64–65

re-interpreted in the light of contemporary environmental perils.

More commonly anthropocentric theories can be categorized as homocentric. These can be grounded in rights-based theories of justice, or in utilitarian considerations of general welfare. Utilitarians may argue that the stewardship of nature is an important concern, but they do so because this in turn is thought to contribute to aggregate human happiness. This can be given an ecological slant; human happiness depends ultimately upon the natural systems which deliver the necessities for life, so these systems must be protected. But stewardship can also be promoted on aesthetic grounds. It can be argued that human beings take pleasure in the richness and diversity of the natural world, so the loss of bio-diversity, for example, is of concern because it threatens these satisfactions.

Marxism is similarly a homocentric theory. Marx saw science and technology as the key to meeting basic human needs, and post-Marxist social ecologists such as Barry Commoner (1972, 1990) and Murray Bookchin (1982, 1989) trace the roots of environmental problems to the power relations which exist in capitalist society. They suggest radical solutions which involve the elimination of hierarchy and patriarchy. They have a vision of a decentralized society based upon ideals of local autonomy and self-sufficiency. Modern science is placed under democratic control and a homocentric ethic determines the kinds of research which are carried out and the technologies which are implemented. Thus technology is put to the service of human needs but within a framework that recognizes the importance of non-human nature.

It is possible to hold a 'weak homocentrist' position which admits the intrinsic value of things other than human beings. A distinction can be made between the belief that only human beings have intrinsic worth and the belief that while humanity has the greatest value, other things may have lesser, yet nevertheless intrinsic, values of their own. On the analogy of an athletic competition, the greatest merit goes to the winner, but those who come second or third are not without merit of their own.

As will be seen below, the ethics of 'sustainability' or of 'sustainable development' can be classified as homocentric. Sustainable development in particular tries to balance an essentially utilitarian concern for the stewardship of nature with an attempt to remedy both the unjust distribution and consumption of resources between rich and the poor countries in the contemporary world, and the potentially unjust distribution of such resources between the present and succeeding generations.

NON-ANTHROPOCENTRIC ETHICS

Non-anthropocentric theories can be classified into biocentric and ecocentric subdivisions.

Biocentric ethics

Biocentric theories extend the boundaries of moral significance to include life forms other than humans. Those who support animal rights base their ethics upon an extension of utilitarianism. The greatest good of the greatest number is no longer restricted to human beings, but is enlarged to include all sentient life forms. Extensionists see this move as a development of the process which has widened the moral community in the past to include formerly excluded groups like other races, slaves, women or the disabled. It is worth noting in passing that the concept of sustainable development, as usually formulated, involves a similar kind of widening of the boundaries of moral consideration, because it includes a potentially very large group, the 'as-yet-unborn', who have not traditionally been included in the ethical community. The activities of animal rights activists draw attention to the significant changes society will have to make, particularly in areas such as agriculture and laboratory practice, if the extensionist stance is generally accepted, but from the point of view of environmental ethics it is a fairly conservative position, at least when compared with the concept of 'biocentric egalitarianism' which we will consider next.

According to some philosophers, human beings are not just part of nature, they are an equal part of nature. The Norwegian philosopher, Arne Naess suggests that all beings have 'the equal right to live and blossom' (Naess, 1973; Naess and Rothenberg, 1989). With ethical extensionism, the test of moral standing was sentience or the capacity to feel pain, a test which might allow us to discriminate between higher mammals with well-developed nervous systems and life forms without such development. For biocentric egalitarians there is no such test. 'Every man is equal' must yield to 'every life form is equal'. While it is relatively easy to discern the ethical implications of the extensionist position, the consequences of biocentric egalitarianism are harder to determine, and much intellectual energy has been devoted to working them out. The position raises questions about the circumstances in which a species, and particularly the human species, may be justified in encroaching upon the interests of other species. This discussion turns upon notions of basic and non-basic needs, for it is felt that such aggression may be justified to defend basic survival needs, such as the need for food or shelter, but not for non-essential needs. What is certain is that biocentric egalitarianism entails a radical reappraisal of humanity's dominance over other species. As a homocentric theory, sustainable development, however, has little to say about such matters.

Ecocentric ethics

Ecocentric ethical theories differ from biocentric theories in that they locate ethical value not in the individual plants, animals or species which constitute ecosystems but in the ecosystems themselves. While biocentrists may seek to protect ecosystems, they do so because they see this as the best way of conserving the individuals of which they are comprised. Ecocentrists, however, believe that our over-riding duties are to the ecosystems or, in some formulations, to the whole environment. Leopold's 'land ethic' was an early statement of such a position. It can be seen as an even more radical form of extensionism whereby not only animals, but also plants, rocks, soils, or collectively the land have moral standing. For ecocentrists, the whole is more significant than the parts.

If it is the system that has value rather than the individuals that comprise it, the value of those individuals becomes a question of their contribution to the overall integrity or stability of the broader entity. Within the literature of landscape architectural theory there is one clear expression of ecocentric thought. This is to be found in Ian McHarg's *Design With Nature* (1969, p. 121) where he suggests that plants, and particularly marine plants, are the supreme creators of value because they are the biosphere's prime creators of negentropy. McHarg tries to salvage a role for humanity by suggesting that our superior 'apperception' allows us to become the 'agent of symbioses' and 'stewards of the biosphere' (ibid., p. 124).

James Lovelock's *Gaia* hypothesis (Lovelock, 1979), which has entered into the popular imagination, also lends itself to ecocentric interpretation. It is really a metaphor which suggests that the whole biosphere, including living beings, air, oceans and land surface, can be seen as a single organism capable of regulating conditions on the planet to maintain conditions which are suitable for life. Lovelock himself has elucidated this central image by a series of further analogies; the earth is like a termites' nest, where the insects shape their own house but could not exist without it, or like a great tree, which we would recognize as a living organism even though the only parts which are truly living are the leaves, growing points and a thin layer of cambium just beneath the bark.

Deep ecology

If homocentric theories redefine humanity as the stewards of nature, and the non-anthropocentrists seek, in Leopold's words, to change 'the role of homo sapiens from conqueror of the land-community to plain member and citizen of it' (Leopold, 1949, pp. 224–5), deep ecologists seek an even more radical redefinition of humanity's status. They seek to escape from the anthropocentric–non-anthropocentric dichotomy entirely by an identification of human beings with nature so close that the need for an environmental ethics evaporates because we see that to harm nature is to harm ourselves. The philosophical underpinning for this position was provided by Arne Naess (1973) (Naess and Rothenberg, 1989) who drew both upon Hindu and Buddhist cosmology and upon the philosophy of Spinoza to propose a metaphysic of interconnectedness. Merchant (1992, p. 88) cites sources for deep ecology which range from the teachings of St Francis Assisi, to the pronouncements of native American leaders, to the philosophies of Leibniz, Spinoza, Santayana, Whitehead and Heidegger, and to the interpretations of eastern philosophies offered by Alan Watts and Fritjof Capra. This seems like an impressive pedigree, but its very breadth lays deep ecology open to accusations of woolliness and mysticism. The label 'deep ecology' is heavily value laden and seems to imply that any other approach to environmental ethics is superficial and does not address the real issues. Such approaches may be labelled 'shallow ecology', a term which is often used pejoratively. For deep ecologists, sustainable development, with its homocentric emphasis upon human aspirations would, despite its concern for social justice, certainly be found wanting. On the other hand, deep ecology may be criticized for its political and socio-economic naïveté. A greater degree of identification between humankind and nature may indeed be desirable, but given the urgency of our present predicament, what seem to be needed are practical steps that can be taken immediately. Whatever its shortcomings, sustainable development suggests pragmatic policy measures, and this no doubt accounts for the willingness of governments to accept its central tenets.

Overview

It will be clear from this brief overview that the main tension within environmental ethics is between homocentrism and the various varieties of non-anthropocentrism. This has been a creative influence and the positions are constantly being refined and developed. We should not expect these matters to be settled one way or the other – or certainly not in the short term. Sustainable development, it appears, belongs squarely in the homocentric camp.

However, there are those who believe that in terms of practical policy the gap between the homocentrists and the non-anthropocentrists is not as wide as it may first appear. Sterba (1994) has argued that when these positions are given their most favourable interpretations, they converge to support the same principles of environmental justice. Similarly, Norton (1997) has advanced his 'convergence hypothesis' which maintains that, from an empirical point of view, 'policies designed to protect the biological bequest to future generations will overlap significantly with policies that would follow from a clearly specified and coherent belief that nonhuman nature has intrinsic value' (ibid. p.99). Merchant (1992) recognizes that homocentrism occupies the centre ground between deep and shallow ecology, and that while it prioritizes human values, it need not lead to the destructive, short-term thinking that characterizes egocentric *laissez-faire* attitudes. While these notions of convergence have been contested, for example by Steverson (1996) who thinks that they underestimate the self-interested latitude that homocentrists will allow the human species, there is clearly a body of thought which suggests that a homocentric ethic can go a long way to meet the concerns of deep ecology. Even though sustainable development is essentially a homocentric notion, this does not necessarily mean that within it there is no space for the idea that non-human nature has intrinsic value and should be protected.

SUSTAINABILITY

Environmental sustainability

The word 'sustain' has two principal meanings. The first is 'to support or hold up' (from the Latin, *sustinere*). Breadwinners sustain their families; generals sustain the morale of their troops. The second is 'to prolong'. To sustain a discussion is to keep it going. A sustained note in music is one which is held for longer than usual. These senses converge. Something is 'sustainable' if it is possible to support it, to keep it going or in existence, over a significant period of time.

In the environmental discourse, 'sustainable' is often used as shorthand for longer and more precise phrases such as 'ecologically sustainable' or 'environmentally sustainable'. It is only within the second half of the twentieth century that humanity has come to fully understand that its continued existence depends upon a complex web of natural processes. The capacity of these systems to support life is finite and indeed may be diminished by many of the demands placed upon them. Human activities may be considered 'ecologically sustainable' if they do not reduce the capacity of natural systems to support life. They are 'ecologically unsustainable' if they cannot be continued over the long term without threatening the very systems which make life possible.

The expression 'carrying capacity' has been used in ecology to refer to the maximum number of a species that a given area can support indefinitely. This has been applied in a Malthusian sense to suggest that there are limits beyond which the human population cannot grow (IUCN, 1980, p. i). However, this overlooks the differences between cultures, which vary widely in the demands they place upon their land. Costa Rica and Cameroon, for example, are clearing their forests faster than Guatemala and Zaire respectively, despite having lower population growth rates (*The Ecologist*, 1993, in Kirkby *et al.*, 1995). There is a poor correlation between population growth and environmental degradation. Human history also contains many instances of technological innovations which have allowed societies to transcend apparent resource limits. The suggestion that there may be such a thing as a global carrying capacity remains controversial. On one hand, we find technological optimists who see no qualitative difference between our present situation and the difficulties faced and overcome in the past. On the other, there are the warnings of those like United Nations Environmental Programme (UNEP), who suggest that wasteful patterns of consumption are driving us towards an environmental precipice (UNEP, 1999), or Friends of the Earth, who regard the mounting data on global warming and loss of biodiversity as evidence that 'we already have one foot over the edge' (McLaren *et al.*, 1998, p. xii).

Sustainable growth and yield

Environmentalists do not have exclusive use of the word 'sustainable', however, and it appears in contexts where its significance may be quite antagonistic towards the objective of ecological sustainability. The most obvious of these is the use made by economists and politicians of the concept of 'sustainable growth'. Year on year increases in a nation's GNP have been taken to be an index of the health of its economy and the prosperity and wellbeing of its citizens. However, an economy which is growing in this sense is likely to be one in which land is being taken for development and natural resources are being consumed at alarming rates.

Lyle (1994) has labelled our current technological modes of production 'degenerative' because they exploit increasingly scarce resources while filling natural 'sumps' like oceans, land and atmosphere with waste products. Moreover, it is becoming clear that in developed economies economic growth is no longer a guarantor of enhanced well-being. Quite apart from spiritual malaise or a pervading sense of alienation, both of which are difficult to quantify, there is mounting empirical evidence that more does not necessarily mean better. The clearest example of this is the growth in car ownership, which has brought obvious disbenefits in the form of more polluted city air, which in turn has been linked with health problems such as irritation of the respiratory system and stress upon the cardiovascular system (Tolley *et al.*, 1982, pp. 1–11).

Similarly, the concept of 'sustained yield' is used, principally by agronomists and foresters, to refer to a harvestable surplus which can be gathered year upon year. Unlike fossil fuels which are finite, or metallic ores which are finite but recyclable, some natural resources, such as crops, game, fish and timber, would seem to be indefinitely renewable. But, as Callicott and Mumford (1998, p. 33) point out, the concept of sustained yield, although not immediately antagonistic to the idea of environmental sustainability, is symptomatic of a view which treats nature as little more than a cupboard of resources for human exploitation. It is certainly not an adequate basis for biological conservation, since most of the species in danger of local extirpation or global extinction are not at risk from over-harvesting, but from the pollution or destruction of their habitats. Indeed, it is easy to see how agricultural developments driven by notions of sustainable yield could accelerate the destruction of 'non-productive' habitats.

Sustainable development

However, by far the most prevalent use of the word 'sustainable' is within the concept of 'sustainable development', an idea which was born of the Stockholm Intergovernmental Conference on the Human Environment in 1972. It appeared in the World Conservation Strategy (WCS) (IUCN, 1980) a document which promoted a conservationist environmental agenda, but came of age upon publication of the report of the World Commission on Environment and Development (UNWCED, 1987) (usually referred to as the Brundtland Report, after the chair of the commission, the former Prime Minister of Norway, Gro Harlem Brundtland). Although there are many competing definitions of 'sustainable development', that of the Brundtland Report itself has become the most widely quoted. Sustainable development is development that 'meets the needs of the present without compromising the ability of future generations to meet their own needs' (ibid., 1987, p. 43).

At the Stockholm conference it had become clear that the interests of environmental conservation, promoted by representatives of developed Northern countries, clashed with the development aspirations of the poorer countries of the South. Perceiving that the North was unlikely to donate more than token amounts to the South, the only way that those in the South could improve their living conditions was to pursue policies of development and economic growth. The Brundtland Report sought to address both the environmental issues and the question of the fair distribution of resources between North and South. This ethical aspiration is expanded to consider not only the lives of the present generation, but of unborn generations to come. The Brundtland Report gave priority to the basic needs of the world's poorest inhabitants for food, shelter, energy, water, sanitation and employment, while urging that the global population must be stabilized.

In 1992, five years after the publication of the Brundtland Report, representatives of 176 nations met at the Earth Summit in Rio de Janeiro. The intention was to build upon Brundtland's recommendations by agreeing global treaties on matters such as biodiversity, climate change and forest management. They also agreed what amounted to a global action plan for the twenty-first century – Agenda 21 – which was designed to deliver sustainable development, in accordance with Brundtland's twin principles of environmental protection and the alleviation of poverty. Although Agenda 21 has never been ratified as a treaty and remains a 'voluntary declaration', many of its objectives have been incorporated into policy at levels which range from the European Union's governing treaties to the planning statements of local authorities.

The idea of sustainable development is ambiguous in that it can be given a homocentric slant, in which environmental conservation criteria are traded off against economic development criteria, or a more radical, ecocentric spin, which emphasizes the constraints on human activity that must be accepted if biospheric systems are to be protected against further life-threatening deterioration (Healey and Shaw, 1993). The Brundtland Report is inclined to regard species and ecosystems as resources for humans rather than things which have intrinsic value. However, it recognizes that the quality of human life can only be guaranteed if it does not put excessive demands upon the carrying capacity of the supporting ecosystems.

Intergenerational justice

The concept of the just distribution and use of resources is central to the notion of sustainable development. The philosopher, John Rawls, has promoted the idea of justice as fairness, as the idea that the institutions which prevail in human society should not confer lifelong advantages upon some people at the expense of others (Rawls, 1989). He asks us to consider a hypothetical situation in which we do not know the most significant facts about our lives – our race, religion, social standing, natural abilities, etc. In such a position, behind what he calls the 'veil of ignorance', what social institutions would we hope to create? Not knowing our position in society, we would be driven towards more egalitarian arrangements which would give priority to avoiding the worst possible life prospects. Sustainable thinking extends the scope of this conception, so that we must consider not only the inequalities which presently exist between the rich nations of the North and the poor nations of the South, but also the distribution of resources between the present generation and generations to come.

A useful notion here is the concept of 'natural capital' which includes not only material resources, but also other capacities and services which are supplied by the biosphere (Pearce et al., 1989, p. 3). The analogy here is with a stock of wealth which may generate an income to support life, but which may be squandered by the present generation leading to the unjust impoverishment of future generations (see Chapter 3).

Material resources are usually divided into renewable and non-renewable categories. Renewable resources are generally derived from animals and plants and are not necessarily depleted when a crop is taken. To guarantee intergenerational justice, we must ensure that we use them at rates no greater than those at which they can regenerate. Non-renewable resources are mostly minerals, like ores or fossil fuels, which are only replenished on the scale of geological time. Any use of such resources means a depletion of the future stock, yet it would make little sense to stop using them altogether, for what would be the point of handing on the entire stock to a future generation if they too would be constrained to preserve it for their descendants? What seems to be required is wise use of non-renewables so that we hand on as large a stock as possible for the future. The use of non-renewable resources is justified in the development of renewable technologies – for example, the steel and fossil fuels that may be consumed in the manufacture of wind farms.

The capacity of the atmosphere, oceans and terrestrial ecosystems to assimilate waste products can be thought of as another form of natural capital with much in common with renewable resources. Just as we should not use renewable resources faster than they can be replaced, so we must not burden these natural 'sinks' with wastes at rates faster than they are able to process them without negative ecological consequences.

The biosphere also provides us with more general services which are essential for the continuation of life, including the maintenance of breathable air, stable global temperatures and dependable weather patterns. The decay of the ozone layer, observable global warming and signs of increasing fluctuations in climate, such as the El Niño phenomenon, warn us that we cannot remain complacent about the continuation of these services.

Economic, political and social dimensions

The previous discussion may have given the impression that moves towards sustainable development are largely a question of environmental science and appropriate technology, and it is certainly true that there is already substantial knowledge of the sorts of technology – from solar, wind and wave energy generation to the treatment of wastes using reedbeds and the production of crops through systems of permaculture – in which we should be investing for the future. However, David Reid lists the following obstacles to sustainable development: 'lack of awareness of the issues, the political unacceptability of "obvious" steps forward, the opposition of entrenched interests, and the inadequacy of institutional mechanisms for integrating environment and development' (Reid, 1995, p. 129). Note that none of these is technical. All are concerned with the

manner in which society is organized, its culture, its goals and values and its institutions.

Western society's belief in material progress is closely linked to the idea that economic growth, crudely measured by GNP, will deliver better lives, and the optimistic notion of a 'technological fix' for every problem that may arise. The proponents of growth see it as a panacea and as an option for all. Countries are labelled as either 'developed' or 'developing', the implication being that the 'developing' will be able to 'catch up' with 'developed' and enjoy equivalent levels of material affluence. Furthermore, they imagine that the economic pie can continue to grow, and that a 'natural' process of 'trickle-down' will provide benefits to the poor without the need for any drastic disturbance of the status quo. This is a very comfortable notion for affluent Western consumers and for the politicians they elect.

Yet even within the developed counties of the North there is ample evidence that this world view is flawed. Ekins has divided people into three categories – there is a minority who benefit from the workings of the present economic system since they have skills which are valued in the marketplace; there is a much larger group who serve the system in humdrum jobs; and there is a permanent underclass, amounting to almost 20 per cent of the population, who live below the poverty line (Ekins, 1992, p. 202; Reid, 1995, p. 143). It would seem that the present economic system increases inequalities, wastes human abilities and destroys social cohesion. In our consumerist economy people define their socioeconomic status by the acquisition of material goods, yet complain about the erosion of moral and spiritual values and feel an increasing sense of hollowness and alienation. Ultimately the unrelenting quest for well-being through consumption is self-defeating. As Reid puts it 'ultimately the process is futile: there is no advantage in standing on tiptoe if everyone else in the crowd is doing the same. If there is more to life than material possessions, it is pointless to seek more material wealth' (1995, p. 137).

Consumerist society is antagonistic towards sustainable development. Sustainability will not be achieved while we continue to hold our prevailing beliefs in economic growth and persist in equating our well-being with the amount that we consume. But changing these attitudes is a Herculean task. Thomas Kuhn gave the name 'paradigm shift' to any revolutionary scientific breakthrough which overthrew an orthodoxy (Kuhn, 1970). What seems to be needed is a 'paradigm shift' in our conception of a good society. Such a change cannot be effected suddenly. It will be the result of an accumulation of small steps. Every action which helps to build social cohesion, which provides support for the disadvantaged, or which liberates human potential, can contribute towards the new world view which sustainability requires (see Chapter 4). Thus it can be argued that initiatives as various as the improvement of crèche facilities, or a programme of continuing education, or the creation of a community park, all may contribute towards the conditions in which sustainable living might be possible. Sustainable development is not just about saving rainforests or fitting solar collectors to the roof.

THE ROLE OF THE PROFESSION OF LANDSCAPE ARCHITECTURE

The range of professionals who consider themselves to be particularly concerned, in one way or another, with the environment is extremely wide (and seems to get ever wider). Broadly it might be divided into scientists and technologists, on one hand, who seek to understand environmental processes, identify potential threats and suggest solutions either in terms of new technologies or policy initiatives, while, on the other, we find an array of planners, engineers, managers and designers who might loosely be called 'environmental design professionals'. Contemporary landscape architects consider themselves to be important members of this latter group. In the light of the discussion above, we are now in a position to examine this claim. If landscape architects are environmentalists, what ethical positions do they adopt, and to what extent can the profession be said to be furthering the cause of sustainable development?

Woolley and Whittaker (1995) usefully distinguish between four varieties of ethics which have a bearing upon the landscape practitioner – personal ethics, business ethics, professional ethics and environmental ethics (see Figure 2.1). Their analysis is somewhat incomplete, since it does not take account of the aesthetic values which practitioners may seek to promote, nor of any obligations they may feel towards the well-being of individuals, communities or society as a whole. Nevertheless, it draws attention to the extent to which the profession's ethics are matters of business or professional propriety and suggests the possibility that the obligations imposed upon a landscape architect by a client could conceivably clash with others derived from environmental ethics. The main purpose of Woolley and Whittaker's paper was to criticize the Landscape Institute, as the professional body for landscape designers, managers and scientists in Britain, for dropping certain phrases from its Code of Conduct which had placed ethical constraints upon members in relation to the preservation of the 'national landscape'. It is interesting to note that new wording in the Royal Charter, granted to the Institute in 1997, which seeks to define the purposes of the profession, recognizes that landscape architects have a role in the promotion of 'aesthetically pleasing, functional and ecologically and biologically healthy' landscapes, but also makes special mention of their responsibility for 'the appraisal and harmonious integration of development and the built environment into landscapes.' (Landscape Institute, 1997, Section 5(2) d). These purposes seem rather mixed. The value systems which are inherent in landscape architecture are complicated (and, one might say, muddled) embracing, as they do, aesthetic and social goals alongside environmental concerns. Indeed, the social and aesthetic agendas have a longer pedigree than the environmental. The first designers to style themselves as 'landscape architects' were Frederick Law Olmsted and Calvert Vaux who won the competition for the design of New York's Central Park in 1858. Peter Walker has described Olmsted's conception of Central Park as 'an uncommon fusion of social and aesthetic intentions' (Walker and Simo, 1994, p.17). A prominent social reformer, Olmsted believed the park would, in Walker's words, 'civilize people, offering views of natural scenery that would calm the nerves and refine the sensibilities, working its magic

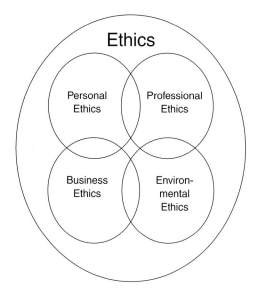

Figure 2.1 Ethical concerns for the landscape professional.

Source: After Woolley and Whittaker (1995)

over the mind like music, imperceptibly yet permanently' (ibid., 1994, p. 17).

In Britain, where the Institute of Landscape Architects was formed in 1929, the predominant concerns of mid-century practitioners were the visual quality of the landscape which was seen to be under threat from urban sprawl and ribbon development. Brenda Colvin tried to show in *Land and Landscape* (1970), first published in 1947, that human use is not incompatible with landscape beauty. Thus a social agenda was placed alongside an aesthetic one. It was paramount to establish that a visually attractive landscape could also be a functional and productive one.

Accommodation

In terms of Tim O'Riordan's (1981) classification of contemporary trends in environmentalism (see Table 2.2), Colvin could be categorized as an 'accommodator'. Landscape architects of her generation had not lost faith in the modernist belief in progress. On balance, technology was still seen as a great social good, and if some of its manifestations were ugly, then ways had to be found to accommodate them. Another prominent landscape architect of the era, Sylvia Crowe, even wrote a book called *The Landscape of Power* (1958) in which she recommended ways in which the impact of large industrial structures like nuclear power stations, dams and the masts of the National Grid might be lessened (see Figure 2.2).

It is revealing that the dust-jacket notes for this book said that Crowe 'accepts the essential need for the construction of immense oil refineries, nuclear reactors, power stations and the network of the electricity grid.' Her suggestions for the visual amelioration of such hardware range from camouflage – a small transformer station can easily be screened by landform or planting – to attempts to nudge society towards a new aesthetic in which the sphere of the Dounreay reactor or the massing of cooling towers beside a coal-fired power station are seen to have a beauty of their own.

Much of this sort of work still goes on, though the phrase which landscape architects use to describe it is not 'accommodation' but 'landscape mitigation'. Thus landscape architects are still commissioned to lessen the aesthetic disturbance caused by major pieces of infrastructure such as the Channel Tunnel Terminal. European Community legislation introducing the requirement for developers to submit Environmental Impact Assessments in relation to major projects as part of the development control procedure has greatly stimulated this area of practice (Greed, 1996, pp. 186–8). Landscape offices also receive a large percentage of their fees from more routine development work associated with business and retail parks, new housing estates and out-of-town shopping centres. According to wording contained in the Royal Charter (Landscape Institute, 1997), the landscapes with which practitioners are concerned must, when required, 'be able to accommodate the built environment in all its forms' (Section 5(2)). One landscape architect interviewed in the course of a recent piece of research said that he had realized that most landscape work was 'related in one form or another to development. It's either repairing the land after development, it's planning for development, or

Table 2.2 Contemporary trends in environmentalism

Technocentrism		Ecocentrism	
Belief in the retention of the status quo in the existing structure of political power, but a demand for more responsiveness and accountability in political, regulatory, planning and educational institutions.		Demand for redistribution of power towards a decentralized, federated economy with more emphasis on informal economic and social transactions and the pursuit of participatory justice.	
Intervention	*Accommodation*	*Communalism*	*Gaianism*
Faith in the application of science, market forces and managerial ingenuity.	Faith in the adaptability of institutions and approaches to assessment and evaluation to accommodate environmental demands.	Faith in the co-operative capabilities of societies to establish self-reliant communities based on renewable resource use and appropriate technologies.	Faith in the rights of nature and of the essential need for co-evolution of human and natural ethics.
Business and finance managers; skilled workers; self-employed; right-wing politicians; career-focused youth.	Middle-ranking executives; environmental scientists; white-collar trade unionists; liberal-socialist politicians.	Radical socialists; committed youth; radical-liberal politicans; intellectual environmentalists.	'Green' supporters; radical philosophers.
	Most landscape architects?	Some radical landscape architects?	Some radical landscape architects?

Source: Adapted from O'Riordan (1981)

it's actually physically designing something to accommodate development' (interview transcript).

This interviewee was using the word 'development' as a near synonym for 'construction', a usage which is common within the profession. In terms of the wider ethical and political debate about sustainable development it is a narrow and skewed use of the term. Attfield (1999, pp. 98–101) reviews contemporary meanings of 'development' and suggests that it is best understood in opposition to 'underdevelopment', where the interconnected evils of 'poverty, disease, illiteracy, high infant mortality, low life expectancy, low productivity, and poor medical and educational facilities' prevail. The process of development moves towards prosperity, health, literacy, low infant mortality, higher life expectancy and better medical and educational facilities; it is clearly not synonymous with 'construction', nor should it even be equated with economic growth. Indeed, as Attfield proceeds to say, economic growth may even conflict with development, thus understood, if it fails to meet basic needs or increases social inequalities, while meeting such needs may require the constraint of undesirable aspects of growth through 'regulation, social planning or public accountability' (1999, p. 99).

Landscape architecture, at its present stage, remains predominantly a First World profession. It would seem that the livelihoods of many (or even most) landscape architects depend upon a close association with construction projects and economic growth. From the viewpoint of environmental ethics, this involvement may be laudable if the kinds of projects with which landscape architects associate themselves exemplify sustainable principles, or if the landscape architect strives to introduce such principles into a project which otherwise lacks them. However, it may be that there are some undertakings which are so inimical to the sustainable ideal that to work on them is tantamount to collaboration in causing environmental harm. The difficulty is in knowing where to draw this line.

Figure 2.2 Drax Power Station, Yorkshire. The accommodation of this major facility within the landscape involved the creation of a new hill built from the pulverized fuel ash produced by the generating process.

Periodically an ethical debate surfaces in the professional press about the kinds of work which landscape architects should shun. For example, in 1989, John Whitelegg, a prominent campaigner against society's over-dependence on the motor car, wrote an editorial for *Landscape Design* entitled 'The Nightsoil Profession', in which he attacked the profession for playing a merely cosmetic role in the development process:

> Too many road schemes have been pushed through with the help of a hefty shove from the landscape architectural profession and justified or excused on the grounds that the environment will be improved by the scheme. This approach can become very arrogant as in the case of the Oxleas Wood route for the east London River Crossing. At this inquiry the Department of Transport argued that it would improve the several thousand-year-old woodland by its imaginative planting after road construction.
>
> (*Landscape Design*, No. 185, p.2)

A month later, in a letter to the same publication, Chris Baines condemned those landscape practices which were, in his view, aiding and abetting the destruction of unique habitats in their role as consultants to the Cardiff Bay Development Corporation. The proposal that had angered him so much was the Barrage which would create a freshwater lake in the place of tidal mudflats, a scheme also opposed by the Royal Society for the Protection of Birds and the Royal Society for Nature Conservation. 'One thing which might bring the government to its moral senses,' he protested 'is a refusal by the landscape profession to play a part in this destructive project' (*Landscape Design*, No. 186, p. 3).

Predictably perhaps, there was a backlash. Peter Youngman entered the fray with a letter headed 'In Defence of Beauty.' In this he deplored the 'emotive terminology' used by Whitelegg and Baines. Planning issues are complex, he argued, and the profession's role is to provide clear thinking and objective analysis in the interests of 'the reconciliation of the inevitable conflicts between genuine interests'. Youngman then succinctly stated his own value system: 'For me reconciliation comes first; but where it is unattainable people matter more than birds and beauty more than scientific interest' (*Landscape Design*, No. 192, p. 3). This is a clear statement of a homocentric ethics employing a utilitarian notion of the greatest good. It also places the social and aesthetic agendas above the environmental, while the latter is demoted to a matter which could only be of interest to scientists – and not, the implication seems to be, of much concern to the rest of us. Perhaps it should not surprise us to discover that landscape architecture is essentially homocentric in its concerns; indeed, it is hard to imagine how a profession which solves design problems on behalf of paying clients and human users could be anything other than homocentric. However, as we saw above, such a position does not exclude the possibility of recognising inherent worth in non-human nature.

There are two possible responses to Youngman. One is to say that nature matters, not just because it interests scientists or even because we find it beautiful, but simply because it is worthy of moral consideration in its own right. This is the response of the ecocentrist. The second argument, which is used by the environmental philosopher, Laura Westra, is to argue from our own ultimate self-interest that the integrity of natural systems is foundational (Westra, 1998). Without them we could not continue to live. This is an ecologically-informed piece of homocentrism, though Westra is better known for advancing a tough biocentric line.

This discussion has alerted us to the possibility that landscape architecture may not always be on the side of the environmental angels. There is the possibility that through taking part in environmental assessments, visual impact assessments and mitigation works, the profession actually helps non-

sustainable projects into existence. If anyone should doubt this, just consider the hours that are spent on drawing boards or computers designing car parks. This realization may be a shock to those who have always thought that landscape architecture was an entirely virtuous occupation.

There are, fortunately, many more positive aspects to the landscape architect's role which are entirely consonant with a commitment to sustainability, and it is to these brighter facets that we turn next.

Landscape architecture and ecology

The term 'ecology' was coined by Ernst Haekel in the 1860s from the Greek work *oikos* meaning 'household' or 'home'. Thus ecology was to be the study of living organisms in their home environments. Ecology thus pre-dates landscape architecture, but its influence was slight until the middle years of the twentieth century. For British landscape architects it was the publication of Arthur Tansley's *The British Islands and their Vegetation* in 1939 which had the most influence. There is ample evidence that landscape architects of that period were aware of the significance of this still relatively young science. In 1948 Brenda Colvin was able to describe ecology as 'the science of landscape' (Colvin, [1948] 1970, p. 65) and with the support of Sylvia Crowe and Brian Hackett it was included in the Institute of Landscape Architect's first examination syllabus. Moreover, when Hackett established Britain's first post-war full-time postgraduate course in Landscape Design at the University of Newcastle upon Tyne in 1949, he expressly stated that it was to be a course based upon ecological principles of design.

Although the term 'sustainability' was not then in currency, Hackett utilized some of the then current concepts derived from ecology, such as stability, balance and diversity, to create a paradigm for the healthy landscape, and it is one which, with its emphasis on self-renewal, we might today call sustainable. Hackett believed that the aesthetic satisfactions a landscape might provide were a by-product of its health, and therefore, if landscape planning is undertaken along ecological lines, the visual aesthetics will, more or less, take care of themselves

(Hackett, 1971). Where Colvin had sought to combine human use and landscape beauty, Hackett sought to combine human use with the ecological health of landscapes (with beauty as a necessary by-product). An ecologically healthy landscape can be regarded as one in which natural capital is passed on intact to future generations.

Meanwhile across the Atlantic, the Scottish *émigré*, Ian McHarg, published his seminal *Design with Nature* in 1969. His thesis, radical at the time, that human development should be planned in a manner which took full account of natural values found ready adherents in a society which had been alerted to the possibility of ecological harms by Rachel Carson's *Silent Spring*, first published seven years previously. Environmental concern continued to mount throughout the decade. When the first pictures of the earth from space were beamed down from Apollo VIII in 1968, it was revealed to be a uniquely beautiful planet, and seen against its vast empty backdrop it also appeared bounded and vulnerable. In *Design with Nature* McHarg imagined an exemplary people, the Naturalists, who lived close to nature in what we today might call an ecologically sustainable society. In the chapter called The Plight he wrote:

> Clearly the problem of man and nature is not one of providing a decorative back-cloth for the human play, or even of ameliorating the grim city: it is the necessity of sustaining nature as a source of life, milieu, teacher, sanctum, challenge and, most of all, of rediscovering nature's corollary of the unknown in the self, the source of meaning. (McHarg, 1969, p. 19)

Design with Nature was important not just because it articulated a philosophical position, but because it provided methodological tools for landscape planning in the form of the sieve overlay technique, which has since been developed to greater levels of sophistication using GIS technology, a point to which Kristina Hill returns in Chapter 14. The work of Hackett, McHarg, and Philip Lewis, who had been developing an approach to large-scale landscape planning along similar lines at the University of

Figure 2.3 Birchwood, Warrington New Town, a testing ground for the 'Ecological Approach' to landscape design.

Illinois from the late 1950s, strengthened the landscape profession's theoretical base. Rather than being sidelined as dreamy aesthetes, landscape architects could be seen to be addressing important questions about humanity's place in nature and to be doing so from a scientifically informed position.

The ecological approach

As long ago as the 1920s and 1930s the American landscape architect, Jens Jensen, was advocating the use of native plants in a way which reflected the local landscape. (Jensen, 1939). At the same time in The Netherlands, Jacques Thijsse was pioneering a new type of urban park which brought the plant communities of the polders into town. His 'instructive gardens' recreated habitats such as hornbeam woodlands and heather moorland from the Utrecht Hills. In the 1970s interest in these approaches revived, first in Holland and then in Britain, where Alan Ruff (1979) set out the principles behind what became known as the 'Ecological Approach'. In essence, this was a method of quickly establishing woodland plantations using native species. In theory, this was supposed to be a low cost/high return landscape in which maintenance costs would decrease as the scheme grew towards greater ecological stability and required less human intervention. At the same time the social benefits of intimate contact with nature would increase. In Britain the approach found favour with many practitioners, particularly those working for the New Towns, and it was particularly successful in Warrington New Town (see Figure 2.3) and the new city of Milton Keynes.

In technical terms the Ecological Approach was an undoubted success, although dense plantations of native trees and shrubs proved to be inappropriate in many inner city areas where they were seen to make residents more fearful of crime. The Ecological Approach was the precursor of today's interest in sustainability, for the landscapes it sought to create were intended to work with natural processes rather than against them. Energy inputs and applications of herbicides could be minimized. Such landscapes might be seen as investments for future generations. What unites the McHargian approach to landscape planning and the Ecological Approach to planting design is an understanding of natural processes and a desire to harmonize human activities with them. This is entirely compatible with sustainable thinking, and Nigel Dunnett and Andy Clayden say more on this in Chapter 10.

New technologies, new aesthetics

If sustainability is adopted as a guiding principle it has both ethical and aesthetic consequences for landscape architects. For planners, sustainable development seems to suggest the need for more compact and contiguous growth patterns at higher densities and for greater reliance on mass transportation. This is the general thrust of a large body of literature, but many of the implications of sustainability for strategic planning are still contested. For a discussion of this topic see Barton (1998) and Chapter 9. From science it demands new technologies which minimize resource consumption and promote recycling, but which in their turn will need to be accommodated in the landscape just as were the previous generation of power stations and dams. From landscape architects and planners it requires not just the avoidance of development on ecologically sensitive lands, but new visions of the landscape informed by the emerging discipline of landscape ecology, a theme developed further in Chapters 7 and 8. Many landscape architects have started to think along these lines and two have already published important books which consider some of the possibilities just mentioned. These are John Tilman Lyle's *Regenerative Design for Sustainable Development* (1994) and Robert Thayer's *Gray World, Green Heart* (1994).

Regenerative design

Lyle addresses the twin problems of resource depletion and environmental degradation. His thesis is that industrial society is a world-wide one-way throughput system in which materials are taken from the earth at rates far greater than those at which they can be replenished, and waste products are deposited in sinks – the atmosphere, lakes, rivers and the sea – which are loaded beyond capacity. His remedy is 'regenerative design': 'A regenerative system provides for continuous replacement, through its own functional processes, of the energy and materials used in its operation' (Lyle, 1994, p. 10).

Following Patrick Geddes (1949), Lyle uses the term 'Palaeotechnic' to describe a society based upon linear, non-regenerative technology, and 'Neotechnic' to describe one based on cyclical, regenerative processes. The parallel is with Palaeolithic and Neolithic societies.

Lyle's compendious book bulges with examples of such technologies, ranging from the anaerobic digestion of biomass to zero run-off drainage systems and from polycultural agriculture to the use of wind scoops and thermal chimneys for natural air-conditioning. He notes that because regenerative technologies are often very specific to their locality, they can, like older technologies, have a considerable visual impact. Indeed, they may have a greater impact, for whereas a power station is a concentrated source of visual impact and can be hidden away, disguised and mitigated in various ways, regenerative design will distribute smaller but more localized impacts far more widely. Lyle cites the case of wind-farms which some people regard as intrusive. This point is also central to Thayer's book. He urges us to look for a new aesthetic, arguing that much landscape practice has been devoted to the camouflaging of inappropriate technologies, whereas in the new sustainable landscape (which we must all play our part in creating), this will be unnecessary. Our technologies will be 'transparent' because they are a source of pride rather than guilt. Thayer's ecotopia is a decentralized one based on small communities. He also goes further than most landscape architects have done in advocating fundamental changes in the way society is organized. This places him on the ecocentric side of O'Riordan's ecocentric–technocentric dichotomy (see Table 2.2).

Irreversible actions

A corollary of the sustainability principle is that we must be on our guard against irreversible actions. This principle has been to the fore in recent British planning battles. It won the day in the case of Oxleas Wood, when in 1993 the government cancelled a proposed trunk road which would have damaged a Site of Special Scientific Interest, but was over-ruled in the regrettable case of Twyford Down, where a hill of enormous landscape significance was bull-dozed to make way for the M3 motorway (Adams, 1996, p. 78) and also in the case of the Newbury

Figure 2.4 Wetlands at Bold Urban Common, where a community-based initiative guided by Groundwork St Helens, Knowsley and Sefton, is restoring social, ecological and aesthetic values to an area of neglected wasteground.

Bypass which went ahead in 1996 despite the damage it would cause to two SSSIs and 12 sites of archaeological interest (Jenkins, 1997, p. 12). Adopting a technocentrist stance, the landscape profession has seen itself as offering objective advice in such circumstances. In a quasi-legal situation landscape architects often appear as expert witnesses on both sides of the argument, leaving the profession open to the charge of aiding and abetting damaging projects. This charge carries some force if landscape architects confine themselves to commenting on the aesthetic implications of proposed building developments. It can be defused if practitioners also regard themselves as ethically responsible for evaluating proposals objectively in terms of their contribution towards sustainability.

Social dimensions

Planning for sustainability requires that some priorities should be reversed. Rather than planning the human habitat first, by allocating land for housing, industry or recreation, and only then seeking to preserve what remnants of other habitats remain, we should be putting the best habitats first while also taking steps to ensure that the hydrological cycle is disturbed and polluted as little as possible (Punter and Carmona, 1997). Only by reordering our priorities in this way can we hope to protect the natural processes upon which our continued existence ultimately depends.

The move towards sustainability and away from damaging forms of development would seem to involve a rejection of consumer-oriented lifestyles in favour of ones which emphasize community, interpersonal links, and connection with the environment (Chapter 4). In his suggested checklist for ecovillage development, Ted Trainer (1998) describes the features of an ideally sustainable settlement. He divides his list into things which are 'simple and easy' because they involve the adoption of new technologies or new approaches to town planning, and things which are difficult because they involve changes in people's fundamental attitudes and lifestyles. At the simple and easy end of the continuum we find all sorts of initiatives in which landscape architects are

already involved such as greening cities, the creation of wildlife corridors and urban commons, the provision of cyclepaths, site planning for solar efficiency, permaculture and alternative water collection and sewage systems (see Figures 2.4 and 2.5).

The more socially engaged members of the profession are also engaged in activities which attempt to transform society at the difficult end of Trainer's checklist. These range from environmental education and the improvement of school grounds to the creation of sustainably and locally managed neighbourhood parks, described further in Chapter 11 and especially Chapter 12. All of these activities can be said to foster the kind of social cohesion

Figure 2.5 The Ridgacre Canal near West Bromwich, where a redundant waterway has been transformed into a recreational and educational resource by Groundwork Black Country. This entrance feature was designed by local children.

which seems to be the necessary condition of any shift towards more sustainable lifestyles.

New aesthetics

To be credible the ethical realignment needs to be accompanied by visions of what sustainable landscapes could look like. The move towards sustainability requires an innovatory aesthetics. Landscape ecology would seem to have the potential to place the new aesthetics on a sound theoretical footing, indeed Dramstrad *et al.* (1996) have sought to interpret the principles of landscape ecology diagrammatically for use by designers and planners. Some useful work in this direction has also been done by Ann Rosenberg (1986) who suggests in her paper 'An Emerging Paradigm for Landscape Architecture' that:

> Instead of admiring a landscape that is ornamental, paved, groomed, and relatively static, an alternative design language would emphasise a diversity and complexity that the human component can interrelate with – water resources, wildlife habitats, edible landscapes, and urban woodlots.
>
> (1986, p.81)

Similarly, in her aptly titled 'Messy Ecosystems, Orderly Frames' (1995), Joan Nassauer observes that many indigenous ecosystems and wildlife habitats violate cultural norms regarding tidiness and order when retained or introduced into the urban fabric. She suggests that designers should provide 'cues to care' which tell the public that an apparently untidy landscape is part of a larger intended pattern. 'Orderly frames,' she says, 'can be used to construct a widely recognised cultural framework for ecological quality' (ibid., p.169).

If the advocated paradigm shift is to happen, there will be aesthetic casualties, because our admiration of formal landscapes and architectural grand gestures, whether classical, modern or whimsically post-modern will be necessarily tempered by consideration of their ecological suitability. On the other hand, the development of a new ecologically-informed aesthetic is the most exciting challenge facing the landscape design profession today.

Sustainability and the profession

It should be clear from this chapter that the concept of 'sustainable development' is just one possible approach to environmental ethics among many. Debates between homocentrists, biocentrists and ecocentrists are likely to continue and those who, like landscape architects, are involved on a day-to-day basis in making environmental decisions cannot wait for the philosophers to settle their differences. Landscape architecture may draw upon many ethical ideas which lie outside the homocentric domain of sustainable development. In particular, the desire to produce landscapes which are ecologically healthy seems to owe much to a non-anthropocentric position close to Leopold's 'land ethic'. Although the majority of landscape architectural work is concerned with aspects of the humanized landscape, many within the profession would also seem to be committed to the conservation of wilderness, and although this can be given an anthropocentric justification, it would seem to be more firmly founded on the non-anthropocentric notion that wild areas have intrinsic value and should be protected for their own sakes.

Nevertheless, this chapter has argued that the broad ethical position taken by the profession of landscape architecture is homocentric, and that sustainable development, by virtue of its concern for human well-being, justice within and between generations, and for the integrity of supporting environmental systems, offers a system of values which can, with some thought, be assimilated by environmental design professionals. Despite some of the failures and weaknesses of 'sustainable development', the concept still offers the most pragmatic way to move forward, and it was largely for this reason that it was embraced by the United Nations Conference on Environment and Development at Rio in 1992. It has also percolated into many levels of policy-making throughout the world through the widespread adoption of Agenda 21 by local authorities. Environmentalists sometimes bemoan the lack of progress since Rio and complain that the idea of sustainability has been appropriated by governments representing the forces of economic orthodoxy, but as Robin Attfield insists, 'crucial concepts and telling theories do not become incoherent or void through partial acceptance by the powerful; and sometimes their acceptance betokens their near indispensability' (1999, p. 112).

This chapter has weighed the extent to which the current practice of landscape architecture can be said to embody principles of sustainable development. Unsurprisingly, there are entries on both sides of the balance sheet. On one side, landscape architects may be open to the accusation that they have, whether willingly or unthinkingly, been complicit in the promotion of unsustainable development. On the other, they have demonstrated concerns for the conservation, enhancement and creation of bio-diverse habitats and a commitment to working with communities in ways which foster the communal values essential for a sustainable existence. It has also suggested, in brief, some of the directions in which landscape architecture may develop as it takes sustainable development to the heart of its concerns. Some of these directions will be explored in more detail in the chapters that follow.

REFERENCES

Adams, W. M. (1996) *Future Nature: A Vision for Conservation* (London, Earthscan).

Attfield, R. (1999) *The Ethics of the Global Environment* (Edinburgh, Edinburgh University Press).

Barton, H. (1998) Eco-neighbourhoods: a review of projects, *Local Environment*, 3(2), 159–177.

Bookchin, M. (1982) *The Ecology of Freedom* (Palo Alto, CA, Cheshire Books).

Bookchin, M. (1989) *Remaking Society* (New York, Black Rose Books).

Callicott, J. B. and Mumford, M. (1998) Ecological Sustainability as a Conservation Concept, in J. Lemon, L. Westra and R. Goodland (eds) *Ecological Sustainability and Integrity: Concepts and Approaches* (Dordrecht, Kluwer Academic Publishers).

Carson, R. (1963) *Silent Spring* (London, Hamilton).

Colvin, B. (1970) *Land and Landscape, Evolution, Design and Control* 2nd edition (London, John Murray).

Commoner, B. (1972) *The Closing Circle* (New York, Bantam).

Commoner, B. (1990) *Making Peace with the Planet* (New York, Pantheon).

Crowe, S. (1958) *The Landscape of Power* (London, Architectural Press).

Dramstad, W. E., Olson, J. D. and Forman, T. T. (1996) *Landscape Ecology Principles in Landscape Architecture and land use Planning* (Harvard, MA, Island Press).

The Ecologist (1993) Carrying capacity, over-population and environmental degradation, in J. Kirkby. P. O'Keefe and L. Timberlake (eds) (1995) *The Earthscan Reader in Sustainable Development* (London, Earthscan), pp.101–103.

Ekins, P. (1992) *A New World Order: Grassroots Movements for Global Change* (London and New York, Routledge).

Geddes, P. (1949) *Cities in Evolution* (London, Williams & Norgate).

Greed, C. (1996) *Introducing Town Planning*, 2nd edition (London, Longman).

Hackett, B. (1971) *Landscape Planning: An Introduction to Theory and Practice* (Newcastle upon Tyne, Oriel Press).

Hardin, G. (1968) The tragedy of the commons, *Science*, 162, 1243–1248.

Healey, P. and Shaw, T. (1993) *The Treatment of 'Environment' by Planners: Evolving Concepts and Policies in Development Plans*. Working Paper No. 31 (Department of Town and Country Planning, University of Newcastle upon Tyne).

International Union for the Conservation of Nature (1980) *World Conservation Strategy: Living Resources for Sustainable Development* (Gland, Switzerland, IUCN).

Jenkins, T. (1997) *Less Traffic, More Jobs: The Direct Employment Impacts of Developing a Sustainable Transport System in the United Kingdom* (London, Friends of the Earth).

Jensen, J. (1939) *Siftings* (Chicago, Ralph Fletcher Seymour).

Kuhn, T. (1970) *The Structure of Scientific Revolutions,* 2nd edition (Chicago, University of Chicago Press).

Landscape Institute (1997) Royal Charter (London, Landscape Institute).

Leopold, A. (1949) *A Sand County Almanac* (London, Oxford University Press).

Lovelock, J. (1979) *Gaia: A New Look at Life on Earth* (Oxford, Oxford University Press).

Lyle, J. T. (1994) *Regenerative Design for Sustainable Development* (New York, Wiley).

McHarg, I. (1969) *Design with Nature* (Garden City, NY, The Natural History Press).

McLaren, D., Bullock, S. and Yousuf, N. (1998) *Tomorrow's World: Britain's Share in a Sustainable Future* (London, Earthscan).

Merchant, C. (1992) *Radical Ecology: The Search for a Liveable World* (London and New York, Routledge).

Naess, A. (1973) The shallow and the deep, long-range ecology movement, *Inquiry*, 16, 95–100.

Naess, A. and Rothenberg, D. (1989) *Ecology, Community and Lifestyle* (Cambridge, Cambridge University Press).

Nassauer, J. I. (1995) Messy ecosystems, orderly frames, *Landscape Journal*, 14(2), pp. 161–170.

Norton, B. G. (1997) Convergence and contextualism: some clarifications and a reply to Steverson, *Environmental Ethics*,19, 87–100.

O'Riordan, T. (1981) *Environmentalism*, 2nd edition (London, Pion).

Pearce, D., Markandya, A. and Barbier, E. B. (1989) *Blueprint for a Green Economy* (London, Earthscan).

Punter, J. and Carmona, M. (1997) Cosmetics or critical restraints? The role of landscape in design policies in English development plans, *Journal of Environmental Planning and Management*, 40(2), 173–197.

Rawls, J. (1989) *A Theory of Justice* (Cambridge, MA., Harvard University Press).

Reid, D. (1995) *Sustainable Development, An Introductory Guide* (London, Earthscan).

Rosenberg, A. (1986) An emerging paradigm for landscape architecture, *Landscape Journal*, 5(2), 75–82.

Ruff, A. (1979) *Holland and the Ecological Landscapes* (Stockport, Deanwater Press).

Sterba, J. P. (1994) Reconciling anthropocentric and nonanthropocentric environmental ethics, *Environmental Values*, 3, 229–244.

Steverson, B. K. (1996) On the reconciliation of anthropocentric and nonanthropocentric environmental ethics, *Environmental Values*, 5, 349–361.

Tansley, A. G. (1939) *The British Islands and their Vegetation* (Cambridge, The University Press).

Thayer, R. L. (1994) *Gray World, Green Heart: Technology, Nature and the Sustainable Landscape* (New York, John Wiley and Sons).

Thompson, I.H. (2000) *Ecology, community and delight* (London, E & FN Spon).

Tolley, G. S., Graves, P. E. and Cohen, A. S. (1982) *Environmental Policy: Air Quality* (Cambridge, MA, Ballinger Publishing Company).

Trainer, T. (1998) Towards a checklist for ecovillage development, *Local Environment*, 3(1), 79–83.

United Nations Environmental Programme (UNEP) (1999) *Global Environmental Outlook 2000* (London, Earthscan).

United Nations World Commission on Environment and Development (UNWCED) (1987) *Our Common Future*, The Brundtland Report (Oxford, Oxford University Press).

Walker, P. and Simo, M. (1994) *Invisible Gardens: The Search for Modernism in the American Landscape* (Cambridge, MA, The MIT Press).

Westra, L. (1998) *Living in Integrity* (Lanham, MD, Rowan & Littlefield).

Woolley, H. and Whittaker, C. (1995) Ethical practices in the landscape profession: a research note, *Landscape Research*, 20(3), 147–151.

3

THE LANDSCAPE OF SUSTAINABLE ECONOMICS

Colin Price

SUMMARY

Economists need not accord special status to sustainability or landscape value: these ideas are embraced in the standard theory of pricing. In a sustainability context, retained landscape may be priced by the cost of preserving it; lost landscape, by the cost of restoring it. Where restoration is infeasible, the cost of creating landscape offering similar services, or even alternative forms of enjoyment, may be used. Where different services are offered, sustainability requires measurement of landscape values, to assure that substitutes have at least equivalent value. However, change of relative values through time is not properly reflected in standard investment appraisals. Abandoning such appraisal techniques offers more to future generations than imposing sustainability constraints.

INTRODUCTION

There is no one view among economists about the meaning of sustainability. Like other professionals, they have defined the concept variously, to suit their own interests. Indeed, by no means all economists agree that sustainability ought to be an overriding – or even an interesting – goal. For example, Beckerman (1994) favours 'optimal development', in which neither environment nor future generations have any special claims.

There are also many views among economists about how, if at all, landscape values are to be incorporated in economic analysis generally. Their inclination to render environmental values in money terms is the most contested aspect of environmental economics, drawing criticism from both within and outside the profession. There are some logical and actual links between particular views about how landscape values might be expressed in money terms, and those about sustainability.

Moreover, sustainability raises unresolved questions about how future landscape values are to be treated. Should it be at parity with current values, or according to normal protocols of investment analysis? And if so, using what interest rate?

The dominant, neo-classical, view of economics has been subjected to repeated attack, particularly where it bears upon public policy and upon evaluation of projects which substantially affect the environment and the interests of future generations (Self, 1976; Sagoff, 1988; Lowe *et al.*, 1993). But the neo-classical paradigm is not the only one to which those calling themselves economists would subscribe. And neo-classical economics is itself a many-headed monster – one might say a many-headed Aunt Sally – and to strike off one head using sharply honed argument is to risk the growth of two more.

This chapter reviews some interpretations that economists may put on sustainability, in a landscape

context. It explores how and why particular interpretations are associated with particular valuation
schemes, then questions whether techniques of
giving a present equivalent to future values, as commonly practised in cost–benefit analysis, are actually
compatible with the presented views of sustainability.

NEO-CLASSICAL ECONOMICS, LANDSCAPE AND SUSTAINABILITY

The neo-classical paradigm in economics might be
characterized somewhat as follows.

- Consumers derive utility or value from consumption of goods and services.
- Consumers have relative preferences for different
  goods and services, reflected in greater willingness
  to pay a high price for those which they value
  more.
- Respecting consumers' preferences as expressed in
  willingness to pay is central to democracy, and
  should motivate governments' interventions in
  the economy.
- Producers striving for high profits have a price
  incentive to produce those goods and services
  which are highly valued by consumers.
- At the same time, they economize on resources
  whose high price indicates that they are either
  scarce, or highly valued as a base for alternative
  productive activities.
- A freely operating market mechanism tends to
  create the best of all possible worlds, resources
  being channelled to maximize consumers' aggregate satisfaction.
- Crucially, in the context of sustainability, time,
  like other goods and services, has its price.
  Consumers forgo interest in order to satisfy their
  preference for consuming goods early rather than
  late: this interest is the price of earliness. The price
  is incorporated by *discounting* the value of goods
  and services which *lack earliness*, that is those
  produced in the more-or-less distant future.
  Numerically, this is accomplished by dividing a
  presumed willingness to pay for a future product

by 1 + [interest rate], once for every extra year
into the future that its consumption is delayed.
This leads to the familiar *present value* formula:

$$PV = \frac{FV}{(1 + i)^t}$$

where PV = present (discounted) value, FV =
future value, i = interest rate, and t = years of
delay to consumption.

Rearranged, this formula is equivalent to the
compound interest formula, which converts a
present sum of money into its future value.

- If the discounted value of an investment's present
  and future revenues exceeds the discounted value
  of its costs, it has positive net present value and
  should be adopted.
- In this sense, future values are nothing special:
  they can be treated by routine application of neo-
  classical economics.
- While markets have virtuous properties, they are
  absent for certain products, for explicable reasons;
  for other products markets function imperfectly,
  being seriously distorted, for example, by
  monopoly power, taxation or government regulation.
- These defects may be addressed by creating
  markets where none exist, by alleviating distor-
  tions where possible, and, where neither of these
  is possible, by deriving a set of theoretical prices
  which reflect the real utility of products and
  shortage of resources.

Within this neo-classical paradigm, landscape – or
rather *experience* of landscape – is a product like any
other. It is produced from a composite resource
consisting of natural capital – the land form and its
enveloping biotic cover – and fabricated capital – the
artefacts of human land use – mixed in different
proportions. It may have some special characteristics, but these fall within classes of special characteristics well recognized by neo-classicists.

STRICT SUSTAINABILITY AND THE LAND RESOURCE

Of all the myriad definitions of sustainability and sustainable development, the one most often quoted is that of the Brundtland Commission (1987): 'Sustainable development is development which meets the needs of the present without compromising the ability of future generations to meet their own needs.' Thus, in its most rigid form, strict sustainability does not allow current use of land to degrade its ability to render services – material or aesthetic – to future generations. This restriction is most obviously burdensome for non-renewable and non-recyclable resources such as fossil fuels. Utilization destroys them, and so makes them useless to future generations (see Figure 3.1). Even recyclable metals undergo irreversible attrition through several cycles of use.

Self-regenerating resources such as forest ecosystems can be exploited sustainably, and indeed have been so exploited for centuries, both in subsistence economies and under classical European forest management systems. However, when stocks are exploited faster than their regenerative capacity replaces them, meeting future needs is compromised: either because the production rate of a depleted growing stock is reduced, or because restoring full productivity requires a period of deliberately curtailed production.

Exploitation of any of these resource elements which physically constitute the landscape – and equally of non-depletable resources like river flow – may adversely affect visual qualities. But the aesthetic qualities of landscape *themselves* have the character of products – such as lighthouses or national defence – recognized by economists as 'public goods'. At least

Figure 3.1 COBEX: mining for the future. Is even mineral exploitation perceived as a difficulty under some interpretations of sustainability?

up to the point of congestion, aesthetic enjoyment by one individual is not destroyed or impaired through its being enjoyed by others. The ability of future generations to enjoy those aesthetic qualities remains uncompromised by any number of previous generations enjoying them. It is even arguable that artistic capital, built up by earlier painters, poets and musicians responding to those aesthetic qualities, may enhance enjoyment of favoured landscapes such as Wenlock Edge or the Lake District.

Thus, a strict sustainability criterion is easily met for purely aesthetic purposes. Sustainability only becomes an issue when exploitation is not of the aesthetic qualities, but of those other qualities, such as mineral composition or topographical configuration, on which landscape depends.

INTOLERABLE COSTS

But, then, a universally strict interpretation of sustainability, which permits no individual aesthetic resource to be damaged, would not only arrest human development, but reverse it traumatically. Indeed, if a resource might be preserved only by preventing its use in perpetuity it ceases to be a resource. Sustainable use of non-renewable resources is unintelligible, except in terms of sustaining the flow of *general services* offered by a *particular resource*. For example, a scenario is sustainable if fossil energy resources are replaced by investment in renewable substitutes such as wind or hydroelectric power. What matters to consumers is availability of electricity, not the location or means of its generation. What matters to producers is that renewable substitutes should be developed at least as fast as fossil resources are depleted.

Once again, landscape is conspicuously different. It is consumed in its raw state at source; and its location, precise configuration and personal and cultural associations are intrinsic to its value. Yet it is simply infeasible to leave every 'nook of English ground secure from rash assault', as Wordsworth might, in theory, have preferred it to be.

Even the more modest and pragmatic ambition, of not violating future generations' access to 'the best' and 'the fullest range' of landscape experience, is problematic. To maintain this limited strict sustainability requires a definition of critical natural capital and safe minimum standards that are inviolable in the face of development. Such a view is not entirely foreign to economists: actually the ideas of safe minimum standards (not to be breached) and critical natural capital (not to be depreciated) can be traced to a land economist, Ciriacy-Wantrup (1947), rather than to conservationists. Constraints of this kind, imposed selectively, might be admissible to mainstream neo-classical economists, at least those who recognize that market economics is not the whole scope of political economy.

Costing intolerability

Nevertheless, with economists nothing is absolute: each and every good can in principle be traded (provided the price is right) or (what amounts to the same thing) exchanged for other goods of equal or greater value. The constraints of safe minimum standards and critical natural capital are *normally* to be enforced, but not if there are 'intolerable costs' in so doing. The role of economists is to determine the cost of imposing the constraint. Such costs comprise the financial outlays required to maintain a cherished landscape, as, for example, in Environmentally Sensitive Areas (Whitby, 1994). They also include opportunity costs – the net revenues or benefits forgone when lucrative development is precluded by the constraint. Judging whether these costs are intolerable is left to political and legislative processes. Sagoff (1988) is one opponent of the full neo-classical treatment who would nevertheless advocate this limited role.

If the cost of the constraint is known, and political judgement indicates willingness by society's representatives to bear that cost, then that might be deemed a minimum cash valuation of the landscape so preserved, or of its contribution to the national portfolio of landscapes.

But here lies the problem. By what criteria were past costs of preservation deemed tolerable? By what criteria might future costs of keeping the status quo be judged intolerable? For one actor, intolerable costs of landscape preservation may be anything that commutes maximum profit. For another, they are ones that threaten not just livelihoods but lives: depression of the UK rural economy has increased the suicide rate among farmers, even if reduction of food surpluses *per se*, rather than environmental constraints on production, has been the leading cause.

Selective and not-quite-strict sustainability

The national parks of England and Wales show just how plastic the concept of strict protection may be, in the face of commercial imperatives. (Adrian Phillips has more to say on protected areas in an international context in Chapter 5.) Legislative protection prohibits development which conflicts with landscape conservation except under the joint conditions of

1   overwhelming national need;
2   absence of any feasible alternative (National Parks and Access to the Countryside Act, 1949).

The parks have nevertheless succumbed to every kind of aesthetic insult: mineral extraction, nuclear power stations, water resource development, ploughing up of heather moorland, blanket afforestation. In 1974 the Sandford Report reviewed the protection afforded by national park status. A minority viewpoint among the membership held that core areas of parks should be afforded absolute protection, but this did not prevail as a majority recommendation. Even if it had done, that would not protect landscapes from permanent aesthetic scars resulting from the parks' other main purpose: recreation provision (see Figure 3.2).

Nearly 10 per cent of England and Wales lies within national parks, and a further 15 per cent

Figure 3.2 Conflict of interest in the Peak District National Park: the recreation objective threatens the long-term aesthetic objective.

in Areas of Outstanding Natural Beauty (AONBs). A much greater proportion of land capable of delivering some special goods and services (high quality limestone, pure water resources, sites for telecommunication aerials) lies within them. It is thus abundantly clear that even a limited sustainability objective – to protect absolutely all designated landscapes – *would* impose intolerable costs in the eyes of many, not least, those of the areas' residents.

Two definitional problems now become apparent:

1 how are geographical limits of areas 'worth protecting' to be set?
2 what economic criteria can be applied within such areas, which recognize that landscape should be treated more protectively than normal, while ensuring that 'intolerable costs' are identified and avoided?

The protected area has grown beyond what was originally envisaged: the Snowdonia National Park is two-and-a-half times the size proposed by Dower (1945), and some designated AONBs were not even mentioned in the 'reserve list' of his report. The greater the protected area, the more inclusive will become the list of costs considered intolerable – particularly as it becomes increasingly likely that land possessing special qualities is found exclusively within designated areas. The greater, too, will become the need for compromise criteria, maintaining some priority to landscape while admitting the possibility of material development. Some such criteria are discussed in Price (1977), for example:

● using aesthetic rather than commercial aspects of proposed developments to identify potential locations for fuller evaluation;
● where uncertainty exists, giving 'the benefit of the doubt' to aesthetic considerations.

But, precisely because they admit the possibility of compromise, criteria like these cannot guarantee the future maintenance of aesthetic resources when they conflict with other considerations.

QUASI-STRICT SUSTAINABILITY, RESTORATION AND REPLACEMENT

Even after some softening of its margins, strict sustainability is a difficult test to meet – impossible if applied to all landscape resources. Practical ways of escape focus not on the inviolability of individual resources, but on maintaining the overall landscape resource.

Restoration

Aesthetic degradation by developments such as wind turbines and pylon lines is not irreversible. Should future generations wish to forgo the benefits of material consumption – of electricity in this case – in favour of an improved visual landscape, they are not precluded by the actions of present generations from dismantling the development (see Figure 3.3).

Such a dispensation provides another perspective on pricing future landscape experience. In order that future generations' consumption is not compromised by having to meet the cost of restoration, the present generation must endow a fund to pay for decommissioning developments and restoring landscape to its prior state. And, if future generations concur with the present generation's judgement – that electricity is worth more than landscape – they can leave the development, and take the interest on the endowment too, provided that the restoration fund is kept intact for *their* successors. The endowment becomes the effective price of landscape.

In other cases, a more deliberate-paced restoration takes place. For example, at Bardon Hill roadstone quarry in Charnwood Forest, not only are former contours progressively being restored by dumping overburden from elsewhere, but occasional large boulders have been scattered artistically on the reconstructed hillside (see Figure 3.4). A public footpath has been reinstated on its old line, and tree planting is beginning to restore the former woodland character.

A payment per tonne exploited into a (real or notional) restoration account is one means by which present exploitation pays to sustain the future landscape.

Replacement

A particular landscape resource may be irreparably degraded by development. However, future generations may be compensated by creating new landscape resources. Bowers and Hopkinson (1994) argue that attractive landscape lost, for example in road development, should be matched by attractive landscape

Figure 3.3   Temporary interruption to service? Wind turbines on a moorland skyline.

created elsewhere: a step beyond 'accommodation' or 'mitigation' described by Ian Thompson in Chapter 2. Francis *et al.* (1992) examined ways of recreating an attractive woodland flora in new farm woodlands, offering a replacement for woodlands destroyed by development. While techniques of creating habitats (Gilbert and Anderson, 1998) have usually had a primary ecological purpose, they can equally serve aesthetic ends. In principle, it is easy to cost the operations involved.

Laudable in purpose, these means of sustaining the aggregate of aesthetic resources are not without difficulties. One problem is how to treat medium-term benefits lost during prolonged mineral extraction and restoration, or between loss of woodlands and the maturity of their replacements. An accounting approach, when an aesthetic feature is replaced in a different location, is to cost replacement from the time when it would have been necessary to establish the replacement, so that it was

mature before the original resource was destroyed. For such features as oak woodland, the inclusion of interest cost over a two-hundred-year aesthetic maturation period dramatically increases the cost: for example, for a hectare costing £2,000 to establish,

$$£2,000 \times (1 + 5\%)^{200} \approx £35,000,000$$

Of course retrospective investment in replacement can be no more than an accounting fiction. Nonetheless, to calculate what it *would have cost* is salutary, and could become an actual basis for compensation.

SUSTAINING AGGREGATE CAPITAL

Sustainability has so far been cast in terms of preventing depletion of the inventory of natural and

Figure 3.4   Please replace after use: restoration of the rocky character of Bardon Hill.

semi-natural capital which constitutes landscape. This falls under the heading of 'strong sustainability' as defined by Pearce *et al.* (1993). A less restrictive requirement, dubbed 'weak sustainability' is to maintain the sum of natural, semi-natural and wholly fabricated capital: thus future generations are compensated for loss of some means of production by gain of other means. Unfortunately for this interpretation, long debate has established no satisfactory means of valuing different kinds of capital on a common scale (Harcourt, 1972) except, that is, by reference to their economic productivity. Hence sustainability might be reinterpreted as maintaining the ability to deliver an undiminished flow of total aesthetic services; or, somewhat more flexibly, undiminished *opportunities* for aesthetic experience by future generations. The shift of approach by various

environmental agencies (CAG Consultants and Land Use Consultants, 1997) – from protecting particular environmental capital towards identifying significant environmental services – aligns with this changed perspective. Thus, in circumstances where exact or even close replicas of lost landscape are problematic to create, creation of a resource rendering aesthetic services *of equivalent value* might sufficiently discharge obligations to future generations.

To ensure that at least equivalent value is created requires evaluation in aesthetic terms both of what has been lost and of what is to be gained. Many methods of performing such evaluation have been proposed (Fines, 1968; Linton 1968; Price, 1994a), but none has been universally – or even widely – accepted. This deficiency threatens the practical application of sustainability constraints.

Nor can maintaining pure aesthetic quality guarantee equivalence between contributions of new landscape and old to the national portfolio of landscape, as documented by the Countryside Character Programme (Countryside Commission, 1994). Richly varied pastureland and barren mountains might score similarly in Fines's system, but they do not offer substitutable aesthetic experiences. Adequate replacement becomes impossible if the meaning of landscape is considered to include its historical significance and cultural value: *how landscape came to be* and its impact on those who have experienced its degradation.

Moreover, landscapes of equivalent aesthetic value at different locations and of different type affect different beneficiary groups, as defined by geographical and psychological characteristics. Environmental philosophers (e.g. Parfit, 1984) have wrestled inconclusively with the question of *which* future people have entitlement to sustained pleasures: the biological descendants of those who lost a particular aesthetic experience; the new members of a lineally continuous interest group; or only 'some group or other' which in each generation benefits from whatever environmental advantages a replacement site is able to offer? In practice neo-classical economics may pool all people as 'equally entitled consumers', but its theory is agnostic about comparing the well-being of different individuals. This consideration of different persons does in one sense alleviate the sustainability problem. After all, we do not know what future generations' tastes will be. Tastes for particular forms of landscape have changed, as was evident in the shift from the formal seventeenth-century garden style in Britain to the naturalistic park style of the eighteenth. It might reasonably be assumed that future generations would welcome the opportunity to experience something close to wilderness, and to rurality, and to the kind of fine townscapes that ancient civilizations, as well as ourselves, appreciated. But such general prescriptions can be met, without preserving either particular landscapes, or even particular landscape styles. Moreover, unspecified future generations have not yet acquired particular associations which make change in landscape so painful to presently living people. Mortality progressively wipes the slate clean: new generations form their associations and their norms of design from whatever landscapes they are born into (see Chapters 4 and 14).

Oddly, it is sustainability of the aesthetic experience of *present* generations that is so difficult to provide. And, even for presently living people, accustomization to new forms and treatments of landscape, and distancing from the sense of loss, make what has been sacrificed less grievous, and what replaces it more acceptable, as time goes on (Price, 1993, Chapter 14). Such considerations might persuade us to be less fastidious in requiring preservation of particular forms of aesthetic experience.

In summary, the problems reviewed above mean that equivalent *aesthetic* value does not imply equivalent *economic* value. But it is noteworthy that they are problems of aesthetics and psychology, not of economics *per se*: they cannot be evaded by eschewing an economic approach.

THE NATURAL RESOURCE CONSTRAINT

Creation of attractive landscape to replace losses elsewhere depends on an unlimited supply of available landscapes wherein schemes of improvement can be discharged. Neo-classical economics tends to be optimistic about such availability: everything, the sub-text reads, is available at a price. Moreover, technology has, so far, provided new resources: as landscapes are destroyed, so advancing transportation technology allows access to world-wide landscape resources.

Suppose, on the other hand, we are not disposed to accept the open-endedness of this process. Suppose we doubt the sustainability of long-distance tourism with its attendant resource depletion and pollution. Does technology then have anything to offer to aesthetic sustainability? Assuredly it has!

Sustaining virtual landscape

The leisure use of virtual reality has mostly developed as a means of mimicking exotic or thrilling experiences. Nothing in its technical nature, however, precludes it from offering the sensation of being within a familiar landscape. Indeed, such capabilities already exist in landscape design CAD packages, with rapid improvement in realism of representation. Potential exists for combining this with the physical sensations of moving oneself through the landscape, and aesthetic data such as bird song (already part of multi-media experience), the feel of the wind in one's hair (not too challenging technically) and 'rich country smells' (perhaps some decades from realization?).

Provided the image of landscape as it now is can be captured before degradation or destruction, any particular aesthetic experience can, in a way, be sustained. The price of destroying landscape *experience* is the cost of technical resources required to recreate it. This virtual experience can be provided in the home, or at least locally, without the resource depletion and pollution involved in travel to the original aesthetic resource.

The question now arises, however, of whether virtual reality is genuinely and completely a *substitute* for experience of the real world, or whether it is an independent experience, understood and enjoyed for what it is, but not confused with what the real world provides. There is even an argument that virtual reality and the real world are complements: experience of one enhances experience of the other. If so, virtual replicas of landscapes may actually aggravate the sense of loss, by perpetuating awareness of what has been destroyed, and giving insight into a conceivable present that past decisions have now rendered unattainable. On the other hand, if consumers accept virtual reality as a genuine substitute, that might activate serious unease about the meaning of real life, and the susceptibility of populations to manipulation. There is a Brave New World aura about it.

Compensation in something-close-to kind?

An alternative response to a perceived land resource limit is that exploited landscapes, rather than being abandoned in favour of replacements, are redeveloped to sustain a flow of psychic benefit, even though of a different kind. For example, in 1971 Rio Tinto Zinc expressed interest in copper mining a 5-square-kilometre tract in the Snowdonia National Park (Zuckerman, 1972). The period of exploitation would have been 20 years, whereafter an extensive outdoors activity site could have been created, with, no doubt, tasteful shaping of spoil heaps and utilization of pits and ponds for water sports (something at which mineral exploiters and public bodies have become increasingly adept). This is restoration of a sort, but with a major shift in the stream of experiences offered (see Figure 3.5). Like is no longer being replaced with like.

Figure 3.5 Any method, but not all objectives: Thames Valley landscape restored to different, recreational use.

Figures 3.6a and 3.6b   Pay as you view: prospect of Rügen's cliffs available only to paying visitors.

SUSTAINABLE WILLINGNESS TO PAY?

As compensating consumption becomes more different from what is actually forgone, so less reliance can be placed on physical and psychological measures of experience, and more must hang on economic indicators of equivalent value. Here perforce we enter a new realm in valuing landscape: no longer by the costs of restoring or re-creating temporarily lost benefits; no longer via establishing equivalents in aesthetic terms, but, much more controversially, through directly monetizing benefits of landscape experience.

Purchase?

Landscape experience is sometimes directly marketed: especially where topography or tree cover enables a view to be treated in an exclusive and proprietary way. Aesthetic resources have been fenced off and made subject to an entry charge, for example, at Swallow Falls in North Wales, or the chalk cliffs of Rügen in Germany (see Figure 3.6). Voluntary contributions may also be solicited, most successfully where an evident cost is incurred by the proprietor in maintaining car parks (Forest Enterprise) or routes of access to viewing points (National Trust).

There are, however, doubts about what such contributions for aesthetic resources really mean

(Price, 1994b). On one hand, they may represent what the user perceives as the cost of provision: on the other, they may express a psychological need to align symbolically with environmental causes. There is a contrary possibility that mandatory or suggested charges will provoke resentment about commoditization – profit-orientated packaging and marketing – of what are considered common heritage or God-given resources (Lowe *et al.*, 1993). This may prompt refusal to pay anything for a resource, even though it is actually highly valued.

In any case, exclusion from experience of landscape is usually infeasible, and voluntary contributions, if solicited at all, are derisory. Recourse must then be made to indirect or hypothetical markets for existing or new landscapes. Some adherents of the neo-classical tradition see, in this extension of economics, welcome scope to increase their own sphere of influence. While perhaps preferring a world where everything is bought with hard cash, they might accept that some things are *not* directly paid for, and that this absence of a market demands corrective treatment.

Hedonic pricing

Perhaps the most acceptable means of monetary valuation to such economists is deriving willingness to pay for aesthetic experience from payments made for *access* to the experience. Hedonic pricing (Griliches, 1971) is a method for deducing the value of a *particular characteristic* of a marketed commodity, from prices of a range of products which variously embody that characteristic. In essence, it entails regression analysis of prices on variables representing what are deemed the desired characteristics. In recent years, records of house prices have formed the basis for valuing components of the view such as woodland type, or presence of a river (Garrod and Willis, 1992). The expectations might be that rivers would improve views and prices, and extensive conifer woodland depreciate them.

The equivalent approach for landscape which is visited rather than inhabited is to record differential willingness to pay for travel to sites which embody features deemed aesthetically attractive. Thus visitors on the whole will travel further to enjoy landscapes containing mountains and vernacular field boundaries, than to wire-fenced flatlands.

Although the theory is appealing, in practice the results have been both disappointing (Hanley and Ruffell, 1993) and puzzling (Price, 1995): disappointing, because expected attractive features seemed to exert no significant influence on distance travelled; puzzling, because features such as age of trees sometimes influence house price contrarily to what might be expected.

A fundamental problem is that landscape value depends not just on a collection of positively signed ingredients (steep topography, varied land uses, presence of water bodies) but also, crucially, on the combination or composition of these elements. It is the former collection that hedonic pricing aims to quantify, on the premise that the value of each component is separable from that of components with which it is conjoined. (Actually, if this were so, sustainability could be delivered without a pricing process, merely by maintaining the overall supply of the valued characteristic: felling woodland in one place *is* balanced by planting trees in another.) In practice, however, aesthetic composition is a subtle and plastic concept, which effortlessly defies attempts to reproduce it in additive or other form intelligible to computers.

Valuing aesthetic quality, holistically and subjectively assessed (Price, 1978; Abelson, 1979), runs counter to the neo-classical credo of objectively recording scientifically measurable entities. Nevertheless, at least one study (Bergin and Price, 1994) has attempted to scale holistic landscape values on the basis of high travel costs to the best quality landscapes.

On this foundation, Thomas and Price (1999) have conjectured a value for landscapes created by planting farm woodlands, via the following steps:

● create aesthetically-orientated designs for a representative range of plantable sites;

- score landscape with woodland and without it on a 'pure' aesthetic scale;
- relate intervals on this scale to increments of willingness to pay to travel to landscapes of greater quality;
- scale up according to the number of leisure visitors.

Assessed aesthetic benefit was of similar magnitude to the expected cost of woodland creation. Such new landscapes might be seen as compensating for loss of trees and hedgerows in the old (Westmacott and Worthington, 1974).

Contingent valuation

Given the problems of interpreting actual payments and hedonic prices, it is unsurprising that much emphasis has recently been placed on contingent valuation. Beguilingly simple in concept, contingent valuation entails asking people directly what monetary compensation they would be willing to accept (for example, from intending developers) for loss of valued landscape experience, or what they would pay to gain landscape benefits (if it was institutionally possible to create a market for the replacement landscape). In theory, when these two values are the same, the aesthetic services of the overall landscape resource have been sustained, provided both development and replacement actually proceed. Alternatively, when consumers are indifferent between a sum of money and the experience of landscape, it can be claimed that exchange of landscape for cash sustains the same level of utility for the respondents (Randall, 1994).

Despite its simplicity, in practice the method encounters a host of technical problems (Mitchell and Carson, 1989), some having particular relevance to sustainability:

- envisaging the hypothesized change in existing and proposed landscape and how this relates to cash sums – consumers may lack both sufficient imagination and any familiarity with buying and selling aesthetic experience;

- believing in institutions for making payments and delivering compensation;
- part–whole bias – consumers offer a symbolic value for environmental conservation generally, rather than for the particular resource.

Among the most enduring problems is that willingness to accept compensation for loss of a particular benefit is usually much greater than willingness to pay to gain or retain that same benefit (Rowe et al., 1980). Moreover, 'protest bids' – zero or implausibly high willingness to pay or accept compensation – are frequently encountered among responses, perhaps reflecting political rejection of the valuation of aesthetic resources in money terms (Sagoff, 1988). But more specifically and quite separately they may reveal a judgement that no amount of money would sufficiently compensate the loss. Economic theory recognizes two explanations for this.

- The value of a particular aesthetic experience may have, or be perceived as having, indefinite value, since, unlike most economic products, it may have no close substitute and is lost, if at all, in its entirety. Even the offer of a replacement landscape of apparently equivalent quality might consistently be rejected, on the grounds that the associations of a particular landscape in a particular place cannot be recreated.
- Cash has diminishing marginal utility: each extra addition to wealth has less value than previous additions, as the thirst for consumption is successively slaked and satiated. Even an infinite amount of extra cash may have finite value, less than the value of cherished aesthetic experiences.

This propensity has serious and evident consequences for sustainability, whenever this is interpreted as providing new resources to the same value as that of resources lost. It needs only one indefinite evaluation (whatever its cause) to render sustainability, even in this laxer interpretation, impossible to achieve.

Nor does hedonic pricing escape the problem: house prices are formed by negotiations between willing sellers and buyers. When landscape is degraded or destroyed, those who experience loss do not voluntarily sell up and purchase elsewhere. That the value of a location may exceed its market price is evident from the need to apply compulsory purchase to properties required for development: owners are definitionally unwilling to surrender the package, in which aesthetic components are often important, that their home offers, and certainly not at the market price.

The new way

The monetization concept might be seen as economists' special contribution to the sustainability debate. These tools, imperfect though they are, address sustainability in a new way. Monetization does not in the end avoid the problem of indefinite values. But these are intrinsic to displacement of one kind of entity by another, not to monetary measurement.

Compensation – trading with any old thing

The new form of sustainability is free from requirements to maintain any particular *means* of producing, or any particular *form* of product. Let us take, as the means of sustaining the well-being once imparted by landscape experience, additional consumption of candy-floss (cotton-candy for readers in North America): this may serve as a symbol of what money buys. Aesthetes might react with horror to the fundamentals of their value system being so casually displaced. But economists might argue that it is for individuals to decide what they value. If they are willing to pay, in actuality, as much for candy-floss as they may be imputed to be for beautiful sunsets, then it is not the place of aesthetic experts to challenge their judgements and preferences: the neo-classical consumer is sovereign. What is lost by landscape degradation may be sustained, provided only that the resources needed to supply additional

Figure 3.7   Would they be content with candy-floss and circuses instead? Future generations contemplate a hole in the ground.

candy-floss are made available (see Figure 3.7). The cost of *those* resources becomes the price of landscape.

SUSTAINING EQUIVALENT VALUES

But even the neo-classical philosophy in its most sentiment-free form now has a problem (whether it knows it or not). Virtual reality experience and candy-floss may be valued to the extent that certain quanta elicit the same willingness to pay as a certain quantum of aesthetic experience. If all types of consumption were complete substitutes for each other, it would be a matter of indifference whether the future basket of experiences were rich in landscape, or in active outdoor recreation, or in virtual reality, or in candy-floss: sustaining the *aggregate value* of experience, not its composition, is what counts. An efficient economy delivers more and more of those products for which technology makes delivery an ever-cheaper option. If technological advance renders production of candy-floss increasingly efficient, as time goes on the quantity of resources needed to provide the compensating candy-floss diminishes. Virtual reality is certainly becoming rapidly cheaper to provide.

If, however, these commodities are not substitutes, the neo-classical analysis becomes quite different. Trade-offs between goods are usually illustrated in economics textbooks as indifference curves (see Figure 3.8). These curves show the following.

- For a consumer at A, rich in landscape experience but poor in candy-floss, a small increment of candy-floss (10 units) is adequate compensation for loss of 20 units of landscape experience (movement to B).
- From B, a greater increment of candy-floss consumption (20 units) is needed to compensate for the same number of units loss of landscape experience (movement to C).
- A future in which affluence increases consumption of candy-floss, but natural resource limits

keep landscape experience at its present level, also increases the amount of candy-floss required to compensate for loss of landscape experience (movement from D to E). Even if the resources required to make each unit of candy-floss are diminished by improving technology, it remains possible that more resources might be needed to replace landscape experience by candy-floss.

- In a future of material affluence but aesthetic poverty, loss of 20 units of landscape experience would entail yet greater candy-floss compensation (movement from E to F). A situation is perfectly conceivable in which no amount of candy-floss could compensate for further loss of aesthetic experience. Compensation in material things may become unattainable for future generations satiated with material goods (Price, in press).

DISCOUNTING AND THE ROAD TO METAPHORICAL SUSTAINABILITY

According to the definition by Pearce *et al.* (1989) strong sustainability means maintaining consumption in each future time period. If, despite landscape change, all future time periods are provided, in kind or otherwise, with consumption at least as valuable as would have been attained without the landscape change, there should be no disagreement between generations that an overall improvement has been achieved.

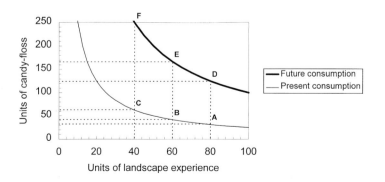

Figure 3.8 Indifference curves showing shifting trade-offs.

There is, however, a less demanding notion of sustainability: 'weak sustainability' in the terminology of Pearce *et al.* (1989), but more like 'very weak sustainability' in the taxonomy of Pearce *et al.* (1993). This requires only that the discounted value of future landscape losses imposed by a development does not exceed the discounted value of the development. This is no different from saying that the net present value of development should be non-negative – the normal, pre-sustainability criterion for an acceptable project. It is at first difficult to see how such a concept could have been registered as a legitimate offspring of sustainability. However, neo-classical economists might argue that the net present value criterion is justified on one of the following arguments.

Growth of the compensation fund

By investing cash gains from early exploitation of land resources, present generations can finance ever-increasing compensation to future generations, as the fund grows at compound interest. The earlier the gains, the larger the fund grows; the later the losses, the smaller the amount needed to generate a given compensation. Table 3.1 illustrates the point, using an interest rate of 8 per cent (approximately the pre-tax and inflation-adjusted rate of return on share investment). For simplicity of illustration, it is assumed that the investment produces two equal tranches of revenue at times 5 and 10, and that aesthetic degradation occurs suddenly at time 11.

Note the following:

- The early contribution, at time 5, offers more to the fund, by way of compound interest, than that at time 10.
- Once compensation begins to be paid at time 11, compensation paid equals interest generated, so that the real value of the fund is sustained at the same level.

Provided net present value is positive (revenues at times 5 and 10 exceed £1,000,000), in theory, gainers from the investment could pay sufficient into a sinking fund, that compensation could be given to losers, such that they too would become gainers. The future pay-outs either compensate future generations for loss of landscape values or supply resources for completely satisfactory restoration or replacement of landscape.

Limitations

Investing early proceeds of the project is only possible if they come in cash form: investments yielding early returns in environmental gain only cannot be so treated. Second, as noted already, a given cash sum, even if inflation indexed, may not suffice to pay adequate compensation for loss of environmental experience which is becoming scarcer relative to material consumption.

Finally, the justification for the argument hangs on endowments *actually* being made, and growing at compound interest, with no withdrawals except for compensation. Many respected economists (e.g. d'Arge *et al.*, 1982) have challenged whether such an investment policy would really be maintained

Table 3.1 Compensation accounts

Time	Contribution to sinking fund	Accumulated fund size after adding interest	Required compensation for environmental loss
5	1,000,000	1,000,000	–
9		1,360,489	–
10	1,000,000	2,469,328	–
11		2,666,874	213,350
–		2,666,874	213,350
100		2,666,874	213,350

over the relevant periods of time. Past experience – of private heritage being squandered on present pleasures; of insufficient provision being made to compensate for industrial diseases; of state pensions being funded from current taxation, because past taxation funded only historical outlays – does not encourage optimism.

Nor has the introduction of an explicit sustainability objective much altered the aspect of the playing field. In a World Bank publication on sustainability, El Serafy (1989) asserts without comment that 'reinvestment of the proceeds [of natural resource exploitation] is only a metaphor'. This yields yet another economic concept of sustainability: metaphorical sustainability, which guarantees nothing for future generations, other than that they will be treated with exactly the same contempt as is accorded to them by less nebulous and less sanctimonious philosophies than that of sustainability. There are precedents for this remarkably cavalier treatment. According to the neo-classical interpretation of redistribution, it is only necessary for compensation to be *potentially* payable: but such an interpretation is ethically void (Layard, 1972).

The equity counter-argument

Another train of thought asks why we should provide more for future generations. Their level of well-being will be maintained above ours in any event. However, this is an equity argument, not one of sustainability. The sustainability requirement is that actions of present generations do not compromise the well-being of future generations, not that future generations' well-being must not decline below that of the present. We might act *justly* by securing to ourselves a greater material well-being at their expense; and to them, a greater aesthetic well-being at our expense. But this would not be sustainability.

Time preference

A desperate final justification for discounting rests in consumers' preferences for consumption now rather than later. At this point, economics and sustainability appear to reach irreconcilable opposition. Sustainability is only upheld as a priority objective if future generations' interests are given undiminished importance: but discounting in line with present generations' preferences compromises the importance of future generations, just because they *are* future generations.

Time preference conventionally interpreted does not include the preferences of future generations. Yet their preferences are likely to reflect those of present generations – that consumption now (that is to say, within their own generation) is more important than consumption in any other generation. In this, all generations think alike: taking account of all time preferences, all generations are entitled to the same consideration.

Nor is rejection of discounting alien to all strands of economic thinking. The classical utilitarians, to whom welfare economics owes its foundations, were of a near-unanimous view that futurity was of itself no reason to give less weight to well-being accruing in future. Sidgwick (1874) famously remarked that 'the value of a man's happiness cannot depend on the time when it occurs'.

SUSTAINING THE STATUS QUO

A final fault to find with economic conceptions of sustainability lies in its nature as a mere negative constraint. In a general sense, sustainability enjoins us to install the present state of affairs as our benchmark: no one should become worse off in future as a result of present actions. Sustainability prohibits us from replacing admired broadleaved woodlands by commercial forests which in due time will offend the eyes of rich neo-rustics (unless we can and do compensate them adequately, which may be very, or indefinitely, expensive). But, whatever interpretation may have been laid on it for political purposes, 'sustainable' actually means only 'capable of being maintained at the same level'. The Brundtland definition explicitly precludes 'compromising the ability of future generations to meet their own needs', but it makes no reference to *promoting their cause actively*. Thus, in itself, sustainability contains no injunction to improve the townscapes of trapped inner city residents. However 'strongly' the sustainability dispensation is interpreted, it remains silent on the merit of making permanent improvements to the aesthetic environment – unless these should incidentally be the cheapest means of compensating for landscape lost elsewhere, or unless such improvements are clearly necessary to stave off social disintegration. 'Development' such schemes may be: but the customary concatenation of words in 'sustainable development' does not make everything that is development also a part of 'sustainability'.

Meanwhile, the normal process of discounting in investment appraisal (Department of the Environment, 1991) trivializes the merit of investing in long-term enhancement of landscape. To regard sustainability as a sufficient guarantor for future generations' well-being is to do no more than defend the status quo, and to shore up existing privilege. Perhaps that is part of the purpose of the sustainability debate: to divert our attention from resolving the inequity existing within our own generation?

CONCLUSION

So, what does economics have to say about sustainability, that has relevance for landscape? A great deal, but not much of it has practical value. In a discipline which, among the social sciences, piques itself on its mathematical precision, economic sustainability is an astoundingly flexible concept. It has the potential to elide from strict safe minimum standards (except when intolerable costs exist) to metaphorical cash compensation (which would often be inadequate, even if it were to be paid).

Sustainability is most valuable when treated literally and uncompromisingly in key areas:

- protecting the very best absolutely, for the benefit of this and later generations;
- protecting the very good relatively, by taking care with aesthetic evaluations.

The most effective general protection we can offer future generations is not to leave them prey to the plastic concepts of sustainability-based economics, but instead to not-discount their well-being. Arguably, it is only because of discounting that there was ever perceived to be a need for a sustainability constraint. Without discounting, the potential benefits to future generations of maintaining *and creating* good landscape are given full value. Such a dispensation does allow that landscape may sometimes be sacrificed to things that people would prefer to have in its stead, in the projected conditions of the future. It also authorizes us to accept great present benefit if available at trivial future sacrifice; and to improve landscapes for the putative benefit of far-distant future generations (by creating oak woodlands now, rather than when the moment of compensation looms). Unless we further debase the meaning of the term by equating it with 'promoting the good of the future', these fine deeds lie outwith the remit of sustainability.

REFERENCES

Abelson, P. (1979) *Cost–Benefit Analysis and Environmental Problems* (Farnborough, Saxon House).

Beckerman, W. (1994) 'Sustainable development': is it a useful concept? *Environmental Values*, 3, 191–209.

Bergin, J. and Price, C. (1994) The travel cost method and landscape quality, *Landscape Research*, 19 (1), 21–23.

Bowers, J. and Hopkinson, P. (1994) The treatment of landscape in project appraisal: consumption and sustainability approaches, *Project Appraisal*, 9, 110–118.

Brundtland Commission (1987) *Our Common Future* (Oxford, Oxford University Press).

CAG Consultants and Land Use Consultants (1997) *What Matters and Why: Environmental Capital: a New Approach* (Cheltenham, Countryside Commission).

Ciriacy-Wantrup, S. von, (1947) *Resource Conservation: Economics and Policies* (3rd ed., 1968) (Berkeley, University of California Division of Agricultural Sciences).

Countryside Commission (1994) *The New Map of England: a Directory of Regional Landscape*, Countryside Commission Publication 445 (Cheltenham, Countryside Commission).

d'Arge, R. C., Schulze, W. D. and Brookshire, D. S. (1982) Carbon dioxide and intergenerational choice, *American Economic Review Papers and Proceedings*, 72, 251–256.

Department of the Environment (1991) *Policy Appraisal and the Environment* (London, HMSO).

Dower, J. (1945) *National Parks in England and Wales* (London, HMSO).

El Serafy, S. (1989) The Proper Calculation of Income from Depletable Natural Resources, in Y. J. Ahmad, S. El Serafy and E. Lutz (eds) *Environmental Accounting for Sustainable Development* (Washington, DC, The World Bank).

Fines, K. D. (1968) Landscape evaluation: a research project in East Sussex, *Regional Studies*, 2, 41–55.

Francis, J. L., Morton, A. J. and Boorman, L. A. (1992) The establishment of ground flora species in recently planted woodland, *Aspects of Applied Biology*, 29, 171–178.

Garrod, G. D. and Willis, K. G. (1992) Valuing goods' characteristics: an application of the hedonic price method to environmental attributes, *Journal of Environmental Management*, 34, 59–76.

Gilbert, O. L. and Anderson, P. (1998) *Habitat Creation and Repair* (Oxford, Oxford University Press).

Griliches, Z. (ed.) (1971) *Price Indexes and Quality Change* (Cambridge, MA, Harvard University Press).

Hanley, N. D. and Ruffell, R. (1993) The contingent valuation of forest characteristics, *Journal of Agricultural Economics*, 44, 218–229.

Harcourt, G. C. (1972) *Some Cambridge Controversies in the Theory of Capital* (Cambridge: Cambridge University Press).

Layard, R. (1972) *Cost–Benefit Analysis* (Harmondsworth, Penguin).

Linton, D. L. (1968) The assessment of scenery as a natural resource, *Scottish Geographical Magazine*, 84, 218–238.

Lowe, P., Clark, J. and Cox, G. (1993) Reasonable creatures: rights and rationalities in valuing the countryside, *Journal of Environmental Planning and Management*, 36, 101–115.

Mitchell, R. C. and Carson, R. T. (1989) *Using Surveys to Value Goods: The Contingent Valuation Method* (Washington, DC, Resources for the Future).

Parfit, D. (1984) *Reasons and Persons* (Oxford, Oxford University Press).

Pearce, D. W., Markandya, A. and Barbier, E. B. (1989) *Blueprint for a Green Economy* (London, Earthscan).

Pearce, D. *et al.* (1993) *Blueprint 3: Measuring Sustainable Development* (London, Earthscan).

Price, C. (1977) Cost–benefit analysis, national parks and the pursuit of geographically segregated objectives, *Journal of Environmental Management*, 5, 87–97.

Price, C. (1978) *Landscape Economics* (London, Macmillan).

Price, C. (1993) *Time, Discounting and Value* (Oxford, Blackwell). [Out of print, but available from the author.]

Price, C. (1994a) Literature review [of landscape valuation], *Landscape Research*, 19(1), 38–55.

Price, C. (1994b) Donations, charges and willingness to pay, *Landscape Research*, 19(1), 9–12.

Price, C. (1995) Pros and cons of alternative evaluation methods, in K. G. Willis and J. Corkindale (eds) *Environmental Valuation: New Directions* (Wallingford, CAB International).

Price, C. (in press) Discounting compensation for injuries, *Journal of Risk Analysis*.

Randall, A. (1994) Contingent valuation: an introduction, *Landscape Research*, 19(1), 12–14.

Rowe, R. D., d'Arge, R. C. and Brookshire, D. S. (1980) An Experiment on the Economic Value of Visibility, *Journal of Environmental Economics and Management*, 7, 1–19.

Sagoff, M. (1988) *The Economy of the Earth* (Cambridge, Cambridge University Press).

Sandford, J. C. E. (1974) *Report of the National Park Policies Review Committee* (London, HMSO).

Self, P. (1976) *Econocrats and the Policy Process* (London, Macmillan).

Sidgwick, H. (1874) *The Methods of Ethics* (London, Macmillan).

Thomas, A. L. and Price, C. (1999) Landscape valuation of farm woodlands, in P. J. Burgess, E. D. R. Brierley, J. Morris and J. Evans (eds) *Farm Woodlands for the Future* (Oxford, Bios).

Westmacott, R. and Worthington, T. (1974) *New Agricultural Landscapes* (Cheltenham, Countryside Commission).

Whitby, M. (1994) *Incentives for Countryside Management* (Wallingford, CAB International).

Zuckerman, S. (1972) *Report of the Commission on Mining and the Environment* (London, Commission on Mining and the Environment).

4

THE SOCIAL DIMENSIONS OF LANDSCAPE SUSTAINABILITY

Maggie H. Roe

SUMMARY

Social structure and social learning are identified in this chapter as two major themes which are central to the discussion surrounding social sustainability in relation to landscape architecture. The chapter introduces these themes by examining the background to the crisis which communal life and landscapes in the UK are perceived to have suffered during the 1970s to the 1990s. Concepts of democracy, public participation, empowerment, landscape exclusion and social justice, communities and decision making are discussed under the theme of social structure and some potentials for more integrated and responsive decision making structures are identified. Under the theme of social learning, concepts of community building, rights and responsibilities, volunteering and citizenship, cultural diversity, identity and character are examined. Changing perceptions of the city and city communities, their behaviour, attitude and lifestyles are also identified. Finally, the author examines ways of building more integrated thinking through community projects and the way community projects are funded. A number of important points emerge from this discussion. These are summarized in the conclusion and some ideas are provided on the way forward for the landscape profession in thinking about this complex and difficult subject.

INTRODUCTION

The question of what social sustainability[1] is in relation to landscape is a complex one. It meshes with current political debates, such as that surrounding social exclusion, and with concepts of environmental ethics and ideals of democratic decision making. It is generally thought that without changes in social behaviour, values and equality in conjunction with economic and political change, opportunities to develop a more ecologically sustainable lifestyle will be severely limited (see, for example, Bechtel, 1997). There is also a perception among researchers and practitioners that these changes involve the development of a more altruistic society that will help rebuild and redefine the concepts of community and citizenship. Few landscape architects have grappled openly with the problem of defining the social elements of sustainability important in landscape planning and design although social considerations are commonly referred to. However, Thayer, who has written extensively and elegantly about sustainability and the human condition in relation to landscape states that there is a need 'not for business as usual' and that 'it is important to look at sustainable landscapes in terms of the nature and degree of the social change they imply' (1994, p. 317).

It is possible to argue that the development of a lifestyle which is more ecologically sustainable might reduce the physical comforts, convenience and

Table 4.1   A summary of the general characteristics of social sustainability

Social learning	Social structure
Retaining *cultural diversity* and richness through recognition, acceptance, understanding and building upon *identity, character* and difference within and between communities and their *beliefs*, values and histories. Allowing for the development of potentials in *cultural expression* and imagination: art, music, stories etc.	Revising the mechanisms for change within societies and their institutions: the development of a more participatory *democracy* and an effective means whereby citizens and communities can *participate* in the decision making process.
Improving the actual and perceived state of communities – the *quality of life*: health, education and security and ability for self-expression.	*Subsidiarity and decentralization of power*: decisions should be made on behalf of communities by the authorities closest to them.
Building awareness and understanding: the development of comprehensible principles for practical everyday action (Selman, 1996): where we are now, and why; what is our potential; how can we get there; what are the consequences of our actions? Helping to build a 'connectedness with the environment' and an understanding that long-term change is indicated.	Change in the *ability* of individuals and communities to influence decision making and make choices (*empowerment*) through a change in social and democratic structures and the organizational capacity of communities.
Building *integrated thinking* within institutions based on understanding the integrative nature of social, economic and environmental conditions.	Relationships/social interactions/interpersonal links: the social structures that will encourage and allow *consensus* to develop.
A change in the materialist/consumerist culture of western society: a *change in values* that would allow for a reduction on the reliance on non-renewable resources and a fundamental change in social structures. The development of *an attitudinal change* (building a new worldview) in respect of individual *behaviour* and *lifestyle*.	Building a structure of 'individuals-in community' (Wilson, 1997). Building autonomy and self-reliance. Building decision making structures that allow for *integrated and responsive thinking* on social, economic and environmental issues.
Responsibility: the ability and *confidence to take responsibility* for individual and community actions and decisions (citizenship) or being prepared to take collective responsibility.	*Social justice* or 'intra-generational equity': all human needs should be considered and the discrimination between individuals or within communities (social exclusion) should be removed. There should be a just distribution of resources within society providing improved *quality of life* for all and a liberation of human potential.
Change in *perceptions* of the capability or skills of individuals and communities to influence decision making and make their own choices about the conditions under which they live and the condition of their environment (*empowerment*). The self-confidence or ability to develop *consensus*.	*Inter-generational equity or justice*: society should ensure that conditions which support life are *at least* as good as those found at present.
Relationships, social interactions, interpersonal links or building *social capital* and *social cohesion*: the generation of understanding, compassion, trust and an inclusive concept of community.	

freedoms enjoyed by the privileged majority in the short term. However, the major discussion focuses on intra-generational justice – or the development of equity between communities and individuals within communities rather than the benefits bestowed on individuals themselves – and inter-generational justice or the belief that the conditions which we bequeath to future generations should be at least as good as those experienced at present. There is an understanding that landscape sustainability and

human happiness are desirable goals. However, we
have to ask, are these goals compatible, and is the
second dependent upon the first? Chapter 2 argues
that these two goals connect through the concept of
sustainable development that provides us with a pragmatic way of improving human conditions and
happiness through the maintenance of natural
systems. Obstacles to this depend largely upon the
way society is organized – its goals, values, beliefs
and institutions. It follows that the imperative for all
those concerned with the landscape is to find long-
lasting solutions to the problems in society which
restrict the potential to improve landscape sustainability. This is the starting point for the discussion
in this chapter.

It is not easy or always desirable to separate the
thinking concerning the social aspects of sustainability into discrete sections, but it is possible to
identify two major themes, *social structure* and *social
learning,* which concur with Thayer's (1994, p. 250)
statement that 'sustainable landscapes require
concurrent social structures and cultural values
which support sustainability' and these are summarized in Table 4.1. In this chapter the components
of these themes which are generally understood to
be central to the social dimensions of landscape
sustainability are examined and in some cases where
it is not useful to separate the discussion, consideration of social learning and social structure is
combined. Since links are commonly made between
the state of the environment and the condition of
society, the chapter starts by examining the changing
state of communities – what is happening and why?
Within the discussion based on our two themes, the
growth of these links is further examined and in
particular the idea of community and landscape
regeneration by focusing on sustainability and the
city. The main area of direct involvement by landscape professionals in the social aspects of landscape
– that of community projects – is traced and the
characteristics of policy and funding for these
projects is discussed. Finally, some conclusions are
provided as to where this leaves society, communities and landscape professionals in relation to the
sustainability debate.

THE CHANGING STATE OF COMMUNITIES AND THEIR LANDSCAPES

In common with communities around the world,
forces of social, technological and political change
have affected the UK's communities in a way that
they feel is beyond their control. Since the early
1970s the economy has undergone structural change
as a result of the move away from the industrial base
and the effects of globalization. Old certainties have
crumbled such as the ending of the Cold War, the
privatization of public services, and the erosion of
channels for political action and expression that were
established by the trades union movement. The most
significant effect of this change on communities
was the end of 'full employment' and a shift from
primary industry to service industry. This dramatically changed the profile of the workforce. Many
communities found themselves facing an uncertain
future situated within redundant post-industrial and
often derelict landscapes. Communities and landscape degradation were thus affected by the development of a society which was increasingly based on
liberalized capitalism (see, for example, Marshall,
1999). Agricultural change and intensification accel-
erated and produced increasingly environmentally
unfriendly conditions in rural areas (see Chapter 8).
Cuts in public sector spending led to poor or unsustainable landscape management practices (see the discussion in Chapter 13). In spite of targeted spending
in particularly badly hit areas, the legacy of polluting
industrial practices combined with these more recent
factors related in particular to management practice,
left much of the landscape of the UK under threat or
in a state of degradation and disrepair. Observers
began asking questions concerning the mechanisms
by which the land is planned and managed and why
communities were changing so rapidly. A particularly
bleak picture was captured by commentators such as
Will Hutton (1995) who called for a complete rein-
terpretation of what 'democracy' meant for society,
the environment and for an overhaul of the institutions and structures of democracy in the UK.

Hutton (1995) traces the move away from any
thought that 'community' or 'society' could be

positive structures. His thesis was that 'the collapse of social cohesion [is the result] when the market is allowed to rip through society'. The social consequences are 'profound' resulting in 'marginalization, deprivation and exclusion' (ibid., p. 175). He writes that during the years of Conservative Government the emphasis on the 'superiority of the private, the self-regulated and the voluntary' grew with 'little sense of the common weal or responsibility to . . . fellow citizens' (ibid., p. 319). By the mid-1990s the UK's democracy had 'silted up' (ibid., p. 320) and it compared with the 1630s, 1680s, 1830s, 1900s and 1940s where there were periods of 'conflation of economic, social and political crises which forced the decaying network of institutions to admit new demands for inclusion and participation' (ibid., p. 324). Hutton proposed that an example must be set by the state because 'the extent to which the state embodies trust, participation and inclusion is the extent to which those values are diffused through society at large. What is needed is the development of a new conception of citizenship' (ibid., p. 25). 'This idea of citizenship could subsume differences of gender and race, and instil a sense of obligation to our natural environment – a victim of uncontrolled economic forces' (ibid., p. 26).

In particular, the communal urban environment (see Figure 4.1) is perceived as having suffered in this period. Local authority tower blocks and housing estates were poorly maintained and managed. Architectural fashions and beliefs in the high rise solution to housing problems shifted as a result of events such as the Ronan Point tower block disaster in 1968. Five people were killed following a gas explosion on the 18th floor that triggered the collapse of part of the building. The investigation

Figure 4.1 Although this picture of tower blocks in Sheffield is now over ten years old, the 'communal urban environment' in many residential areas has changed little from the sterility seen here.

following this gave proof to the increasing allegations of poor building quality, poor workmanship and brought the tower block into disrepute. The increasing dominance of the car and the effects of transport policy also began to have a severe effect, not only on the structure of and way landscape was used, but on communities – on the feelings of disconnection and isolation that individuals felt.

During the 1960s and 1970s links began to be made between human poverty and ecological degradation as described in Chapter 6. The further rise in 'green' awareness during the 1980s and 1990s led to a significant change in the approach to the design and management of specific landscapes as well as a general rise in interest groups, activism and direct action related to the environment. One of the characteristics of this environmental concern was often

the tendency to look back to some kind of 'golden period' (usually unspecified) where landscape and society, as well as the links between them, were in a better condition than at present. Environmental renewal became linked to economic renewal through the urban development and regeneration initiatives, but these initiatives placed little emphasis on social regeneration or community structure to support the initiatives. Although investment in regeneration and renewal characterized by major landscape 'flagship' projects tackled large and often prominent pockets of dereliction in inner city areas, the projects themselves did little to address the emerging much wider environmental agenda and concerns, or solve the problems of an increasingly fragmented society.

In the post-war period the landscape has also been affected by new avenues of thought brought

Figure 4.2 Communal vegetable plots in a housing area near Amsterdam. Initiatives such as the 'city as garden' in Germany and the Netherlands go much further than the Woonerf or 'Home Zone' ideas and include the provision of communal vegetable plots within housing to encourage people to become more self-sufficient.

by the larger social changes that have also created new patterns in family life and in communities. Disengagement, lack of community structure, exclusion and poor 'backdoor' landscapes have been seen as primarily urban problems and the common but ill-conceived vision of life in the countryside is still often that of a rural idyll. However, there has recently been a move to re-examine rural landscapes as a whole as a result of the crisis now occurring in rural areas which hinges on agricultural and economic change, but where communities also feel disenfranchised by the urban majority and where the traditional community structure is disintegrating and traditional values and links to the landscape are rapidly being lost. Here, more than in many urban areas, the existence and character of the community spaces are determined by a few people within the community willing to take on responsibility. In the inner cities the move to create 'home zones' by some local authorities in the UK can be seen as a positive response to calls to make more appropriate and 'people-friendly' local landscapes. But this is a belated and limited response to similar initiatives such as 'Woonerfs' in the Netherlands or the more comprehensive planning of some German city areas under the sustainability label, such as Kronsberg suburb in Hanover where 'ecological optimization' is planned and 'city as social habitat' and 'city as garden' projects are now in place (see Figure 4.2).

Blowers observed that the perception of crisis now felt in many areas of society can lead to negative social attributes such as fatalism (self-loathing) or a 'search for transitory satisfactions', such as vandalism, but it may also provide more positive opportunities such as 'major shifts in attitudes and values' (1997b, p. 160). Marshall states that although it was recognized by most political economists that environmental degradation has a profound effect on people, 'systematic treatment of the environment is omitted from mainstream models of political economy' (1999, p. 254) and action to pull environmental thinking into mainstream theory has been an *ad hoc* effort or theoretical afterthought rather than an activity at the core of government policy-making. However, the emergence and adoption of the sustainability agenda by government can be seen in

the light of and in response to this broad picture: while a new environmental awareness produced a better understanding of the critical condition of the environment, the crisis in the economy moved people to find new solutions, or at least a new way of looking at both problems. What was perceived as a social crisis led to calls for the 'rebuilding' of communities and 'community spirit'. The use of participation in the development process was seen as a way for communities to regain some feeling of control over their lives and develop hope or a 'feel-good factor'.

THEME 1: SOCIAL STRUCTURE

Democracy and sustainable landscapes

The main discourses for social change highlight the two approaches of (a) total lifestyle and institutional change, and (b) working within the system to change the system. In landscape terms, so little is known still about what underpins landscape change that developing approaches to manage the changes which are regarded as a problem is difficult, if not impossible. However, much landscape planning and design depends on the character of social structures, institutions and systems which have control over the change. Considerations of the nature and functioning of social structures are now regarded to be of vital importance in creating more sustainable conditions in the landscape.

The planning profession in the UK has been at the forefront of the development of theories and techniques which focus on the importance of social sustainability and which identify its role in physical environmental change. The aim to achieve social equity and political participation is reflected in one of the five goals of the Town and Country Planning Association Working Party on sustainability (Matthews, 1996) where core values are focused on the ideals of the 'social city' as originally conceived by Ebenezer Howard (Blowers, 1993; Matthews, 1996). The role of existing social and institutional systems and structures has been questioned – in particular, the existing system is often seen not to have the potential to deliver greater self-determination or 'improved democracy' which is closely linked to social sustainability in communities. It is therefore pertinent to ask in our own society what systems, structures and institutions will deliver a more sustainable landscape or what has democracy to do with sustainable landscapes? What does a democratic landscape look like? Will 'improved' or more sustainable landscapes incline people to behave in a different way – to treat each other as equals? 'Will better buildings diminish the rage of our own young?' (Sennett, 1999, p. 68). This can be seen simply as an extension of the environmental determinism debate brought to the attention of the profession by Oscar Newman (1972) and Alice Coleman (1985, 1986), but in fact it is much more complex and far-reaching in its questioning of social and environmental conditions, the social structures which control them and the physical environment which can be created.

Concepts of what the spaces which might promote increased democracy might be like vary according to definitions of democracy. But in general there is a feeling that permeability and accessibility are important. Modern, mainly urban, lifestyles have been criticized as fostering an isolated way of life through the use of 'personal' space (car, home, garden, office) and an increased pace of life (see Levine *et al.*, in Bechtel, 1997, p. 350) which encourages no 'messiness' in personal contacts or daily life. Although the Greek society (from which democratic ideals originate) was far from democratic by our own standards, examination of the central spaces of ancient Greece – the town square and the theatre – provides some useful ideas in design terms. Sennett (1999) writes that the square (the *Agora*) 'stimulated citizens to move beyond their personal concerns and acknowledge the presence and needs of other citizens' (ibid., p. 68). The theatre (the Pnyx) helped 'citizens focus their attention and concentrate on decision making' (ibid., p. 68). According to Aristotle, the mixture of activities in which citizens took part in the Pnyx and the design of the space encouraged and supported discussion of differing views and conflicting interests and an understanding of them. The configuration of the spaces fostered a breakdown in

isolation and helped build consensus and a 'tolerance of difference' (ibid. p. 69) among those groups who were allowed to use the spaces through the encouragement of physical interaction.

Examinations in this country of what is perceived by many to be a degraded democracy have been bolstered by a concentration on the local and the idea of subsidiarity. One of the major reactions to the many characteristics of globalization now affecting us has been to re-examine the significance and potential of the 'local' in many different forms, from local landscape character to local governmental power structures. Subsidiarity is the belief that decisions should be made on behalf of communities by the authorities closest to them (Selman, 1996). Some believe that by taking up the local theme central government has simply passed the buck to local authorities in terms of environmental responsibility and so there is now a void between the supra-state decision making (e.g. by the EU) and the local (see Agyeman and Evans, 1997). However, decentralization, or power based at the local level with participation as the central part of decision making, is seen as important in a number of areas linked to landscape planning and design. More community involvement or *participation* (reviewed in more detail later in the next section) in environmental decision making is regarded as a necessary prerequisite for sustainability (ibid.). This concept is embodied in the Local Agenda 21 programme which is recognized as having a central role in the move towards a more devolved government. This decentralist tendency has implications for the design of city landscapes as well as social and political structures. It could remove the need for large central civic spaces in cities but increase the need for smaller gathering spaces, for a more permeable landscape. However, it might also create a fragmentation, a lack of coherence (Sennett, 1999), a lack of identity in design terms and a loss of common interest or purpose.

Concepts of community and community participation

The structure and attributes of communities are closely entwined and so form part of both the social learning and social structural themes we examine in this chapter. The concept of *community* is a 'chimeric notion' (Evans, 1994, in Freeman *et al.*, 1996). It is a term used now as often and with as many meanings as 'sustainability'. Complex spiritual, emotional and economic values are placed upon communities and ideas of what a particular community is in relation to landscape is difficult to unravel. Selman (1996) argues that communities which are linked together by common interests and to a particular place are no longer the norm and they tend to be 'diffuse networks of people with particular interests and activities in common rather than a single, all-purpose cluster of people in a locality' (ibid., p. 144). Healey discusses the problems with using the traditional view of community as a 'place-based' notion in contemporary society and concludes that the ideal of a 'place-based community culture [with], a moral order, is as much romantic illusion as historical fact' (1997, p. 123). Communities are now recognized as existing as a variety or network of social relations as well as having connotations of opposition to an external force – such as a government institution. However it may still include a place or landscape-based idea. Healey believes that 'collaboration among neighbours can provide helpful solutions to a lot of the challenges of accomplishing daily life' (ibid., p. 124) whether they are neighbours in the street, the city or the region. The challenge is to find 'ways of collaborating which can deal with different perspectives and priorities among "neighbours", and develop the capacity to transform wider structures of power which make everyday life difficult' (ibid., p. 126). Such mobilization of communities is usually understood to be through increasing *participation* in the decision making process.

Community participation can be generally defined as 'where people living in an area are able to articulate their desire for change by being involved in the planning and enactment of that change and maintaining and building on that change in the future' (Rowe and Wales, 1999). 'Good' participation involves the community developing a deeper sense of these abilities and building their potential to use them. A term commonly used in connection with these community attributes is *empowerment*.

Embedded in this is the belief that local people have or could have the ability to be their own agents for change – the catalysts and movers towards more sustainable landscapes – as well as being about change in other aspects of life such as economic conditions and health. Good participation is seen as requiring local authorities to have a clear understanding of how they relate to the community and who they can identify as specific stakeholders in the participatory process (Freeman *et al.*, 1996).

A large body of work has been carried out by social scientists and planners concerning the systems and structures of participation. Landscape architects, on the whole, have not been concerned with building a social theory that can be applied to how landscape design is determined, in spite of considerable involvement by the profession over the years in the design and management of social projects (see Chapter 12). Arnstein's (1969) 'Ladder of Citizen Participation' is commonly referred to by researchers as the basis for assessing the spectrum of participation from simple community consultation to community instigation. Although it is now widely questioned because of its hierarchical structure and has been reinterpreted many times (e.g. see European Commission, 1997, p. 35), it is still used as a way by which the extent or type of participation can be assessed. Arnstein describes the simple kind of consultation which commonly takes place in landscape projects as 'tokenism' with no 'follow through, no "muscle," hence no assurance of changing the status quo' (p. 217). But simple dialogue cannot be considered better or worse than full partnership or community instigation of a project, it simply depends upon what people want and what is appropriate. There is therefore a continuing debate on *how* to provide an inclusive participatory process as well as the ethical dimension of *who* to include as part of the relevant community.

Empowerment

The emphasis on devolved democracy and participation encompasses the concept of empowerment. This is now commonly used to describe how communities are provided with the ability to take decisions concerning their own lifestyles and environments through the structure of the decision making system and through a change in the perception of their capability to influence and make choices about the conditions under which they live. Some of those who attack the present government's concentration on empowerment believe that it is simply an excuse by which government and large corporations are able to renege on their own duties to tackle social and environmental problems. Such critics also believe that social and environmental problems cannot be solved by a simple shift of power to communities. Irvine (1999) comments that empowerment 'might lead to some very nasty consequences, from the return of capital punishment to repression of "deviant" minorities' (1999, p. 330). Globalism has been linked to such aspects of local community action and it has been blamed for the rise of oppressive forces and social practices, such as forms of fundamentalism, by generating social, economic and ecological insecurity (Shiva, 1999). Similarly, in terms of the environment, local community action may lead to more intense environmental destruction that might undermine citizen freedom rather than enhance it. However, a more positive community empowerment model is found in Colenutt (1997, p. 116) who describes the usual meaning of empowerment – that of mutual learning and actions established between experts and citizens:

> Community empowerment is quite different from empowering local authorities, or local hospital trusts, or regional development agencies. Empowering communities means empowering residents acting together. Genuine community and local empowerment is essential for a democratic planning system . . . through giving local residents resources and discretion to act for themselves (sometimes with the state, sometimes through development trusts or public/private-sector partnerships).

A conclusion from Petts' (1995) study on consensus-building approaches was that

> empowerment of the public is not contrary to representative democracy, but rather should be viewed as a means of enhancing effective decision making through an opening-up of the decision process to challenge and the exposure of decision makers to public views and concerns.
>
> (ibid., p. 533)

As with many terms surrounding sustainability, empowerment is a highly loaded and an emotive political issue which is not easily unravelled. The critical question here is what empowerment has to do with landscape sustainability. Whether or not empowerment really provides us with more sustainable landscapes is not yet possible to determine since so little research has been carried out in this area. However, community landscape architects have been working for some time on the premise that a form of empowerment – or power over decision-making – provides communities with more appropriate landscapes (see Chapter 12). The critical consideration is that issues that concern landscape professionals about how the landscape is changed and maintained cannot be divorced from considerations on how those decisions are taken. Whether a more sustainable landscape will result from a structure which is based on a 'bottom-up' decision making process, with many decisions taken at the local level by local people, or whether a 'traditional' representative democratic structure, where the decision making process is devolved to certain individuals and groups, is more likely to provide sustainability is impossible to say since good and bad examples of both can be found. In relation to the local versus national or international decision making debate, it is important to remember that there is no one solution and that local decision making, however democratic and inclusive, may not provide the desired effect. decision making concerning the landscape needs to be carried out at an 'appropriate level' in relation to the problem since landscapes do not always comply with politically or culturally imposed borders. In consideration of issues such as landscape and environmental designations, it is obviously important that a hierarchy of possibilities is examined – internationally important sites, national, regional and local – and that the 'big picture' can only be effectively assessed at the larger scale as described in Chapter 5 and the local at the local scale.

Whatever assessment is carried out, it is important that the 'matrix' – or the bits in between those considered important internationally, nationally or locally – does not become forgotten and degraded whether in rural or urban locations. Put another way, the concentration on community landscapes should not result in 'islands' of highly protected or valued landscapes in a desolate, semi-derelict 'sea' because this is anathema to any idea of whole landscapes upon which concepts of landscape sustainability are based.

Landscape, exclusion and social justice

Providing social justice or intra-generational equity is one of the major components in the consideration of how social structure can be changed to provide social sustainability. This means that 'all people currently alive have an equal right to benefit from the use of resources, both within and between countries' (Selman, 1996, p. 15) and that discrimination between individuals or within communities should be removed. In spite of the broadening palette of methods for participation the question of *who* to include in landscape decisions is still a problem. Social exclusion occurs in the landscape as in every other sphere of life, being particularly experienced by women, the elderly and children. It is interesting that these are the groups also most likely to become involved in local landscape change through community projects (see Chapter 12). It is possible to see this in almost every landscape, for example, think of suburbia – where are the collective playing areas to explore, experiment and 'grow up'? The suburban landscape can be seen as a parking space and bin-collection area with private (grown-up determined) spaces surrounding each house. Colin Ward (1979) identified the significance of the childhood experience:

Behind all our purposive activities, our domestic world, is this ideal landscape we acquired in childhood. It sifts through our selective and self-censored memory as a myth and idyll of the way

things ought to be, the lost paradise to be regained.

(ibid., p. 2)

In spite of his calls for a 'city where children live in the same world' as adults there has been little movement towards his thinking in the past twenty years. We can still ask: who do inner-city housing estate landscapes respond to? It would be reasonable to deduce that it should be that of a child because children spend most time in it. But even an adult could see that most estate landscapes are far from exciting, appropriate or challenging and do not allow for much innovation or developmental advance. Ward provides a compelling case for examining the city through a child's eyes (see Figure 4.3) and as designers surely we should

seek a shared city, rather than a city where unwanted patches are set aside to contain children and their activities . . . We have enormous expertise and a mountain of research on the appropriate provision of parks and play-spaces for use by children of different ages, but the ultimate truth is that children play anywhere and everywhere . . . If the claim of children to share the city is admitted, the whole environment has to be designed and shaped with their needs in mind, just as we are beginning to accept that the needs of the disabled should be accepted as a design factor.

(1979, p. 204)

Bradshaw's (1997) analysis of the traditional 'scales of life' identifies seven main scales in the environment in which patterns of life or activities occur: individual; family/household; street/neighbours; neighbourhood; city/town/region; national-state; global. He believes that functions are carefully allocated to these different scales and problems occur when they are reallocated. The impacts of this are felt mainly on children, the elderly, the poor and the disabled and ill – i.e. the disadvantaged or 'excluded' who then actually make up a majority in society. The city is therefore designed for the minority AAAs (Active, Affluent Adults). For example, parks become

Figure 4.3 A child's landscape – North Shields, 1987.
Source: Sirkka-Liisa Konttinen

fewer and further apart, with poorer facilities and cities are dominated by considerations of car transport.

Primary Environmental Care (PEC) has been put forward as a way of obtaining basic rights and needs while providing environmental care through community empowerment (Jackson, 1994). It encompasses ideas of responsible action by communities to satisfy their social and economic needs. It has usually been connected to action taken in developing countries although it has been used in the UK by the Countryside Commission (see Selman, 1996, p. 154) where the link is made between 'enabling'

good citizens to respond to the need of the local environment as a way of self-education on conservation issues and more sustainable lifestyles. However, PEC has been criticized for not recognizing that communities consist of groups with different agendas and characteristics, some of whom are likely to be excluded from the community consensus for reasons such as gender. Jackson argues that 'participatory approaches to development assume that communication is unproblematic and ungendered . . . There is no recognition of the degree to which views expressed by participants reflect dominant/dominated models and knowledge as "false consciousness" or mutedness' (1994, p. 120). Those disempowered in the participatory process may be unwilling to put their view because of the conflict within the group or community that it might instigate. PEC often portrays women in particular as 'altruistic actors – a portrayal that allows community work to come to mean voluntary work by women' (ibid., p. 120).

Chapter 2 reviews the concepts of *social justice.* This includes the idea that there should be 'intra-generational equity' or a just distribution of resources within and between societies not only to remove discrimination and liberate the potential of those presently suffering social exclusion but to provide improved *quality of life* for all. It also encompasses the important concept of inter-generational justice, or equity between generations. This is of vital importance to the concept of social sustainability: whatever actions we take at the present time should not damage or destroy the potential of future generations to have the same quality of life. As Colin Price argues in Chapter 3, this may not necessarily provide for *improved* conditions in the future although the term sustainable *development* would indicate that *change* is part of this thinking and it would be reasonable to surmise that this should be change for the better.

Communities and decision making

It appears that much of the present demand for solutions to the problems found in communities is coming from within communities themselves, with the desire for a sense of connection, ownership, personal investment and pride in their localities. People now expect greater accountability and a direct role in the decision making process. Yet, the raised levels of expectation and public demand are not necessarily evidence of an increasingly empowered population calling for more sustainable modes of living. It could be translated as a crisis of faith among authorities and policy-makers, searching to justify public policy and expenditure in the vacuum left by the decline of party politics. Two things may be happening here: first, the apparent demands of the community are being projected onto communities by policy-makers. If community demands can be

seen to be framed in this particular way, policies can be devised that appear to aim to meet them. Second, policy is being framed in order to pre-empt critics. If communities appear to have chosen their own outcomes, then they cannot legitimately criticize the policy-makers.

Community empowerment implies a certain degree of self-reliance or autonomy in the decision making process. The concept of raising self-reliance can be seen as an attempt to reduce *intervention,* usually to reduce resource expenditure. However, in order to achieve more self-reliance it appears that a certain level of intervention is necessary – the majority of attempts to provide self-reliance have occurred through the intervention of government, police, agencies and the regeneration industry. The assumption, however, is that self-reliance or *autonomy* (European Commission, 1997, p. 38) is desirable, and the aim is for actions that do not create the need for more interventions particularly in the form of financial support. Blowers (1997a) puts the case for more intervention on the regulatory side to ensure 'restraint and sacrifice of present economic interests' and to assert the common public interest of sustainability. However, it is perhaps most useful to realize that nobody has all the answers because no one solution or prescribed solution is possible.

Future potential: the development of integrated and responsive structures

In response to the criticisms that the main obstacles to participation are the attitudes and education of professionals and the structure of institutions, the main concentration has been on how local government can 'recast itself in a more porous role in local governance structures and yet still exercise leadership and provide strategic direction in the allocation of its own resources and those of others from business to local community groups' (Freeman *et al.*, 1996, p. 65). The Local Agenda 21 (LA21) initiative has been put forward as a way to achieve this porosity. Many community landscape initiatives are now being pulled under the LA21 umbrella. Freeman *et al.* (1996) identified three models reflecting structural differences in the six LA21 initiatives studied. The study found that a primary aim in the long term was to devolve responsibility for LA21 to the community. The model which approached broad 'grass-roots involvement' indicated an optimistic picture with each local authority expressing 'a deep sense of commitment to the ideal of "entering into a dialogue with their citizens" and to the process of "consultation and consensus-building"' (ibid., p. 74). Other commentators have identified how tensions frequently appear within the LA21 process (e.g. see Smith *et al.*, 1999) and the need for positive lessons to be learnt from government initiatives such as Going for Green which aims to change environmental attitudes and behaviour at community level. Marvin and Guy (1997) put forward a strong note cautioning reliance on LA21 and the way the emphasis on a new localism 'strives to create both the good citizen and ideal city from within, using local government as the main instrument of change' (ibid., p. 317) rather than a 'more ambitious debate' concerning new structures which bring in 'new participants and asks new questions about what a policy might achieve and for whom' (ibid., p. 317). Whatever structure is used, it needs not only to facilitate community building and community action to bring about change in local environments in the foreseeable future, but also to support continued management of change in communities and their landscapes over long periods of time. Both landscape and communities in the UK have suffered in the past from inappropriate quick-fix approaches based on political expediency and economic fluctuation. Perhaps one of the most exciting visions to emerge from the new sustainability agenda for both landscape and communities is the possibility of social structures which might provide truly *integrated* and *responsive* thinking to built development and management frameworks which respond to long-term cycles of growth and change. Although the Urban Task Force Report (DETR, 1999) appears to have little innovative or new thinking for the creation and management of city spaces, the emphasis on local government responsibility and control recommended in the report may help move the emphasis from the short-term provision of

capital funding to the longer-term provision of revenue funding for landscape regeneration.

THEME 2: SOCIAL LEARNING

Rights and responsibilities

Many of the components of our second theme of social learning provide the basis for communities to gain in strength and skills which will allow them to demand changes in social and political decision making structures. In addition to this, debates about how social and political structures should respond to environmental conditions have instigated calls for cultural and social regeneration. Underlying this are ideas based on what is believed to represent quality of citizenship and the perceived need to regenerate civic life. Links have been made between the rehabilitation of degraded landscapes and moral 'regeneration' where 'citizenship' includes the taking on of responsibilities for the environment as well as exercising rights over it. This concept is derived mainly from ancient Greek civil society where 'citizenship' and 'civicness' within a community are terms often used to describe a sense of civic pride and a collective responsibility towards the local arena (Selman, 1996) as well as to the environment. Selman and Parker (1997) identify two broad types of citizens. The 'passive' citizen believes in individual rights and benefits while the 'active' citizen engages with the community, taking on moral responsibility, duties and rights (ibid., p. 145). The participatory role of active citizenship assumes that people are inclined to *consensus* and to actually want to volunteer to take participatory action on environmental issues. Although the issue of volunteering can be seen as part of the theme of social structure, it is examined here because of its close links with concepts of citizenship.

Volunteering and citizenship

One of the characteristics of the environmental planning system in the UK has been the traditional preference for a voluntary approach to problem-solving through negotiation, persuasion, self-regulation, co-operation and informal agreement by government at the local level. There is a growing dependence on voluntary activity by pressure groups and stake-holders for policy implementation and environmental management activities. Volunteering in the form of tenants' and residents' associations, youth clubs, etc. is now being promoted as an antidote to the various threats to social order such as teenage rebellion and broken communities but there has been a drop in volunteering rates, in the period 1991–97, particularly among young people. However, although there was a drop in the number of volunteers, the number of hours volunteers actually worked for has risen.[2] Both positive and negative aspects of volunteering can be identified. Those who do not volunteer may lose access to the decision-making process and are therefore effectively excluded, detached and powerless. There are also often changed expectations when people are relied upon to do unpaid work. The growth in funding to the voluntary sector has coincided with local councils off-loading liabilities in terms of premises and running costs and there also appears to be a growth in single-issue pressure groups run by voluntary action. However, a project which encourages volunteering can add thousands of hours of people's freely given time to local community development – or provide added value. The fact that freely given time is often neglected in economic evaluations of projects has been identified as a problem by government bodies (EC, 1997). Some organizations already account for voluntary time and can use it to raise 'match funding' by being counted as a 'gift in kind'. This is important because the voluntary sector is rapidly becoming a third sector in areas such as housing interests and therefore it is likely that it will be increasingly taken into account by development agencies. Volunteering has also encouraged the emergence of a new breed of citizen who is involved in the new forms of 'deliberative democracy' (Kuper, 1997) such as citizens' juries and focus groups. The idea of the citizen's jury is based on bringing together a randomly selected group of people to hear expert opinion, question witnesses and through collective discussion and deliberation make informed recommendations on the issue put before it (ibid., p. 139). Focus groups may include randomly selected or specifically chosen individuals brought together to provide views on particular topics. They are often used at a local level to obtain the views of those such as teenagers who are often regarded as excluded or unable to express their views in other participatory processes (see Woolley, 1999 *et al.*, for example).

Direct action or civil protest can be seen as an extreme form of volunteering and has been regarded as the ultimate form of empowerment or the taking on of civic responsibilities. But since most concepts of citizenship dictate the need for the individual to abide by the legal limits set by a country and much direct action runs contrary to this, defining it in terms of citizenship is difficult. Direct action often takes on controversial single issues concerning the landscape such as pollution, access to the country-side and road developments such as the Twyford Down case.[3] Expressing opinions on such issues has mostly been beyond the realm of debate in the professional landscape journals that tend to steer a less controversial line or highlight the amelioration that can be achieved by 'good landscape design'; but professionals can be found on both sides of such debates about 'difficult' landscape issues. Those promoting the idea of citizenship in the political arena often ignore the issue of direct action precisely because the limits of rights and responsibilities are blurred.

Selman argues that

collectively, modern citizenship theory is strongly influenced by ideas of addressing poverty and extending civil rights to non-human components of the biophysical environment. Both of these are, in a sense, concerned with empowering the powerless and they are profoundly relevant to sustainable development.

(1996, p. 147)

However, it has also been argued that in the past citizens 'just were' and some now feel that the idea that citizens can be made or trained degrades the concept of citizenship and creates a new 'us and them' distinction. The present concentration on citizenship in the name of sustainability can also be seen as a moralistic critique on society or simply part of the mood or *Zeitgeist* promoted by the present government in the UK. The problem with a policy which focuses on the regeneration of civic life to redress the breakdown of communities is that it fails to take into account the massive structural economic changes that have occurred in the past thirty years. It concentrates on changing behaviour and immediate environments without necessarily addressing the causes of perceived decline. It is worth remembering that participation does not often equate to taking any power or achieving any environmental change, let alone achieving equal power. Similarly, active citizenship does not necessarily increase the ability to make decisions about the environment by communities.

Building social capital

The emphasis moves from the attributes of the individual as citizen to those of the community as a whole, or the 'web of individuals-in-community' (Wilson, 1997, p. 756) and is summarized by the concept of 'increasing social capital'. Social capital is the term used to describe the outcomes of promoting social learning and is commonly used to describe the aims of community participation. Healey describes the need to find 'a stable, enduring and legitimate way of addressing the dilemmas of co-existing in shared spaces' (1997, p. 70) and that in order to find 'sustainable practices' communities need to develop social capital or mutual trust, and a shared understanding and ability to collaborate. Social capital has been described as the 'neighbourhood glue' or the 'organisations, structures and social relations which people build up themselves' (Selman and Parker, 1997, p. 175). This encompasses the idea of justice between generations – that is the present generation should leave to the next a stock of 'capital' which is assumed to have the capacity to produce well-being at least equivalent to that which is enjoyed at present (Cowell and Owens, 1997). It is also now understood that the recognition of social capital can help local economic development and increase the productive potential of a community in a number

of ways (Wilson, 1997). Methods for building social capital in communities and shared capital between stakeholder groups are well documented. However, translating this capital into action is much more difficult (see Margerum, 1999; Wilson, 1997) and landscape professionals are now developing a new 'toolbox' of techniques in order to address this problem (see Chapter 12).

Cultural diversity, identity and character

The sustainability debate has instigated discussion concerning diversity in many different forms including ecological diversity, economic diversity and cultural diversity. In all three there appears to be a belief that diversity equates to resilience and that this is generally understood to be a characteristic of sustainable systems. The focus in retaining and promoting cultural diversity and richness is on the recognition, acceptance and understanding of difference in society which is exhibited through identity, character, beliefs, values, cultural history and cultural expression. Articulations of identity, including those expressed through landscape character, are often regarded as a fundamental democratic right. Identity is the expression of an individual's or a community's cultural character (who I am, what I do, where I live, my background, what my values are, etc.). Landscape matters to many people because individuals and communities create a view of their own identity through experiences of both their social and physical location (Breakwell, 1992, in Matthews, 1996). Perceptions of sustainable landscapes are now being linked to issues of identity through the quality of life movement, the idea that a community defines and is defined by the landscape, and that the character of one therefore reflects that of the other. Embedded in this is the understanding that many of a culture's roots and traditions are linked to landscape and the feeling that 'to belong to a locality implies that you belong along with all kinds of other things such as houses, factories, services and pasts. Belonging entails a claim on, and a connection to, those things and, therefore a say in any changes to them' (Edwards, 1998, p. 161). Many myths are built up around landscape features and these express certain elements of a society's beliefs or way of life and this may explain the fierce defence by communities of what appear to outsiders to be insignificant landscape features. The concept of identity and distinctiveness or character in the landscape has been taken up by a number of agencies, such as the Countryside Agency, which is developing new policy frameworks to improve landscape structure, functioning and appearance. As described in Chapter 7, the countryside character and landscape character initiatives are rapidly become the baseline for landscape assessment and planning in this country. They represent an important step forward in the move towards more integrated thinking between ecological and cultural identities and how these can be used in the planning and managing of environments in a more sustainable manner. It seems that landscape identity should be examined at a variety of scales to make it relevant to individuals, to small communities such as villages or neighbourhoods, and larger communities such as cities or regions. There is no single answer to the question, 'What has human perception of identity to do with landscape sustainability?' But what emerges from the discussion is a great emphasis on providing communities with the ability to build, restore and express identity. The potential to do this now exists partly as a result of the moves towards a more participative, and devolved, rather than a representational democratic structure of local governance now emerging in this country.

Empowerment and changing perceptions: sustainability and the city

Much of the concentration on landscape and societal renewal has focused on urban areas. Rees (1997) estimates that approximately 80 per cent of the populations of industrial (high-income) countries live in cities and that 50 per cent of all people in the world will be urban dwellers by the beginning of 2000. He argues that people in cities rarely think of themselves a part of 'ecology' because they are distanced both spatially and psychologically from the landscape that supports them.[4] The crisis felt in urban communities has been partially blamed on a

failure in post-war planning policy, or as the natural consequence of postmodernity, but also as a result of this removal from an understanding of natural processes. Bechtel describes the majority of the inhabitants of western Europe as having 'been forced indoors since the world became largely urban in the latter half of the twentieth century' and that life there has become 'increasingly threatening' (1997, p. 37). The tendency has been for the prosperous middle classes to retreat to residential areas in the suburbs leaving behind them 'ghettos' of poorer people where there is moral, social and environmental decline (the 'hole' model).[5] Much of the activity of urban planning authorities over recent years has been to try and draw the middle classes back into the city in order to bring spending power into the poorer areas and ameliorate inner city problems – a philosophy supported by the recent report by the Urban Task Force (DETR, 1999). It is sometimes purported that inner-city communities value their environments less because they are not leafy – like the suburban middle-class areas. However, this is dismissed by Colenutt (1997) who says 'on the contrary, they have more to lose because they start off with a poorer environment in the first place' (ibid., p. 111). More often communities in poor inner city areas simply lack political muscle and are unable to articulate their viewpoints concerning what they value about their environment.

The belief that part of the problem lies with the disassociation between urban humans and natural processes has led to the idea of using the urban landscape to help raise environmental awareness and self-reliance within communities by the development of community gardens to grow food. Rees puts forward the idea of reducing the city's parasitic relationship with other landscapes by integrating open-space planning with other policies to increase local independence and providing a change in thinking not just in action. He believes that the high ecological footprint of cities is a 'reflection of individual values and behaviour and would occur whatever the settlement pattern' (1997, p. 309). We therefore need to focus 'less on trying to fix our cities and more on fixing ourselves'. The less land space is available, the more urgent the need for communities to build consensus to determine its planning and management.

Behaviour, attitude and lifestyle

Many agencies in the global environmental forum concentrate on the creation of sustainable communities as the means by which to create a more sustainable environment, not sustainable landscapes *per se*. Certain environments are the subject of intense scrutiny, particularly in urban areas. The focus of this concern is on the housing estates, tower blocks, polluted ex-industrial landscapes, parks and open spaces, streets and town centres. The main problems are perceived as those derived from *behaviour* and *lifestyle*: crime, noisy neighbours, children out late, gangs and groups, drugs, racial tension, vandalism, litter, dumping, graffiti and motoring offences – most of which have spatial dimensions. In reaction to this, Tenants and Residents Committees take on the role of leaders (sometimes self-appointed) and improvers of the community, trying to define who can use spaces and for what. However, such action often raises tensions and conflicts emerge over the use of communal landscapes such as playgrounds, stairwells, open spaces and flowerbeds. Much of the conflict focuses on the relationship between young and old, with older people calling for young people to be barred from spaces. Young people are being simultaneously presented as inadequate victims (illiterate, innumerate, drug- and alcohol-dependent,

suffering low self-esteem) and antisocial ingrates (noisy, inconsiderate, threatening, hanging around, vandalizing). This picture is reinforced by sections of the recent Crime and Disorder Act 1998 that allows for the breaking up of groups, imposition of child curfews and the rounding up of young people perceived to be a nuisance. Analysts of the situation have identified that there is considerable scepticism about the scale of the problem and little hard evidence used in the construction of the powers (Leng *et al.*, 1998) that may indicate that the perception of the problem is much greater than the problem itself. However, increased levels of policing and the installation of CCTV in open spaces such as outside residential areas are commonly regarded as a solution to such problems by communities. Commentators often define these problems as deriving from social exclusion – a term that describes the complex overlapping problems and perceptions of problems of long-term unemployment, alienation from the democratic process and poverty – but also as a result of perceptions of risk (see Table 4.2).

The preoccupation with risk and risks seems now to pervade all parts of society in this country in a variety of ways, but it has been particularly linked to urban societies. The term *risk society* was coined by Ulrich Beck (1992) and is described by Halfman (1999) as a feeling in industrial societies that risk is a negative factor in life linked to danger and 'angst' rather than a positive challenge with poten-

Table 4.2 Perceived problems in different landscapes

Landscape	Examples of perceived problems or risks
Housing estates and tower blocks	Social exclusion, community breakdown, environmental degradation, poor design, lack of maintenance.
New Towns	Road rage, noisy neighbours, poor quality environments.
Polluted ex-industrial landscapes	Mismanagement and irresponsibility, fears about pollution-related health hazards.
Parks and open spaces	Criminal activity and antisocial behaviour e.g. flashing, drug abuse.
Rural areas	Loss of economic viability, precarious employment.
Streets and town centres	Drunken disorder, football hooliganism, urination in shop doorways.
Suburbia	Property and car crime and security, groups of youngsters with 'nowhere to go'.

tial benefits. It has encouraged the idea for the need to transform society and the rise in social movements based on risk avoidance e.g. anti-genetic engineering. Actual risks are often not distinguished from perceived risks and the discussion often ignores the characteristic of unevenness found in both risks and communities. For example, Blowers (1997a) states that the ability of the environment to cope with human instigated problems is uneven and societies are therefore also affected unevenly with the benefits and burdens of risk unequally shared. Halfman (1999) describes the way risk reflects the uncertainties felt in societies over present decisions on future conditions, whether economic, social or environmental. The rise in risk movements has also provided a way of examining how different communities respond to what are considered common goods

(e.g. health and safety) and their perceptions of how those actors such as government, big industry or big science at the 'centre' increase the threats to 'life chances'. There is much discussion and criticism on the applicability of Beck's theories to countries other than Germany and Scandinavia (see Marshall, 1999). However, in the UK it certainly seems that a concentration on risks has brought about a more cautious society where the main preoccupation arises over perceptions of risk or individual vulnerability as well as giving rise to social movements and public interest or community groups.

Concerns of risk connected with the landscape are linked to environmental conditions such as pollution and they also encourage calls for the provision of 'safe' routes to schools and measures such as the removal of vegetation in public areas to counteract muggers

Figure 4.4 Community woodlands: the movement towards the development of multiple-use community woodlands on the urban fringe of UK cities has highlighted the need for a better understanding of why certain groups are excluded from using woodlands and the development of methods to overcome such problems.

hiding in the undergrowth. Demands for action indicate that people are often unwilling or unable to cope with what are perceived as risks, and want that responsibility removed from the individual. The reasons for this are complex and the solutions to problems of risk in the landscape bring new demands for or actual increases in regulation over previously unregulated areas of life – such as the installation of CCTV. Oc and Tiesdell (1999) identify and discuss the merits of four planning and urban design approaches now used to counteract feelings of vulnerability in city centres: 'Fortress', 'panoptic' (or all-seeing), 'regulatory' and 'animated'. In particular, they favour the regulatory and animated approaches which 'frequently reinforce or complement each other' and which include encouraging more people to use public city spaces. These are citizen-based approaches rather than those based on 'private-minded behaviours' which simply reinforce exclusion in such spaces. Burgess and Woolley have both carried out useful research in relation to perceptions of personal risk and the landscape. Burgess's (1995) research on understanding people's perceptions of urban fringe woodlands (see Figure 4.4) highlighted the particular problems which children, women and ethnic groups face. It indicated the need for more people simply to be in the landscape because the 'strongest contribution to feeling safer is the presence of others' (ibid., p. 35) and that overcoming this single problem would allow woodlands to be used by the 'whole community' (ibid., p. 5) thus reinforcing the 'animated' approach identified by Oc and Tiesdell (1999). Woolley *et al.*'s (1999) research concerning children's perceptions and experience of city centres showed that 'the attractiveness of urban areas can relate directly to [the children's] perceptions of safety and danger' (ibid., p. 288). An additional important point found by Woolley was that urban areas were generally 'valued, much used and . . . clearly becoming part of [the children's] personal and social identity' or as is surmised 'early and secure attachment to place is a good basis upon which to develop a stable personal identity' (ibid., p. 300).

Problems of risk are usually presented as deriving from the environmental conditions rather than people's perceptions of them and particular landscapes are characterized by a range of different problems and anxieties attached to them (see Table 4.2). Although the solutions to these problems have now been linked to political and social restructuring, environmental professions have for some time recognized the importance of work at the interface between community and landscape. This builds community confidence and an ability to overcome feelings of vulnerability to risk by increasing the input which people have in determining the character and management of the landscapes. These potentials have now been taken up by funding bodies who have also become keen to support community-based work and are beginning to recognize the complexities of the links between environmental degradation and social inequalities.

Building integrated thinking: community projects, funding bodies and regeneration

The methods by which communities have become involved in changing their landscapes have encompassed changes in social learning and social structure. The development of community-based work represented a small-scale move towards more integrated thinking within institutions. It was based on the idea that multiple benefits could be derived by involving communities in the decision making process. The community project movement originally grew as a result of problems associated with urban living. It took public authorities in the UK until the end of the nineteenth century to begin to address the problems associated with a rapidly growing urban population. Housing in inner cities was established specifically to cater for the poor urban masses and for the first time this included public facilities or 'social architecture' (Towers, 1985, p. xiii). The Garden City movement provided social housing on the outskirts of urban areas in landscapes as well as buildings that were more humane and spacious. However, over time these settlements were taken over by the middle classes and the poor still predominantly remained in the urban ghettos of the inner cities. The 1950s and 1960s brought the high rise answer to overcrowding and urban renewal but the redevelopment often destroyed communities and large parts of old cities. The umbrella term 'community architecture' was used in the 1980s for a new approach to the development process undertaken by all those involved in the built environment which was based on the principles of co-operation and user participation in the design process. In community architecture the built environment was designed 'to reflect the needs and demands of users, rather than the concerns of designers or developers' (Towers, 1985, p. xv) and the movement as a whole sought 'to improve the lot of the poorer members of society' by empowering groups who had least control over the determination of their own environment.

In contrast to the community architecture movement, Urban Development Corporations (UDCs) emerged from the 1980s ideas of demand-led development planning. This period was also characterized by deregulation and ideas of 'anti-planning' (Colenutt, 1997). The solution to urban problems was to redevelop the built environment of an area on the assumption that social and economic benefits would 'trickle down'. Development Corporations swept away dereliction, but they also swept away landscapes where natural regeneration was occurring and often removed or provided a new interpretation for landscape features which formerly embodied the memories of the community. UDCs generally worked on the concept of providing big solutions to big problems. Large buildings were built and inhabited by corporations (such as themselves) and in many cases the landscape design reflected this 'flagship' approach with the creation of sanitized

Figure 4.5   Teesside Canoe Slalom: although some major new public facilities were created, the communal environments created by Urban Development Corporations were mostly typical of a large-scale, somewhat clinical 'flagship' approach to regeneration.

landscapes consisting of 'boulevards' along infra-structure networks, mass single-species planting and extensive sealed surfaces – paving, tarmac, buildings. New housing was usually of the executive type – such as on the Newcastle Quayside – with little or no attempt to provide low-cost housing or 'family' facil-ities for remaining local residents. The assumption by many developers, as shown particularly in UDC areas, that the inner city is for childless people and suburbia is for families, remains unaddressed. However, UDCs had a difficult task and in some cases extensive new parks and recreational facilities were included in the redevelopment (e.g. the canoe slalom on Teesside (see Figure 4.5) or Chirton Dene Park adjacent to Meadowell, Newcastle-upon-Tyne) and some UDCs were quite active in seeking local opinion. On the whole, the philosophy was of land-scape transformation for commercial interests and attention was not directed towards building upon the local vernacular or local identity. UDCs were their own planning authority which meant they were able to bypass existing local democratic planning structures and ignore local opinion if they wished.

The City Challenge programme (1991–92) repre-sented a move towards more integrated thinking. It linked the private, public and voluntary sectors emphasizing the idea of planning *in partnership* with the local community and voluntary sectors. It gave some financial and planning power back to local authorities (Colenutt, 1997) and created new approaches to physical, economic and social renewal. All regeneration programmes are now covered under the Single Regeneration Budget (SRB) with its inte-grated approach and built-in community participa-tion (EC, 1997). This kind of partnership-building has become a characteristic of urban renewal linked to the sustainability agenda and it often allows for new sources of funding to be brought into projects from private sponsors in addition to other benefits such as widening the 'ownership' of the project. However, the local community is often underprivi-leged, poorly organized and poorly articulated, and the voluntary sector lacks financial clout. An inequality therefore may remain in the decision making process with big business, government and other financially powerful agencies in the dominant

positions. Although it has been seen as a step for-ward for collaborative planning, the SRB has been criticized for precisely this reason – another prop-erty/development-led initiative which through the aim of bringing in private-sector investment allows private interests to determine the pattern of new development.

Dramatic shifts in emphasis of urban policy can thus be seen in the past thirty years – from the area-based initiatives of the late 1970s, to the UDCs of the 1980s and the contemporary New Deal for Communities.[6] Over the years a number of initia-tives have tried to solve problems in society and land-scapes through a variety of participatory methods with varying success. Distinctions are usually made between community involvement and the process by which communities are involved in projects (social structure), and community development that equips people with skills to become involved (social learning). Both now are seen to play an important role in regeneration projects in the UK (EC, 1997). This represents a change of emphasis from restruc-turing the landscape as a catalyst for social and economic regeneration and simply removing indi-viduals or the landscape features which are seen as the 'problem', to the need to provide the means to regenerate social, environmental and economic conditions in a more integrated manner.

The regeneration of community life has been the defining feature of urban policy in the 1990s. A second important development – especially for the building design professions – has been the emergence of a professionalized regeneration industry, within which a range of design professionals work, includ-ing landscape architects, urban designers and artists. This is supported by an increasingly powerful volun-tary sector, but one which is increasingly reliant financially on local authorities (Leach and Wilson, 1998) that provide the financial backing for many voluntary operations and projects.

Communities are being offered new opportuni-ties to participate in regeneration projects that affect their locality. In rural areas the focus has been on the regeneration of common areas such as village greens which are still at the hub of much of village life (Figure 4.6). The move to create millennium greens and develop parish maps by many rural communities can be seen as a positive response to the need to improve community spaces and a recognition by funding bodies that communities in rural areas need financial and institutional help in the same way as inner city areas in order to strengthen and sustain community character and structure. To take up many of these new opportunities, the community needs to give itself a voice through an organized committee such as a Tenants' and Residents' Association, New Deal Trust or focus group. These groups are generally managed and attended by members of the community on a voluntary basis and considerable power is being delegated to such groups to steer local regeneration – power to shape local landscapes through choices such as whether to create private gardens or a communal play area. These processes pose a number of challenges for local democracy:

1 A decision making system is emerging that completely bypasses the traditional representative democratic process. Power is being devolved to communities without answers to the questions: who should have a vote? Who belongs to a community? This process represents a crisis of faith in traditional channels and perhaps says negative things about a fundamental loss of confidence in authority and positive things about community empowerment. Taking part or participating is not the same as taking power.

2 It is assumed that the strength of the new decision making channels is their ability to represent the community as a 'people's committee'. However, such groups are not necessarily any more representative than traditional structures. Ethnic groups for example tend to be underrepresented, as do adult males of working age. This is not surprising: it is often difficult for

Figure 4.6 Dancing around the maypole in a village in Yorkshire: many such areas are still at the hub of village life and communal activity in rural England.

parents to find time to get involved and some people prefer to steer clear of bureaucracy or lack confidence to speak out in meetings. People who are desperate to live somewhere else will not be inclined to become involved and others may feel no desire to do voluntary work.

3   Those who do not get involved are likely to lose access to a decision making process that has the power to affect the area in which they live. This raises the question: Should people be obliged to get personally involved in the process of local change if they wish to have a say or should they be able to continue to exercise their rights as citizens to delegate decision making to local or national government where accountability is, at least in theory, relatively clearly defined?

CONCLUSION

There is a growing concentration on breaking down the human-constructed constraints to action for sustainable development (Selman, 1996) rather than those based on a lack of scientific knowledge concerning the condition of the environment. Interdisciplinary co-operation and thinking are increasingly called for and a wide variety of professionals now acknowledge that sustainability encompasses this need. This includes considerations of social sustainability since 'people co-operating or working together appears important, so that competition for space and resources does not destroy the necessities of a sustainable environment' (Forman, 1995, p. 492). However, economic conditions driven by political considerations remain the fundamental factors which affect social conditions in the communities and many of the landscapes which are most in crisis – whether they are, for example, the inner city neighbourhoods or the hill farmers in the north of England. The inequalities that exist within and between communities will not be solved by outsiders tinkering with the physical environment and landscape professionals should be under no illusion that communities or society can become more sustainable by addressing this single issue. Sustainability theory demands integrated thinking where all aspects

of life are considered in relation to each other. Where communities are helped to take decisions and power over the change in their environment this may act as a catalyst to help create new connections within communities, release the energy and develop the potentials, which can alter economic as well as social conditions. Indeed, the European Commission has identified that such thinking is commonly found throughout Europe and that there appears to be 'no lack of citizen initiatives, contrary to what people wish to believe if they see in society only the rise of individualism. The stumbling block for these initiatives is due to ignorance or to their containment by the institutional environment' (EC, 1997, p. 34). Underpinning present conditions is the political framework, the market economy and professional and institutional attitudes. The problems which can be found in communities such as those in inner city areas in the north of England will not be solved simply by moving workers away from their established family and community networks to jobs in the south, or by knocking down chunks of the built environment.

A number of important points can be identified from this analysis of the social sustainability debate in relation to landscape. *Social structure* matters to the landscape in that its form determines the way the landscape is planned, designed and managed both now and in the future. The condition and make-up of communities matter because the balance within a community can have an important influence on the character of the decision taken. The ways decisions are made are important because individual and institutional views about landscape can vary very strongly from communal views and treatment. Communities make very different decisions about their local landscapes and see a very different picture to policy-makers (and many landscape professionals) who may be working on a larger even global basis. *Social learning* matters because concepts of community, identity and locality are inextricably bound with landscape character, distinctiveness and the way the landscape is perceived. Social ideals, beliefs and values can have a major affect on reshaping the landscape and on the way funding is provided for landscape projects. Perhaps, above all, integrated thinking is important in both our understanding of and our decision making concerning landscape processes and change.

While it has been suggested that the adoption of the sustainability agenda by many (including government) is a measure of convenience and is still based on *ad hoc* action rather than part of core policy thinking, others believe that in spite of many problems there is a more optimistic picture. This is based on the idea that there is potential for considerable alterations in relationships within communities and those between communities and the landscape which can be made on the back of the sustainability agenda. The analysis of the social sustainability debate in relation to landscape put forward in this chapter reveals two important messages:

1 The focus on local and community issues and potentials provides a new way to examine the importance of human resources and reassess identity, uniqueness and awareness of local environments. Landscape identity must be considered at a variety of scales – individual, neighbourhood and regional. Two strong caveats are that (a) community participation cannot alone answer either the problems found in communities or those found in the landscape, and (b) participatory theories and methods commonly used at a local or 'neighbourhood' scale may not be transferable to a larger 'landscape scale' (see Jones, 1999).

2 Integrated thinking and changing democratic structures which affect the mechanisms by which projects are instigated, implemented and managed demand that professionals develop a greater understanding and expertise in working directly with community groups and their representatives as diverse multi-disciplinary professional teams. This theme is further developed in Chapter 12.

It is perhaps easy to make calls for change, it is much less easy to act as a successful catalyst for this change. A practitioner who has worked on community projects for some years recently remarked in a professional journal that the situation in practice is now much more complex and 'ethically charged' and landscape design needs to acquire a 'sociological imagination as another string to its bow' (Julings, 1999, p. 7). It is clear that no one action or no one aspect within the three areas of ecology, society and economics is going to solve our present problems, retain the good characteristics of what we have now or provide an improvement in those elements that need it. No one component of our two major themes of social learning and social structure will solve the problems of social sustainability or sustainability in the landscape and perhaps Irvine's (1999) comment provides us with a summary of some of the thinking behind this chapter:

> government action is not an alternative to other avenues of change but a part of what can only be a comprehensive process of change, top-down and bottom-up, global and local, individual and collective. Direct action is a vital part of the fight for a sustainable world. So too is individual lifestyle change. Yet enlightened use of the tiller of government will be always critical in the testing times ahead. We must think and act locally, regionally, nationally and internationally. The fundamental principle is that the level of action should be the lowest one appropriate, the one closest to the source of the problem and to those suffering from it. That framework could range from a village, a watershed, an existing nation-state, or, yes in some situations, the United Nations.
>
> (Irvine, 1999, p. 331)

Landscape professionals need a willingness to grapple with problems traditionally seen as outside the sphere of their responsibility. We need intellectual agility, flexibility and visionary creativity as well as a new 'toolbox' of professional skills to be able to take advantage of the opportunities which the sustainability agenda offers to become involved in the improvement of conditions in both communities and landscapes.

ACKNOWLEDGEMENTS

Thanks to Maisie Rowe for lively discussion on the content of this chapter and contributions to it. Thanks also to Rose Gilroy for sane and helpful comments on the content and structure of the chapter.

NOTES

1   The term 'sustainability' is used throughout the chapter to denote both retaining the good characteristics of the existing situation *and* the improvement of undesirable or poor characteristics.

2   A recent survey by the Institute for Volunteering Research, London (1997) reveals that during the period 1991–97 rates of formal and informal volunteering fell. The proportion of the adult population volunteering fell from 51 per cent to 48 per cent or approximately 23 million to 22 million people taking part in activities. But there was a marked increase in the number of hours people were volunteering for – up from 62 million hours of formal volunteering a week in 1991 to 88 million hours in 1997. Rates of volunteering for middle-aged people fell from 60 per cent–57 per cent and for 18–24 year olds it fell from 55 per cent–43 per cent, for 25–34 year olds from 60 per cent–52 per cent. It is not yet clear why these changes have occurred although the survey suggests some improvements have taken place in organizational practice – more recognition given to volunteers and more of their expenses are reimbursed.

3   The M3 road development which destroyed part of Twyford Down became infamous because of the considerable direct public action – resulting in the jailing of some of the demonstrators – and the feeling that the environmental assessment process had been perverted for political and economic expediency. The route went through a landscape that was supposedly well protected by statutory designations: it destroyed Scheduled Ancient Monuments, sliced through Sites of Special Scientific Interests and degraded an Area of Outstanding Natural Beauty. The public protests against the development became increasingly acrimonious as legal battles fought by groups such as Friends of the Earth (FOE) and the Twyford Down Association emerged unsuccessfully and with high court costs. The FOE even pulled out of the campaign because the organization felt they could not risk a hefty fine following the injunction imposed on them forbidding its representatives from demonstrating on the site. The Landscape Institute condemned the route and suggested that the decision-process was flawed (see *Landscape Design* (1990, p. 5, Editorial comment). However, landscape architects were found on both sides of the battle. The late Sir Geoffrey Jellicoe showed his colours in a letter to *Landscape Design* (1994, 232, p. 3) where he asked 'Are we not ashamed?' and others questioned whether the Landscape Institute could be so named following the destruction of this landscape (see Percy, 1994, *Landscape Design*, 234, p. 3).

4   In conjunction with Wackernagel, Rees developed the concept of the *ecological footprint* to assess what resources particular settlements use and how much land is therefore required to support a community, (see Wackernagel and Rees, 1995). Rees (1997) notes it has been estimated by the IIED that London's ecological footprint for food, forest products and carbon assimilation is 120 times the surface area of the city proper and that this kind of figure is common to the cities of high-income countries in Europe.

5   Bechtel (1997) describes the emergence of two urban patterns following the Second World War: the 'hole' as commonly found in the USA and Europe where richer communities desert the city centre for the suburbs and the 'doughnut' model – found mostly in developing countries where the poorest migrants cluster around the outer edges of the cities.

6   The *New Deal for Communities,* which is described by Schlesinger (1999) as the 'most significant housing regeneration initiative for some time' (ibid., p. 345), was set up in 1998. It has been applied through 17 pilot projects and is based on partnership schemes focused on selected worst case neighbourhoods of about 3,000 houses. Some £20–£50 million is being made available to each partnership. Although the emphasis is on partnership within the community Schlesinger believes that the structure, timing and funding limitations of the scheme will still result in an emphasis on a 'bricks and mortar' approach, or trying to solve problems through physical improvement, rather than providing the holistic programme needed to solve the dire and complex problems in these areas. He believes that although the programme reflects the 'real concern' of the government about social exclusion and conditions on many housing estates the programme is 'experimental in conception and limited in its application' and what is really needed is 'new delivery mechanisms and institutions' (ibid., p. 347).

REFERENCES

Agyeman, J. and Evans, R. (1997) Government, sustainability and community, *Local Environment,* 2(2), 117–118.

Arnstein, S. R. (1969) A ladder of citizen participation, *Journal of the American Institute of Planners,* July, 216–224.

Bechtel, R. B. (1997) *Environment and Behaviour* (California, Sage).

Beck, U. (1992) *Risk Society: Towards a New Modernity.* Trans. M. Ritter (London, Sage).

Blowers, A. (1993) The time for change, in A. Blowers (ed.) *Planning for a Sustainable Environment*: a report by the Town and Country Planning Association (London, Earthscan).

Blowers, A. (1997a) Environmental planning for sustainable development: the international context and society, in A. Blowers and R. Evans (eds) *Town Planning in the 21st Century* (London, Routledge).

Blowers, A. (1997b) Sustainability: the context of change for planning, in A. Blowers and R. Evans (eds) *Town Planning in the 21st Century* (London, Routledge).

Bradshaw, C. (1997) Using our feet to reduce our footprint: the importance of scale in life, *Local Environment,* 2(1), 90–94.

Burgess, J. (1995) *Growing in Confidence*, a report for the Countryside Commission CCP457 (Cheltenham, Countryside Commission).

Coleman, A. (1985) *Utopia on Trial: Vision and Reality in Planned Housing* (London, Hilary Shipman).

Coleman, A. (1986) Dangerous dreams, *Landscape Design*, 163, 29–31.

Colenutt, R. (1997) Can town planning be for people rather than property? in A. Blowers and R. Evans (eds) *Town Planning in the 21st Century* (London, Routledge).

Cowell, R. and Owens, S. (1997) Sustainability: the new challenge, in A. Blowers and R. Evans (eds) *Town Planning in the 21st Century* (London, Routledge).

Department of Environment, Transport and the Regions (DETR) (1999) *Towards an Urban Renaissance*, Final Report of the Urban Task Force (London, Spon).

Edwards, J. (1998) The need for a 'bit of history': place and past in English identity, in N. Lovell (ed.) *Locality and Belonging* (London, Routledge).

European Commission (EC) (1997) *Community Involvement in Urban Regeneration: Added Value and Changing Values* (Luxembourg, European Communities).

Forman, R. T. T. (1995) *Land Mosaics: The Ecology of Landscapes and Regions* (Cambridge, Cambridge University Press).

Freeman, C., Littlewood, S. and Whitney, D. (1996) Local government and emerging models of participation in the Local Agenda 21 process, *Journal of Environmental Planning and Management*, 39(1), 65–78.

Halfman, J. (1999) Community and life-chances: risk movements in the United States and Germany, *Environmental Values*, 8, 177–197.

Healey, P. (1997) *Collaborative Planning: Shaping Places in Fragmented Societies* (Basingstoke, Macmillan).

Hutton, W. (1995) *The State We're In* (London, Jonathan Cape).

Institute for Volunteering Research (1997) *The 1997 National Survey of Volunteering*, Research Bulletin (London, Institute for Volunteering Research).

Irvine, S. (1999) The globalisation debate, *The Ecologist*, 29(5), August/September, 330–331.

Jackson, C. (1994) Gender analysis and environmentalism, in M. Redclift and E. Benton (eds) *Social Theory and the Environment* (London, Routledge).

Jellicoe, G (1994) Letter to the Editor, *Landscape Design*, 232, 3.

Jones, S. (1999) Participation and community at the landscape scale, *Landscape Journal*, 18(1), 65–78.

Julings, P. (1999) Social side to the urban renaissance, Letter to the Editor, *Landscape Design*, 286, 7.

Kuper, R. (1997) Deliberating waste: the Hertfordshire citizen's jury, *Local Environment*, 2(2), 139–259.

Landscape Design (1990) *Tragedy on Twyford Down*, Editorial comment, 189, 5.

Leach, S. and Wilson, S. (1998) Voluntary groups and local authorities: rethinking the relationship, *Local Government Studies*, 24(2), 1–18.

Leng, R., Taylor, R. D. and Wasik, M. (1998*) Blackstone's Guide to the Crime and Disorder Act 1998* (London, Blackstone).

Margerum, R. D. (1999) Getting past yes: from capital creation to action, *Journal of the American Planning Association*, 65(2), 181–192.

Marshall, B. K. (1999) Globalisation, environmental degradation and Ulrich Beck's Risk Society, *Environmental Values*, 8, 253–275.

Marvin, S. and Guy, S. (1997) Creating myths rather than sustainability: the transition fallacies of the new localism, *Local Environment*, 2(3), 311–318.

Matthews, J. (1996) Social processes and the pursuit of sustainable urban development, in S. Buckingham-Hatfield and R. Evans (eds) *Environmental Planning and Sustainability* (Chichester, Wiley).

Newman, O. (1972) *Defensible Space* (New York, Macmillan).

Oc, T. and Tiesdell, S. (1999) The fortress, the panoptic, the regulatory and the animated: planning and urban design approaches to safer city centres, *Landscape Research*, 24(3), 265–286.

Percy, P. (1994) Serving the members, Letter to the Editor, *Landscape Design*, 234, 3.

Petts, J. (1995) Waste management strategy development: a case study of consensus-building in Hampshire, *Journal of Environmental Planning and Management*, 38(4), 519–536.

Rees, W. E. (1997), Is 'sustainable city' an oxymoron? *Local Environment*, 2(3), 303–310.

Rowe, A. M. and Wales, A. (1999) *Changing Estates A Facilitator's Guide to Making Community Environment Projects Work* (London, Groundwork Hackney).

Schlesinger, A. (1999) New deal for communities – one year on, *Town and Country Planning*, 68(11), 345–347.

Selman, P. (1996) *Local Sustainability* (London, Chapman).

Selman, P. and Parker, J. (1997) Citizenship, civicness and social capital in Local Agenda 21, *Local Environment*, 2(2), 171–184.

Sennett, R. (1999) The spaces of democracy, *Harvard Design Magazine*, Summer, 68–72.

Shiva, V. (1999) The two fascisms, *The Ecologist*, 29(3), May/June, 198–199.

Smith, J., Blake, J., Grove-White, R., Kashefi, E., Madden, S. and Percy, S. (1999) Social learning and sustainable communities: an interim assessment of research into sustainable communities projects in the UK, *Local Environment*, 4(2), 195–207.

Thayer, R. L. Jr. (1994) *Gray World, Green Heart: Technology, Nature and the Sustainable Landscape* (New York, Wiley).

Towers, G. (1995) *Building Democracy: Community Architecture in the Inner Cities* (London, UCL).

Wackernagel, M. and Rees, W. E. (1995) *Our Ecological Footprint: Reducing Human Impact on the Earth* (Gabriola Island, BC, New Society).

Ward, C. (1979) *The Child in the City* (Harmondsworth, Penguin).

Wilson, P. (1997) Building social capital: a learning agenda for the twenty-first century, *Urban Studies*, 34(5–6), 745–760.

Woolley, H., Dunn, J., Spencer, C., Short, T. and Rowley, G. (1999) Children describe their experiences of the city centre: A qualitative study of the fears and concerns which may limit their full participation, *Landscape Research*, 24(3), November, 287–302.

5

INTERNATIONAL POLICIES AND LANDSCAPE PROTECTION

Adrian Phillips

SUMMARY

This chapter reviews the place of landscape at the international level. It argues that landscape was slow to become a suitable subject for international discourse because there was no consensus on the concept until recently, but that its relevance to the sustainability debate has changed this. Significant developments have been: the incorporation of cultural landscapes within the World Heritage Convention; IUCN's work on Category V protected areas, or Protected Landscapes; Action Theme 4 of the Pan-European Biological and Landscape Diversity Strategy; and the proposed European Landscape Convention. The chapter analyses the significance of these developments and reviews their relevance to the UK. It concludes by predicting that the international dimension of landscape protection, management and planning will be increasingly important in the UK.

INTRODUCTION

Until recently, environmental policy-makers have neglected landscape as a topic at the international level. Certainly it has received much less attention than nature conservation, and pollution control and

abatement. But that is changing. The inclusion of 'cultural landscapes' within the scope of the World Heritage Convention a few years ago (Rossler, 1995), and the emergence of protected landscapes as a focus of special attention from IUCN – the World Conservation Union – point to a growing interest in the topic at the global scale. At the European level, landscapes were treated as a separate issue in the Dobris Assessment (Stanners and Bourdeau, 1995), and identified as an action theme in the Pan-European Biological and Landscape Diversity Strategy (Council of Europe, 1996; McCloskey, 1996); now there is the possibility of a European Landscape Convention. Thus 'the decade [of the 1990s] has seen landscape conservation move to the mainstream of the conservation movement' (Buggey, 1998).

This chapter will consider the background to this trend, review the global and European developments, and examine briefly the implications for the UK. It will argue that the development of an interest in landscape at the international level is in part linked to the growing consensus about the need to find more sustainable paths of development. Though the author's perspective is primarily that of nature conservation, drawing heavily on his IUCN experience, it is recognized that a similar story can be told from the perspective of the conservation of the cultural heritage.

LANDSCAPE: A UNIFYING CONCEPT

As recognized in Chapter 1 and elsewhere in this book, landscape is a peculiarly complex concept and has been the subject of numerous definitions. Yet in the policy field at any rate, the strength of the concept lies in the way in which it focuses on the interaction between people and nature. Landscape is both a way of viewing the environment which is more than objectively scientific, and a means of describing the world about us so as to include both its natural and the human aspects. Jacquetta Hawkes caught all the major elements in a single sentence when she saw the landscape of the UK as being shaped 'in *time* by *geological processes*, by *organic life*, by *human activity* and *imagination*' – the five key concepts are given emphasis (Hawkes, 1951, p. 238).

Thought of in these terms, the notion of landscape has certain distinctive characteristics:

- it contains both natural and cultural values and features, and focuses on the relationship between these;
- it is both physical and metaphysical, with social, cultural and artistic associations. While landscape is how we see the world, it is much more than mere scenery and appearance. We take it in with all our senses;
- while we can experience landscape only in the present, it is the sum of all past changes to the environment: it is where past and present meet;
- landscape is universal – it exists throughout each country;
- landscape gives identity to place, and hence diversity to the settings of our lives.

(Phillips, 1998, p. 14)

In policy terms the appeal of the idea of landscape is that it unifies rather than disaggregates the factors at work in our relationship with the environment. In particular, since landscape is about seeing the world as 'nature plus people', it has a special resonance in the post-Rio period. If sustainable development has any generally agreed meaning, it is that

we should pursue human well-being and environmental protection together, not at each other's expense; and that society needs a holistic approach to the management of the development process, embracing economic, social, cultural and ecological considerations. Landscape is a framework within which this can be done. 'It is *par excellence* a factor in the incorporation of environmental concerns in other sectoral policies and hence a factor in sustainable development' (Prieur, 1997).

Indeed, 'landscape' is more likely to concern the man in the street, or the woman in the field, than is 'biodiversity'. Landscapes – whether distinguished or degraded – provide the day-to-day settings for human lives. Thus everyone is familiar with landscapes. Moreover, unlike biodiversity, landscapes offer us a welcome, because the concept explicitly recognizes that people have a place in the environment, interacting with nature. Therefore it links people to nature, treating them as part of the natural world and not as separate from it. It also appeals to our sense of history and continuity. 'Reading' landscape is a way of understanding how our ancestors survived and shaped the world around them. Thus landscape provides a connection to our past, even though it is a living, evolving concept. Further, it is a way in which people can recognize what is distinctive about one area as against another – and thus it provides a sense of identity and of place, a theme picked up again by Kristina Hill in Chapter 14. No wonder then that, in exploring the significance of sustainability and in endeavouring to make its relevance to people more apparent, policy-makers around the world are now showing a growing interest in the context which landscape can provide.

But if landscape is indeed such a powerful concept, and universally relevant, why has it taken so long for it to appear on the international agenda? Two reasons may be advanced. First, since landscape is a social construct, it follows that it is viewed very differently in different parts of the world; and also that each society has its own distinctive view of landscape and its values. That is indeed evident in the way in which each culture celebrates its landscape. Moreover, two cultures may look upon the same piece of landscape in quite different ways: for example, Australians of European origin saw the outback of that continent quite differently from the aboriginal peoples who had lived there for millennia, and the Masai in East Africa saw the wildlife spectacle of Serengeti through different eyes to those of the white safari tourist. As a result, landscape was not initially a comfortable topic for international discourse. In particular a 'euro-centric' view of landscape, with its heavy emphasis on a shared cultural heritage of painting, literature and music, had little appeal to those whose culture leads them look on landscape very differently. It seems reasonable to assume that landscape could not become a topic for international debate until its advocates were ready to recognize and respect the diversity of views and attitudes towards the subject.

Another reason for the delay in addressing the topic at the international level may be that landscape is a multi-disciplinary meeting ground. Its study involves ecologists, archaeologists, historians, geographers, geologists, geomorphologists and others. It unites the natural and social sciences. It therefore also seems reasonable to assume that until multi-disciplinary approaches to the understanding of our environment had become acceptable, even desirable, landscape was doomed to be everyone's interest, but no one's responsibility.

THE WORLD HERITAGE CONVENTION AND CULTURAL LANDSCAPES

This treaty, the full title of which is the Convention Concerning the Protection of the World Cultural and Natural Heritage, is now one of the oldest environmental agreements: it was adopted in 1972, the year of the Stockholm Conference, and came into force three years later. Some 156 states are now members. It is instructive that landscape was not incorporated within the World Heritage Convention at the outset; indeed, it took twenty years before it was accepted as a suitable subject for the convention's attention.

The convention aims to promote co-operation among nations to protect and conserve natural and cultural heritage of 'outstanding universal value'. It does this primarily through the inscription of sites on the List of World Heritage properties. World Heritage sites must be endowed with exceptional natural and/or cultural values. The World Heritage List (at the end of 1998) included 582 sites: 445 sites of these are cultural sites (such as the Pyramids of Egypt, the Taj Mahal of India, the Great Wall of China and Westminster Abbey); 117 are natural sites (such as the Grand Canyon of the United States, Serengeti in Tanzania or St. Kilda in Scotland); 20 sites are mixed (such as Machu Picchu in Peru) (UNESCO, 1999).

The World Heritage Committee, consisting of representatives from twenty-one nations, administers the convention. Its main task is to consider properties that have been nominated by member states for inclusion in the World Heritage List. Other functions include the removal from the list of properties that have lost their World Heritage values, the placement of endangered properties on the World Heritage in Danger List and the administration of the World Heritage Fund. The World Heritage Committee is serviced by the World Heritage Centre, a free-standing unit provided by the Secretary General of UNESCO. The Committee is advised by three international NGOs, the International Council of Monuments and Sites (ICOMOS), the World Conservation Union – IUCN, and the International Centre for the Study of the Preservation and Restoration of Cultural Property (ICCROM) (UNESCO, 1999).

Although the convention brings together cultural and natural sites under one framework, until recently there was no way of recognizing sites which were important precisely because of the interplay between cultural and natural values: i.e. outstanding cultural landscapes. This became a source of concern during the 1980s for several reasons. First, the split between culture and nature in the implementation of the convention was felt to be unhelpful – for example, it made it effectively impossible for the World Heritage Committee to consider the UK's nomination of the Lake District as a World Heritage site in 1985. As a result, a number of places around the world, which seemed to be clearly part of the world's heritage, could not receive recognition (Jacques, 1995).

Second, the inability to address landscape within the convention seemed at variance with many of the key messages which emerged in the run-up to the Rio Earth Summit in 1992. Although the word itself hardly appears in the whole of the Agenda 21 action plan adopted at Rio, landscape is directly relevant to the core messages of the Earth Summit: the earth's environmental capital is in danger of being exhausted, solutions cannot be found unless they are based on equity and environmental respect, and the whole of society must be involved in finding those solutions. Landscape can itself be seen as a form of environmental capital; and with its stress on the links between nature and culture, and between people and their environment, landscape is well suited as a medium by which Agenda 21 strategies can be pursued. The failure of the World Heritage Convention to bridge the gap between nature and culture, despite the fact that in its title and mechanisms it embraced both concerns, was clearly a shortcoming that had to be corrected.

Third, the gulf between nature and culture in the implementation of the convention ignored an increasing volume of evidence that shows that in practice there is very little, if any, truly 'natural' environment to be found, since the influence of humanity is much more all-pervading than previously thought (e.g. McGibben, 1990). In landscapes as varied as the Australian outback, the savannahs of East Africa, the North American prairies and the Amazon rainforest, scientific study has revealed that what was once thought to be a 'natural' landscape is in fact heavily modified by human influences over thousands of years.

Finally, a reassessment was also called for because of the importance which much current work placed on the subjectivity of landscape assessment. Such studies recognize that the associations to which landscape gives rise in the human mind may be more important than so-called objective assessment of landscape quality (Lowenthal, 1978). In its most sophisticated form, we find the ideas of the Australian Aborigine landscape-based cosmology, the significance of which has been made universally accessible through Bruce Chatwin's *The Songlines* (1988).

These arguments came to a head in a concerted move to put cultural landscapes firmly onto the World Heritage agenda. As a result, in 1992 criteria were adopted to allow cultural landscapes to be recognized under the World Heritage Convention as World Heritage sites. The criteria have been drawn up under the cultural side of the convention but the Committee recognized the importance of the natural values in many such areas. Several sub-categories were identified:

- designed landscapes;
- organically evolved landscapes (sub-divided in turn into living and 'fossil' landscapes of this type);
- associative landscapes.

(Rossler, 1995)

In the years since 1992, a number of cultural landscapes have been added to the World Heritage List. The first two were associative sites, Tongariro National Park (New Zealand) and Uluru-Kata Tjuta (Ayer's Rock) National Park (Australia). This choice is interesting evidence of a very catholic view adopted by the World Heritage Committee towards the idea of landscape and its values. The communities whose association with the landscape was recognized by these decisions were the Maori and Aboriginal peoples, respectively. Other cultural landscapes now on the list include the rice terraces of the Philippines Cordillera in Luzon (accepted under the organically evolving category) (Figure 5.1) and the designed landscapes of Sintra (Portugal), and Lednice-Valtice (Czech Republic). By 1999, twelve cultural landscapes of all kinds had been added to the World Heritage List, as listed on the UNESCO web site. Many more are on the way for assessment in the coming years as countries become more familiar with the concept; as we shall see, the UK is among those planning to nominate candidate cultural landscapes.

The inclusion of cultural landscapes in the World Heritage has been significant for several reasons. First, it enables landscapes of outstanding universal

Figure 5.1 Rice terraces, Luzon, Philippines Cordillera: a World Heritage (Cultural Landscape) site and effectively a Category V site. Parts of this landscape are some 2,000 years old and the whole area depends for its survival on maintaining strong cultural traditions.

value to take their place on the list alongside the world's great cultural monuments and natural sites. In the language of economists, it recognizes them as part of the world's environmental capital. Second, it sends a signal to all concerned with the better understanding and protection of the environment that landscapes merit attention at the international and – by extension – the national level too. Third, through its threefold division of landscapes types, the convention is encouraging debate around the idea that landscapes may be designed, may evolve organically, or may be found in the mind.

But the inclusion of cultural landscapes has not been entirely straightforward. Jacques was wrong in his assumption that IUCN would resist the idea of a convergence between nature and culture under the convention on the grounds that nature conservationists 'have particular difficulty in acknowledging that their subject arises from their cultural values'. In fact, IUCN experts have been pressing for the ultimate integration of the two arms of the convention by the consolidation of the still separate natural and cultural World Heritage criteria (Lucas, 1997). However, other difficulties have emerged. For example, how should the convention deal with the rich heritage of cultural landscapes in Europe? Since there is already a disproportionate number of World Heritage cultural monuments from that region, the addition of numerous landscapes would skew the convention still more towards a celebration of all things European at the expense of heritage values from elsewhere around the world. (A partial answer to that may emerge through the operation of the proposed European Landscape Convention – see below.) How can an organically evolving cultural landscape be managed when the values associated with the sites are dependent on the viability of a particular land use? In the case of the rice terraces of the Philippines, for example, a complex set of cultural traditions has ensured the communal management of soil, water, etc., but these are breaking down as young men leave for Manila (Villalon, 1995). There is, too, the question of whose associations matter most in relation to landscape – the American West is a landscape of myth and legend but the significance of place is very different for the Native North Americans, for whom this is their ancestral homeland, and for those Americans of European descent reared on tales of pioneer heroism (see Kristina Hill's Chapter 14 for another perspective on these issues). Finally, there is the question of universality. As Jacques points out, the associative significance of the Lake District depends on whether one considers Wordsworth and Ruskin as universal influences – maybe Beatrix Potter has had more impact in conveying the values of the area around the world (Jacques, 1995, p. 99).

IUCN, PROTECTED AREAS AND PROTECTED LANDSCAPES

IUCN, the World Conservation Union, is the leading international body for nature conservation and the sustainable use of natural resources. As part of its global mission, it has a World Commission on Protected Areas (WCPA), which is a world-wide body of experts in national parks, nature reserves, etc. working to promote the cause of site-based protection. IUCN defines a 'protected area' as 'an area of land or sea especially dedicated to the protection and maintenance of biological diversity, and of natural and associated cultural resources, and managed through legal or other effective means' (IUCN, 1994a). Under such a definition, there are currently some 30,000 plus sites held on the database of the World Conservation Monitoring Centre at Cambridge, UK. Over 12,750 of the larger of these sites (i.e. those over 1,000 ha in extent) are listed in the so-called United Nations List of Protected Areas (IUCN, 1998).

Within the overall definition given above, protected areas are set up for many purposes: the protection of species or ecosystems; scenic or landscape reasons; tourism and recreation; education, science or research; watersheds, forest and fisheries protection; and increasingly for the sustainable use of natural resources by local people. To bring some logic to this complex situation, and as a basis for listing of protected areas and for its other work, IUCN has developed and promoted definitions of management categories of protected area (IUCN, 1994a). This system contains the following six categories:

I   Protected area managed mainly for (Ia) science or (Ib) wilderness protection (Strict Nature Reserve/Wilderness Area).
II   Protected area managed mainly for ecosystem protection and recreation (National Park).
III Protected area managed mainly for conservation of specific natural features (Natural Monument).
IV   Protected area managed mainly for conservation through management intervention (Habitat/Species Management Area).
V   Protected area managed mainly for landscape/seascape conservation and recreation (Protected landscape/Seascape).
VI   Protected area managed mainly for the sustainable use of natural ecosystems (Managed Resource Protected Area).

At the risk of over-simplification, Categories I to III focus on areas which are in a broadly natural state, (subject to the important proviso entered above that in practice there is little if any truly natural environment remaining anywhere). Categories IV and VI are subject to rather greater manipulation, that of Category IV sites for conservation purposes and that of Category VI sites so that the local communities can derive natural resources sustainably. Category V involves the greatest degree of modification: it represents the idea of protecting humanized, managed landscapes – landscapes in which people live, work and exploit natural resources. This fifth category is also of especial interest in the context of landscape protection as it specifically recognizes a class of protected area established for this purpose.

The relative number and area of sites in these categories in the latest version of the UN list are set out in Table 5.1. The distribution of protected areas categories varies widely around the world (see Table 5.2). Category V areas represent a significant part of protected areas estate in Europe, but not so much elsewhere (see Figure 5.2).

Article 8 of the Convention on Biological Diversity requires all signatories to develop systems of protected areas. In its advice on how this should be done (Davey, 1998), IUCN emphasizes that all protected area management categories are often needed in a national system of protected areas. While it recognizes that in many countries the priority is to enlarge and extend the number of more strictly protected areas (I to IV), there is currently a growing interest at the international level in the use of Categories V and VI, and especially Category V.

The origins of this can be traced back to the Lake District Symposium, an IUCN event organized by the then Countryside Commission in 1987 in order to promote international interest in the value of protected landscapes (Countryside Commission, 1988). This in turn led to the adoption of a resolution at the IUCN General Assembly in Costa Rica (1988) calling for the wider use of the approach. The publication of a *Guide to Protected Landscape* (Lucas, 1992) and the establishment at Aberystwyth of the International Centre for Protected Landscapes (ICPL) helped to carry the message more widely. In 1996, the Global Biodiversity Forum (an NGO assembly associated with the Convention on Biological Diversity) noted the potential importance of Category V and VI areas (IUCN, 1997a). A resolution (1.33) adopted at the Montreal session of the IUCN World Conservation Congress in 1996 (IUCN, 1997b) gave renewed impetus to this work in IUCN. In June 1999, the ICPL and the Atlantic Center for the Environment (ACE) (both mentioned in resolution 1.33) convened a further IUCN work-

shop to launch a global programme and a regional initiative in the Andean countries to progress work on Category V (Brown *et al.*, 2000).

These developments have to be put in the context of an emerging set of new ideas about protected areas as a whole. In the past, such places were planned and managed against people; now it is believed they should run with, for and – in some cases – by them. Where talk was of 'setting aside' areas, now the stress is on how such places can serve social and economic objectives, as well as habitat preservation and the assurance of biodiversity. Each protected area tended to be developed separately in the past; now the aim is to plan them as part of a national or even international system. Most protected areas were managed as 'islands'; now there is interest in developing networks, where strictly protected areas are buffered and linked by green corridors, issues picked up by Paul Selman in Chapter 6 and again by Rob MacFarlane in Chapter 8. Scenic preservation used to drive protected areas' establishment; now scientific, economic and cultural reasons are often more influential. Visitors and tourists used to be the managers' first concern; more often now it is local people. Protection was all; now restoration also plays a part. And where the initiative used to lie mainly at the national level, now it is also to be found at the local and international levels (Brown *et al.*, 2000). These ideas are summarized in Table 5.3.

This new paradigm is the context in which all protected areas will be managed in the coming century. But it gives a particular importance to the protection of those places where people live and work, as well as more natural areas where the human presence is less evident. In the language of IUCN's protected area management categories, such places are Category V areas, or Protected Landscapes. These are lived-in, working landscapes, which have special natural and cultural values deserving recognition and protection (Figure 5.3). As with the new category of cultural landscapes under the World Heritage Convention, the concept is based on the links between nature and culture, not their separation. Local communities are central to the management of protected landscapes. The economic, social, cultural and environmental aims for the landscape

Table 5.1 Protected Areas by IUCN Management Category: global data, 1997

Management category	No. of sites	%	Extent sq. km.	%
Ia	4,389	14	978,698	7
Ib	809	3	940,360	7
II	3,384	11	4,001,605	30
III	2,122	7	193,021	1
IV	11,171	37	2,459,703	19
V	5,578	18	1,057,448	8
VI	2,897	10	3,601,440	27
Total	30,350	100	13,232,275	100

Source: IUCN (1998)

Table 5.2 Protected area categories: global and Europe, 1997

IUCN Management Category	I	II	III	IV	V	VI	Total
Global	1.3%	2.7%	0.2%	2.0%	1.0%	1.8%	8.9%
Europe % of total land area	0.6%	1.4%	<0.1%	1.7%	7.1%	0.3%	10.9%

Source: IUCN (1998)

Figure 5.2 Yorkshire Dales National Park – UK: typical landscape scene in Northern Europe, and a recognized Category V site – village, farmland and moorland scenery.

Table 5.3 A new paradigm for the world's protected areas

As it was – protected areas were:	As it is – protected areas are:
planned and managed against people	run with, for and – in some cases – by them
set aside for conservation	run also with social and economic objectives
developed separately	planned as part of a national or international system
managed as 'islands'	developed as networks (strictly protected areas buffered and linked by green corridors)
set up more for scenic preservation	often set up for scientific, economic and cultural reasons
managed for visitors and tourists	managed with local people more in mind
about protection	also about restoration
initiated at the national level	initiated also at the local and international levels

Figure 5.3 Corsican Regional Nature Park – France: typical landscape scene in Southern Europe, and a recognized Category V site – village, farmland and mountain scenery.

embody the community's traditions and values. Protected landscapes thus maintain the integrity of the relationship between people and their environment.

The use of the protected landscape approach has many benefits. By including working landscapes that are rich in biodiversity, and that demonstrate sustainable use of natural resources, the protected areas' estate can be extended. Protected landscapes can also reinforce more strictly protected areas by surrounding them and linking them with landscapes managed for conservation and sustainable use. They can help to conserve both wild biodiversity and agricultural biodiversity, and to conserve human history alongside nature. They can support and reward the stewardship of natural resources, sustain rural economies and help communities resist pressures from outside which could undermine their way of life. Skills and standards developed within such areas can be applied elsewhere, both in rural areas in general and in more strictly protected areas. In this way, protected landscapes can become 'greenprints' for a more sustainable future. Not only can protected landscapes play this important role, but more generally this analysis shows how landscapes can be an effective forum in the pursuit of strategies for sustainability.

So far, the protected landscape approach has been most used in Europe (see Table 5.2), but there is evidence around the world to show that it has potentially wider application. For example, protected landscapes are being created in small island states in the Pacific and Caribbean, the mountains of the Andes, traditional coffee-growing areas of Central America, the landscapes of New England, and – as seen above – the rice terraces of the Philippines (Phillips, 1999). What is emerging is a new kind of protected area, in which people live and work – a model well suited to the new protected area paradigm. IUCN sees great potential in the wider adoption of the protected landscape approach, alongside other more strict categories of protected area. Through WCPA, it plans to promote it vigorously in the years leading up to and through the next World Parks Congress in Durban, South Africa, September 2002.

LANDSCAPES AND EUROPE

The discussion so far has been global in context and focused on the protection of special areas. In fact, the interest in landscapes and a landscape approach to conservation is particularly strong in Europe. It has a long history: for example, schools of French and German geographers from the nineteenth century onwards have studied landscape; the painting of landscape has been a strong tradition in many countries; and the English landscape protection movement took root with the founding of the National Trust in 1895 (Waterson, 1994). As a result, many European countries have developed systems to identify and protect the best of their landscape heritage. England and Wales were among the forerunners with 1949 legislation to establish National Parks and Areas of Outstanding Natural Beauty based on landscape quality, the first such national legislation of its kind. The importance of outstanding landscapes as environmental assets worthy of protection is now recognized in many other countries, as shown by the dominance of Category V areas in their protected area estate (see Table 5.4).

However, the current interest in landscapes is no longer confined to the outstanding areas which deserve special identification and measures of protection. Rather, it is based on a growing appreciation in the diversity and wealth of the landscape heritage as a whole. Thus in several countries, such as Sweden (Sporrong, 1995), Ireland (Aalen, 1997), Spain (Mendoza 1999) and England (Countryside

Table 5.4 The importance of Category V areas in the larger European countries (1997)

Country	Total protected area coverage as a percentage of land area	Category V as a percentage of protected land
France	10.2	86.3
Germany	27.0	94.0
Italy	7.3	71.2
Poland	9.4	91.5
Spain	8.4	53.6
UK	20.4	94.1

Source: IUCN (1998)

Commission 1998; Countryside Agency, 1999), nation- or region-wide exercises have recently been undertaken to survey, record and understand landscapes.

However, the interest in landscape as a European asset has been far slower to emerge. While a European-wide agreement for the conservation of nature was adopted in the Bern convention in 1979, and two powerful nature conservation directives have been adopted for the EU Member States (for birds in 1979 and habitats in 1992), no such measures have yet been formally adopted specifically to encourage the protection and management of landscapes across and between states. Though landscape figures in several advisory recommendations from the Council of Europe in recent years (Prieur, 1997), in general landscape issues have been treated as an essentially national or even local concern, appropriate therefore for national level action, including legislation. Recently, however, an appreciation has emerged of the value of landscape at a European scale, partly no doubt because of a growing sense of European identity generally and partly in response to Europe-wide threats to each nation's landscape heritage – threats which therefore require, in part at least, an international response. The dangers are broadly of three kinds: insensitive land use and development, neglect and abandonment, and pollution and resource abuse.

While there are some examples of late twentieth-century development demands leading to new and better landscapes, in general most modern development has been large in scale, insensitive in design and dominating in its impact. As a result, it diminishes the quality of the landscape. This is most apparent in the results of intensified agriculture, evident throughout Western Europe (see Chapter 8 for more on this and for new policy responses and initiatives). Now, through the eastward extension of the Common Agricultural Policy, this threatens to have a similar impact on those remaining traditional landscapes of Central and Eastern Europe which survived the devastating impact of collective farming under Communist rule. Standardized designs and materials too often replace vernacular architectural styles and local materials, thus destroying the distinctive character of local landscapes. Coastal, lakeside and mountain areas with a particular landscape appeal have often suffered from unsympathetic tourism development (Stanners and Bourdeau, 1995, pp. 181–185).

In contrast to the pressures of development, other landscapes of Europe have suffered through abandonment and neglect. In some remoter mountainous regions, especially around the Mediterranean basin, carefully tended farmland systems, e.g. terracing, have broken down and the land has reverted to scrub, buildings have become derelict and the whole landscape is deteriorating. Landscapes around cities are also vulnerable to abandonment, as traditional land uses become impossible to maintain under pressures from nearby urban centres (ibid., p. 182).

A third group of problems is associated with pollution and misuse of the resources of land, air and water. Sometimes these are fairly localized, but long-range pollution (such as that caused by acid rain) has an impact on forest landscapes throughout Europe (ibid., p. 558). Excessive abstraction lowers water tables with damaging impact on wetland vegetation; so too does the canalization of rivers. Insidious forms of pollution affect soils, freshwater and coastal areas – and all have an impact on the landscape. Climate change and rising sea levels are also bound to have a far-reaching landscape impact.

In summary, the pressures upon the landscape heritage of Europe are inducing many changes, some subtle and some obvious; some occurring gradually, some with great speed. The combined effect is the degradation of distinctive landscape features, the diminution of natural and cultural values, and the weakening, and even breaking, of the links between people and the land. 'The overall result is that the diversity, distinctiveness and value of many landscapes in Europe are declining rapidly' (ibid., p. 186).

TOWARDS THE DEVELOPMENT OF A EUROPEAN LANDSCAPES CONVENTION

It was these kinds of concerns that led to proposals from NGOs and concerned individuals for the development of an international agreement, or convention, on landscape. This would complement existing conventions developed under the auspices of the Council of Europe on the European heritage of nature conservation (Bern – see above), architecture (Granada, 1985) and archaeology (Valetta, 1992). The case for such a landscape convention was made in 1992 at an Anglo-French colloquium in Blois, France, which heard a call for 'a European level initiative in the form of a convention, to secure better recognition and protection of the landscape heritage of our continent' (Phillips, 1995, p. 95). The arguments were based upon the values in Europe's landscapes, the threat to these, and the need for international action to strengthen national efforts at landscape protection. This call was reinforced in the IUCN programme for protected areas in Europe, *Parks for Life* (IUCN, 1994b) which issued an appeal for the development of a Convention on the Conservation of Rural Landscapes of Europe. It also meshes well with the interest shown within the European Union in sustainability.

The inter-governmental response can be traced back to the publication of the so-called *Dobris Assessment* of Europe's Environment in 1995, which devoted a chapter to landscapes issues (Stanners and Bourdeau, 1995, Chapter 8). This argued the international values of the landscape heritage and the need for European-level action to counter the threats posed to it. The text specifically referred (ibid., p. 187) to the arguments for a European convention on landscape. The *Dobris Assessment* was presented to the European Environment Ministers at their meeting in Sofia in October 1995. They adopted a Pan-European Biological and Landscape Diversity Strategy (Council of Europe, 1996). Though the title of this programme – soon shortened to PEBLDS – was a mouthful, it was significant in putting landscape diversity alongside biological diversity as an aim for international action. Within PEBLDS, moreover, there is an Action Theme 4 on Landscapes, which seeks to provide a framework for European action in this regard. This aims to compile a comprehensive reference guide to landscape diversity in Europe, establish guidelines for landscape management, set up a Code of Practice

for landowners in landscapes of biological importance, investigate the link between traditional landscapes and rural economy, and develop an action plan for European landscapes. Responsibility to co-ordinate Action Theme 4 now lies with the European Centre for Nature Conservation, based in the Netherlands, under the auspices of the United Nations Economic Commission for Europe, the Council of Europe and the United Nations Environment Programme (McCloskey, 1996).

PEBLDS as adopted declined to support the proposed landscape convention, which at that time did not enjoy inter-governmental support. 'No legal basis is envisaged because of the difficulty of one European legal instrument being able to cover the variety of landscape types and cultural approaches and policy instruments in the various countries in Europe' (ibid., p. 23). However, an initiative was begun in 1994 by the Standing Conference (now Congress) for Local and Regional Authorities of Europe (CLRAE). CLRAE, which is a constituent part of the Council of Europe, proposed to draw up a 'framework convention on the management and protection of the natural and cultural landscape of Europe as a whole' (Hittier, 1997, p. 2). Under CLRAE's auspices, a draft European Landscape Convention has been developed by a group of experts. Its legal adviser, Prof. Michel Prieur of Paris University, advised that, although several conventions, including the World Heritage Convention, contained measures relating to landscape,

> none deals with landscape as such. This is a clear justification for seeing that in the absence of a general convention on landscape, there is room for a regional landscape convention. This would be a timely response in view of the growing interest on the part of politicians, governments and the public. It would at the same time be innovatory in presenting a global vision of landscapes not confined to aesthetics and public monuments.
>
> (Prieur, 1997, p. 80)

A draft text for such a European landscape convention was adopted by the congress in 1998. During 1999, the text was reviewed by the inter-governmental machinery of the Council of Europe with a view to its being open for signature by states in the year 2000. The prospects are therefore good that the convention will become law as part of the Council of Europe millennium campaign 'Europe, a common heritage'. It is also significant that Action Theme 4 of PEBLDS now accepts that the convention should be pursued as an integral part of its own programme (Council of Europe, 1999b). As will be seen in the following section, the draft convention seeks to address the PEBLDS's concern about being over-prescriptive by concentrating on the *process* of landscape protection, management and planning.

THE DRAFT EUROPEAN LANDSCAPE CONVENTION[1]

The draft convention (Council of Europe, 1998; 1999) does not take a protectionist view of landscape but recognizes that landscape will and should evolve to meet society's changing needs. This is especially so in a crowded part of the world, like Europe, where the rising demands from its people for food, timber, minerals, water supplies, building land, leisure space, transport and so forth all have to be met within the landscape. But while there are bound to be major impacts upon the landscape, present trends are needlessly destructive in a number of ways (Hittier, 1997).

The issue then is how to ensure the survival of Europe's rich heritage of landscapes in a period of accelerating economic and social change. This presents a dilemma. Landscape reflects the way that human needs are pursued in the environmental context; 'it is always a cultural product' (ibid., p. 4). Apart from a very few 'museum landscapes', it is therefore unrealistic to try to 'freeze' a landscape at some particular point in its long evolution. Rather, the goal should be to manage the process of change. This means aiming to reduce the damaging affect of activities on the landscape, and on the natural and cultural values which it contains, and at the same time encouraging the creation of new landscape values. The objective should be to sustain and even enrich the diversity and quality of Europe's landscapes within the context of social and economic development. This is the challenge which the draft European Landscape Convention seeks to address.

The preamble of the draft convention lists a number of principles, from which three central propositions appear to emerge:

● recognition of the value and importance of landscapes to the people of Europe;
● belief that it is possible to guide the process of change affecting landscapes so that variety, diversity and quality are enhanced;
● conviction that people must be involved in making this happen.

The draft text seeks to build on these principles by promoting actions at the national (Chapter II) and at the European level (Chapter III).

NATIONAL LEVEL ACTION UNDER THE DRAFT CONVENTION

The draft convention recognizes the need to raise public and professional awareness of landscape. Landscape is 'a peoples' issue'. Everyone's quality of life is affected by the landscapes around, and everyone – farmer, forester, house-owner or industrialist – can, by their own actions, make an impact on the landscape in their care. This is why the draft text seeks to establish the legal principle that the landscape is an essential component of the surroundings of human populations, an expression of the diversity of their shared heritage and the foundation of their identity (draft Preamble, especially para. 4). It also emphasizes that 'Landscape is important everywhere; in human settlements and in the countryside; in degraded areas as in areas of high quality; in areas recognised as outstanding as well as everyday areas' (Preamble, para. 5). At a more practical level, it commits parties to undertake information and awareness campaigns for the public (Article 6.1), and programmes of training and education in landscape-related studies at school and university

(Article 6.2). Landscape should be included as a cross-cutting theme in school education: it is relevant to the teaching of history, geography, natural sciences and the arts, and it is the ideal outdoor classroom. Throughout there is much resonance with the ideas in Agenda 21, further evidence of the link between landscape and sustainability strategies.

Public awareness should be built upon knowledge about our landscapes. As noted, there are a number of countries where work has been undertaken to survey, record and understand landscapes. Some pioneer work of this kind has also been done at the European level (e.g. Stanners and Bourdeau, 1995, Chapter 8). What such exercises have in common is a focus on identifying the distinctive character of each area, with its natural and man-made elements (the technique is sometimes called Landscape Character Analysis – see Chapter 7). The power of such analytical work has been greatly enhanced in recent years by technical advances in survey,

including remote sensing, and GIS mapping; and also by the results of cross-disciplinary research in institutions across Europe which have drawn out the connections between ecological and historical aspects of the landscape. Such landscape character information is a prerequisite for the evaluation of landscapes, that is the process of informed judgement about what is distinctive in each landscape, and where landscape improvement should be sought. In the spirit of the draft text (Article 6.3), this should be done by professionals working with the local communities who live in the landscape concerned.

The final strand of national action is the definition of policies and their implementation for each landscape area, including through the definition of 'landscape quality objectives' (Article 6.4 and 5). The draft convention (Article I) draws a most useful distinction between policies for three purposes: protection, management and planning, see Box 5.1. Of course, in any single area it is likely that a mix

---

Box 5.1

Landscape protection, planning and management (from Article I of the draft European Landscapes Convention)

Landscape protection is defined as 'action to conserve a landscape's features, justified by its value derived from its natural configuration or from the type of human activity for which it is used'. Landscape protection is an appropriate policy for a country's finest landscapes, and many countries have indeed designed protected areas for this purpose. IUCN recognises these as Category V Protected Areas (IUCN, 1994).

Landscape management is defined as 'action to ensure the regular upkeep of a landscape and to harmonise changes necessary for economic and social reasons'. This is a process of deliberate stewardship to maintain the quality and diversity of each landscape and prevent its erosion by aban-

donment, neglect and abuse. Landscape management is a suitable approach for most areas, certainly for the great tracts of rural Europe where the landscapes, though not outstanding, still retain their distinctive qualities.

Landscape planning means 'forward-looking action to enhance, restore or re-create landscapes', through a process of plan-making, design and construction. Landscape planning is about landscape enhancement and is suitable for areas which have been left derelict from past industrialisation, degraded by intensive agriculture or subjected to a whole range of pressures in peri-urban areas. Landscape planning is a conscious investment in landscape enhancement for future generations, for example through the creation of new forests around cities.

Source: Derived from Article 1 of the draft European Landscapes Convention

---

Box 5.2

Legal, administrative, fiscal and financial means of implementing landscape policies

- Plan-making, based on a good understanding of landscape – and including also landscape plans for degraded areas, or areas under pressure.
- Development control, to ensure compatibility with landscape requirements (including landscape considerations in EIAs).
- Inclusion of landscape quality objectives in publicly-funded infrastructure programmes, affecting design and location.
- Support for traditional land use practices (e.g. agri-environmental incentives, advice, tax incentives).

- Underpinning of aspects of economy that respect or 'use' the landscape (e.g. sustainable tourism).
- Ownership by public, quasi-public or voluntary bodies committed to landscape management and protection.
- Agreements with private owners of land to manage landscape in public interest.
- Identification and designation of special areas for protection or restoration measures (including establishment of special agencies for their management).
- Education and public awareness for all.

Source: Derived from Appendix to the 1998 draft of the European Landscapes Convention

---

of these approaches will be appropriate but in general the scale 'landscape protection/landscape management/landscape planning' is appropriate to 'outstanding/moderate/degraded landscapes'. Thereby the point is reinforced that all landscapes are appropriate for landscape policies, from the finest scenery of remote mountains and coastal areas to the degraded environment around our cities. These are followed up later in the book, especially in Chapters 6, 7, 8 and 9.

During the development of the draft, work was done to identify the range of legal, administrative, fiscal and financial instruments needed to achieve the policies of landscape protection, management and planning, see Box 5.2. Though these do not appear in the final 1999 draft, they are a good guide to how the convention's aims might be achieved.

INTERNATIONAL LEVEL ACTION UNDER THE DRAFT CONVENTION

The draft convention proposes to complement the national level of landscape protection, management

and planning with a Europe-wide set of actions. It specifically calls on governments to recognize that 'European landscapes constitute a common resource, for the protection, management and planning of which they have a duty to co-operate' (Preamble, para. 10). Under the overall guidance of a Standing Committee of Contracting Parties (Article 10), there will be four kinds of co-operative action: support for national effort; support for trans-frontier landscapes; recognition of outstanding achievements in landscape protection, management and planning; and, possibly, recognition of landscapes of European significance.

Co-operation between parties to the convention should: cover all technical and scientific aspects of landscape protection, management and planning; involve exchange among the staff engaged in landscape work around Europe; include exchange of experience on the implementation of the Convention itself; and promote public awareness and understanding of landscape issues at the European scale (Article 10).

One particular area of interest is collaboration in the protection and management of trans-frontier landscapes. Many European countries share common areas of landscape with their neighbours, mountain ranges or river valleys in particular (see Brunner, 1999). It is desirable that work on one side of the boundary should be co-ordinated with that on the other. In some cases this can be done through the framework of agreements already established between neighbouring protected areas. But the scope for collaboration extends far beyond that, and the draft landscape convention encourages such trans-frontier co-operation (Article 9).

The central purpose of the convention would be to promote higher standards in landscape protection, management and planning. To help encourage these, a European Landscape Award is proposed, which would be a way of conferring such distinction, recognizing outstandingly successful efforts and promoting them as examples to be followed elsewhere in Europe. Its presentation would carry with it a commitment to continued high standards in the care of the area (Article 11).

While the landscape award is to be given for the quality of landscape protection, planning and management, the Convention also introduces the idea of a list of Landscapes of European Significance as an award for the quality of the landscape itself. Based upon criteria to be drawn up and agreed by the Committee of Ministers, the countries of Europe would be invited to nominate areas which are regarded as outstanding in terms of landscape quality. Examples might include the Puzsta of the Hungarian Plains, the hills of Umbria and Tuscany in the Northern Apennines, the valleys of the Lot, Tarn and Dordogne of South West France, the waterways vistas of the Netherlands or the Lake District in Northern England. Such areas have inspired writers and artists, drawn travellers and achieved fame far beyond the immediate locality. If the conservation of Venice, Granada or Prague is a European concern, so too should be that of such important landscapes. As with the Landscape Award, trans-frontier landscapes could be included, provided all concerned countries submit a joint request.

In earlier drafts of the convention, it was emphasized that any landscapes that are nominated should have already been recognized as significant at the national level, and that the countries concerned

would commit themselves to continued protection. Arrangements would be put in place for the removal of landscapes from the list should it be determined that they no longer meet the criteria for inclusion. However, in the latest 1999 version, the concept has been watered down: the requirement is only that the Standing Committee should consider 'the desir-ability of identifying as appropriate, Landscapes of European Significance and/or a "label" for quality of landscape and quality of management' (Article 10 f). It would appear that some governments are resistant to another layer of international designation, and will object to its inclusion in the final text put before Ministers for adoption in the year 2000. The future of this proposal is therefore still uncertain.

Its loss would represent a setback, because – if it were to come about – the concept of landscapes of European significance would usefully complement the World Heritage Status which UNESCO has recently extended to the field of cultural landscapes (see above). It is for that reason that the draft convention has been welcomed by the World Heritage Centre as supporting the World Heritage Convention's efforts at the global scale. Thus the convention would effectively put in place the middle tier in a three-tier level of landscape recognition: landscapes of national importance (normally identi-fied as protected landscapes, i.e. Category V); land-scapes of European significance (recognized under the proposed Landscape Convention); and cultural landscapes of 'outstanding universal value' recog-nized under the World Heritage Convention.

Despite the importance of the idea of landscapes of European significance, it is worth repeating that in general the draft convention is about all landscapes. For the convention, landscape is seen as deliberately comprehensive and relevant to the setting of everyone's life. Its philosophy can be captured in the phrase 'nowhere is nowhere, and everywhere is somewhere'.

IMPLICATIONS FOR THE UK

The above account shows that landscape has become a matter of growing international interest in recent years. Through the World Heritage Convention, there is now an opportunity to accord global recognition to certain universally outstanding landscapes. IUCN is promoting the use of landscape protection designations as part of national protected areas systems, and 'talking them up' as being at the forefront of protected areas thinking. Through PEBLDS and now the draft Europe Landscape Convention, the notion of a European interest in landscape is becoming well established, alongside that for nature conservation and historic and archaeological sites of importance. What will this mean for conservation and land use in the UK as the impacts of each of these international systems 'bites' more on domestic landscape management practice?

The effect of introducing cultural landscapes into the World Heritage Convention is already apparent. At the behest of Chris Smith, Secretary of State for Culture, Media and Sport, a review has been undertaken of the UK's World Heritage sites, based on advice from an expert committee and a consultation paper (DCMS, 1998). In the Government's response (DCMS Press Release 86/99, April 1999), twenty-five new sites are put forward for submission over the next five to ten years to the World Heritage Committee in the new 'Tentative List' (a procedural step required of all states before formal submission of candidate sites). These include two sites that will be nominated as cultural landscapes, the Lake District and the New Forest.

This announcement is brief but the earlier consultation paper has a fuller discussion, pointing out that the inclusion of this new category under the convention 'arose largely from its previous consideration of the Lake District as a candidate for inscription'. It states that 'Britain as a whole contains a large number of areas of high importance falling into the categories' of planned gardens and parklands, organically evolved landscapes and landscapes with strong associative qualities. Examples of possible planned parks and garden sites for nomination include Stowe in Buckinghamshire and Mount Stewart, Co. Down in Northern Ireland (in fact Mount Stewart is on the list put out in April 1999, but oddly not as a cultural landscape). 'A number of possibilities were considered, but further work is needed before a represen-

tative selection could be made. Such an evaluation should be put in hand before the Tentative List is next reviewed.'

But nonetheless, the expert group recommended and the consultation supported the case for putting the Lake District and the New Forest on the Tentative List now, listing the various World Heritage natural and cultural criteria that these sites are considered to display. The consultation paper emphasized the natural qualities of the New Forest and the associative qualities of the Lake District – not only that of the Lakeland poets and painters but also as the 'birthplace of the National Trust and UK's National Parks movement'.

The significance of these developments for landscape policy issues in the UK would appear to be threefold:

1 The actual process of nomination of the Lake District and the New Forest will raise intense local interest in World Heritage issues.
2 The 'further studies' of cultural landscapes called for in the consultation paper, and already being pursued by UK ICOMOS, will generate a wider interest in the idea of international recognition of landscape quality (especially if this study is also done partly as a response to the European Landscape Convention – see below).
3 The attention given to cultural landscapes under the World Heritage Convention seems likely to widen the debate about cultural landscapes in general and how they can be better recognized in all land management action and land use planning decisions.

World Heritage nomination is a very rigorous process (and it is by no means certain that all the UK's list of candidate sites will in fact be inscribed). By comparison, the categorization of protected areas by WCMC and WCPA for inclusion in the UN list has been less exacting and generated far less interest. But that may change as the system of protected area management categories becomes more widely known and used. The UK members of IUCN are in the process of establishing a protected areas forum, one of whose functions will be to assist in the categorization of protected areas. This should help to ensure that the next UN list, due to be published in time for the World Parks Congress in South Africa in 2002, is as accurate as possible. Although this will affect all protected areas, one of the areas of predictable argument is whether the degree of protection given to such landscape designations as AONBs, Heritage Coasts and (in Scotland) National Scenic Areas is such as to justify their continued inclusion in the UN list. If experience in some other European countries is anything to go by (e.g. in Germany and Austria where the categorization of protected areas is a matter of intense conservation debate), this could become a lively issue in future in the UK as well. At the core of the debate will be the question of whether all the UK landscape designations are sufficiently rigorous to deserve international recognition. As in the case of the World Heritage Convention, the discussion generated by such rather technical questions is likely to spark a wider interest in how UK landscape protection measures up at the international level.

Finally, European level initiatives, such as PEBLDS Action Theme 4 and the European Landscape Convention (assuming it is adopted during 2000) are likely to generate an increased interest in landscape matters in the UK. The convention in particular, with its idea of an award for outstanding protection, management or planning, and perhaps a system of recognition for outstanding landscapes, could well bring to the fore the question of the international status of some of our own landscapes. It would be logical in this connection to ensure that the review of potential cultural landscapes foreshadowed in the DCMS consultation paper (see above) also covers potential sites for nomination as landscapes of European significance, should this element find its way into the convention as adopted.

CONCLUSION: MESSAGES FOR US IN THE UK

Developments at the international level have set the stage for the topic of landscape to be given more attention in the UK in future. This development owes much to the way in which landscape has come to be recognized both as an environmental resource in its own right and as a medium through which sustainability policies can be pursued. It seems likely, therefore, that in international circles over the next few years we shall hear landscape and biodiversity conservation spoken of more and more together as matters of equal and closely linked environmental concern, as has already happened with the PEBLDS.

The implications for the UK are of two kinds. On the one hand, the interest in landscape will open up a debate about what the international implications of our own landscape heritage are and what should be our global and European responsibilities for its protection, management and planning. The UK will have to measure up to international standards in landscape management (see Chapter 13). It will have to show too how its systems of both nature conservation and landscape protection relate to each other and help secure our international responsibilities.

But the emergence of landscape as an issue of more importance at the international level also offers opportunities to the UK to play a full role in the European and world-wide debate. The UK has a rich heritage of landscape. Some of its public agencies have an impressive record in the field of landscape study and policy work. It is an area where bodies like the National Trust have outstanding achievements to their credit. Also it is a topic which stirs interest in the public mind. Against that background, landscape could well become an area where the UK could exercise some leadership on the world's environmental stage.[2]

ENDNOTES

1   The Committee of Ministers of the Council of Europe decided, on 19 July 2000, to adopt the Convention. It was open for signature by the 41 States of the Council of Europe at a ceremony in Florence on 20 October 2000.

2   Since this chapter was written, many of the ideas within it, and especially their relevance to the UK, were given powerful support by the adoption of the Oxford Declaration on Landscape in May 2000. This statement was drawn up at a conference convened by ICOMOS (UK), IUCN (UK) and the University of Oxford's Department of Continuing Education. The full text of the Declaration is at http://www.landscape.co.uk/oxford.html (accessed 9 August 2000).

REFERENCES

Aalen, F. (ed.) (1997) *Atlas of the Irish Rural Landscape* (Cork, Cork University Press).

Brown, J., Mitchell, N. and Sarmiento, F. (eds) (2000) Various articles in: The George Wright Forum, 17, 2000, i12–79.

Brunner, R. (1999) *Parks for Life: Transboundary Protected Areas in Europe* (Ljubljana, Slovenia, IUCN).

Buggey, S. (1998) Historic landscape conservation in North America: roaming the field over the past thirty years, *APT Bulletin*, Special Thirtieth Anniversary Issue, pp. 37–44.

Chatwin, B. (1998) *The Songlines* (London, Vintage Books).

Council of Europe (1996) *Pan European Biological and Landscape Diversity Strategy* (Strasbourg, Council of Europe).

Council of Europe (1998) *Draft European Landscapes Convention* (Strasbourg, Council of Europe).

Council of Europe (1999a) *New Version of the Draft European Landscapes Convention* (Strasbourg, Council of Europe).

Council of Europe (1999b) *Strategy Bulletin,* 14 April, pp. 4–5 (Strasbourg, Council of Europe).

Countryside Agency (1999) *Countryside Character;* Vols 4: East Midlands; 5: West Midlands; 6: East of England; and 7: South East England and London (Cheltenham, Countryside Agency).

Countryside Commission (1988) *Summary Proceedings of the International Symposium*, Lake District, UK, 5–10 October 1987 (Cheltenham, Countryside Commission).

Countryside Commission (1998) *Countryside Character;* Vols 1: North East; 2: North West; and 3: Yorkshire and Humberside (Cheltenham, Countryside Commission).

Davey, A. (1998) *National System Planning for Protected Areas* (Cambridge and Gland, IUCN).

Department of Culture, Media and Sport (1998) *UNESCO World Heritage Sites: A Consultation Paper on a New United Kingdom Tentative List of Future Nominations* (London, DCMS).

Department of Culture, Media and Sport (1999) Chris Smith announces final UK nominations for World Heritage status, press release 86/99, 6 April (DCMS, London).

Hawkes, J. (1951) *A Land* (Boston, Beacon Press).

Hittier, P. (1997) *Report on the Preliminary Draft European Landscape Convention*, Council of Europe document CG (4) 6, part II (Strasbourg Council of Europe).

IUCN (1994a) *Guidelines for Protected Area Management Categories* (Cambridge and Gland, IUCN).

IUCN (1994b) *Parks for Life: Action for Protected Areas in Europe* (Cambridge and Gland, IUCN).

IUCN (1997a) *Global Biodiversity Forum – 1997* (Cambridge and Gland, IUCN).

IUCN (1997b) *World Conservation Congress – Montreal,* October 1996 – Resolutions and Recommendations (Cambridge and Gland, IUCN).

IUCN (1998) *United National List of Protected Areas 1997* (Cambridge and Gland, IUCN).

Jacques, D. (1995) The rise of cultural landscapes, *International Journal of Heritage Studies,* 1(2), 91–101

Lowenthal, D. (1978) Finding valued landscapes, *Progress in Human Geography*, 21(3), 373–418.

Lucas, P. H. C. (1992) *Protected Landscapes: A Guide for Policy-Makers and Planners* (London, Chapman & Hall).

Lucas, P. H. C. (1997) From Caracas to Montreal and beyond, *PARKS*, 7(2), 15–26.

McCloskey, C. (1996) *PEBLDS Explained* (Cambridge, IUCN).

McGibben, B. (1990) *The End of Nature* (London, Viking Books).

Mendoza, J. G., (1999) *Los Paisajes de Madrid: Naturaleza y Medio Rural* (Madrid, Spain, Fundación Caja) (in Spanish).

Phillips, A. (1995) The conservation of the rural landscapes of Europe – proposal for a convention, in *Paysage and Amenagement*, 21 October, 74–77.

Phillips, A. (1998) The Heritage Lottery Fund and the landscape, in: *Our Environmental Heritage: Proceedings of the Heritage Lottery Fund Seminar* (London, HLF).

Phillips, A. (1999) Working landscapes as protected areas, in S. Stolton and N. Dudley (eds) *Partnerships for Protection: New Strategies for Protected Areas Planning and Management* (London, Earthscan).

Prieur, M. (1997) Preliminary draft report on the Law Applicable to Landscape in Comparative and International Law, in P. Hittier, *Report on the Preliminary Draft European Landscape Convention*, Council of Europe document CG(4)6, part II (Strasbourg, Council of Europe).

Rossler, M. (1995) UNESCO and cultural landscape protection, in B. Von Droste, H. Plachter and M. Rossler (eds) *Cultural Landscapes of Universal Value* (Stuttgart, G. Fischer Verlag).

Sporrong, U. (ed.) (1995) *Swedish Landscapes* (Swedish Environmental Protection Agency, Stockholm).

Stanners, D. and Bourdeau, P. (eds) (1995) *Europe's Environment: The Dobris Assessment* (Copenhagen, EEA).

UNESCO (1999) *World Heritage Newsletter 1999*, numbers 19 and 20 (Paris, UNESCO).

Villalon, A. (1995) The cultural landscape of the rice terraces of the Philippines Cordilleras, in B. Von Droste, H. Plachter, and M. Rossler (eds) *Cultural Landscapes of Universal Value*, (Stuttgart, G. Fischer Verlag).

Waterson, M. (1994) *The National Trust: The First Hundred Years* (London, National Trust and BBC Books).

6

LANDSCAPE SUSTAINABILITY AT THE NATIONAL AND REGIONAL SCALES

Paul Selman

SUMMARY

Landscape is a concept most commonly understood at the local scale. The regional and national scales, however, have traditionally been important in safeguarding fine scenery: this approach continues today, and is complemented by more sophisticated methods of defining and managing landscape character. Moreover, our understanding of landscape has progressed beyond the purely visual, to include ecosystem functions, as well as a range of other natural and human factors. In addition to policies specifically for landscape at the larger scales, it is important also to recognize the contribution which landscape makes to other fields of national and regional policy, most notably those associated with liveability, biodiversity and prosperity.

INTRODUCTION

Landscape is a term which is familiar to most people. It is, however, most commonly understood at the local scale, as a gaze which extends, perhaps, over a kilometre or two. Often, this relates to the framed scene of a painting or photograph. In the case of exceptionally dramatic or cherished areas, the scale may extend to the sub-region, and people may have a mental image of the 'Cotswold' or 'Snowdonia' landscape, for example. Yet a visual tract of land-scape can no more be isolated from its regional setting or from wider economic and social forces than can a species survive on a fragmentary nature reserve surrounded by an ecological desert. If tracts of land are not simply to be preserved or have a merely touristic value, then they must be related to wider frames of spatial and temporal reference. It is this broader context which makes the difference between a dynamic and self-sustaining landscape, and pretty scenery.

However, the national and regional dimensions of landscape, and the ways they may contribute to sustainable development, are ill-defined and difficult to specify. They require a degree of abstraction which surpasses our natural instincts and emotions: we find it difficult to respond to visual and ecological properties which transcend the local. This chapter argues that the wider scale is best framed in two ways: in terms of the scientific and social factors which underpin the sustainability of macro- and meso-scale landscapes themselves; and in terms of the contributions which landscape can make to the attainment of regional and national sustainability objectives. The former requires the development of approaches which enable comprehension and comparison of bioregions in terms of their environmental, economic and cultural dynamics. The latter rests upon a framework of policy, planning and guidance, within which the contribution of landscape can be assessed and articulated with mainstream policy. The factors affecting ecologically and aesthetically valued land are associated with national and even global trends. Our response, if it is to be anything other than piece-meal and reactive, needs to be similarly grounded in scale and strategy.

THE NATURE OF NATIONAL AND REGIONAL SUSTAINABILITY: A BRIEF RÉSUMÉ

Sustainable development has become an important organizing principle for environmental, social and economic policies. Although critics complain of tokenism in governmental policy commitments to sustainability, compounded by the imprecision and fragility of its key concepts, the present discussion must work on the assumption that sustainability is now a significant influence on public policy. The priority themes of sustainable development are increasingly expressed as a 'quality of life' agenda, and the term 'liveability' is often preferred to 'sustainability'. 'Landscape', as a product of our physical and cultural environment, is inescapably connected to policy initiatives which seek to improve quality of life, including the natural systems which support life itself.

Environmental issues first made a serious impact on the popular imagination during the 1960s. A nation which had shaken off the privations of rationing and conscription, and whose urban areas had largely recovered from wartime damage and industrial squalor, was beginning to confront the problems of affluence. Amenity became a priority, and concerns grew over traffic congestion, car-borne outdoor recreation, pollution, noise, tree protection, and greenfield development. The impact of *Silent Spring* (Carson, 1962) led us to realize that chemi-cally subsidized agriculture was not the global panacea that people had hoped. The forestry plan-tations which had been sweeping across the uplands since the 1920s were starting to accede to the influ-ence of the landscape architect (Crowe, 1966). However, this environmental re-awakening brought with it a false antithesis: implicit in the 1960s' meta-narrative was an implication that environmental quality and economic development were mutually incompatible.

The environmentalism of the 1970s brought a greater awareness of the links between human poverty and ecological degradation, as well as a glob-alization of concern. The effect of the Stockholm Conference in raising public consciousness, com-bined with a growing body of national and interna-tional policy and legislation, ensured environment's place on the political agenda. However, the devel-opment of North Sea hydrocarbon resources attested to the concern that one 'cannot live off the scenery': issues of amenity and marine ecology were thrown into sharp relief against national dependency on oil imports and the economic and social regeneration of the far-North. This paradox was confronted during the 1980s, with some success, by organizations which sought to demonstrate that long-term econ-omic progress and ecological integrity were in-escapably interconnected rather than implacably polarized. Thus, for example, the World Conserva-tion Strategy (IUCN, 1980) pivoted upon the notion of 'resource conservation through sustainable development', the Brandt Commission (ICIDI, 1980) held trade and debt inequalities to lie at the heart of economic–environmental inefficiency, while the Brundtland Commission (WCED, 1987) sought a pattern of development which met the needs of the present without compromising the well-being of future generations.

During the 1990s, sustainable development drew ever closer to the political heartland. Initially, it was reflected through landmarks such as the 'second World Conservation Strategy' (IUCN, 1991) and the 'Earth Summit' (UNCED, 1992). Subsequently, it became enshrined as a policy principle in a myriad of transnational, national and corporate strategies, and even the terms of reference of certain public bodies. For all its faults, the notion of sustainable development was weaving an influential 'liveability' agenda from a set of economic, social and environ-mental policy issues. The 1990s also produced a complementary political debate (which had been bubbling under the monetaristic and materialistic policies of the 1980s) focused on inclusion and identity. In this context, sustainable development was not only a means of elevating the political status of animate and inanimate nature, but also of people who hitherto had been 'othered' for reasons of ethnicity, gender, poverty or colonialism. An important feature of the sustainability agenda has, therefore, been a strong interest in participatory methods of policy development and implementation, assisting the inclusion of an extended range of voices and helping to merge expert and lay knowledge (e.g. Buckingham-Hatfield and Percy, 1999, and Chapter 4).

A number of commentators suggest that effective governance for sustainability requires to be based on bioregional landscape units. These constitute areas defined by climate, soil, landforms, plant and animal communities, watersheds, and human cultures and activities. The bioregional line of argument proposes not only that natural patterns and processes, rather than historical administrative boundaries, provide the essential basis for policy action, but also that the landscape forms natural units within which ecological self-sufficiency can be pursued (McGinnis, 1998). While this radical proposition still may seek widespread endorsement, it is notable that, in the UK, 'wider landscape' plans are already being produced for river catchments (Environment Agency, 1997), offshore coastal 'cells' of sediment movement (MAFF, 1995), and areas of relative internal ecological homogeneity (English Nature, 1998). These plans display physical aspects of bioregionalism, and also include a cultural dimension through the use of consensus- and trust-building methods (e.g. O'Riordan and Ward, 1997).

Landscape can thus not simply be viewed, in policy terms, as attractive scenery which satisfies the tourist gaze; nor is it located at the outer margins of political interest. Instead, landscape is a key element within a nationally and internationally significant policy agenda. It is a means of improving the 'quality of life' of all people, for example, through aesthetic beauty, tranquillity and opportunities for wholesome exercise. It is a principal means of enhancing the 'identity' of places, associated with senses of stability, continuity and attachment. It is a setting and a resource for the attraction and indigenous

growth of sustainable industry. It supports biodiversity and the functioning of environmental life-support systems. Participatory approaches to landscape policy can ensure that local perceptions of place are blended with expert analyses of capacity and character; people can also contribute to the future conservation and development of their own cherished places.

Numerous other examples of the importance afforded to landscape by recent political events could be cited, but it is clear that it is no longer simply of local or specialist interest. Landscape, instead, impinges on a spectrum of regional and national agendas, and we need to develop ways of comprehending it at these wider scales and of articulating it with mainstream policy domains.

COMPREHENDING REGIONAL AND NATIONAL LANDSCAPES

Sustainable development requires a sea-change in the traditional, functional approach to governance, in which action focuses upon a department's narrowly defined remit. Policies for the management and planning of, and human relationship to, the environment are moving away from a sectoral and reductionist approach towards a holistic and transdisciplinary one (Selman, 2000). Indeed, the concept of landscape is one which contributes to our ability to frame integrative policies: it fuses the patterns and processes of rivers, soils, rocks, vegetation, animals and people, and thus acts as a basis for addressing complex sustainability issues (see Figure 6.1). Landscape is thus starting to underpin our approach to the use of natural capital more generally, with planning and management units based more on bioregional units and less on administrative boundaries.

Paralleling our earlier account of the evolution of sustainable development, we may observe that the landscape studies during the 1960s were strongly associated with a quantitative approach: landscape was something to be measured and evaluated, so that it could be fed into the emergent breed of strategic/sub-regional land use plans (e.g. Fines, 1968). Seminal work on island biogeography also

Figure 6.1   The North Devon coastline, part of the Exmoor National Park.

alerted us to the need for a 'landscape scale' in our protection of nature (MacArthur and Wilson, 1967). The 1970s and 1980s witnessed an increasing concern to rationalize our fragmented approaches to landscape protection, and to reflect the multiple dimensions of landscape in decisions related to the environmental impact of new developments. Partly, this reflected a growing concern for the broader scale: both landscape and nature conservationists were increasingly aware of the dangers of protecting 'the best' at the expense of 'the rest', so that the notion of 'wider countryside' crept into policy jargon (e.g. Hodge *et al.*, 1994). Island biogeography was broadened into the science of 'patch dynamics', extending and generalizing the principles affecting the use of habitats by species (Wu and Levin, 1994). The 1980s also saw greater attention being given to more humanistic interpretations of large-scale landscape, especially its phenomenological attributes and its

associations with historical events and literary texts. Thus, while some landscape analysts aimed to reduce the landscape to its measurable sub-components, and then interpret their character and qualities through the application of statistical or psychometric techniques, others sought for meaning within individual personal experience (Mezga, 1993 and Kristina Hill in Chapter 14). Landscapes thus contain profound associations, both personal and collective, reflecting insiders' experiences of joy, tragedy, plenty and famine, which are often concealed to the outsider.

This constructive tension between qualitative and quantitative paradigms has profoundly influenced our current understandings of the wider landscape. On the qualitative side, phenomenology has been promulgated as a problem-solving approach centred on the search for meaning within individual personal experience of landscapes. Fundamental to this view is the notion that objects and people within one's environment take on meaning only in terms of a person's intentions, emotions and goals. Thus, landscape cannot be described as a biophysical artefact solely on the basis of its natural processes: it is a social construct, in which are coded messages to be revealed through glimpses into the world of its insiders. Some of these messages are national ones, with metaphorical associations of identity and collective culture (e.g. Lowenthal, 1991; Daniels, 1993). Some have associations with events and shared histories, or with distinctively regional artists, composers and writers. Many more, at the sub-regional scale, are understood in more intimate ways by their inhabitants, containing 'special' places which contribute to local affections and security. Thus, our mapping and management of landscape have had to become more highly sensitized to 'insider' perceptions and less reliant on the judgements of expert 'outsiders'.

Moreover, landscape can also be shown to be linked to the concepts of 'nation' and 'region' through concepts of morals and civics. The ways in which UK landscapes have been 'imaginatively constructed' have not only reinforced national identities and sentiments, associated with the connections between quintessential 'countryside' and attachment to one's 'country', but they have also sustained powerful myths of regionalism. Brace (1999), researching the ways in which regional landscape identity has been constructed in the Cotswolds, suggests that the representation of imageable regions informed a discourse of national unity, especially during the inter-war years. In a similar fashion, Matless (1997) illustrates how a sense of national duty to be healthy and adventurous was cultivated in relation to the UK countryside during the 1930s and 1940s. For example, the National Fitness Campaign of the 1930s can be related to the three cultures of the landscape – the intellectual, the physical and the spiritual – such that the countryside offered sites whereby good citizenship could emerge.

The cultural interpretation of the significance of the regional and national scales of landscape has, however, been accompanied by a reaffirmation of the contribution of quantitative methods. Notably,

advances in information technology and analytical power have assisted the comprehension of meso- and macro-scale environments, and the conversion of copious data into flexible management information. Geographic information systems and relational databases have facilitated the synthesis and interpretative mapping of comprehensive datasets on diverse environmental attributes enabling, effectively for the first time, the display and interpretation of regional landscapes (e.g. Haines-Young et al., 1993; O'Callaghan, 1995). Entire river catchments, mountain ranges, regional forests and national parks, for instance, can be modelled to understand their present dynamics and alternative futures. To the planner and landscape architect, therefore, it becomes possible to conceive these geographical units as self-organizing, evolutionary systems rather than as static designations whose appearance is to be controlled by reactive planning. Complementary advances have been made in automated landscape classification, permitting large-scale patterns to be discerned from otherwise impenetrable and overwhelming datasets. In particular, the former Institute of Terrestrial Ecology's land classification methodology has revealed natural and fundamental divisions between landscape units, providing new bases for formulating monitoring and management strategies (e.g. Cooper, 1992).

A further hallmark of landscape governance in the 1990s was the growing integration of scientific and aesthetic policies. The practices of nature conservation and landscape protection had been artificially sundered in the UK by the creation of separate bodies and statutory provisions since the 1949 National Parks and Access to the Countryside Act. This separation led to increasing tensions during the 1980s as recognition grew, on the one hand, of the cultural traditions which support the maintenance of nature conservation value, and, on the other, the natural processes underlying landscape aesthetics (Bishop et al., 1995). This growing awareness of the inseparability of visual and ecological qualities partly underlay the merger of countryside organizations in Scotland and Wales in 1992, and the closer working between English Nature and the Countryside Agency, especially over joint mapping initiatives. A significant outcome of this has been the wider scale and more integrated fashion in which we have approached landscape management and planning (Chapters 7 and 8).

One factor driving this more integrated approach is the science of landscape ecology which, in particular, has led to analyses focused on meso- and macroscales. Landscape ecology has its antecedents in island biogeography and patch dynamics, and so requires a conceptual framework based on extensive geographical areas. In essence, it proposes that species behave within metapopulations, rather than isolated, self-contained breeding units, and that their life-cycle needs have to be considered in terms of the suitability of the wider landscape. The growing ability to perceive patterns and processes in the 'wider countryside' through GIS and land classification systems has also assisted the momentum of landscape ecology. Its precise character varies according to its country of origin, but typical themes include: the large-scale improvement of landscapes which have been degraded by pollution or soil erosion; the creation of compensation areas to support species whose habitats have been lost to development; the retention or creation of large-scale habitat conditions around the life-cycle needs of particular species; the rejuvenation of agricultural landscapes as part of land re-parcelling programmes; connectivity of corridors and habitats to facilitate species' modification of 'ranges', for example, in response to climate change; and the creation of multi-purpose linear corridors, or greenways (Hawkins, 1999). While the scientific principles underlying landscape ecology remain controversial, its basic vocabulary and tenets have become very influential. Thus, acknowledgement of the 'landscape scale' (ranging from a few kilometres to the sub-continent) has led to the widespread adoption of concepts such as corridors, connectedness, porosity, permeability and shape, which can find application in the production of sustainable land use strategies (e.g. Farina, 1998).

Additional momentum towards integrated approaches has been the perceived need to reverse visual and ecological fragmentation, which had grown from a failure to see the 'wider picture'. To protect and regenerate scenic distinctiveness, it has been necessary to develop a basis for producing

policies focused once more on the 'landscape scale'. In relation specifically to the rural landscape, the historical pattern has become fragmented and degraded during long periods of urbanization, agricultural modernization and infrastructure construction, leading both to a loss of cohesion and increasing regional uniformity. Rob MacFarlane says more on this in Chapter 8. The Countryside Agency's Countryside Character programme has attempted to re-assert the distinctive qualities of large-scale landscapes, first, by gathering qualitative and quantitative data on the vestiges of inherited character and, second, by directing policy measures at the re-establishment of landscape components associated with the 'placeness' of each area (see Figure 6.2). Brooke (1994) noted that the Countryside Character Programme sought both to describe and celebrate the English Landscape, and to 'paint its portrait' from a regional perspective. It drew upon an analysis of the elements making up the landscape (geology, topography and drainage, ecological associations, land use, historical and cultural associations, and population density), and also on public perception studies which provided a counterpoint to professional judgement. Similarly, English Nature (1998) has divided the country into Natural Areas, which possess characteristic associations of wildlife and natural features. The two were resolved in a single mapping exercise of the 'Character of England' (Countryside Commission/English Nature, undated), which for the first time displayed 'bioregions' of wildlife, visual and natural features.

An influential theory of the past decade has been that of 'risk society' (Beck, 1992), in which environments were increasingly seen to be vulnerable to generalized risks and hazards (including some which were 'dread', such as major nuclear accidents). Enabling citizens to engage with the nature and causes of these threats has become an important theme of sustainable development. Landscape provides the arena of environmental risk, and it can be related to various human ecological factors which predispose societies to such hazards, namely, vulnerability and adaptability of people and places; intervening conditions of danger; and the capacity for human coping and adjustment. Natural hazards

Figure 6.2 The English Lake District, showing the coincidence of the Cumbria High Fells character zone with the Cumbria Fells and Dales natural area.

may be atmospheric (e.g. hurricanes), hydrological (e.g. floods, drought), geological (e.g. earthquakes) or biological (e.g. forest fires). Added to these are technological (such as nuclear power, particularly the 'rear end' activities) and war hazards (Hewitt, 1997; Blowers, 1999). It is not difficult to imagine how, even in the UK's relatively benign environment, certain regions may preferentially be associated with landscapes of hazard and risk. Parts of south-east England have become semi-arid, and subject to chronic drought, while some regions may host clusters of industrial waste hotspots or be vulnerable to marine transgression. Contestation of such 'landscapes of risk' is an inescapable part of sustainable development, the social dimensions of which have already been discussed in Chapter 4.

PLANNING REGIONAL AND NATIONAL LANDSCAPES

Our changing appreciation of the nature of large-scale landscape, both aesthetic and ecological, is now influencing approaches to planning and management at regional and national levels. Thus, the approach to landscape protection which has prevailed over the past fifty years, based on ring-fencing, has been progressively supplanted by strategies based on active management and re-creation, and integration of ecological–aesthetic parameters within development policy more generally (see Table 6.1). Since 1949, a series of *safeguards* has been introduced aimed at retaining distinctive large-scale landscapes. These have been based on the concept of designation, or greenlining, in which an administrative unit

Table 6.1   Safeguards, systems and sustainability – phases in the development of large-scale landscape policy

	Safeguards	*Systems*	*Sustainability*
Territorial inclusiveness	Separation of town, country, coast; designations have sharp administrative boundaries; protected land is either 'in' or 'out'; emphasis on 'special' landscapes	County-wide evaluations; increasing use of locally sensitive policy instruments	Completely inclusive – all areas deemed to possess natural capital in the form of character and biodiversity
Integration of landscape and nature conservation	None – separate specialist agencies	Landscape and nature conservation seen to be increasingly inter-related – recognition of nature conservation value of amenity land and vice versa	Landscape ecology; merger of nature and landscape conservation in Scotland and Wales; integration of policy objectives in England through 'characterization'
Affordances (elements of landscapes which 'afford' opportunities for particular human uses)	Land and water perceived as venues for active outdoor pursuits and car-borne visitors	Application of 'recreation ecology', including attempts to reconcile and zone multiple uses; marketing and interpretation of landscape opportunities; increasing awareness of appropriate levels and types of use in different environments	Attempts to work within environmental capacity and not exceed limits of acceptable change; places of tranquillity, relaxation, personal fulfilment and, occasionally, noisy pursuits; opportunities for personal and community identification with 'local distinctiveness'; recognition that perceptions of opportunity/ enjoyment/risk vary with age, gender, education, experience and ethnicity.
Approach to landscape management	Little active management; emphasis on planning control and protection	Increasingly active approach to countryside management; use of wardens and area-based project officers	Increasing integration of landscape management with economic land uses; expectation that farming and forestry must change to deliver aesthetic–ecological outputs; landscapes as living cultures
People in landscapes	People as visitors, providers of facilities, and landworkers	People as consumers; interpretation of landscapes to audiences	People integral to landscapes; landscapes underlain by cultural systems; phenomenological qualities of landscapes, with inscriptions reflecting people's times of prosperity, hardship and trauma

is encircled for the application of stricter planning measures and the limited application of area-based project work. This approach continues as the principal means of countryside protection today, and its strengths have been identified as its ability to provide a reasonable degree of safeguard and a variety of benefits. However, its weaknesses have included: a tendency to treat areas as 'islands' set apart from the surrounding landscape; a failure to integrate conservation into other sectors; and an inadequate recognition of the role of the local population in deriving their livelihoods and sustaining the landscape's qual-

Figure 6.3 Traditional grazing pasture on the washlands of Cambridgeshire.

ities (Bishop *et al.*, 1995). Adrian Phillips has already discussed these issues in an international context in Chapter 5.

As our understanding of the properties of large-scale landscapes has developed, so the policy framework surrounding them has changed. During the 1970s and 1980s, the notion of environmental *systems* became more popular, as computer models improved our understanding of the dynamic processes and interconnections between land, water and air. Landscapes were thus viewed, not only as scenic areas requiring special planning controls, but as the integrating units for interactions between farming, forestry and the environment, and for the active management of visitor pressures. Over the same period, the increasing regionalization of agriculture led to responses which recognized both the need to create valid new agricultural landscapes, and

the retention of those farming practices which were regionally distinctive (see Figure 6.3 and Chapter 8). The protection of landscapes became increasingly important as a means of reversing the erosion of socio-cultural capital and damage to critical life-support systems: there has been an increasing recognition not only of the folly of restricting landscape policy to designated enclaves, but also of separating it from mainstream policy in other economic and social sectors.

Most recently, our approach to the regional landscape has been influenced strongly by *sustainability* concepts. These emphasize inclusivity, environmental capacity and cultural-natural capital. Thus, perceptions of landscape have moved firmly in the direction of recognizing the value of all areas, recognizing that visual distinctiveness and environmental functionality are universally present. Of particular note has been the previously mentioned integration of aesthetic capital and biodiversity into a single mapping framework, assuring the application of landscape policy to all areas. The rather limited notion of ecological carrying capacity, which had rather unsuccessfully been transferred to recreational site management, has become an influential conceptual tool for sustainability management. Thus, landscape units, such as estuaries and mountain ranges (and, indeed, townscapes), can be analysed in terms of their environmental capacity, or 'limits of acceptable change' (e.g. RSPB, 1994). Landscape once more becomes the organizing unit within which we might 'tread more lightly on the earth'. The effects and needs of people have also gained in prominence: links between society and characteristic, distinctive landscapes include influences as varied as vernacular irrigation systems, use of regional breeds of livestock in pastoral farming, low intensity traditional agricultural practices, and the socio-economic spin-offs of hunting to hounds. In other words, the sustainability phase of landscape policy leads to the pursuit of landscapes which 'work' insofar as they are self-maintaining, regenerative of natural capital and supportive of human quality of life. To take an example, much effort has latterly been invested in forest design and planning in order to create new lowland forests possessing rich ecosystems, access and recreation opportunities for all sectors of the population, and a commercially viable timber reserve (see Chapter 8 for more on this). Ideally, all of these objectives are mutually reinforcing, leading (hopefully) to woodlands which are ecologically complex, enjoy public support and pay their way.

LANDSCAPES WITHIN REGIONAL AND NATIONAL SUSTAINABILITY STRATEGIES

Finally, it is important that landscape takes on a regional and national dimension through its contribution to mainstream sustainability policy. While sustainable development strategies include specific components on landscape *per se*, they are also more generally about 'liveability', offering opportunities for landscape to contribute more generally to the attainment of socio-economic goals. Policy contexts

---

Box 6.1

A Better Quality of Life: key themes relevant to landscape

- Farming and the countryside – food standards, reform of CAP towards environmental and rural development measures.
- Tourism strategy.
- Building sustainable communities (e.g. improving local surroundings).
- Better planning and design – re-using previously developed land, extending existing urban areas rather than building isolated new settlements, encouraging a high quality environment with the provision of green spaces, and improving local environmental quality (including the improvement of open space and wildlife habitats in and around towns, and initiatives such as community forests and the central Scotland forest).
- Landscape and wildlife – reversing the decline in biodiversity and encouraging well-managed change in the countryside (this includes protection of the wider landscape in terms of identifying important character, designating special landscapes and promoting public access and enjoyment; promoting sustainable land management, notably agriculture; and protecting individual features and local heritage).
- Forests and woodlands – seeking sustainable management of forests and woodlands, protecting ancient semi-natural woodlands, promoting new woodlands and forests, and producing 'sustainable' timber.

Source: DETR (1999)

are provided at various levels. For example, at the European scale, as well as explicit landscape policies and programmes, the EU promotes sustainability in numerous ways which impinge on the landscape. Agri-environment policy, including Agenda 2000, the Environmental Action Programmes, and nature conservation directives and biodiversity strategy, are among the more obvious examples (CEC, 1979, 1992a, 1992b, 1997, 1998). However, it is likely that EU policies generally will be 'balanced off' in terms of their contribution to sustainability. Sustainability at the national level is allegedly central to a range of policies across government departments, while the Regional Development Agencies have the pursuit of sustainable development as part of their remit (Sue Kidd has more to say on this in Chapter 7).

National priorities for sustainable development reflect a perceived need for prosperity to be based on economic growth (DETR, 1999). While this basic assumption may be debatable, its conditions are less controversial. Thus, growth is expected to be of higher quality, more equitable, associated with higher quality urban and rural environments and compatible with our global responsibilities. Within the overarching goals, various key themes are identified, including those which relate to the contribution which towns and countryside make to quality of life. As already noted, though, landscape can contribute to the attainment of a wide range of themes (see Box 6.1). Progress towards national sustainability is measured through a suite of indicators and, of particular relevance to landscape, are those which relate to: participation and community empowerment (see Chapter 12); better recognition of sustainable development in the planning system (see Chapter 7); and reform of the Common Agricultural Policy (see Chapter 8).

The opportunities for landscape to contribute to policy developments at national and regional scales are also reflected in policy statements from government agencies and non-government organizations. For example, the Countryside Agency (1999) is framing a policy agenda which reflects people's concerns about loss of tranquillity and scale of new development, and is thus seeking a countryside of:

- diverse character and outstanding beauty;
- prosperous and inclusive communities;
- economic opportunity and enterprise;
- sustainable agriculture;
- transport that serves people without destroying the environment;
- recreational access for local people and visitors.

More generally, while the regional dimension has been rather muted in the UK since the 1970s, it is once more impacting strongly on the way in which policy is devised and implemented. This is occurring most notably through new parliaments/assemblies in Scotland, Wales and Northern Ireland, and regionalization in England, leading to a more differentiated policy response to environmental management. Of more subtle significance is the increasing devolution of planning matters along the same lines, requiring a regional landscape context as a framework for urban expansion, mineral extraction and transport development (see Chapter 7). It is clear that landscape can provide an important basis on which different parts of the UK can represent their distinctiveness and, perhaps most significantly from the point of view of the economic regeneration functions which have been devolved, provide conducive settings for inward investment. A prime example is the community forest, which as well as creating a multi-functional landscape, provides an attractive setting where previously there was nondescript or degenerate landscape.

The likely areas in which landscape will contribute to national and regional sustainability objectives appear to be threefold. The first is its role in underpinning the human economy, that is, providing a setting for human prosperity, encouraging economic uses which create and maintain (either spontaneously or through policy support) valid landscapes, tourism which respects environmental capacities, and distinctive regional landscapes which underpin the promotion of inward investment. A second role is that of underpinning delight, placeness and beauty – landscape for human quality of life, facilitating human enjoyment of landscape within the intrinsic limits of environmental capacity, and maximizing the 'affordances' of landscapes so

Figure 6.4 A visitor centre in an Ontario provincial park.

that people have opportunities for recreational activity, tranquil relaxation, visual stimulation, and attachment to place (see Figure 6.4). Finally, landscapes can underpin nature's economy, i.e. landscape for nature, seeking to ensure that land cover and the maritime zone meet the life-cycle requirements of species, that human manipulation of the physical environment does not disrupt physical systems (such as river flows or wave regimes), and that the integrity of life-support systems (e.g. soil fertility and replenishment of air quality) is maintained.

CONCLUSION

Landscape is an important policy domain in its own right, and much of the expression of landscape policy has been at the regional and national scales. Of undiminished importance are the key designations of National Parks and AONBs, with nature conservation and agri-environment designations also often being of sufficient scale to bolster regional landscape distinctiveness. While statutorily confirmed designations such as these will be a mainstay of conservation policy well into the twenty-first century, they are likely to be re-interpreted through mapping, analytical and management procedures which reflect their intrinsic qualities. Rather than standing aside from their host regions, designated areas are likely to be treated as places which are inseparably connected to their surroundings through visual, ecological and hydrological continuity. Indeed, they may even be viewed as 'source' zones from which neighbouring landscape can be re-populated with native species or receive inspiration for the reconstruction of visual character.

Landscape will also be seen as an important integrating framework for sustainable development. It is the essential amalgam of people and place, providing a context for integrated and holistic policy development. Sustainable development policy requires the meshing of people's stories (see Chapter 14), indigenously based economic wealth, and sensitive use of natural resources. Landscape character, even as a weak form of bioregionalism, provides natural units within which these disparate attributes and purposes can converge.

As with all aspects of the environment, though, if it is really to contribute to sustainable development, then landscape must be integrated into the drivers of regional and national change rather than treated as a sectoral activity. Thus, the essential policy framework within which landscapes are managed is likely to comprise:

- liveability – the need for aesthetic surroundings, safety and wholesome air/water/food;
- biodiversity – the provision of viable core and matrix areas in which nature can thrive and extinctions be avoided;
- prosperity – the development of an economically viable landscape supported by farming, forestry, indigenous manufacturing and services, water and leisure.

Landscape is thus a natural candidate as a framework for the integrative and transdisciplinary tasks of sustainable development. To fulfil such a role, landscapes must be understood not only as localized, particular expressions of people and place, but also as the regional and national frames for the analysis and maintenance of fundamental patterns and processes.

REFERENCES

Beck, U. (1992) *Risk Society: Towards a New Modernity* (London, Sage).

Bishop, K., Phillips, A. and Warren, L. (1995) Protected for ever? Factors shaping the future of protected areas policy, *Land Use Policy*, 12(4), 55–74.

Blowers, A. (1999) Nuclear waste and landscapes of risk, *Landscape Research*, 24(3), 241–264.

Brace, C. (1999) Finding England everywhere: regional identity and the construction of national identity, 1890–1940, *Ecumene*, 6(1), 90–109.

Brooke, D. (1994) A Countryside Character programme, *Landscape Research*, 19(3), 128–132.

Buckingham-Hatfield, S. and Percy, S. (1999) Keys to a Sustainable Environment: Education, Community Development and Local Democracy, in S. Buckingham-Hatfield and S. Percy (eds) *Constructing Local Environmental Agendas: People, Places and Participation* (London, Routledge).

Carson, R. (1962) *Silent Spring* (Harmondsworth, Penguin).

Commission of the European Communities (1979) *Directive on the Conservation of Wild Birds*, 79/409/EEC (Brussels, CEC).

Commission of the European Communities (1992a) *Directive on the Conservation of Natural and Semi-Natural Habitats of Wild Fauna and Flora*, 92/43/EEC (Brussels, CEC).

Commission of the European Communities (1992b) *Towards Sustainability: A European Community Programme of Policy and Action in Relation to the Environment and Sustainable Development*, COM (92) 23 (Brussels, CEC).

Commission of the European Communities (1997) *Agenda 2000: For a Stronger and Wider Union* (COM (97) 2000 Final) (Luxembourg, Office for Official Publications of the European Communities).

Commission of the European Communities (1998) *A European Community Biodiversity Strategy*, COM (1998) 42 (Brussels, CEC).

Cooper, A. (1992) A structured method of landscape assessment and countryside management, *Applied Geography*, 12(4), 319–338.

Countryside Agency (1999) *Tomorrow's Countryside – 2020 Vision* (Cheltenham, Countryside Agency).

Countryside Commission/English Nature (undated) *The Character of England: Landscape, Wildlife and Natural features*, pamphlet (Peterborough, English Nature).

Crowe, S. (1966) *Forestry in the Landscape* (London, HMSO).

Daniels, S. (1993) *Fields of Vision: Landscape Imagery and National Identity in England and the United States* (Cambridge, Polity Press).

Department of Environment, Transport and the Regions (1999) *A Better Quality of Life* (London, DETR).

English Nature (1998) *Natural Areas: Nature Conservation in Context*, CD-ROM (Peterborough, EN).

Environment Agency (1997) *An Environmental Strategy for the Millennium and Beyond* (Bristol, EA).

Farina, A. (1998) *Principles and Methods in Landscape Ecology* (London, Chapman & Hall).

Fines, K. D. (1968) Landscape evaluation: a research project in East Sussex, *Regional Studies*, 2, 41–55.

Haines-Young, R., Green, D. and Cousins, S. (eds) (1993) *Landscape Ecology and Geographic Information Systems* (London, Taylor & Francis).

Hawkins, V. (1999) Landscape Ecological Planning: A Study of the Principles and Methods of Landscape Ecology and their Application to the Planning and Management of Rural Land Use Change in Britain, unpublished PhD thesis, University of Bristol.

Hewitt, K. (1997) *Regions of Risk: A Geographical Introduction to Disasters* (Harlow, Addison-Wesley Longman).

Hodge, I., Adams, W. M. and Bourn, N. A. D. (1994) Conservation policy in the wider countryside: agency competition and innovation, *Journal of Environmental Planning and Management*, 37(2), 199–213.

Independent Commission on International Development Issues (1980) *North–South: A Programme for Survival* (Brandt Commission) (London, Pion).

International Union for the Conservation of Nature and Natural Resources (1980) *World Conservation Strategy* (Gland, IUCN).

International Union for the Conservation of Nature and Natural Resources (1991) *Caring for the Earth* (Gland, IUCN).

Lowenthal, D. (1991) British national identity and the English landscape, *Rural History*, 2, 205–230.

MacArthur, R. H. and Wilson, E. O. (1967) *The Theory of Island Biogeography* (Princeton, NJ, Princeton University Press).

McGinnis, M. V. (ed.) (1998) *Bioregionalism* (London, Routledge).

Matless, D. (1997) Moral geographies of the English landscape, *Landscape Research*, 22(2), 141–155.

Mezga, D. (1993) Phenomenology and Auschwitz: seeking practical application of the paradigm in design analysis, *Landscape Research*, 18(2), 66–77.

Ministry of Agriculture, Fisheries and Food (1995) *Shoreline Management Plans: A Guide for Coastal Defence Authorities* (London, MAFF).

O'Callaghan, J. R. (1995) NELUP: an introduction, *Journal of Environmental Planning and Management*, 38(1), 5–20.

O'Riordan, T. and Ward, R. (1997) Building trust in shoreline management: creating participatory consultation in shoreline management plans, *Land Use Policy*, 14(4), 257–276.

Royal Society for the Protection of Birds (1994) *Capacity Planning: A Practical Application of Sustainable Development Concepts in the Land Use Field*, Proceedings of a conference, 24 February, Nottingham (Sandy, RSPB).

Selman, P. (2000) *Environmental Planning*, 2nd edition (London, Sage).

United Nations Conference on Environment and Development (UNCED) (1992) *Agenda 21 – Action Plan for the Next Century* (Rio de Janeiro, UNCED).

World Commission on Environment and Development (1987) *Our Common Future* (The Brundtland Report) (Oxford, Oxford University Press).

Wu, J. and Levin, S. A. (1994) A spatial patch dynamic modelling approach to pattern and process in an annual grassland, *Ecological Monographs*, 64, 447–464.

7

LANDSCAPE PLANNING AT THE REGIONAL SCALE

Sue Kidd

SUMMARY

Landscape planning in the UK tends to concentrate on the site and the landscape scales. Concepts of sustainable development and the new-found importance of regional level planning suggest, however, that there is a growing case for the landscape community to develop a regional planning perspective and to engage in wider areas of decision-making in order to forward landscape planning goals. This chapter explores these challenges with particular reference to the North West of England which through the work of an organisation called Sustainability North West and the production of a Regional Landscape Strategy has been at the forefront of regional level landscape planning in the UK. The chapter provides an account of the production of the Regional Landscape Strategy and some reflections on the experience, highlighting some the problems and potential of the approach. An outline of the new regional arrangements in England is then given and their relevance to landscape planning interests is highlighted. Movement towards sustainable development is a central element in the new regional planning structures and the chapter concludes with some discussion of the links between landscape and sustainability thinking with particular reference to the regional scale.

INTRODUCTION

Landscape planning in the UK tends to operate on two main scales. The first is the site level and is concerned with the design and construction of relatively small sites often as settings for built development (see Chapter 9). The second is the landscape scale covering tracts of countryside at least several kilometres wide (Selman, 1999). From a landscape ecologist's perspective landscape can be defined as consisting of: 'distinct, measurable unit(s) defined by . . . recognisable and spatially repetitive cluster(s) of interacting ecosystem(s), geomorphology and disturbance regimes.' (Forman and Godron, 1986, p. 11). Thus, landscape scale can be determined by, for example: the extent of natural processes; the incidence of a particular habitat; the location or potential location of a particular type of land cover; or by incidence of a discreet landscape character which reflects the interaction of ecological conditions and human land use. It may also be determined more arbitrarily by land ownership or jurisdiction. Planning activity at the landscape scale is principally concerned with environmental protection and enhancement and/or resource management and is often expressed in the form of plans. These plans may promote preferred patterns of resource use, provide a framework for more effective co-ordination and collaboration between agencies working in an area, and/or set out detailed action plans related to the management of

Table 7.1   Examples of landscape scale plans in the UK

Determinant of scale	Type of plan
Natural processes	Local Environment Agency Plans Shoreline Management Plans
Natural habitats	SAC and SPA Management Plans
Incidence/potential incidence of particular land cover	Forestry and Woodland Strategies Community Forest Plans
Landscape character	AONB Management Plans
Land ownership/jurisdiction	Whole Farm Management Plans Estate Plans Local Authority Nature Conservation Strategies

specific sites and areas. Table 7.1 provides some examples of the range of landscape scale plans currently being produced in the UK.

The focus of landscape planning activity at the site and landscape scales reflects the need for spatial precision in dealing with many landscape planning concerns and the practicalities of implementation which require the engagement of agencies and individuals who can directly affect change on the ground (see Chapters 9–11). Beyond the site and landscape scales the scope for spatial precision may be reduced and the ability to link planning activity to site level action may be less apparent (Forman, 1995). There is, however, a growing case for landscape planners in the UK to look beyond the site and landscape scales and to engage in planning activity at higher levels. In addition, there is a developing appreciation that landscape planners should be prepared to engage in wider areas of decision making in order to achieve landscape planning goals, as Paul Selman has advocated in Chapter 6.

Emerging concepts of sustainability are significant in both these developments. They have highlighted the need for a more integrated approach to environmental planning and management in recognition of the trans-media and trans-boundary nature of environmental processes and the trans-sectoral nature of environmental policy-making (Blowers, 1993). So, for example, it is increasingly understood that concerns about environmental protection and enhancement are directly linked in many instances to agriculture, transport, energy and other policy

areas (Chapter 8). Chris Patten, a former Environment Secretary in the UK government, underlined this situation when he observed that 'the most important parts of environmental policy are handled elsewhere – the levers aren't in my office' (O'Riordan, 2000, p. 74). This understanding has in turn emphasized the need for a more strategic approach to environmental planning with action necessary at international, national, and regional levels to complement and support, and where appropriate to direct, activity at the local and site scales. As a consequence, the region is increasingly being seen as an important level for sustainable planning and management. It is a level at which many macro-level sustainability issues, such as acid deposition in the uplands, the problems of ground level ozone in the lowlands and poor water quality in many of the UK's estuaries, can begin to be effectively addressed (Handley et al., 1998).

The case for landscape planners to look beyond the site and landscape scales is also influenced by the new-found importance of regional level policy and statutory planning in the UK. This trend has been underpinned by a number of factors including: the adoption of the region as the common denominator of government both within the European Union and within a wider Europe; the growing importance of European regional programmes; and the need to provide a stronger strategic planning framework for metropolitan and other areas which have seen institutional fragmentation as a result of local government reorganization (Roberts, 1997; Baker, 1998).

It is in this context that stronger and new regional institutions have begun to emerge, culminating in 1998 in the establishment of the Scottish Parliament and Welsh Assembly and Regional Assemblies in England. As a consequence, regional level planning is achieving a new level of significance and there is the prospect of a much stronger regional influence over national policy and greater regional direction of local policy and local spending priorities. It is therefore critically important that landscape planners engage with these new arrangements to ensure that environmental concerns are given due attention alongside economic and social considerations.

Engagement with the region does, however, present UK landscape planners with a challenge. How can their fine-grained understanding of landscape at the site and landscape scales be translated effectively to the macro-level perspectives of the region in a way which maintains an effective influence over action on the ground? Equally, how can landscape planning concerns be integrated into broader regional planning objectives in a way which is relevant to both the landscape planning constituency and to those concerned with other aspects of regional policy?

This chapter explores these challenges with particular reference to experience in the North West of England which through the work of an organization called Sustainability North West and the production of a Regional Landscape Strategy has been at the forefront of regional level landscape and sustainability planning in the UK. The chapter begins with an account of the production of the Regional Landscape Strategy which sets out the context for the project and the study method. This is followed by a reflection on the North West experience highlighting some of the problems and potential of the approach. An outline of the new regional arrangements in England is then given and their relevance to landscape planning interests is highlighted. Movement towards sustainable development is a central element in the new regional planning structures and the chapter concludes with some discussion of the links between landscape and sustainability thinking with particular reference to the regional scale.

GREENING THE NORTH WEST: A REGIONAL LANDSCAPE STRATEGY

Regional context

The North West Region of England stretches from the uplands of Cumbria in the north to the lowland landscapes of Cheshire in the south. It is flanked to the east by the Pennine ranges and to the west by the Irish Sea. It is a region of great landscape contrast encompassing areas of the highest international quality such as the Lake District and coast as well as substantial areas of environmental degradation and dereliction associated with its industrial heritage and more recent economic restructuring. Concern to protect and improve the environmental quality of the region has been a long-standing feature of regional level planning in the North West dating back to the publication of the first regional strategy in 1973 (North West Joint Planning Team, 1973). This theme was retained as a central element in the new regional strategies produced in the middle of the 1990s – The Regional Economic Strategy for the North West (North West Regional Association/North West Business Leadership Team, 1993) and North West Regional Planning Guidance known as RPG13 (Government Office for the North West/Government Office for Merseyside, 1996). Both documents encompassed a vision for the North West as:

- a world-class centre for the production of high quality goods and services;
- a green and pleasant region;
- a region of first-class links to the rest of Europe and the world.

In 1996 Sustainability North West (SNW) was established as the environmental arm of the North West Partnership, a coalition of local government and business leaders which was a predecessor of the new regional arrangements mentioned above. SNW was charged with assisting in the realization of the vision for the North West as 'a green and pleasant region'. In order to help in this task one of the first initiatives taken by SNW was the commissioning of a Regional Landscape Strategy. This had as its overall objective the fuller articulation of the North West vision of a 'green and pleasant region'. The detailed remit was to review landscape condition and appraise current strategic environmental initiatives with a view to identifying the scope for co-ordination, reinforcement and innovation. The work was sponsored by the then Countryside Commission, United Utilities and English Nature and was undertaken by a small team drawn from the Department of Planning and Landscape at the University of Manchester and the Department of Civic Design at the University of Liverpool.

Approach to the work

Two underlying principles permeated the Study Team's approach to the work. First landscape was

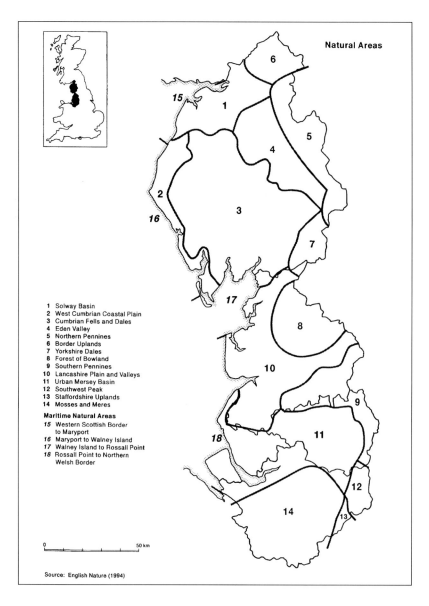

Natural Areas

1   Solway Basin
2   West Cumbrian Coastal Plain
3   Cumbrian Fells and Dales
4   Eden Valley
5   Northern Pennines
6   Border Uplands
7   Yorkshire Dales
8   Forest of Bowland
9   Southern Pennines
10   Lancashire Plain and Valleys
11   Urban Mersey Basin
12   Southwest Peak
13   Staffordshire Uplands
14   Mosses and Meres

Maritime Natural Areas

15   Western Scottish Border
     to Maryport
16   Maryport to Walney Island
17   Walney Island to Rossall Point
18   Rossall Point to Northern
     Welsh Border

0   50 km

Source: English Nature (1994)

Figure 7.1   North West Region Natural Areas.

interpreted in its broadest sense following the Forman and Godron definition of landscape cited earlier and that of Zonneveld who defines landscape as: '(A) part of the space on the Earth's surface, consisting of a complex of systems, formed by the activity of rock, water, air, plants, animals and man and that by its physiognomy forms a recognisable entity.' (Zonneveld, 1990, p. 55). For the purposes of the study, therefore, landscape was considered both as a set of features embracing both natural and built elements, and as a dynamic entity affected by all aspects of its environment and human use. Hence air and water quality as well as the nature and condition of land was regarded as important. In addition, the more intangible significance of landscape as 'symbolic expressions of cultural values, social behaviour and individual actions worked upon particular localities over time' (Meinig, 1979) was encompassed.

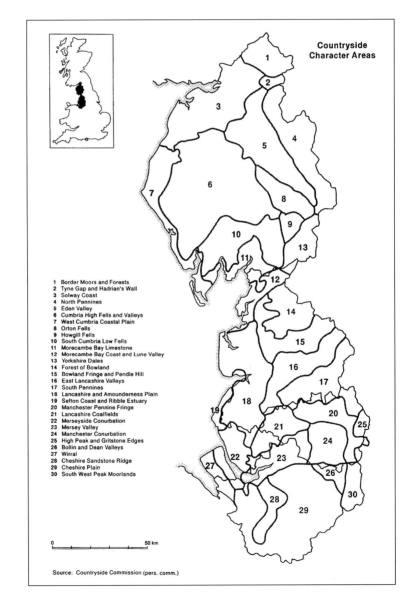

Countryside Character Areas

1 Border Moors and Forests
2 Tyne Gap and Hadrian's Wall
3 Solway Coast
4 North Pennines
5 Eden Valley
6 Cumbria High Fells and Valleys
7 West Cumbria Coastal Plain
8 Orton Fells
9 Howgill Fells
10 South Cumbria Low Fells
11 Morecambe Bay Limestone
12 Morecambe Bay Coast and Lune Valley
13 Yorkshire Dales
14 Forest of Bowland
15 Bowland Fringe and Pendle Hill
16 East Lancashire Valleys
17 South Pennines
18 Lancashire and Amounderness Plain
19 Sefton Coast and Ribble Estuary
20 Manchester Pennine Fringe
21 Lancashire Coalfields
22 Merseyside Conurbation
23 Mersey Valley
24 Manchester Conurbation
25 High Peak and Gritstone Edges
26 Bollin and Dean Valleys
27 Wirral
28 Cheshire Sandstone Ridge
29 Cheshire Plain
30 South West Peak Moorlands

0   50 km

Source: Countryside Commission (pers. comm.)

Figure 7.2 North West Region Countryside Character Areas.

Reflecting this broad-based definition the Study Team was fortunate to be able to draw upon work which had been recently completed for the Countryside Commission and English Nature related to the definition of Countryside Character Areas. The Countryside Character Areas drew upon the earlier definition of Natural Areas by English Nature (see Figure 7.1) and defined areas of distinct landscape character which expressed the interaction of people with the natural environment. Some thirty such areas had been identified for the North West region (see Figure 7.2) and these were seen to provide a solid foundation and important building blocks for landscape strategy development.

The second principle underlying the Study Team's approach to the work was the perception that it was critical to create a direct relationship with the established regional policy framework set out in the Regional Economic Strategy for the North West and North West Regional Planning Guidance (RPG). These documents were key determinants in directing new investment and development in the North West and it was considered that the Landscape Strategy would have greater status and a better chance of influencing implementation agencies if it was seen as an extension of these established regional policy approaches.

These two considerations permeated all aspects of the work which was divided into two stages (See Figure 7.3). In Stage One the Study Team under-

Table 7.2   Environmental Agenda of RPG13

Natural environment	Built environment
Natural heritage	Built heritage
Coast	Recreation and sport
Urban fringe	Energy
Water and air quality	Urban greenspace
Non-energy minerals	Derelict land
	Waste

took two parallel baseline surveys – a Regional Landscape Assessment and a Review of Strategic Environmental Initiatives in the region. Both these exercises were structured to reflect the environmental agenda identified in RPG 13 which covered the elements set out in Table 7.2.

While this broad-based definition of landscape potentially extended the task in hand and posed the risk of losing a tight focus to the work, it was considered that such problems were more than offset by the benefits of its adoption. The extent of coverage was generally consistent with the Study Team's commitment to a holistic definition of landscape with all the RPG categories impinging to a significant extent on the quality and character of the landscape in the region. The categorization also offered the benefit of having some statutory weight with the outputs of the survey stage being capable of being related back to RPG13.

The output from the Regional Landscape Assessment was a compendium of regional level information grouped under each of the environmental themes with associated commentary (Wood *et al.*, 1996). The exercise revealed areas of particular information scarcity especially in relation to built environment themes such as urban greenspace, and waste. However, for most areas it was possible to bring together much valuable information on the current state of the North West landscape. The key conclusions of the assessment included a clear recognition of the great landscape diversity of the region and the extent of nationally and internationally important environmental assets of great aesthetic, cultural, recreational and ecological value. Among

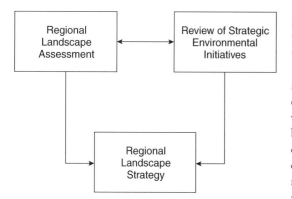

Figure 7.3   Development of the North West Landscape Strategy.

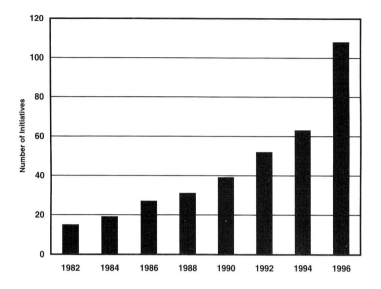

Figure 7.4 Development of North West Strategic Environmental Initiatives.

these assets was the built inheritance of the industrial revolution but the assessment also highlighted that this phase in the region's history had also created a legacy of environmental damage. Current problems were typified by increasing urbanization of the land- scape, a growth in derelict land in the lowlands, acid deposition in the uplands and the prospect of sea level rise along the coast.

The output of the review of Strategic Environmental Initiatives was a regional directory of

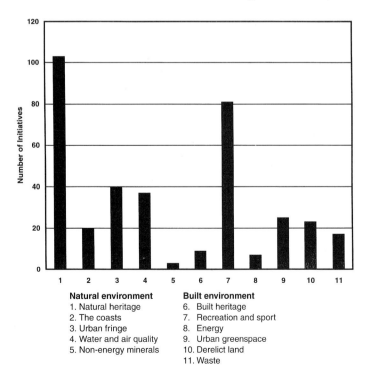

Figure 7.5 North West Initiatives by RPG theme.

non-statutory, collaborative and promotional environmental initiatives which were of significance at a district level or above (Kidd *et al.* 1996). The directory detailed the objectives, area covered, start date and lead organization(s) of each initiative. ThisCdirectory was accompanied by an overview of the development, coverage and orientation of environmental initiatives in the region. The exercise revealed the great diversity of environmental activity in the region and the substantial increase in the number of initiatives since the beginning of the 1990s (see Figure 7.4). The durability of initiatives was also significant. Once established they tended to continue even in difficult funding circumstances. Environmental initiatives were a feature of all parts of the region. The majority were multi-dimensional with nature conservation and recreation being the most common concerns (see Figure 7.5). Finally it was clearly evident that the public sector played a prominent role in directing and nurturing initiatives but the private and voluntary sectors also contributed significantly through funding and manpower.

The results of these two baseline surveys informed the second stage of the work which entailed the development of a Regional Landscape Strategy itself (Sustainability North West/Countryside Commission (1998)). This took as one of its starting points the thirty Countryside Character Areas which had been identified for the North West. These reflected distinct physical and cultural parameters which combined to make each area unique. In theory therefore the Countryside Character Areas provided an appropriate scale at which to develop landscape planning responses. However, from a regional perspective the level of disaggregation was unhelpful as it required a level of detail in policy which is difficult to accommodate at the regional scale. The challenge for the Regional Landscape Strategy was to provide a meaningful framework for landscape planning at the regional scale which could be effectively translated into action at the local level. In assessing the merits of the Countryside Character Areas the Study Team noted that while each had a unique identity, many significant attributes recurred in different areas. With this in mind the Team sought to aggregate Countryside Character Areas which had

Table 7.3 Criteria for defining landscape domains

Domain	Criteria
Coast	Character areas abutting coast or estuary
Urban Core	Character areas over 90 per cent urbanized
Urban Fringe	Character areas abutting the urban core and/or over 25 per cent urbanized
Rural Lowland	Character areas contiguous with CIS* arable/pastural zones but not urban core
Rural Upland	Character areas contiguous with CIS upland/marginal zones

*Countryside Information System (DETR).

common physical characteristics and management issues associated with them and this was achieved by the definition of five landscape domains:

- the Coast
- the Urban Core
- the Urban Fringe
- the Rural Lowlands
- the Rural Upland.

The criteria for defining the landscape domains are set out in Table 7.3.

The landscape domains were felt to be valid in both an abstract and a real sense: abstract in that they represent a broad 'feel' for the landscape, real in that there are distinct physical characteristics and management issues associated with them. They were felt to be helpful as a means by which issues of common interest to geographically disparate areas could be explored.

In developing the content of the Landscape Strategy the Study Team again tried to build upon the established policy framework set out in the Regional Economic Strategy and RPG13. Close consideration was given to the environmental objectives of both these documents and these were drawn together to form the six objectives for the Regional Landscape Strategy (see Figure 7.6).

With the spatial framework and general objectives defined, the Study Team then began to flesh out the

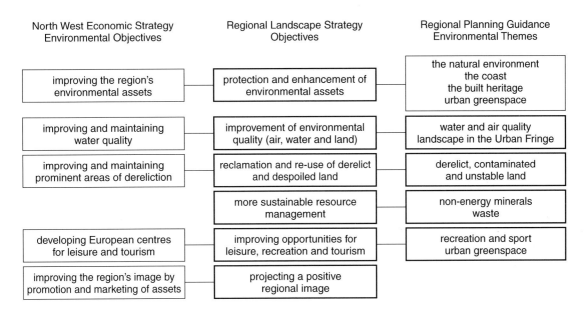

Figure 7.6 Regional Landscape Strategy objectives.

detailed content of the Regional Landscape Strategy which in line with its original remit sought to provide a framework for current and future environmental action and provide guidance on its reinforcement and co-ordination and indicate areas where innovative activity may be required.

Strategy development was undertaken at two levels. For each of the domains a standard approach was adopted. A descriptive environmental profile of the domain and a review of relevant strategic environmental initiatives set the context. This was followed by discussion of the environmental future of the domain and priorities for action were then grouped under each of the six landscape strategy objectives. Finally, links with other domains were considered. Table 7.4 provides a flavour of the approach with reference to the Urban Fringe domain.

The priorities for action for each of the domains were designed as pointers for bodies, public, private and voluntary, with a common interest in the domain. It was recognized that many of the actions highlighted were already being addressed through local policy mechanisms, such as local development plans and the wider Local Agenda 21 initiatives. However, it was the first time that these issues had been brought together in a way which could provide a basis for policy development at both regional and sub-regional level, uniting the neighbourhood with the Countryside Character Areas and the region (see Figure 7.7).

From a regional level perspective a number of issues emerged from the domain accounts which were clearly of common concern and these informed the development of a region wide landscape agenda again grouped under the six landscape domain headings.

REFLECTIONS ON THE NORTH WEST LANDSCAPE STRATEGY

The North West Landscape Strategy remains, perhaps, a unique example in the UK context of a landscape plan at the regional scale and, as previously indicated, it appeared as a result of a very particular combination of circumstances. These included the emergence of new regional level organisations,

Table 7.4 North West Landscape Strategy – some examples of findings for the Urban Fringe domain

Environmental profile	Environmental initiatives in train	Priorities for action
Buffer between town and country	Alt 2000	Environmental assets
	Beal River Valley Project	• protect and improve wildlife
Complex but distinct character	Bollin River Valley Project	corridors and spaces linking
	Canal and Countryside Project	town and country
Arena of intense activity	Darwen River Valley Project	• safeguard industrial heritage
	Groundwork Macclesfield and Vale	
Problems of:	Royal	Environmental quality
• degraded and despoiled land	Groundwork Blackburn	• maintain and improve water and
• pressures for waste disposal and	Groundwork East Lancashire	air quality
mineral extraction	Groundwork Manchester	• enhance landscape quality
• urban pollution	Groundwork Oldham, Rochdale and	through positive management of
• fragmented farmland	Tameside	Green Belt
• low-grade management practices	Groundwork Rossendale	
• poor environmental quality of	Groundwork Salford and Trafford	Derelict and despoiled land
Green Belt	Groundwork St Helens, Knowsley,	• promote strategic approach
	Sefton	ensuring appropriate use of
Positive features:	Groundwork West Cumbria	brownfield sites
• role of Green Belt in preventing	Groundwork Wigan and Chorley	• recognize the process of natural
urban sprawl	Groundwork Wirral	colonization in reclamation
• accessible countryside to large	Knowsley Community Woodland	
urban population	Initiative	Resource management
• opportunities for farm	Leeds Liverpool Canal Management	• promote development of
diversification	Scheme	sustainable energy sources such
• rich industrial heritage	Mersey Basin Campaign	as coppice woodland
• arena for innovative management	Mersey Forest	• integrate plans for landfill with
solutions	Red Rose Forest	community forest objectives
	Mersey Valley Partnership	
	NUVIL Project	Recreation/leisure/tourism
	RIVA2005	• expand and enhance greenways
	Sankey NOW	traversing urban fringe
	Stockport Planting Strategy	• provide new recreation resources
	Wasteland to Woodland	to divert pressure from wider
	Weaver River Valley Project	countryside and reduce leisure
	West Pennine Moors Management	travel
	Scheme	
	Wigan and Salford Mossland	Image
	Strategy	• promote positive image as
		accessible and valued
		countryside

the North West Partnership and Sustainability North West, which were keen to develop regional level environmental action programmes and had the flexibility to do this in a way which was unconstrained by statutory requirements and expectations. This interest coincided with the publication of the Countryside Commission and English Nature's Landscape Character Areas and these organizations were beginning to explore associated policy applications. The resulting North West Regional Landscape Strategy is therefore very much a product of a particular time and place and it has to some extent been overtaken by the new regional order which will be discussed more fully below. It therefore may seem questionable how far this North West experience may be relevant to the current UK context and to wider landscape planning debates. However, it does provide some interesting insights into the particular problems faced by landscape planning in the UK as well as areas of potential development.

Figure 7.7 Components of a Regional Landscape Strategy.

The fact that the Regional Landscape Strategy has to some extent been overtaken by events is in itself of interest. The Strategy was fairly typical of many landscape plans in that it did not have any statutory status and despite the very best efforts of the Study Team to link it into formal policy documents, this limited the extent to which key organizations were prepared to commit themselves to its delivery. Equally, no new resources were available for its implementation and in the context of a rapidly changing regional scene priorities for action were clearly elsewhere. Such problems are common to many landscape-related plans (e.g. Curry, 1992) but as research into collaborative planning has shown, they may be overcome, at least to some extent, by the presence of an appropriate forum for bringing key stakeholders together where commitment and co-operation can be built up over time (Healey, 1997). The timing of the publication of the Regional Landscape Strategy was, however, not conducive to these circumstances. No champion of the strategy has emerged as all the key partners are having to readjust and refocus their activities in light of new regional and institutional arrangements and attention has inevitably been concentrated on galvanizing co-operative effort in relation to new formal regional planning activities. In this context the existence of yet another strategy – the Regional Landscape Strategy – has also not been helpful as organizations become overfaced with a proliferation of such documents.

Despite these circumstances it would not be fair to imply that the North West Regional Landscape Strategy has been without influence. Indeed, there are many illustrations of ways in which it has both directly and perhaps indirectly influenced actions and events. In terms of direct effects one of the most tangible outcomes of the Regional Landscape Strategy has been the establishment of ENWEB, a regional web site providing information on the North West environment and environmental initiatives in the region. This is an updated and extended version of the two baseline studies which fed into the development of the Regional Landscape Strategy and its establishment was one of its key recommendations. A notable feature of the site is its links to other relevant sources of information and this provides the North West with an excellent resource which should benefit landscape and environmental planning at all levels and in all areas of the region.

More subtle influence can perhaps be observed in the new formal regional policy documents that are emerging for the North West. The first to be published has been the new North West Regional Development Agency's Strategy (NWDA, 1999). Interestingly, this has clearly set sustainable development at its heart to an extent which may be unusual in such documents and perhaps reflects the relative sophistication of the North West in this respect as illustrated by the existence of the SNW. With sustainability at its core, it is therefore not surprising that environmental, as well as economic and social concerns feature prominently in the document. Examples of environmental considerations which may have been derived from the Regional Landscape Strategy, and certainly reflect its content, include the weight attached to the protection and enhancement of the region's varied environmental assets. In this context it is significant that the region's built industrial heritage, which has previously attracted little attention in regional policy documents, is highlighted as an area for particular attention with World Heritage Site status proposed for the Liverpool waterfront and the Ancoats area of Manchester. In addition to these concerns the RDA strategy also gives its support to the protection and enhancement of landscape diversity in the region and makes specific reference to the Countryside Agencies, Countryside Character Areas.

North West Regional Planning Guidance (RPG13) is the second key regional policy document in the new regional order. The original version published in 1996 is currently undergoing review and two consultation documents have been produced so far as part of this process (North West Regional Assembly 1999a and 1999b). Resonance with the North West Regional Landscape Strategy is also evident in both of these documents. Indeed, the strategy is specifically mentioned as a key source of advice for the new RPG. Prudent management of environmental and cultural assets and physical regeneration and environmental improvement are highlighted as key themes for policy development and within this broad frame concepts of regional and local distinctiveness are receiving an unprecedented level of attention and support from a wide spectrum of consultees. Equally, a more holistic approach to environmental concerns than in the previous RPG is evident and this is most notable in relation to the coast where research into integrated coastal planning is being commissioned to inform the content of the new document. This emphasis on the coast has perhaps been influenced by discussion of issues at a domain level within the North West Landscape Strategy where the case for action within the Coastal domain was particularly persuasive. There is also a recognition within the RPG consultation documents of the need in preparing the new guidance to consider issues on a geographical basis and the landscape domains are put forward as a potentially useful framework in this respect.

In developing the domain concept the Study Team were aware that it could be of value beyond policy formulation. One aspect of the Study Team's task was to identify the scope for co-ordination, reinforcement and innovation and the domains offered a coherent basis on which to bring together at a sub-regional

scale disparate areas, organizations and interest groups which shared common experiences and challenges. To this end the North West Landscape Strategy proposed the establishment of domain fora which would extend many aspects of SNW's remit to the domain level. These fora would provide an opportunity to improve the co-ordination of initiatives, reduce duplication of effort, disseminate good practice, give added weight to lobbying activities and funding bids and facilitate new areas of work of benefit to the wider domain community. Although so far the domain concept has not been formally developed in this way, a coastal grouping, PISCES, has emerged which illustrates the benefits of the approach.

The North West of England has a strong reputation in the coastal planning field with the work of the Sefton Coast Management Plan dating back to 1978. More recently coastal planning activity in the region has benefited from English Nature's Estuaries Initiative and the work of the Mersey Basin Campaign and by 1997 when the North West Regional Landscape Strategy was produced all but a small section of coastline in Cumbria was covered by coastal or estuary plans (see Figure 7.8). Efforts at that stage had concentrated very much on plan production within each of the plan areas and co-ordination between plans and certainly the development of a clear North West Coast perspective was only beginning to emerge. The organizations involved faced the difficult transition from plan production to implementation and the Regional Landscape Strategy highlighted the very real possibility that the benefits and momentum of all these efforts could be lost through lack of funding and continuing commitment. In response to such concerns PISCES, a grouping of North West coastal and estuarine interests, has developed in order to raise awareness of the strategic importance of the North West Coast. The emphasis being placed on the coast within the review of RPG 13 must partly be attributed to the efforts of this group and it highlights what can be achieved by domain-level action.

The need to take a strategic review of the implications of sea-level change was one of the key recommendations within the Coastal domain section of the

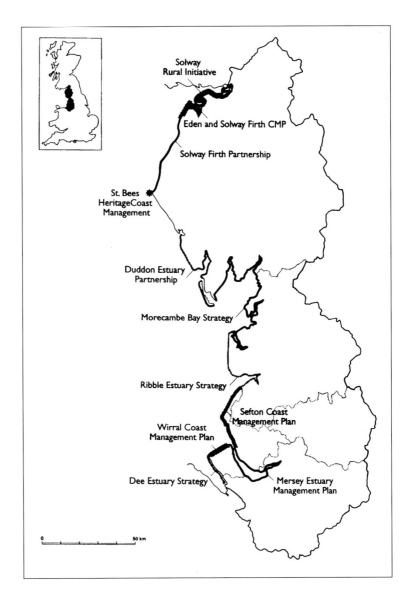

Figure 7.8 North West coastal and estuary plans.

North West Landscape Strategy. SNW has responded to this issue and extended its focus to consider the implication of climate change more generally in the region. In a pioneering study funded by a wide range of North West partners the implications of various climate change scenarios have been considered. This consideration has extended to various economic sectors such as manufacturing industry, tourism and recreation, and insurance. It has also considered the implications for each of the landscape domains. The impacts of climate change will vary between domains with, for example, the coastal experience being quite distinct from that of the rural uplands. This study is a further example of the value of a regional approach to landscape planning and the potential use of landscape domains as a framework for analysis which acts as a bridge between the landscape and regional scales.

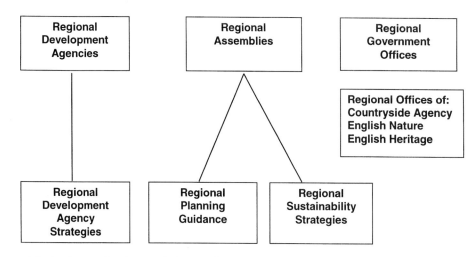

Figure 7.9   The landscape-related regional planning framework in England.

THE NEW FRAMEWORK FOR LANDSCAPE PLANNING AT THE REGIONAL SCALE

The North West Landscape Strategy experience highlights some of the problems and opportunities associated with landscape planning at the regional scale. It clearly demonstrates that established landscape planning concerns related to environmental protection and enhancement and/or resource management are of relevance at the regional level and through the landscape domain framework it can be possible to translate the fine-grained understanding of landscape at the site and landscape-scales to the macro-level perspectives of the region. The pitfalls of developing a separate landscape planning response at the regional level are, however, apparent. The North West experience reveals that important decisions regarding development and investment priorities are increasingly being made at the regional level and it indicates that the landscape planning constituency must be prepared to engage with the new formal regional planning structures in order to ensure that their area of interest is given due weight alongside other regional priorities. Landscape planners therefore require a clear understanding of the new regional arrangements and their relevance to landscape planning concerns. These are discussed below with particular reference to England.

As Figure 7.9 shows, there are now three key bodies responsible for regional level planning in England. These are the new Regional Assemblies made up of local authority, private and community sector representatives, the new Regional Development Agencies and the Regional Government Offices. Over time it can be expected that the latter may begin to assume less significance as the Regional Assemblies and Regional Development Agencies become more established. Alongside these agencies there is also the regional office structure of English Nature, English Heritage and the newly configured Countryside Agency which play an important role in regional affairs.

The main planning outputs of this new regional structure will be the Regional Development Agency Strategies and Regional Planning Guidance. The former is essentially an economic strategy for each region highlighting priorities for investment to sustain regional economic growth over a 20-year timescale. The RDAs have to take into account concepts of sustainable development in preparing these strategies (DETR, 1999a) and they do have the opportunity to place these concerns at the heart of their decision making, so environmental and social concerns will inevitably be considered alongside economic matters. The character of each RDA strategy is determined through regional consultation and the basic thrust of the strategies will be reviewed on a three year cycle. The strategies have an associated Action Programme for the RDA itself and partner organizations which is reviewed and updated annually and will be used to determine spending priorities.

The North West Development Agency's recently published strategy is perhaps indicative of the character of these new documents. It is centred on four related themes:

- investing in business and ideas
- investing in people and communities
- investing in infrastructure
- investing in image and environment.

Under the last theme, Restoring the Environmental Deficit of the Region is set out as a key objective and detailed aims which illustrate the direct landscape implications of the strategy include:

- identifying and enhancing assets of special regional value, in heritage, coast and countryside;
- supporting creative conservation projects, which enhance biodiversity, especially in urban areas;
- planting new woodland and forestry;
- developing new regional park resources close to the main centres of population;
- establishing clear objectives and efficient systems for land reclamation.

The second key regional planning output, Regional Planning Guidance, will increasingly become the responsibility of the new Regional Assemblies with the Regional Government Offices playing a diminishing role. The RPG will in future sit alongside the RDA strategy and provide a long-term indication of areas of development and development restraint and the range of considerations which should be taken into account in the preparation of development plans within the Region. In line with national planning policy guidance, sustainable development again sets the scene for RPG and a sustainability appraisal is

to become a formal requirement of RPG production and review. The content of the various RPGs is of direct concern to the landscape planning community as the land use planning system has traditionally been an important implementation mechanism for many landscape planning concerns. Indeed, it seems likely given the content of the public consultation draft of new Planning Policy Guidance Note 11 on Regional Planning (DETR, 1999b) that the next round of reviewed RPG documents will have a more significant role in landscape planning matters than previously. Greater prominence appears to be given to a number of established landscape-related concerns such as biodiversity and nature conservation and integrated coastal planning. In addition, Draft PPG 11 proposes that regional planners should increasingly try to embrace current thinking related to environmental capacity and to countryside characterization and give closer regard to the impact of development on natural resources.

It is therefore evident that the landscape planning community should feed into the preparation and review of both these documents which will have a strong bearing on regional investment and development patterns. However, from a landscape planning perspective they have their limitations in that they are principally concerned with directing specific types of economic and land use change and do not necessarily focus on some of the broader land and resource management issues addressed in many landscape plans. For example, future patterns of agricultural activity may be largely unaffected by these documents. In this respect, the third key regional planning strategy, the Regional Sustainability Strategy, may be of particular significance to landscape planners. The forerunners of these documents are the draft Action for Sustainability documents produced by the regional government offices (e.g. GONW, 1999). It is envisaged that these will form the basis of new Regional Sustainability Strategies produced by the Regional Assemblies. These wide-ranging strategies aim to develop a shared vision and coherent programme of delivery of sustainable development at the regional level. The significance of these documents is as yet unclear and the problems of uncertain status, levels of commitment and funding are already apparent. However, once the initial focus of attention on the RDA strategies and RPG reviews passes, the Regional Sustainability Strategies may well receive a higher profile in regional affairs. The landscape planning community could be well placed to influence the form and direction of these documents to ensure that they complement and fill the gaps left by the other two key regional policy documents. In this context the scope for adopting a domain level as well as the usual topic based approach to strategy and action plan formulation may prove valuable in linking action for sustainability to differing local contexts.

Box 7.1

Changing interpretations of sustainable development

World Conservation Strategy 1980

- to maintain essential ecological processes and life support systems
- to preserve genetic diversity
- to ensure the sustainable use of species and ecosystems

     (IUCN-UNEP-WWF, 1980, p. VI)

This Common Inheritance 1990

 . . . responsibility to future generations to preserve and enhance the environment of our country and our planet

       (DoE, 1990, p. 10)

Strategy for Sustainable Development for the UK 1999

 . . . ensuring a better quality of life for everyone now and future generations to come

       (DETR, 1999c, p. 8)

REGIONAL LANDSCAPE PLANNING AND SUSTAINABILITY

A key feature of all three of the new regional planning strategies is sustainable development and it appears critical that landscape planners should be able to articulate their interests within this context. Sustainable development is the framework through which disparate economic, social and environmental objectives are increasingly being brought together. It is the setting in which a dialogue between those involved with these differing areas of policy can take place. It could be argued that one of the failings of the North West Landscape Strategy was that it did not adequately articulate connections to the broader sustainability debate, although these were clearly in the minds of the authors throughout. As the other chapters in this book illustrate, the connection between landscape and sustainability is, however, complex and this complexity is only added to by the varying interpretations of landscape and of sustainability. In the final part of this chapter some discussion of the linkages between landscape planning and sustainability at the regional scale will be explored.

As Box 7.1 shows, interpretations of sustainable development have shifted over time. From an initial emphasis on environmental sustainability the concept has increasingly broadened to encompass economic and social sustainability. While it could be argued that the current focus within the UK at least, as illustrated by the new Strategy for Sustainable Development in the UK (DETR, 1999c), is increasingly on these latter two concerns, connection to environmental considerations remains fundamental. With this in mind it is apparent that all planning activities which purport to embrace sustainability must recognize their environmental connections and implications and that a detailed understanding of the physical characteristics of place must be a reference point in policy development. Thus a landscape ecology perspective has a valuable role to play in grounding diverse areas of policy in the realities of environmental constraints and dynamics. Landscape perspectives also have resonance with social sustainability considerations which emphasize quality of life and recognize the importance of connections with cultural heritage (Chapter 4). In both these contexts the landscape planners fine-grained understanding of the particularities of place may assist greatly in meeting broader sustainability objectives.

As we have seen, this fine-grained understanding is not only of value at the site and landscape scales but also can be utilized at the regional level. This appreciation is not new and underpinned the regional planning approaches developed early in the twentieth century by Patrick Geddes and Lewis Mumford (Luccarelli, 1995). Both men emphasized that cities did not exist in isolation of their natural hinterlands and that regional planning was needed to contextualize urban development and ensure respect for natural limits and diversity. Mumford was perhaps the best-known member of the Regional Planning Association of America and there are many dimensions of the RPAA's thinking which have resonance with the current context. The RPAA wanted to recover the link between development and the ecology and cultural significance of place. They were responding to what they perceived to be the predominant Western world view that turned nature into empty space and promoted technological solutions that engulf the complexities of both the urban and natural worlds. These concerns seems as relevant today as they were eighty years ago and they present a useful reminder of a potential pitfall for regional level planning.

More recent concepts of bioregionalism carry forward RPAA thinking in the current context of sustainable development (e.g. Sale, 1985). Bioregionalists believe that the rescaling of communities and the economy according to the ecological boundaries of a physical region will encourage sustainability. The concept seeks to reduce the negative external impacts of cities beyond its natural hinterland defined, for example, by river catchments, geological features or distinctive ecosystem types. As far as possible, resources should be derived from within the region and wastes and pollution dealt with *in situ* rather than exported. It is considered that such an approach would help to increase awareness of the environmental consequences of resource consumption and encourage an associated reduction in resource demands. There are many criticisms of this rather utopian thinking. These include the view that it encompasses an over-simplistic belief in ecological determinism and the ability to define ecologically coherent and discrete regions. Equally, the political unacceptability of potentially relegating a regional economy to underdevelopment in an increasingly nationally and internationally interdependent world has been raised. Nevertheless, bioregional perspectives appear to have merit in helping to develop a greater understanding of sustainability by highlighting the conflicts among a region's interconnected economic, social and ecological networks and indicating areas of healthy regional self-sufficiency and parasitic dependence on other regions' resources (Satterthwaite, 1999).

CONCLUSION

This chapter has considered the case for the landscape community to look beyond the site and landscape scales and to engage in regional level planning. The pioneering development of a Regional Landscape Strategy for the North West Region of England has highlighted some of the opportunities and problems inherent in this type of activity. This work has demonstrated that it is possible and potentially valuable to translate a fine-grained understanding of the landscape to policy development at the regional scale. However, the experience also highlights the well-understood landscape planning pitfalls of strategy proliferation and the need for effective engagement with formal planning frameworks. The emergence of stronger regional organizations and planning functions does, however, present the landscape community with important new opportunities to extend its planning horizons. Concepts of sustainability provide the backcloth against which the new regional arrangements are being developed. The interconnectivity of economic, social and environmental decision making is increasingly being recognized and this means that the environmental implications of all areas of policy are receiving an unprecedented level of attention. Landscape perspectives therefore have the potential to be of growing value in a broad range of policy contexts. However, in order to take up this challenge, the landscape community must gain a full understanding of the wider sustainability debate and be able to articulate its concerns within this context. This will be essential if it is to participate effectively in the new round of Regional Development Agency Strategies, Regional Planning Guidance Reviews and Regional Sustainability Strategies. All these documents seek at least in part to make regions more sustainable and in this context landscape-related ideas of bioregionalism and landscape domains appear to merit further exploration as a basis for regional policy development.

REFERENCES

Baker, R. (1998) Planning for the English Regions: a review of the Secretary of State's Regional Planning Guidance, *Planning Practice and Research*, 13(2), 153–169.

Blowers, A. (ed.) (1993) *Planning for a Sustainable Environment* (London, Earthscan).

Curry, N. (1992) Nature conservation, countryside strategies and strategic planning, *Journal of Environmental Planning and Management*, 35(1), 79–91.

Department of Environment (1990) *This Common Inheritance: Britain's Environmental Strategy* (London, HMSO).

Department of the Environment, Transport and the Regions (1999a) *Regional Development Agencies' Strategies* (http://www.local-regions.detr.gov.uk/rda/strategy/index.htm).

Department of the Environment, Transport and the Regions (1999b) *Planning Policy Guidance Note 11: Regional Planning Public Consultation Draft* (http://www.planning.detr.gov.uk/consult/ppg11/index.htm).

Department of the Environment, Transport and the Regions (1999c) *A Better Quality of Life: A Strategy for Sustainable Development in the United Kingdom*, Command Paper 4345 (London, HMSO).

Forman, R. (1995) *Landscape Mosaics: The Ecology of Landscapes and Regions* (New York, Springer).

Forman, R. and Godron, M. (1986) *Landscape Ecology* (New York, John Wiley).

Government Office for the North West (1999) *Action for Sustainability: Towards a Regional Sustainability Action Plan for the North West of England*, Draft Action Plan – Consultation (Manchester, GONW).

Government Office for the North West/Government Office for Merseyside (1996) *Regional Planning Guidance for the North West* (RPG13) (London, HMSO).

Handley, J., Wood, R. and Kidd, S. (1998) Defining coherence for landscape planning and management: a regional landscape strategy for North West England, *Landscape Research*, 23(2), 133–158.

Healey, P. (1997) *Collaborative Planning: Shaping Places in Fragmented Societies* (Basingstoke, Macmillan).

International Union for the Conservation of Nature and Natural Resources (1980) *World Conservation Strategy – Living Resource Conservation for Sustainable Development* (London, IUCN/UNEP/WWWF).

Kidd, S., Handley, J., Wood, R. and Douglas I. (1996) *Greening the North West: A Regional Landscape Strategy: Strategic Environmental Initiatives*, Occasional Paper No. 54, Dept. of Planning and Landscape (Manchester, University of Manchester).

Luccarelli, M. (1995) *Lewis Mumford and the Ecological Region* (New York, Guilford Press).

Meinig, D. (1979) *The Interpretation of Ordinary Landscapes: Geographical Essays* (Oxford, Oxford University Press).

North West Development Agency (1999) *England's North West : A Strategy Towards 2020* (Warrington, NWDA).

North West Joint Planning Team (1973) *Strategic Plan for the North West* (Manchester, North West Joint Planning Team).

North West Regional Assembly (1999a) *Regional Planning Guidance: Listening to the North West: Consultation Issues Facing the Region* (Wigan, NWRA).

North West Regional Assembly (1999b) *Regional Planning Guidance Review: Choices for the North West: Consultation on Strategic Options for the Region* (Wigan, NWRA).

North West Regional Association/North West Business Leadership Team (1993) *Regional Economic Strategy for North West England* (Warrington, NWRA/MWBLT).

O'Riordan, T. (ed.) (2000) *Environmental Science for Environmental Management,* 2nd edition (Harlow, Pearson Education Ltd).

Roberts, P. (1997) Sustainability and spatial competence: an examination of the evolution, ephemeral nature, and possible future development of regional planning in Britain, in P. W. J. Batey (ed.) *Regional Governance and Economic Development* (London, Pion).

Sale, K. (1985) *Dwellers on the Land: The Bioregional Vision* (San Francisco, Sierra Book Clubs).

Satterthwaite, D. (ed.) (1999) *The Earthscan Reader in Sustainable Cities* (London, Earthscan).

Selman, P. (1999) Landscape Ecological planning for the wider countryside, paper prepared for ECOPLAN meeting, Cheltenham, 29 June (unpublished).

Sustainability North West and Countryside Commission (1998) *Greening the North West: A Regional Landscape Strategy* (Manchester, SNW).

Wood, R., Handley, J., Kidd, S. and Douglas, I. (1996) *Greening the North West: a regional landscape strategy: regional landscape assessment*, Occasional Paper No. 53, Dept. of Planning and Landscape (Manchester, University of Manchester).

Zonneveld, I. (1990) Scope and contents of landscape ecology as an emerging science, in I. Zonneveld and R. Forman (eds) *Changing Landscapes: An Ecological Perspective* (New York, Springer).

8

MANAGING WHOLE LANDSCAPES IN THE POST-PRODUCTIVE RURAL ENVIRONMENT

Robert MacFarlane

SUMMARY

Whole landscape planning is increasingly emerging as a significant idea in the literature on sustainable rural environments. Aesthetic, ecological and amenity perspectives on landscapes often place an emphasis on values and characteristics such as cohesiveness, connectivity and integration between land uses. In reality, however, a fragmented pattern of landholding may exist, across which different landowners and occupiers may pursue very different and often conflicting land management strategies. This often results in discontinuous and degraded ecological and amenity networks and highly discordant features in the landscape. This chapter critically evaluates how recent changes in the policy environment for agriculture and forestry, and emergent initiatives for more integrated landscape management, may contribute to a climate within which whole landscape management may be implemented across increasingly large tracts of land. Such an outcome is by no means a foregone conclusion, and the significance of initiatives that attempt to vision such future landscapes is an important complement to the contributions of the scientific and design disciplines to the whole debate over the feasibility, look, function and accessibility of sustainable rural landscapes.

INTRODUCTION

Agriculture and forestry dominate the rural landscape. The way in which that dominance has come about, and responded in balance to policy signals that have emerged, and in some cases receded, over the course of the past 100 years is the starting point of this chapter. The integrating theme that runs through the chapter is the scope for developing management frameworks which integrate these dominant land uses across land management boundaries, to better meet environmental objectives that are often articulated at a whole landscape, or a regional scale. The debate over the causes and long-term impacts of an aggressively productivist policy framework is by no means concluded. However, the impacts of technically advanced, highly capitalized and often loosely regulated agricultural and forestry sectors on rural landscapes have been widely documented (e.g. Westmacott, 1997). The policy frameworks which promoted output at the expense of biodiversity, local and national cultural heritage and the integrity of regional landscapes have been subject to an extensive critique.

This chapter traces the rise of the productivist era in forestry (in the UK in the immediate aftermath of the First World War) and later in agriculture (in response to the broadly similar imperatives of the Second World War) which initially assumed no conflict with landscape management for non-productive, or secondary objectives. However, these activities proved complex, contentious and unwieldy to deflect onto a more socially acceptable, economically accountable and environmentally sustainable trajectory. In a manner akin to changing the direction of a supertanker, the changes have taken a long time to achieve and, to stretch the analogy, the timescale of further shifts in the European policy agenda of agriculture is complicated by the internal tensions of 'the steering committee' of the European Union. However, over the past three decades, attractive and healthy landscapes have begun to emerge as a product of rural land use and environmental management in their own right, no longer assumed to follow as a by-product or desirable spin-off from productively farmed or forested rural areas. This emergence has been paralleled by policies which have developed to increasing maturity and sophistication, a set of instruments to re-position farmers and other productively oriented land managers as environmental managers in their own right.

There is an important distinction to be made when talking about whole landscape management between two different, but equally legitimate uses of the term. Landscape has been extensively used as a level of spatial organization; 'a crucial organisational level and spatial scale at which the effects of global change will be apparent and at which appropriate responses will need to be implemented' (Hobbs, 1997, p. 2). Further to this it is important as a spatial level at which synergies between local initiatives may be realized, both in an aesthetic and an ecological sense. Landscape is also used in a design and planning context, with a primary concern for the spatial organization of elements and units across a sub-regional area, and with a focus on the aesthetic implications of alternative patterns. Clearly the two uses overlap, and it is a primary objective of this chapter to explore the scope for the design and integration of land use patterns across whole landscapes to meet aesthetic, amenity and ecological objectives.

Analyses of the environmental objectives associated with the Post-Productivist Transition (PPT) have tended to focus on how established actors within land-based product markets are responding to new policy signals and the emerging quasi-markets

for goods such as multi-purpose community woodlands and traditional features in the farmed landscape. Broadly speaking, this body of work may be characterized as research into participation; what makes landowners and land managers get, or not get, involved with such schemes, and what may be required to entice them 'on board'. These policy schemes and the associated research effort constitute a key input into the longer-term attainment of environmental objectives that are articulated at the landscape scale. Implicitly many such references to landscape and whole landscapes are already there in schemes such as the English National Forest, but, as Selman (1993) has noted, the scale of the problems and the scale of the proposed solutions in rural environmental change rarely coincide. This chapter traces the way in which such a spatial mismatch has arisen, evaluates the shortcomings of present policy initiatives that purport to revitalize or re-construct whole landscapes (UK Agri-Environmental Policy and community forests, respectively) and presents a framework within which co-ordinated action by individual landowners could more effectively work towards sustainable rural landscapes. The chapter focuses primarily on the UK in its review of relevant policy initiatives, but the discussion of frameworks for whole landscape management adopts a wider range of examples, drawing on initiatives from North America and elsewhere in Western Europe.

GENERAL PRINCIPLES OF WHOLE LANDSCAPE MANAGEMENT IN REGIONS OF FOOD AND FIBRE PRODUCTION

The notion of whole landscape management has been driven by a number of factors. From an aesthetic perspective, the emergence and development of landscape assessment and evaluation methodologies have placed a variable but increasing emphasis on measures of coherence and compatibility between elements in the landscape. Such a holistic perspective has been at ease with a view of the landscape as a product, and reflection, of the varied, layered and interrelating components (Mills,

1997; Muir, 1999). These components may be historically or geomorphologically inherited, such as landform, soils, land use, archaeology and human settlement, or the more subjective, personal and contestable values of cultural associations, social valuation and aesthetics, which are themselves subject to a range of temporal and ephemeral conditions (Brassley, 1998). The growth of interest in landscape by ecologists is much more recent. One of the most significant shifts of recent years in thinking about nature conservation has been the growth of interest in the landscape, not just as an ecological matrix or aesthetic entity, but critically as a scale of analysis. In turn this has been associated with the growth of interest in landscape ecology, perceived by some as a discipline, and by others as an inter-disciplinary research framework. Vos and Opdam (1993) argue that landscape ecology 'emerged as a fusion of the spatial approach of geographers and the functional approach of ecologists' (ibid., p.xiii). Landscape, in this sense, is thus defined as a scale factor. However, other authors have argued that landscape ecology, with its strong concern for planning, must show an explicit concern for the aesthetics of landscape and issues of cultural valuation (Burel and Baudry, 1995; Nassauer, 1995; Selman, 1993; Naveh, 1995), in addition to physical structure and ecological function (Noss *et al.*, 1998). A number of authors have attempted to offer a definition that is sufficiently inclusive of the different elements (for two useful reviews of general principles see Forman, 1995b or Selman, 1993). Selman (1996) proposes a definition with two components, starting with the issue of scale:

> The emphasis on diverse and extensive tracts of land, and the ways they change over time, should be a diagnostic hallmark of landscape ecological studies. *Equally, landscape ecology explicitly recognises human intervention, including land use planning, treating it as a driving variable rather than an inconvenient complication.*
>
> (ibid., p.29; my emphasis)

Landscape ecology proposes both a scale of analysis and a set of general principles to integrate the management of competing demands on land resources, and uses of the land (notably designated conservation sites and the wider, productively farmed and forested countryside) which can no longer continue in isolation from each other if sustainable rural development is to be achieved (Adams, 1996a). Coupled with the analytical concerns of the discipline, primarily those of connectivity and coherence, issues of design feature strongly in landscape ecology, either starting from an ecological perspective (what might a landscape that is optimized for species X look like?), or from an aesthetic perspective (how might productive, wildlife conservation and amenity interests be accommodated in landscapes that surveys show to be popular or desirable?). What landscape ecology has certainly provided is an emergent discipline which at present makes no real claim to maturity, and is characterized by an openness to inter-disciplinarity, notably a focus on the social dynamics and cultural significance of landscapes (Nassauer, 1997a).

There are a number of conceptual and analytical frameworks that have been developed by researchers into rural sustainability and landscapes in particular. Typically these comprise a breakdown of the pre-requisites for sustainability (Rannikko, 1999) or a target-like pair of axes, along which various present landscapes and potential trajectories may be mapped (O'Riordan *et al.*, 1993). One such framework (van Mansvelt and van der Lubbe, 1999) is drawn from the final report of an EU programme, 'The landscape and nature production capacity of organic/sustainable types of agriculture' (Figure 8.1). It is used in that document to illustrate the conceptual framework for the analysis of landscape management approaches and van Mansvelt and van der Lubbe promote approaches to landscape management that are both more holistic and increasingly progressive. The debate over conservative and progressive conservation philosophies has been well rehearsed, and Bill Adams in particular has forcefully argued the case for a more forward-looking approach to the management of particular sites and regions that is less referenced to scientifically and historically-rooted ideas of appropriateness (Adams, 1996a, 1996b, 1997). Holistic, or more holistic, or even less reductionist approaches to landscape management and nature conservation have thus attracted a lot of attention in recent years. The whole notion of sustainable landscapes is highly contestable, and there are few general principles that will be useful in guiding the transition towards sustainability in any level of detail for specific places and regions, but one over-arching vision might be the development of landscapes that are ecologically viable (with respect to socially defined conservation objectives), visually appealing, culturally meaningful and physically accessible. In specific localities different conditions and demands will of course apply, and very different landscapes may emerge over time. O'Riordan *et al.* (1993) use a simple two-dimensional axis to present the relative dimensions of seven future landscapes (Figure 8.2). Where van Mansvelt and van der Lubbe (1999) present differing perspectives on rural

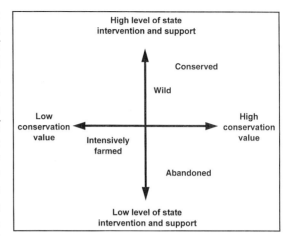

Figure 8.2 Future landscape targets, illustrating the level of state investment and nature conservation returns. No attempt is made to rank landscape quality, in view of the highly subjective nature of such judgements.

Source: Based on O'Riordan *et al.* (1993)

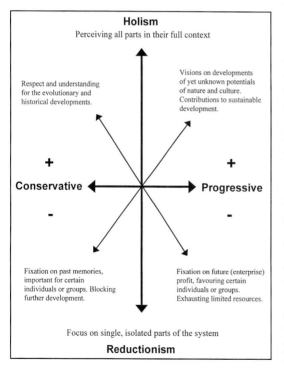

Figure 8.1 Polarization within society (horizontal) and the relation to a narrow or broad perspective on landscape management.

Source: van Mansvelt and van der Lubbe (1999)

resource and landscape management, O'Riordan *et al.* (1993) present the range of possible outcomes as a function of these perspectives and local pressures on the land resource.

In their EU report van Mansvelt and van der Lubbe (1999) define *ecological* coherence as having three components:

1 vertical coherence: on site;
2 horizontal coherence: in the landscape;
3 cyclical coherence: in time.

The first of these, concerned primarily with the dynamics of indicator, umbrella and flagship species and site specific habitats and ecosystems (Simberloff, 1998) is essentially the preserve of 'conventional' conservation ecology. This is coupled with a concern for the effective management and enhancement and perpetuation of sites or landscape elements. The notion of site-in-context (2) as an approach to conservation planning and management has been driven by the emergence of landscape ecology and it is described here by the term horizontal coherence in the landscape. Planning for horizontal coherence is essentially the pursuit of synergies in the landscape, whereby species movement between patches may be accommodated by corridors, feeding ranges may be extended by attention to spatial patterns of habitat patches and potentially conflicting land uses are separated or buffered. Promoting cyclical coherence (3) requires planning to accommodate natural processes and rates of change rather than tightly defined periods of establishment, management and cropping may form part of landscapes that achieve a wider range of the sustainability criteria than at present (Cobb, Dolman and O'Riordan, 1999).

The notion of coherence across space and time may be usefully applied to an analysis of the wider dimensions of landscape that may be significant in the pursuit of sustainability, but present frameworks of landownership and rural land use policy militate against the achievement of such spatially and temporally cohesive ideals. A focus on cohesiveness should not, however, be taken to deny the significance of boundaries, whether 'natural' or 'human'. Boundaries are important in defining patches, mosaics and landscapes; the edge of a plantation forest, a ridge line, river bank or flood plain limit are all geographically identifiable boundaries that have ecological and aesthetic functions in delineating patches, mosaics or whole landscapes (Fry and Sarlöv-Herlin, 1997; Gosz, 1991; Nassauer, 1997b). However, naturally occurring boundaries are generally less distinct than human boundaries in the landscape. For instance, the 'fence effect' that is observed at the interface of overgrazed and appropriately managed heather moorland is spatially immediate, but phenomena such as altitudinally and topographically determined treelines and other similar vegetation shifts are more gradual; human management of the land has imposed these spatial frameworks which underpin the dominant spatial processes of landscape change, summarized by Forman (1995a) as being perforation, dissection, fragmentation, shrinkage and attrition (Table 8.1).

The tensions between nature conservation and landscape management, between ecology and aesthetics and between scientific and lay discourses of 'nature' are widely documented (Macnaghten and Urry, 1998), and I repeat the point that there are no

Table 8.1 Spatial processes of land transformation, leading to a reconfiguration of the landscape-ecological matrix

Spatial processes of landscape change	Causes of land transformation
Perforation	Forest cutting
Dissection	Suburbanization
Fragmentation	Desertification
Shrinkage	Settlement
Attrition	Chronic pollution
	Catastrophic transformations (e.g. flooding)
	Reforestation
	Corridor construction
	Burning
	Agricultural intensification
	Drainage

Source: Based on Forman (1995a)

standard, or universally acceptable, design solutions; the significance of local circumstances in determining what is broadly desirable, as well as viable and attainable, must not be overlooked. The integration of culturally meaningful landscape objectives into this framework is not without its problems, given the divergence of landscape tastes between different groups in society and different groups in particular regions. Ribe's (1999) distinction between aesthetic and cognitive responses to landscape is one axis of division that has serious implications for the appropriate definition of sustainable, meaningful and productive landscapes. Reconciling aesthetics with ecology and reconciling contemporary cultural values with the need to adjust and move forward in landscape management are fraught with difficulties.

The notion of linkages or connectivity across landscapes has been enthusiastically adopted in certain quarters, for example as a significant component of Nature Conservation Strategies in the UK (English Nature, 1994), and it is implicit in the establishment of the Natura 2000 network of

European protected areas (de Jong and van Tatenhove, 1998). This is in spite of relatively limited empirical evidence for the level of potential conservation gains; Fleury and Brown observe that 'there is no precedent methodology for use by landscape architects that would allow translation of the theoretical information into a format useable in the design and development of high quality wildlife corridors' (1997, p. 163). However, at a very general level, a landscape where features of conservation value are effectively connected, and where species movement and behaviour across the landscape is not severely constrained by linear or areal features such as roads, polluted water bodies and intensively managed farm holdings, is preferable to a fragmented landscape which exhibits a lesser degree of connectivity or coherence, less visual and ecological structure, and a diminished aesthetic and conservation value (Andrews, 1993).

Theories of aesthetic landscape design are in less agreement on the value of connectivity; there are no standard design solutions applicable across the range of local and regional landscapes of the British Isles (Bell, 1993). The Forestry Commission (1992) suggests that 'landscape diversity is linked to ecological diversity, but the two are distinct and not necessarily equivalent' (ibid., p. 9). English Nature (1994) goes further, stating that 'it is important not to confuse nature conservation with landscape. While the two are often complementary, there are differences of emphasis and, occasionally, conflicts' (ibid., p. 30). Undoubtedly, there is widespread public affection for, and increasing state protection of, linear features such as hedgerows in farmed lowland and mid-level areas, and the copses and small woodlands which were characteristic of old agricultural estates. In this particular instance aesthetics, cultural valuation and the ecological structure and value of the productive (but not necessarily productivist) landscape overlap very closely and a fragmented landscape has less visual and ecological structure, and a diminished aesthetic and conservation value. However, over-general statements of this type are perhaps best avoided, as Deffontaines *et al.* (1995) illustrate in their analysis of the differing values accorded to landscapes in Lorraine and Normandy by agronomists, ecologists and those with a primary interest in the visual aspect of landscape. Although public landscape preferences have proved dynamic over time, and indeed malleable to a point (Bunce, 1994; Short, 1991), adjusting to the future will entail change, which could embrace the extensification of agricultural systems, the widespread emergence of agro-forestry, the afforestation of lowland landscapes or the creation, through design or abandonment, of wild areas. Many of these potential changes pose a direct challenge to what Nassauer has termed 'aesthetic conventions for the display of care', and care is most commonly associated with the productive use of land: 'both the scenic aesthetic and the aesthetic of care are culturally ingrained and conceptually well developed. They are also resistant to change' (1997b, pp. 67–68).

ENGINES OF CHANGE IN THE RURAL ENVIRONMENT: AGRICULTURE, FORESTRY AND THE PRODUCTIVIST TRADITION

The metaphor implicit in the term 'engine of change' goes a long way towards explaining its popularity in discussions concerning post-war agricultural policy in particular, and the emergence of the twentieth-century productivist era in general. The productivist era in agriculture and forestry is used to describe a period of re-orientation through which both sectors became increasingly capitalized, technologically intensive, integrated with input and output processing sectors and highly mechanized. Associated with this increase in (narrowly defined) efficiency, and sharply increased levels of productivity of food and fibre per unit area, came social changes in the practices of farming and forestry; dwindling labour forces and increases in the size of units of production have been characteristic of the productivist era.

Driving these three primary agents of change in rural Britain is a whole range of forces, a number of which appear in Figure 8.3. All of these drivers of change are further differentiated along sectoral and spatial lines (Hidding, 1993). An example of a policy instrument might be payments under the European

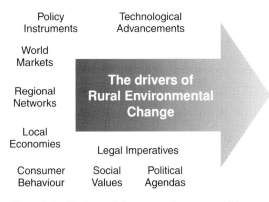

Policy Instruments

Technological Advancements

World Markets

Regional Networks

The drivers of Rural Environmental Change

Local Economies

Legal Imperatives

Consumer Behaviour

Social Values

Political Agendas

Figure 8.3 Engines of change can have many drivers.

Union (EU) Common Agricultural Policy (CAP). A legal imperative could be the cross-compliance of production related payments with certain minimum environmental standards. Technical advancements clearly embrace the whole issue of genetic modification of food and fibre crops. For a specific example of such forces, Poudevigne *et al.* (1997) trace the action and interaction of rural landscape dynamics in an area of Normandy and some of the main impacts of the primary drivers of change have been summarized by Adams (1986) (Figure 8.4).

The primary engines of change in the rural environment are spatially differentiated in terms of their nature and impact, and then yet further differentiated at the level of individual land management units (Potter *et al.*, 1996). Of particular relevance to the rural UK, given the fact that approximately 70 per cent of the land area is farmed in one way or another, is the current backdrop of CAP reform. This policy debate arouses the concerns of the farming lobby that significant withdrawal of support will lead to the widespread collapse of family farms, and the fears of some conservationists that a free market would lead to the spatial-environmental differentiation of 'food factories and parks' (Holden, 1999). That such a simple divide would emerge is highly debatable and the nature of land use response to external change, including market forces and agri-environment schemes, is highly complex (Carr and Tait, 1991; MacFarlane, 1996; McHenry, 1996; Skerratt and Dent, 1996). However, the conservation lobby is itself split on the desirability of such a divide, as evidenced in recent Council for National Parks proposals for the re-creation of extensive wild areas in the UK uplands which would largely depend on the collapse of some UK upland farming systems (CNP, 1998).

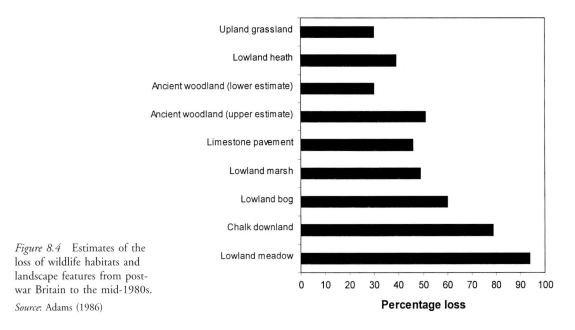

Figure 8.4 Estimates of the loss of wildlife habitats and landscape features from post-war Britain to the mid-1980s.

Source: Adams (1986)

Table 8.2 Some key episodes from Europe and the USA to illustrate the development of productivist agriculture and the partial change of direction associated with the Post-Productivist Transition

Key dates and episodes	Events
1939–1945	The Second World War made the goal of national self sufficiency in agricultural produce a priority for the British and other European countries' governments during the conflict, and in the post-war years.
1947	The UK Agriculture Act formalized the system of guaranteed markets and assured prices for most agricultural commodities, a system which went largely unchanged with the accession of the UK to the European Economic Community in 1973.
Late 1970s	Conflicting estimates of the future agricultural land budget were made by CAS (1976) and Whitby and Thomson (1979). Whitby and Thomson provided the first rigorous analysis to suggest that food surpluses would be much more likely than shortages. More recent forecasts have been made by North (1990).
1970s to 1980s	Transition to surplus production in most food commodities in Europe, and inexorable rise in the public costs of supporting agriculture over much of the developed world.
1981	UK Wildlife and Countryside Act, which entrenched the voluntary principle in agriculture–environment relations, whereby conservation management of farmland could only be forced in extreme circumstances and had to be financially compensated for in all cases.
Early to mid-1980s	Rapid mounting of public concern in Europe over food surpluses in the face of persistent famine elsewhere in the world, and the associated environmental costs of intensive agriculture in the developed world, manifested in the UK by declines in wildlife and in the US by soil erosion.
1984	US Farm Bill, launching the Conservation Reserve Programme (CRP), with a focus on soil erosion control and rooted in non-coercive voluntary participation, the principle of which has characterized soil erosion control in the US since the Dust Bowl of the 1930s. For high-erosion hazard land a strong conservation cross-compliance element was built in to the CRP.
Early to mid-1990s	Evolution of the global and local sustainability agenda with the consequent effect of nudging more focused 'green' issues to the margins of political concern.
1992	MacSharry reforms of the CAP initiated the process of de-coupling production-related payments from direct income support to farmers, and launched a raft of European Agri-Environment Schemes.
Mid- to late 1990s	Significant erosion of the respectable position of farmers with the politically complex and publicly alarming issues of BSE and GM crops, which were themselves preceded by earlier health scares such as Salmonella contamination of battery chickens in the UK.

It is not the purpose of this chapter to review the twentieth-century history of agriculture and forestry in detail, and there are many sources where such information is presented (for instance Gilg, 1996; Winter, 1996). Key periods and episodes in the productivist era and the uneven and rather faltering transition of agriculture and forestry into the post-productivist era are presented in Tables 8.2 and 8.3.

THE POST-PRODUCTIVIST TRANSITION: FROM CONCEPT, TO POLICY, TO LANDSCAPE OUTCOMES

Agriculture

During the 1970s and 1980s the political agenda within which European and national ministries and departments operated was broadened by a realization of the changing position and role of agriculture and

Table 8.3 Staging posts in the uneven transition from low-productivity yet highly productivist forestry, to more evenly distributed, environmentally positive and multiple-purpose forests in the UK

Key dates and episodes	Events
Mid to late nineteenth century	In the decades prior to the First World War there had been no policy decision to promote forest development, assuming that Britain should rely heavily on imports with a consequent concentration on livestock in the uplands. The steadily falling costs of transport and the availability of abundant supplies in North America and Scandinavia, reinforced the policy of *laissez-faire*.
Late nineteenth century	Development of a strong knowledge base and training infrastructure in Britain that was strongly informed by German advances in forestry establishment and management science, and was, in part, a reflection of the significance of forestry in the colonial states of the British Empire, most notably India.
1914–1918	The First World War exposed the errors of this previous policy, or the lack of one. The strategic role of timber had never really been recognized, critically in the mining sector where the wartime increase in energy demands had led to a chronic shortage of basic supplies such as pit props.
1919	Establishment of the Forestry Commission FC, with a dual responsibility for advice and forest establishment. At the time of its establishment the FC had three primary objectives, in order of importance: (i) to replace stock felled prematurely in WW1, (ii) to increase strategic reserve, and (iii) to substitute greater proportion of imports.
Inter-war and post Second World War	Due to financial constraints in public funding, and a general presumption against planting on agricultural land, state planting in this period was largely confined to the uplands of Scotland and Wales.
1939–1945	when the Second World War (1939–1945) started the strategic timber position was actually worse than in 1914. Limited public funding and the general presumption against the 'loss' of agricultural land had combined to limit the effectiveness of the young Forestry Commission.
1945	From the end of the Second World War, there was a substantial reorientation balance of public and private investment in forestry with a significant shift away from direct to contractual control with an emphasis on public grants to induce private sector planting.
1947	The 1947 Agriculture Act formalized the wartime structures of guaranteed prices to farmers in most commodity sectors, which further increased the relative prosperity of agriculture and yet further marginalized forestry, with serious implications for its potential viability.
1957	Another staging post on the path away from single-objective forest promotion was the rather belated realization, accepted in the findings of the Zuckerman Committee of 1957, that the strategic value of timber was an irrelevance in the nuclear era.
Late 1980s to 1990s	Development of the multiple-purpose Community Forest concept, imported from North West Europe into England and Wales, associated with a significant push to increase lowland forestry, focused principally on derelict sites and surplus agricultural land.
1999	The stated objectives of the Forestry Commission are founded in multi-purpose utilization of the forest resource. The objectives embrace a continued commitment to the government's objective of significantly increasing and re-positioning forest areas, to increase the economic efficiency of the sector, and to improve the biodiversity, landscape and cultural heritage of forests and woodlands.

farmers, in relation to rural environment, society and economy. This development has been characterized as a shift from an explicitly agricultural to a more rural policy (Gilg, 1996). It recognized both the social and environmental responsibilities and economic pressures borne by farmers throughout Europe. Many of the monolithic structures of price and farm income support which characterized so much of post-war European agricultural and rural policy are being dismantled and policy signals have become much more complex over recent years. Maximization of output from most developed nations' productive resources is no longer required, and the diversity of rural policy objectives now being promoted by government agriculture departments has increased markedly. Markets are developing to satisfy an increasing level of public demand for countryside goods and services (Curry, 1994) and new policy schemes such as the UK Countryside Stewardship Scheme and Environmentally Sensitive Areas (ESAs) are being targeted at specific non-productivist goals. Wider policy structures are also beginning to integrate agri-environmental objectives (which are linked to production control), for instance extensification and long-term land diversion (Potter *et al.*, 1991; Whitby and Lowe, 1994). This process of institutional re-positioning around new political and social agendas has been a key component of the Post-Productivist Transition (PPT). However, as Potter has observed, individual land managers condition actual environmental outcomes on the ground, with a clear implication for the process of designing, and achieving, desired landscape outcomes: 'Explanations . . . are complicated by the fact that policy, institutional and technological factors affect farmers first and pieces of countryside only second' (1986, p. 193).

A key problem for emergent policy frameworks is how to influence the decisions of hundreds of thousands of individual land managers (and clearly fewer at a sub-regional scale) to achieve the desired outcomes. Ilbery and Bowler (1998) make the point that the PPT (if it is conceptualized as a phased transition away from highly productivist land use towards a more integrated, extensive and accessible multi-purpose area of countryside) should not be seen as either universal in coverage, or even in the rate of transition:

> the productivist farm systems have not been replaced by post-productivist systems: the two diverging pathways co-exist. Thus, intensive, high input-high output farming, with an emphasis on food quantity, is still being encouraged. But this is now being complemented by low input-low output farming, with an emphasis on sustainable farming systems and food quality. These divergent pathways are likely to become more spatially

differentiated, at regional and national scales . . . indeed, the uneven development of the productivist regime seems likely to be deepened during the PPT.

(1998, p. 57)

It has been widely demonstrated (CAS, 1986; Harvey and Thomson, 1985; O'Callaghan, 1996) that policy and market change such as is affecting agriculture at the present time will have regionally differentiated impacts. However, the findings of much of the research into the conservation behaviour of farmers adds a more detailed spatial dimension to the policy outcome pattern. Farmers of the different classes identified by Shucksmith (1993), in respect of post-productivist policy stimuli, and of Morris and Potter (1995), in respect of agri-environment schemes, are not spatially segregated into self-selecting groups. They are distributed across the UK countryside with a consequent complicating effect for new policy initiatives that are fundamentally associated with the PPT. Perhaps the most significant suite of such initiatives relating to the farmed landscape is the development and takeoff of Agri-Environmental Policy from the late 1980s.

The development of agri-environmental policy

Agri-Environmental Policies (AEP) were introduced at a European Union (EU) level as part of the 1992 reforms of the CAP under the EC Regulation 2078/92, which provides CAP funds to encourage environmentally sensitive agricultural practices (MAFF, 1999), and there is a large body of research into the merits and limitations of this emergent policy framework (Evans and Morris, 1997; Hanley *et al.*, 1999; Whitby and Lowe, 1994; Wilson, 1997). The development of AEP schemes, both at a national level and as part of the incrementally reforming CAP, has been greeted with enthusiasm by a wide range of parties, especially since the 1992 reform of the CAP which signalled an annual UK AEP budget of £33 million in 1992/3, rising to £86 million in 1996/7, although expenditure on regulation 2078 was highly variable across the EU (Figure 8.5). For instance, the conservation lobby has been largely won over by the previously unthinkable sums of money now being channelled into agri-environmental management and agricultural impact amelioration. Farmers were supportive on the basis of the same sums which could be available to them in the context of falling farm incomes and future uncertainty in global commodity markets. Policy-makers were attracted by the ability of the schemes to simultaneously control overproduction, thereby saving money, and also to signal their green credentials (Whitby and Lowe, 1994), even though AEP spending accounts for only approximately 2.5 per cent of total CAP spending in the UK, and 3 per cent for the EU as a whole. Since the early beginnings of AEP, the range of schemes and measures available has grown dramatically, to encompass nitrate water pollutant control, support for organic conversion, public access schemes, woodland promotion and management schemes for specific habitats. This extension and diversification have been unequivocally welcomed in many quarters. In spite of these undoubted advances, it has been widely commented on that European AEP is still only a component, and a small component, of the CAP, the fundamental structure of which is inherently insensitive to the social, economic and environmental diversity across the ever-increasing number of members' states. What the Agenda 2000 reforms seem to have achieved is really an extension of the 1992 MacSharry reforms, rather than a more significant change of pace or direction, which looked a more distinct possibility at an earlier stage of the reform negotiations (Lowe

et al., 1996). Under Agenda 2000 the structural and agri-environment funds have been merged to form the Rural Development Regulation (RDR) funds. The principle of increased subsidiarity in the allocation of these funds is accepted, yet the overall allocation to the new RDR is only slightly increased, and that allocation has been capped for the duration of the Agenda 2000 regime, until 2006.

Although AEP has attracted most of the attention in this area, especially in the wake of the financial changes after 1992, two UK precursors should be noted. The Farming and Wildlife Advisory Group (FWAG) was established in 1969 through a joint initiative by landowning and farming groups, Ministry for Agriculture, Fisheries and Food (MAFF) and conservation groups such as the Royal Society for the Protection of Birds (RSPB), with a view to establishing methods of communication and conflict resolution between farmers and conservationists. FWAG soon developed a network of County advisors, who usually came from a farming background, thereby leapfrogging one of the major cultural gaps between the two groups. The organization is judged to have had a very positive effect in disseminating a wider acceptance of the place of conservation practices on farmland. The actual value of some of that advice has been criticized by Winter et al. (1996), but the significance of the cultural shift that has been promoted by this relatively small organization should not be underestimated. From a policy perspective, 1969 also saw the launch of two Upland Management Experiments (or UMEX), as a joint initiative

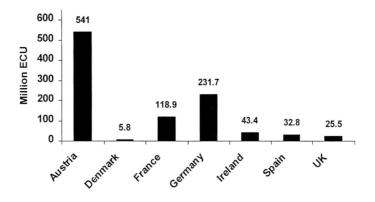

Figure 8.5 Expenditure on agri-environment schemes in selected EU Member States, 1996.

Source: Potter (1998, p. 119)

between the newly formed Countryside Commission and MAFF. The stimulus for the experiment was not the complex and systemic impact of modern agriculture on the farmed landscape, which was only just beginning to emerge as an issue of widespread concern (Shoard, 1980), but the more specific problems experienced in National Parks, especially the Lake District and Snowdonia where the UMEX pilots were established, over the impacts of recreation on the landscape and farm infrastructure. The pilot scheme established a system of small grants for farmers which were based on a management plan to provide enhanced, and more robust, facilities for visitors and to carry out landscape enhancement works. The UMEX was only ever an experiment, and remained highly localized in its impact, but it was extremely significant as the first step in establishing a market for landscape goods and services and also in beginning to re-cast farmers as countryside managers, an initiative that was complemented by the growth in FWAG advisors over time.

The development of the first AEP schemes during the 1980s and the diversification and acceleration of related measures following the 1992 CAP reform have been an important development for a number of reasons. From a landscape ecological perspective, where issues of aesthetics are viewed in conjunction with ecological concerns, the lack of a clear distinction between landscape and habitat/wildlife management in many AEP schemes' aims and prescriptions is an important departure from previous structures for conservation policy and implementation. The post-war separation of landscape and nature conservation in the UK, enshrined in the establishment of the Nature Conservancy in 1949, and the Countryside Commission in 1968, with parallel arrangements in Scotland and Wales, has been widely commented upon. The re-structuring of the national conservation agencies in the early 1990s, which gave rise to the notionally integrated agencies of Countryside Council for Wales (CCW) and Scottish Natural Heritage (SNH), has been critically evaluated elsewhere (Sheail, 1998). Against this backdrop, it has been cause for satisfaction that AEP schemes have steered a path (at least in the definition of their aims and objectives) which embraced both

landscape, ecological and, where appropriate, recreational needs and opportunities (Whitby and Lowe, 1994).

One key concern which has not been addressed, however, is the universally voluntary nature of the UK AEP schemes; it may be financially attractive for some farmers to join the schemes, and as such the carrots have been very effective in places, although notably less so elsewhere. There are instances where MAFF has introduced sticks to enforce certain environmental conditions (the linking of producer payments to minimum environmental performance standards, known as cross-compliance, with respect to issues such as overgrazing and watercourse pollution). However, AEP schemes are voluntary, and rely on attracting farmers through a mix of strategies. These include attractive payments, contract periods which are not perceived as being either overly long and restrictive, or indeed too short in this period of policy and market uncertainty, and tiered levels of participation to attract those with differing levels of commitment to environmental works.

In a number of respects AEP attempts to travel a difficult path. The problems of attracting sufficient land enrolment to maintain their credibility and also effect positive environmental change in areas where ecological and landscape degradation has become the norm, and yet retain budgetary control of limited finances, require a close eye on management agreements' funding rates. From the conservation perspective it is easy to argue the principle that bigger is better in terms of the conservation estate and parcels of conservation management land in the UK countryside. However, in common with the basic economic concepts of economies of scale and marginal utility, there also comes a point where enough must be enough; as Wilson (1996) has argued with reference to the conservation estate of today, there is only so much money to go around, and the Agenda 2000 reforms have clearly signalled that the AEP budget will not be expanding significantly before 2006. The RSPB (1999) has criticized the Welsh Office for only funding Tir Goval to the extent of £3 million in its first year, which they calculate to mean that only 2 per cent of Welsh farms will be able to enter in 1999–2000. Even in the longer term, where a significant re-balancing of land prices might follow further reaching policy reform, which could make the conservation organizations' Euros go further in terms of land purchases and management agreements, competition from existing and new sources will serve to restrict where and how much land can be brought into the conservation estate. Further to these complexities and obstacles, many AEP schemes are attempting to encourage and support farmers onto a trajectory which treads the middle ground between the two most likely responses to the withdrawal of state support and market changes which are depressing farm incomes, that is intensification or land withdrawal and abandonment. In this respect many AEP schemes, especially in the uplands where economic survival is less assured, are something of a delicate balancing act between intensification and farming withdrawal.

Forestry

The UK is very poorly wooded relative to other regions, and in Western Europe only Ireland has a lower proportion of land under trees at 5 per cent (Table 8.4). Rackham (1980) reports that the decline of woodland cover dates back further than is widely believed, suggesting that Norman Britain was only 15 per cent wooded as a result of prehistoric and early historic clearance. The historical processes which led to the reduction, fragmentation and degradation of woodlands and forests in Britain up to the twentieth century has been extensively reviewed by a range of authors (for instance Hoskins, 1955; Reed, 1997) and will not be detailed here but the theo-

retical debate over the so-called 'forest transition' is considered.

Although the strategic case for an ongoing expansion of forestry in the UK had been discredited by the 1960s and the economic rationality of widespread and intensive planting in the uplands was being subjected to an increasing critique, there are a number of factors which have been ushering in a new way of looking at trees in the landscape, in social, economic, ecological and aesthetic terms, including:

- the changing national land budget, notably the surplus of agricultural land, a situation which seemed unlikely to backslide given the rate of technological advancements;
- the emergence of post-industrial landscapes in regions undergoing severe economic decline and the collapse or withdrawal of heavy manufacturing industry (Chapter 7), another situation which seemed unlikely to reverse and rehabilitate wide areas of severely degraded and often heavily polluted urban fringe;
- the rapid growth of environmental consciousness in UK society during the 1980s, which contributed to a sharply increased awareness of the multifaceted local and global value of trees;
- the longer-term, but accelerating, rate of participation in all forms of outdoor leisure and recreation, and the accompanying development of policy measures to provide for and accommodate this rising pressure, most commonly felt in urban fringe and near-urban areas;
- the realization that the formal planning process has often failed to deliver accessible, attractive and diverse environments, notably in urban fringe areas;
- the changing policy context for forestry, which has placed a significant emphasis on multipurpose forestry and social and environmental gains through the expansion of forestry in the landscape.

Table 8.4 Percentages of forest cover in 1995

Country	%	Country	%
Austria	47	Sweden	64
France	27	Finland	66
Greece	51	USA	23
Denmark	12	Brazil	65
UK	10	Japan	67
All EU Countries	33	World	27

Source: Forestry Industry Council (1995)

In the introduction to a chapter on forestry in *Rural Politics*, Winter (1996) writes that he initially set out to title the section 'farming's poor relation', on the

Figure 8.6 The Institute for Terrestrial Ecology dominant land cover types: broadleaved and coniferous woodland cover (in white).

for much of the twentieth century as a residual land use. In fact, the chapter was titled 'farming's rich relation', in reflection of the high and relatively stable levels of direct state support for forest establishment. A range of new policy instruments and schemes have their roots in the 1980s, which was the period over which the UK Forestry Commission cemented its changing role as a responsive, environmentally oriented and publicly aware organization in the redefinition of its objectives as 'the sustainable management of our existing woods and forests, and a steady expansion of tree cover to increase the many, diverse benefits that forests provide' (Figure 8.6). The intricacies of forestry grants are only slightly less complex than those relating to agriculture and will not be reviewed in detail here, but the magnitude of state financial involvement in forestry is underscored by the successes of that policy when considered in purely quantitative terms. With the diversifying policy agenda of the 1980s, driven to a large extent by public disquiet over public money fuelling the primary engines of rural change, there was no significant change in the push for more forests, but the qualitative dimensions of what, where and how became of paramount significance.

The period of transition, from nearly universal naturally occurring tree cover, to what is in the case of the UK a small proportion of land, has been theorized by a number of authors, notably Mather (1992) and Grainger (1995). These authors have attempted to develop an explanatory framework that is sufficiently flexible to account for the diverse environments, histories, economies and cultures of the world's countries, yet is sufficiently robust to predict likely trends of change over time. The term 'national land use transition' is used to define the period over which there is a marked and relatively rapid period of deforestation, during which trees are displaced by other land uses, notably settlement and agriculture, and where the harvesting of trees is increasingly industrialized to support growing demands for timber products. Although the actual rates of loss, measured per year or per decade, have been highly variable historically, much of the developed world has seen a deceleration in that rate of loss and in some cases a marked increase in the forest area. The

basis that new forests are dominantly on the poorest land, implicated in landscape decline rather than all of the cultural associations of landscape quality that farming has historically enjoyed, and has been seen

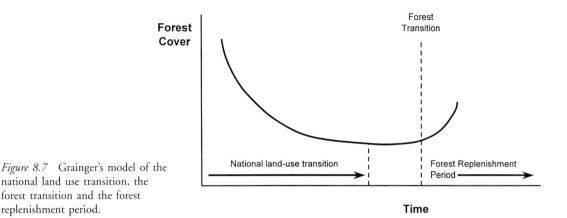

Figure 8.7 Grainger's model of the national land use transition, the forest transition and the forest replenishment period.

UK is a clear example of this turnaround from decline to expansion, with a doubling of the tree cover from 1900 to 1990. This period has been termed the forest transition by Mather (1992), which is followed, in the model at least, by a sustained period of forest replenishment. The reasons for this reversal have been summarized by Grainger (1995) (Figure 8.7) as including economic pressures to provide for future demands, changes in the popular perception and usage of forests and wider changes in the land budget, notably the declining demand for farmland with consequent implications for the location and economics of productive forestry. In landscape terms the quantitative rate of this upturn in land afforestation is important, but of equal significance is the type and changing location of that diversion of land, mostly from agriculture into forestry (Mather and Thomson, 1995).

Mather (1998) presents the notion of a shift in forestry perception and practice between a traditional and a forest ecosystem paradigm. As discussed by Tsouvalis-Gerber (1998), the traditional paradigm dominated most of the twentieth century, with the associated premise that broadleaved woodland was uneconomic, a premise that was itself founded in the projected cycles of establishment to harvest and the relatively poor locations where major plantations were located. A number of factors combined to 'bring forestry down the hill' onto reasonably productive agricultural land, and in much closer proximity to the centres of population. However, the

effectiveness of these intentions, relative to targets, has been largely disappointing and there are a number of reasons for that. The relative returns on hardwood and softwood forests are dramatically different. The growth rate of species such as Sitka spruce ranges between 10 and 20 m³/annum/hectare in comparison to 4–6 m³/annum/hectare for hardwood species such as oak or beech. One consequence of this is that coniferous trees may be harvested many decades before broadleaves, with very clear implications for profitability before grant aid and also the decision to plant in an uncertain policy climate (Green, 1996).

To address the problems of unequal returns, the UK Woodland Grant Scheme (WGS) and Farm Woodland Grant Scheme place premia on grants for broadleaved woodland and to encourage the transition of farmland to woodland. Further heightened payments are available in locally designated areas, which may be associated with community forest schemes, to increase the attractiveness of the carrots offered by the Forestry Commission or the individual community forest development agencies. Associated with new planting and management grants, there have been the changing imperatives and structures for land use change and general re-alignment to emerging patterns of the supply and demand of land. As Mather notes,

one of the most striking manifestations of a changing paradigm is the concept of the national and community forests. The potential for multi-purpose forestry in the lowlands lay at the heart of the idea and the National Forest was envisaged as an extensive area of mixed woodland interspersed with farmland. Mixed species timber would be produced, a recreational resource would be created and environmental enhancement would occur.

(1998, p. 121)

The development of the multi-purpose forest concept, and community forests

The creation of multi-purpose forests near to urban areas builds on experience from a number of European countries, notably Germany and the Netherlands. In the UK it has sprung from a variety of pressures and emergent issues, perhaps most notably the overcapacity in agriculture which has stimulated a focus on trees as the most obvious alternative to food products (Green, 1996, p. 271). Specific agendas have arisen in different parts of the UK, for example in the Scottish Highlands where current initiatives to re-establish native pine forest are closely related to broader cultural agendas of conservation and the appropriateness of land use in any given place (Toogood, 1995; Wightman, 1997). The most notable and spatially significant initiative is the National Forest and the community forests in England, dominantly located on relatively blighted, post-industrial landscapes in close proximity to major centres of population (Hodge, 1995).

The community forests or woodlands are not owned by local people in the UK; the model employed for the establishment and expansion of these woodlands places a heavy emphasis on the private sector, partnerships between private enterprise and community groups and/or local government, working within the framework of the 'voluntary principle'. This reliance, made with a commitment to reducing public sector outlay on the attainment of policy objectives, has led to a slow start to the National Forest and other community forests. The very ambition of the vision has not been met by the relatively opportunistic pattern of planting that has characterized the short-term growth of many of the

Table 8.5 Objectives of the National Forest and the mechanisms intended to realize them

Objectives of the National Forest	Mechanisms to achieve objectives
1 A functional and working forest (though under multiple ownership and management)	1 The planting and management should be done by choice, not compulsion
2 An environmentally sensitive area, blending the trees into the historical, ecological and cultural character of the area	2 The strategy should be achieved in a politically acceptable and cost-effective manner involving the private and voluntary sectors
3 Geographically diverse, with a mixture of land-uses, varying in intensity	3 Full use should be made of all existing measures to encourage planting and other forest-related activities. New measures should be introduced if there is a shortfall in these mechanisms
4 A sustainable forest, with appropriate and related development being welcomed	

Source: Bell (1993)

present community forests; there are many places in the UK where trees have simply been planted in the absence of significant alternatives, for instance in the scattered, but widespread land reclamation projects of the former mining areas of the English Midlands, South Wales and Central Scotland (Table 8.5). The design principles for community forests are rooted in the acceptance that while this may be an exercise in whole landscape planning at the conceptual level, it will be founded in the participation of individual land and forest owners and managers in reality. The design guidelines reveal this tension:

means must be found for describing a design strategy as [the forest] builds up so that key locations are identified and explored in a way that remains indicative and as flexible as possible. *There can be no imposed solutions.* The best community forests established in the closing years of this century will be those which combine a tough minimal framework with opportunism.

(Forestry Commission, 1991, p. 5, my emphasis)

Very clearly the National Forest concept, to be complemented by satellite community forests adjacent to many other UK cities, is rooted in the discourse of multi-purpose forestry and accurately reflects the wide remit of the Forestry Commission. However, the National Forest and community forest projects are not just Forestry Commission initiatives. They are anchored in the concept of partnership between government agencies, between different levels of government, between the public and private sector, and, ambitiously, between communities and all of these actors. The discourses of sustainability, landscape, nature, integration and participation have been widely analysed (Cloke *et al.*, 1996; Bell and Child, 1998) but it is something of an embarrassment that land use shifts towards the momentous re-design of whole landscapes envisaged and explicitly planned for in the individual forest development documents, have been both limited and patchy. In certain respects there are parallels with the AEP experience; farmers are a key group and the initiative aims to promote a shift in land management practices. There is a heavy reliance on carrots as distinct from sticks to drive the change, cultural values as reflected in land use decisions are a pivotal issue. The clearly defined limits to state involvement all echo the experience of AEP. However, there are fundamental differences, and most importantly the very nature of the land use transition is perceived by most farmers as extreme, and outwith their frame of reference. The cultural specificity of field afforestation is highly significant; Selby and Petäjistö (1995) report that most grant-aided afforestation in Finland has been carried out by farmers nearing retirement thereby capturing a 'pre-pension bonus', but the literature on inter-generational succession in the UK does not flag this as a significant form of land diversion (Potter and Lobley, 1992). Incentive schemes to encourage the afforestation of agricultural land have historically been of only limited success and, as Crabtree *et al.* comment, 'the long-term and illiquid nature of forestry investment . . . raises difficulties for short-term decision modelling, as does the importance of non-economic factors in the investment process' (1998, p. 307). It is an area of serious conceptual, methodological and practical problems which has hampered the whole national and community forest project.

It is presently inconceivable that the state could intervene to purchase large areas of land, or even *specific* areas of land that may be of local or regional significance in a landscape, ecological or recreational sense. The attainment of the quantitatively ambitious and qualitatively significant levels and patterns of forest establishment therefore seems highly problematic. Issues of economics must surely remain close to the heart of the problem and the effect of the medium- to long-term reform of the CAP on land prices in specific areas is hard to predict. It seems likely that the worth of WGS grants is set to increase relative to the potential return on agricultural production. The time-scale of forestry production systems, especially to farmers who may be watching for the emergence of reliable, longer term signals from key actors such as the EC and World Trade Organization, is a definite obstacle to this group. Although farmers predominate as current land managers in the designated National and community forest areas, large areas of land are post-industrial derelict sites, the particular problems of which are discussed in depth by Moffat and McNeill (1994).

There is an extensive literature on the aesthetic, amenity and ecological implications of various plantation and other forest establishment, management and felling strategies. In the UK even the largest plantation forests such as Kielder Forest in Northumberland, are limited in size when compared to the regional forest landscapes of North America and Scandinavia (Mather, 1990). Ribe (1999) reviews the different perspectives from which landscape judgements are made of such extensive forest areas. A broad division between aesthetic perceptions and more cognitive perceptions can be made, which has far-reaching implications for the design and management process in particular localities. Ribe defines a group of 'disinterested' observers who interact with forest landscapes in largely or purely aesthetic terms. This group might be comprised of

recreational visitors or passers through lacking in a strong or active proprietary or ideological interest in national forests. Or, public perceptions of management may be more cognitive, involving conceptual understandings or associations with what is seen, such as ecological impacts, the perceived value of forestry practices or other normative ideas.

(ibid., p. 102)

There are no universal solutions; as Antrop observes, landscape 'judgement is mainly based upon a particular view of utility or in relation of achieving a particular goal or situation. Consequently, changes are not always perceived by all in the same way and positive and negative evaluations may be conflicting for the same type of change' (1998, p. 155). Such work has been paralleled by research into the relations between farmers and their local landscapes (Deffontaines *et al.*, 1995; Thompson, 1995; Manning *et al.*, 1999). For the purposes of planning for publicly acceptable forest landscapes this poses quite a severe obstacle as cognitive and aesthetic judgements over landscape can be in conflict, for instance where aesthetic judgements of ecologically functional attributes are at odds with their actual or potential contribution to the attainment of species, habitat or wider biodiversity objectives (Nassauer, 1995).

Indicative forestry strategies: whole landscape planning by the back door?

Indicative Forestry Strategies (IFSs) were pioneered in Scotland following a Scottish Development Department circular to local planning authorities in 1990, which was followed by the Department of Environment and the Welsh Office in 1992. Selman has defined indicative planning in this particular context as 'the production of area-based, non-statutory plans which indicate the pattern of land use change which a democratically elected council would wish to see occur within its area' (1997, p. 58). The IFSs were developed using a sieve mapping process, commonly automated through the application of Geographical Information Systems (GIS) (Aspinall *et al.*, 1993), to identify areas as 'preferred', 'potential', 'sensitive' (large-scale planting generally

undesirable) and 'unsuitable' (very high land, urban areas, inland water, etc.). Input layers to these analyses generally encompass factors and constraints such as the land capability for agriculture and for forestry, nature and cultural conservation sites and designated areas, mineral deposits and important recreational areas. IFSs have not been universally pursued with the same enthusiasm or specific outlook across the whole of the UK, as reviewed in depth by Selman (1997). In Scotland, a legacy of high profile and highly damaging (both ecologically and in terms of the credibility of the state conservation agencies) plantation developments spurred the Scottish Office to promote IFSs, and a number of the (now restructured) Regional Councils had developed and implemented strategies by the early 1990s. Implementation of an indicative strategy is, of course, no guarantee in itself of realizing desired outcomes, but the strategies were widely used to structure the evaluation of WGS applications. In this respect, the position of forestry, alongside agriculture, outwith the formal Town and Country Planning System was embedded into a regional strategy for conflict minimization, although strong reservations have been expressed over the 'unsuitability of [the IFSs'] schematic zonal approach to the comparatively intimate landscapes of the lowlands' (Selman, 1997, p. 72).

Following the spirit, rather than the letter, of the IFS circulars, various levels of local authorities, together with bodies such as the National Park Authorities, have developed alternatives to the 'official' IFSs, including forestry and woodland action plans, local woodland projects, community forest plans, urban forestry strategies and highly localized frameworks and agreements to promote woodland management, development or regeneration. While all of these represent local frameworks for the articulation and achievement of landscape objectives, the plethora of such initiatives and designations must be questioned from the perspective of good practice and comparability at spatial scales above the local authority area. Sheail (1997) has reviewed the complexities of carrying a land use and landscape concept, or vision (the National Forest in the English Midlands) through into action; a high level of procedural complexity is often matched by a complex and overlapping system of spatially bounded designations and policy instruments. In addition to the initiatives whereby the conflicts associated with productivist land uses are mediated more or less directly by state agencies and local government, there are a number of largely endogenous trends in land use which are of relevance to whole landscape management. Organic farming and agro-forestry are characteristic of extensive rather than intensive land uses and as such they occupy relatively large areas of land per unit output, with some relevance to whole landscape management. For both of these land use systems the fundamental obstacle to whole landscape management still remains, that is they represent practices which may be significant and positive in their own contribution to the ecological and aesthetic fabric of the landscape, but such impacts will be limited to individual holdings in the absence of an over-arching framework for the integrated management of these features across fragmented landholdings.

Organic farming: landscape implications of low-input, extensive agriculture

Organic farming is often perceived as more than a land use practice, or a tightly-bounded production system. Popular conceptions of organic farming tend to associate the produce and practice with health, natural values, balance and a range of associated, rather vague qualities (Pretty, 1998; Thompson, 1995). Van Mansvelt *et al.* report convincing evidence that 'the fundamentally integrative character of organic agriculture' (1998, p. 210) contributes an enhanced vertical and horizontal structure to the farmed landscape (Table 8.6). They report the findings of ecological research that beetles and earthworms on organic farms and orchards in Denmark, Germany and the Netherlands are between 200 per cent and 2000 per cent more prevalent, and that a wider range of invertebrates, including butterflies and spiders, were between 50 per cent and 700 per cent more common. The amount of organic farms remains small and highly unequal between countries;

Table 8.6 Gains in vertical and horizontal landscape coherence on organic farms reported by van Mansvelt *et al.* (1998)

Diversity gains over conventional farming	Coherence gains over conventional farming
land use – more variation over the farm	land use and abiotic conditions – lower level of intervention and environmental control gives a higher level of fit with local conditions.
Crops – more spatial and temporal diversity	
Livestock – more species kept on the farm	
Shrubs and trees – more species in more types of spatial organization (e.g. hedges and field trees)	land use and farm structure – the layout of the farm represents a use-intensity gradient away from the farm building core, as distinct from a more diffuse pattern of land use
Flora – more non-crop species in and around fields, and on lane verges, etc.	Spatial structures – reflecting the intensity gradient above, field size tends to increase with distance away from the farm buildings.
Sensorial information – more forms, colours, smells and sounds.	

Pretty (1998) reports that there are only 1,000 fully registered (i.e. no longer in conversion) organic farmers in the UK, in contrast to the 18,000 in Austria. Cobb *et al.* (1999) explore some of the reasons for a low participation rate across Europe, and in the UK in particular, focusing on the cost implications and the long time-scale of the conversion process, arguing that the present structure of CAP and agri-environment payments do not bridge the cost gap for farmers, in spite of the demonstrated social and environmental gains of conversion.

These results are interesting and encouraging, especially in light of the increased interest, participation and demand for organic practices throughout much of the developed world (Lampkin, 1996). However, organic farms, in spite of the tendency for stronger co-operative linkages between individual farms, remain individual holdings *within* the landscape and as such do not constitute a significant avenue for whole landscape management, in spite of their widely accepted credentials for sustainability.

RAISING THE SCALE: FROM SITES TO LANDSCAPES

Whole landscape management in areas where the scale of landownership is not extensive is an ambitious objective. Although it represented something of a culture shift at the time, especially for farmers where short-term interests were often best served by a highly reductionist approach to conservation 'features' on their farms, the notion of whole farm conservation management is now widely accepted (FWAG, 1994; Morris and Cobb, 1993) and it is a requirement of entry into many European AEP schemes such as some ESAs and Tir Goval. In contrast, co-operation and collaboration across whole landscapes to achieve conservation objectives that are also articulated at that level is a radical idea, yet it is a firm prerequisite to the kind of regionally consistent environmental planning and management that landscape ecologists and other landscape researchers are calling for (Benson, 1994; O'Riordan, 1994).

Figure 8.8 illustrates what is termed here the landscape research–management gap. The research into the general principles and specific applications of landscape design and landscape ecology theory is a relatively advanced body of work (Forman, 1995a; 1995b) and awareness of these principles is becoming increasingly widespread in the conservation and countryside management professions (Andrews, 1993; Dover, 1992; Kirby, 1995; Ratcliffe et al., 1998). Conservation professionals, in turn, have a relatively uneven relationship with land managers (mostly farmers and foresters) (Lowe et al., 1986; Mather, 1993). Just as the socio-cultural and ecological value of the rural environment is variable over space, reflected in part by the spatial pattern of designated areas such as Nature Reserves and National Parks, relationships between conservation agencies and private landowners and managers are also locally variable and contingent on a range of historical, cultural and personal factors. Researchers have only recently begun to consider these human factors and the nature of relationships between individuals in the regulatory-advisory and productive-land management spheres, which are all-important in achieving successful partnerships and informed land management on individual land holdings. (For example, see Lowe et al. (1997) for a detailed case study of farm pollution, water quality and the emergence of a new environmental ethic amongst the public in one particular locality.) Many farmers and other land managers tend towards suspicion, and occasionally outright hostility, when conservation organizations express an interest in their land (Ramsay, 1993) and tensions between organizations such as Scottish Natural Heritage and the owners and managers of the privately owned sections of the national 'conservation estate' have been well documented (Lowe et al., 1986; Mather, 1993).

So, conservation land management may be *directed* by various state agencies, but it is, or is not, as the case may be, actually carried out by individual land managers on individual sites and landownership parcels. Pierce (1996) observes that, although public ownership is a high proportion of overall landownership in Canada, in the Southern third of the country where 95 per cent of the population is located, the land is overwhelmingly privately owned. As a consequence,

> the conservation gain is becoming increasingly influenced by the ownership question as it is by some simple realities; the need for fiscal restraint, the problem of ongoing management of these lands if removed from the public domain, and the political unsuitability of large-scale purchase of the land.
>
> (ibid., p. 217)

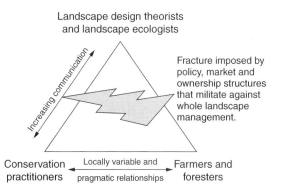

Figure 8.8 The landscape research–management gap.

Visioning future landscapes

The future does not just lie ahead; it is something that we create. More precisely, the future is produced by natural processes and human modification thereof.

(Forman and Collinge, 1997, p. 129)

It is widely believed that many environmental trends are so far-reaching and deep-rooted that it is beyond the power of human agency to influence them, such is the style of media reporting of issues such as climate change and depletion of the ozone layer. Further to this, there is a distinct tendency amongst politicians to ascribe a kind of life force to things such as the CAP budget which renders it nearly impossible to control. This is cynicism indeed, but one of the attractions of landscape as an environmental entity is that is can be perceived, changes can for the most part be observed, and it has a tangible reality and cultural resonance that require no specialist knowledge to interpret or appreciate. This accessibility is one of the reasons for the popularity of landscape-based planning frameworks such as the English Countryside Character Areas and regional equivalents (see Sue Kidd in Chapter 7) among planners and policy-makers; sub-regional landscapes allow for a coming-together of interests and perspectives on the values, resources and future options for these landscapes. Local Agenda 21 as a political project has done much to develop structures for the communication of these resources, and also the gathering of bottom-up information on future conditions. That link, into communities, into mainstream social groupings and into minority groups is the weak one, however, and methodologies to probe and mobilize people's desires for their landscapes into the future are not well advanced (Chapter 4).

O'Riordan *et al.* (1993) and Simpson *et al.* (1997) report two projects which have tried to portray the future landscapes that may be inherent in sector-based or more integrated policies for rural areas (Emmelin, 1996) and use these images as a vehicle for feeding information on public wishes back into the policy debate. There are of course a huge number of examples of this kind of participatory evaluation

in policy formulation and the UK Forestry Commission is just one organization that can point to a recent history of such public involvement to avoid the mistakes of their more distant past (Bell, 1998). O'Riordan *et al.* explicitly address the issue of whole landscape management:

there is no reason in principle why we should not develop the techniques to plan whole landscapes just as, in principle, we can create whole townscapes. One should however be careful to avoid the pit-fall of planning paternalism. Design of large units is dangerous if the affected public are not explicitly involved in imaging the choices available, and guiding the final outcome.

(1993, p. 125)

The procedure evaluated by O'Riordan *et al.* involved six paintings of the same view of the Yorkshire Dales National Park, each depicting a possible landscape future and associated text of the driving forces behind that landscape, and they conclude that the technique has considerable potential in the process of publicly accountable and transparent decision-making in regions of high cultural landscape value.

Landownership and management issues

Landscape design, whether as an exercise in applied ecology or aesthetics, or both, has an explicit concern with geography: the spatial arrangement and interaction of landscape components over space, which must include the socio-economic fabric of the landscape and the cultural legacy of socio-economic structures through history. With reference to the 'grid' of landownership in the USA, Meine comments that

the continuing evolution of the social and political landscape cannot be understood apart from the grid upon which it quite literally rests. The farming community and economy grew out of the grid; the grid, too, has fed the economies of scale that promote farm consolidation and the depletion of those same rural economies and communities.

(1997, p. 54)

We are back with the engines of change and the challenge of how to temper their damaging excesses and to spatially differentiate potential future landscapes that are sustainable yet sufficiently productive to meet local, regional and national needs, from landscapes of conservation, of access and of the wild. Landscape ecology is developing and promoting general principles of spatial organization and interaction for sustainable landscape management that are gaining increasingly widespread acceptance and application in wide area conservation management. However, although the design principles for sustainable landscape management have been established, or at least drafted out (Harms et al., 1993; Kirby, 1995), the control necessary to implement those principles is difficult to attain. Direct landownership may be the most assured avenue for appropriate management by state conservation agencies, but it is simply unrealistic as an avenue to significantly expand existing conservation estates. Even in the USA, where National Parks and other extensive tracts of land such as National Forests and National Grasslands, are state-owned and geographically immense relative to most European comparisons, there are the same pressures to curb public sector spending and to develop effective partnerships with the private sector to achieve many environmental objectives (Bliss et al., 1998).

Pierce (1996) provides an extensive review of various strategies and actions for the conservation of rural environmental resources in North America and Europe, ranging from voluntary frameworks, through economic and trade controls, to direct ownership and management by the state. This encompasses a wide range of interventionist measures for land and landscape management, but Pierce stresses the significant role which has been adopted by non-governmental organizations and partnerships 'to clarify the issues, to establish common ground and galvanise constructive action' (ibid., p. 227). In Wales the Welsh Office Tir Goval (Land Care) scheme (WOAD/CCW, 1999) has taken an impor-

tant step forward in bringing together previously separate AEP schemes under one umbrella, with whole farm management plans being drawn up only once an application is successful, itself a departure from the more formulaic, menu-driven approach of some other AEP schemes. In principle, this represents a shift towards a more integrated, holistic approach to the integration of conservation management with productive agriculture on individual farms. Further to this it establishes a locally sensitive, negotiative model of reaching management plans, which could be extended to encompass more than one holding at a time, which is surely a prerequisite to effective landscape-scale management of ecological and aesthetic features and character across that landscape (O'Riordan, 1994). Precedents for such an integrative approach to separately owned land holdings do exist (Hiemstra et al., 1993, Horwich, 1990; Stevens et al., 1999), and the scope for a UK application of the principle has previously been evaluated (MacFarlane, 1998, 2000). The development of partnerships in environmental management and conservation initiatives has an extensive body of literature (for example, see Michaels et al., 1999; Scott, 1998). It would be naïve to assume that the bringing together of groups of farmers as Franks (1999) suggests, would be an easy task in the first instance, let alone a workable structure for the achievement of scale-dependent conservation outcomes into the longer term. It is, however, a demonstrably significant avenue for policy evaluation and research.

Although vertical coherence and the conservation significance of particular sites can be ensured through sensitive management of patches within the landscape, horizontal coherence is often left to the accidental or fortunate synergies arising from neighbouring land managers' activities and strategies. It is rare, outwith areas of large-scale landownership, that parcels of land owned by various people are managed in a way that encourages these synergies; conversely, the scope for the development of intrusive human artefacts, the destruction of semi-natural or other valued features and fragmentation of linear features such as stone walls or riparian corridors is often high. A focus on site-based conservation as an activity within largely designated areas, and voluntary farmer participation in agri-environment schemes outside of these areas has clearly failed to halt the processes of habitat fragmentation, species decline and loss of biodiversity in the rural environment (Adams, 1986; Adams *et al.*, 1992; 1994; Gorham, 1997). When the conceptual problems of defining meaningful boundaries for whole landscape management (i.e. how many bits make up the whole, and which bits, if any, can be left out) collide with the policy and practical problems of assembling multiple-actor and multiple-agency frameworks for that level of landscape management, the ambitious scale of the task becomes clear.

This chapter builds on previous arguments that certain localities or features of conservation significance are best managed not in isolation from the surrounding landscape, but explicitly in the context of the wider landscape. This will require, for many localities, a way round 'the problem' of landownership, whereby neighbouring land managers are pursuing different strategies and practices on their land which may be either insensitive or actually damaging to the prospects of effectively conserving either particular landscape elements or the wider matrix that makes up the visible landscape. If rural policy is to actively engage with whole landscape planning for the integrated supply of productive, aesthetic, ecological and amenity outputs, one of three shifts is required for the scale of action to meet the scale at which plans are formulated, management objectives are articulated and at which action must be co-ordinated for defined objectives to be realized:

1   the active intervention of government to ensure appropriate management of the landscape matrix to meet defined objectives, both at the aggregate level and in a place-specific sense;
2   the strengthening of the relative ability of Conservation, Amenity and Recreation Trusts (CARTs) such as the National Trust and the John Muir Trust (Dwyer and Hodge, 1996; Hocker, 1996), to engage in the land market to purchase extensive tracts of land over which a cohesive management framework may be implemented;

3   the evolution of the dominantly voluntary framework of conservation participation in agriculture and the indicative and uneven strategic lead in forestry, to develop mechanisms for land enrolment that are more sensitive to the characteristics of the local environment, and the socio-economic context for action.

With respect to these three options, the first is highly unlikely given the almost universal drive to control public expenditure (White and Lovett, 1999). The second is already a reality, albeit a highly localized one, in certain parts of the UK and elsewhere (Dwyer and Hodge, 1996). However, the scope for a significant extension of landholding by CARTs is critically dependent upon longer-term shifts in rural policy and the rural land market, primarily in the uplands. It is the third option which represents the most immediately viable avenue for relating principles of landscape ecology to the regional and local objectives for agri-environment schemes and the significantly extended establishment of new upland, mid-level and lowland woodlands. Implementing this option requires a significantly enhanced level of attention to the spatial pattern of land enrolment and a much greater degree of sensitivity to local environmental conditions in the specification of locally or regionally tailored schemes.

As an ideal, such a call is not highly contentious, but the reality of attaining the required degree of formalized inter-agency communication and co-operation is extremely ambitious. With reference to forestry policy in the UK, Jones has called for 'a synthesis of all the strands of themes [addressed by and affected by UK forestry], which can only be achieved through an integrated national strategy by making forestry answerable to one government minister' (1994, p. 127). It would not be too fanciful to extend this line of argument to embrace a wider range of rural resource and environmental issues which are inherently interconnected in landscape terms, but highly segregated in institutional and policy terms. The Netherlands is widely recognized to have a strong land use planning structure with an emphasis on the regional level, which has attempted to tackle both vertical (levels of government) and sectoral (departments of government) dis-integration, through what Hidding (1993) has termed 'diagonal co-ordination'. In spite of the adoption of regionally-based integrated policies for land use, environment and water planning, Hidding concludes that the elusiveness of a definition of sustainability that is acceptable to the full range of levels and sectors of government has undermined actions to achieve fully integrated and sustainably oriented physical planning objectives and structures.

Even once an acceptable definition of sustainability is achieved, the transition from present states and trajectories to more sustainable pathways is littered with obstacles and clouded in uncertainty. This chapter has traced instances of good practice that are indicative of more sustainable land use practices and structures, but the role of landscape in the transition to sustainability is an uncertain one. Rannikko (1999) presents the various dimensions of sustainability (Figure 8.9), with ecological sustainability as the overarching, long-term priority, the attainment of which is dependent upon effectively addressing and balancing the economic, social and cultural dimensions. The scheme is highly appropriate to a landscape perspective on sustainability, in

that landscape is run through with issues of cultural valuation, there are few landscapes which do not bear the imprint of human activity and many are by-products (and where post-productivist policies support it, products) of human land use. Discussions over the sustainability of regions and landscapes cannot be abstracted from discussions over social structures and economic welfare, if only in recognition of the often pivotal role of land managers in landscape management.

CONCLUSION

Achieving whole landscape management in the context of fragmented landownership is a problem, as Selman (1997) puts it in a forestry context, of land use planning in the absence of planning powers. Where landownership parcels are extensive, for instance in the Scottish Highlands, or vast, such as some US National Parks, there is scope for the design and implementation of whole landscape plans if the landowner is so disposed and a framework of advice and incentives exists to guide appropriate management. Even in this context, however, structural

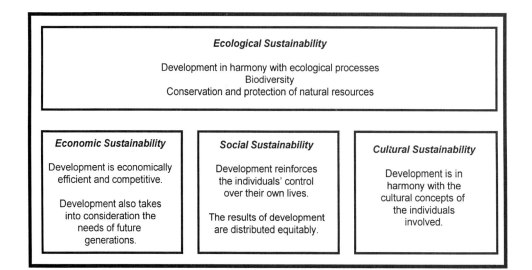

Figure 8.9 Dimensions of sustainable development.

Source: After Rannikko (1999)

features such as communications infrastructure and settlements may hinder the achievement of ecological objectives that may require non-fragmented, non-perforated wilderness areas. However, whole landscape management need not be premised on ecological grounds alone, and a cohesive visual landscape with extensive recreational potential, sustainable productive use of land parcels and appropriate watershed management may support a diverse range of species. This would require due attention to be paid at the planning level to the spatial organization of human, modified, semi-natural and near-natural landscape features, and the enforcement of management that is appropriate to locally defined priorities and practices. For most areas, admittedly, this remains an utopian vision of good practice that is founded in holistic landscape design and landscape ecological principles. Utopian it may be, but progress towards more sustainable rural landscapes requires a significantly heightened attention to spatial patterns of form, use, and function (Forman and Collinge, 1997; Hidding, 1993). Defining desired patterns of form and function in whole landscapes cannot fall to planners alone; a policy framework that provides appropriate incentives to assemble land management structures that can deliver the defined patterns has yet to emerge. Of equal importance, the decision-making process which defines conservation, amenity and aesthetic objectives for regional and sub-regional landscapes needs to bring together scientific, expert and lay discourses in the visioning of these future landscapes to adequately reflect the legitimacy such claims have on future rural environments.

REFERENCES

Adams, W. M. (1986) *Nature's Place: Conservation Sites and Countryside Change* (London, Allen & Unwin).

Adams, W. M. (1996a) Creative conservation, landscapes and loss, *Landscape Research,* 21(3), 265–276.

Adams, W. M. (1996b) *Future Nature: a Vision for Conservation* (London, Earthscan).

Adams, W. M. (1997) Rationalization and conservation: ecology and the management of nature in the United Kingdom, *Transactions of the Institute of British Geographers,* 22, 277–291.

Adams, W. M., Bourn, N. A. D. and Hodge, I. (1992) Conservation in the wider countryside: SSSIs and wildlife habitat in Eastern England, *land use Policy,* October, 235–248.

Adams, W. M., Hodge, I. D. and Bourn, N. A. D. (1994) Nature conservation and the management of the wider countryside in Eastern England, *Journal of Rural Studies,* 10(2), 147–157.

Andrews, J. (1993) The reality and management of wildlife corridors, *British Wildlife,* 5(1), 1–7.

Antrop, M. (1998) Landscape change: plan or chaos?, *Landscape and Urban Planning,* 41, 155–161.

Aspinall, R., Miller, D. R. and Birnie, R. V. (1993) Geographical Information Systems for rural land use planning, *Applied Geography,* 13, 54–66.

Bell, M. and Child, L. (1998) Redesigning a region: the National Forest and quality of life, in M. A. Atherden and R. A. Butlin (eds) *Woodland in the Landscape: Past and Future Perspectives* (College of Ripon and York St. John, PLACE Research Centre).

Bell, S. (1993) *Elements of Visual Design in the Landscape* (London, E & FN Spon).

Bell, S. (1998) Woodland in the landscape, in M. A. Atherden and R. A. Butlin (eds) *Woodland in the Landscape: Past and Future Perspectives* (College of Ripon and York St. John, PLACE Research Centre).

Benson, J. (1994) The landscape resource, in M. Whitby and N. Ward (eds) *The UK Strategy for Sustainable Agriculture: A Critical Analysis* (Newcastle upon Tyne, Centre for Rural Economy, University of Newcastle upon Tyne).

Bliss, J. C., Sisock, M. L. and Birch, T. W. (1998) Ownership matters: forestland concentration in rural Alabama, *Society and Natural Resources,* 11, 401–410.

Brassley, P. (1998) On the unrecognised significance of the ephemeral landscape, *Landscape Research,* 23(2), 119–132.

Bunce, M. (1994) *The Countryside Ideal: Anglo-American Images of Landscape* (London, Routledge).

Burel, F. and Baudry, J. (1995) Social, aesthetic and ecological aspects of hedgerows in rural landscapes as a framework for greenways, *Landscape and Urban Planning,* 33, 327–340.

Carr, S. and Tait, J. (1991) Differences in the attitudes of farmers and conservationists and their implications, *Journal of Environmental Management,* 32, 281–294.

CAS (1976) *Land for agriculture,* CAS Report No.1 (Reading, University of Reading, Centre for Agricultural Strategy).

CAS (1986) *Countryside Implications for England and Wales of Possible Changes in the Common Agricultural Policy* (Main Report) (Reading, University of Reading, Centre for Agricultural Strategy).

Cloke, P., Milbourne, P. and Thomas, C. (1996) The English National Forest: local reactions to plans for renegotiated nature–society relations in the countryside, *Transactions of the Institute of British Geographers,* 21, 552–571.

Cobb, D., Dolman, P. and O'Riordan, T. (1999) Interpretations of sustainable agriculture in the UK, *Progress in Human Geography,* 23(2), 209–235.

Cobb, D., Feber, R., Hopkins, A., Stockdale, L., O'Riordan, T., Clements, B., Firbank, L., Goulding, S., Jarvis, S. and MacDonald, D. (1999) Integrating the environmental and economic consequences of converting to organic agriculture: evidence from a case study, *land use Policy,* 16, 207–221.

Council for National Parks (1998) *Wild by Design in the National Parks of England and Wales* (London, Council for National Parks).

Crabtree, B., Chalmers, N. and Barron, N. J. (1998) Information for policy design: modelling participation in a farm woodland incentive scheme, *Journal of Agricultural Economics*, 49(3), 306–320.

Curry, N. (1994) *Countryside Recreation, Access and land use Planning* (London, E & FN Spon).

Deffontaines, J. P., Thanail, C. and Baudry, J. (1995) Agricultural systems and landscape patterns: how can we build a relationship?, *Landscape and Urban Planning*, 31, 3–10.

de Jong, D. and van Tantenhove, J. (1998) The institutionalisation of Dutch-German Cross-Boundary nature policy, *Sociologia Ruralis*, 38(2), 163–177.

Dover, J. W. (1992) *Kirklees UDP: Green Corridors.* Final report (Liverpool, The Environmental Advisory Unit Ltd).

Dwyer, J. C. and Hodge, I. D. (1996) *Countryside in Trust: Land Management by Conservation, Recreation and Amenity Organisations* (London, Wiley).

Emmelin, L. (1996) Landscape impact analysis: a systematic approach to landscape impacts of policy, *Landscape Research*, 21(1), 13–36.

English Nature (1994) *Nature Conservation Strategies* (Peterborough, English Nature).

Evans, N. and Morris, C. (1997) Towards a geography of Agri-Environmental Policies in England and Wales, *Geoforum*, 28(2), 189–204.

Fleury, A. M. and Brown, R. D. (1997) A framework for the design of wildlife conservation corridors with specific reference to south-western Ontario, *Landscape and Urban Planning*, 37, 163–186.

Forestry Commission (1991) *Community Woodland Design* (Edinburgh, Forestry Commission).

Forestry Commission (1992) *Lowland Landscape Design Guidelines* (Edinburgh, Forestry Commission).

Forest Industry Council (1999) *A Reference for the Forestry Industry* (Stirling, Forestry Industry Council of Great Britain).

Forman, R. T. T. (1995a) *Land Mosaics: The Ecology of Landscapes and Regions* (Cambridge, Cambridge University Press).

Forman, R. T. T. (1995b) Some general principles of landscape and regional ecology, *Landscape Ecology*, 10(3), 133–142.

Forman, R. T. T. and Collinge, S. K. (1997) Nature conserved in changing landscapes with and without spatial planning, *Landscape and Urban Planning*, 37, 129–135.

Franks, J. R. (1999) *In situ* conservation of plant genetic resources for food and agriculture: a UK perspective, *Land Use Policy*, 16, 81–91.

Fry, G. and Sarlöv-Herlin, I. (1997) The ecological and amenity functions of woodland edges in the agricultural landscape; a basis for design and management, *Landscape and Urban Planning*, 37, 45–55.

FWAG (1994) *Guidelines for Environmentally Responsible Farming* (Stonleigh, Farming and Wildlife Advisory Group, National Agricultural Centre).

Gilg, A.W. (1996) *Countryside Planning* 2nd edition (London, Routledge).

Gorham, E. (1997) Human impacts on ecosystems and landscapes, in J. D. Nassauer (ed.) *Placing Nature: Culture and Landscape Ecology* (Washington DC, Island Press).

Gosz, J. R. (1991) Fundamental ecological characteristics of landscape boundaries, in M. M. Holland, P. G. Risser, and R. J. Naiman (eds) *Ecotones: The Role Of Landscape Boundaries in the Management and Restoration of Changing Environments* (New York, Chapman & Hall).

Grainger, A. (1995) The forest transition: an alternative approach, *Area*, 27(3), 242–251.

Green, B. (1996) *Countryside Conservation* 3rd edition (London, E & FN Spon).

Hanley, N., Whitby, M. and Simpson, I. (1999) Assessing the success of agri-environmental policy in the UK, *Land Use Policy*, 16, 67–80.

Harms, B., Khaapen, J. P. and Rademakers, J. G. (1993) Landscape planning for nature restoration: comparing regional scenarios, in C. C. Vos and P. Opdam (eds) *Landscape Ecology of a Stressed Environment* (London, Chapman & Hall).

Harvey, D. R. and Thomson, K. J. (1985) Costs, benefits and the future of the Common Agricultural Policy, *Journal of Common Market Studies*, 24(1), 1–20.

Hidding, M. C. (1993) In search of new concepts of sustainable development of rural areas in the Netherlands, *Landscape and Urban Planning*, 27, 259–264.

Hiemstra, W., Benedictus, F., de Bruin, R. and de Jong, P. (1993) Farmers search for new ways of co-operating: networking in the Friesan woodlands of the Netherlands, in C. Alders, B. Haverkort and L. van Veldhuizen (eds) *Linking with Farmers: Networking for Low-External-Input and Sustainable Agriculture* (London, Intermediate Technology Publications).

Hobbs, R. (1997) Future landscapes and the future of landscape ecology, *Landscape and Urban Planning*, 37, 1–9.

Hocker, J. W. (1996) Patience, problem solving, and private initiative: local groups chart a new course for land conservation, in H. L. Diamond, and P. F. Noonan (eds) *land use in America* (Washington, Island Press).

Hodge, S. J. (1995) *Creating and Managing Woodlands Around Towns* (Edinburgh, Forestry Commission).

Holden, P. (1999) Director of the UK Soil Association, interviewed on BBC Radio Four Today Programme, 23rd February.

Horwich, R. H. (1990) How to develop a community sanctuary – an experimental approach to the conservation of private lands, *Oryx* 24, 95–102.

Hoskins, W. G. (1955) *The Making of the English Landscape* (London, Penguin).

Ilbery, B. and Bowler, I. (1998) From agricultural productivism to post-productivism, in B. Ilbery (ed.) *The Geography of Rural Change* (London, Longman).

Jones, R. B. (1994) National forestry strategy required, *land use Policy*, 11(2), 124–127.

Kirby, K. (1995) *Rebuilding the English Countryside: Habitat Fragmentation and Wildlife Corridors as Issues in Practical Conservation* (Peterborough, English Nature).

Lampkin, N. (1996) *European Organic Farming Statistics* (Aberystwyth, Welsh Institute of Rural Studies).

Lowe, P., Clark, J., Seymour, S. and Ward, N. (1997) *Moralizing the Environment: Countryside Change, Farming and Pollution* (London, UCL Press).

Lowe, P., Cox, G., MacEwen, M., O'Riordan, T. and Winter, M. (1986) *Countryside Conflicts: The Politics of Farming, Forestry and Conservation* (Aldershot, Gower).

Lowe, P., Rutherford, A. and Baldock, D. (1996) Implications of the Cork Declaration, *ECOS*, 17(3/4), 42–45.

MacFarlane, R. (1996) Modelling the interaction of economic and socio-behavioural factors in the prediction of farm adjustment, *Journal of Rural Studies*, 12(4), 365–374.

MacFarlane, R. (1998) Implementing agri-environmental policy: a landscape ecology perspective, *Journal of Environmental Planning and Management,* 41(5), 575–596.

MacFarlane, R. (2000) Achieving whole landscape management across multiple land management units: a case study from the Lake District Environmentally Sensitive Area, *Landscape Research,* 25(2), 229–254.

McHenry, H. (1996) Understanding farmers' perceptions of changing agriculture: some implications for agri-environment schemes, in N. Curry and S. Owen (eds) *Changing Rural Policy in Britain: Planning, Administration, Agriculture and the Environment* (Cheltenham, Countryside and Community Press).

MAFF (1999) Ministry for Agriculture, Fisheries and Food WWW site: http://maff.gov.uk

Manning, R., Valliere, W. and Minteer, B. (1999) Values, ethics and attitudes towards national forest management: an empirical study, *Society and Natural Resources,* 12, 421–436.

Mather, A. S. (1990) *Global Forest Resources* (London, Belhaven Press).

Mather, A. S. (1992) The forest transition, *Area,* 24, 367–379.

Mather, A. S. (1993) Protected areas in the periphery: conservation and controversy in Northern Scotland, *Journal of Rural Studies* 9(4), 371–384.

Mather, A. S. (1998) The changing role of forests, in B. Ilbery (ed.) *The Geography of Rural Change* (London, Longman).

Mather, A. S. and Thomson, K. J. (1995) The effects of afforestation on agriculture in Scotland, *Journal of Rural Studies,* 11(2), 187–202.

Macnaghten, P. and Urry, J. (1998) *Contested Natures* (London, Sage).

Meine, C. (1997) Inherit the grid, in J. D. Nassauer (ed.) *Placing Nature: Culture and Landscape Ecology* (Washington, DC, Island Press).

Michaels, S., Mason, R. J. and Solecki, W. D. (1999) Motivations for ecostewardship partnerships: examples from the Adironack Park, *Land Use Policy,* 16, 1–9.

Mills, S. F. (1997) *The American Landscape* (Edinburgh, Keele University Press).

Moffat, A. and McNeill, J. (1994) *Reclaiming Disturbed Land for Forestry* (London, HMSO).

Morris, C. and Cobb, R. (1993) Agriculture and conservation – the whole farm approach, *ECOS,* 14(3/4), 53–59.

Morris, C. and Potter, C. (1995) Recruiting the new conservationists: farmer's adoption of agri-environmental schemes in the UK, *Journal of Rural Studies,* 11(1), 51–63.

Muir, R. (1999) *Approaches to Landscape* (Basingstoke, Macmillan).

Nassauer, J. (1995) Culture and changing landscape structure, *Landscape Ecology,* 10(4), 229–237.

Nassauer, J. (1997a) Action across boundaries, in J. D. Nassauer (ed.) *Placing Nature: Culture and Landscape Ecology* (Washington, DC, Island Press).

Nassauer, J. (1997b) Cultural sustainability: aligning aesthetics and ecology, in J. D. Nassauer (ed.) *Placing Nature: Culture and Landscape Ecology* (Washington, DC, Island Press).

Naveh, Z. (1995) Interactions of landscapes and cultures, *Landscape and Urban Planning,* 32, 43–54.

North, J. (1990) Future agricultural land use patterns, in D. Britton (ed.) *Agriculture in Britain: Changing Pressures and Policies* (Wallingford, CAB International).

Noss, R. F., O'Connell, M. A. and Murphy, D. D. (eds) (1997) *The Science of Conservation Planning* (Washington, DC, Island Press).

O'Callaghan, J. R. (1996) *Land use: The Interaction of Economics, Ecology and Hydrology* (London, Chapman & Hall).

O'Riordan, T. (1994) Creating whole landscapes, *Countryside,* September/October, 7.

O'Riordan, T., Wood, C. and Shadrake, A. (1993) Landscapes for tomorrow, *Journal of Environmental Planning and Management,* 36(2), 123–147.

Pierce, J. T. (1996) The conservation challenge in sustaining rural environments, *Journal of Rural Studies,* 12(3), 215–229.

Potter. C. (1986) Processes of countryside change in lowland England, *Journal of Rural Studies,* 2(3), 187–195.

Potter, C. (1998) *Against the Grain: Agri-Environmental Reform in the United States and the European Union* (Wallingford, CAB International).

Potter, C., Burnham, P., Edwards, A., Gasson, R. and Green, B. (1991) *The Diversion of Land: Conservation in a Period of Farming Contraction* (London, Routledge).

Potter, C., Carr, C. and Lobley, M. (1996) Environmental change in Britain's countryside: an analysis of recent patterns and socio-economic processes based on Countryside Survey 1990, *Journal of Environmental Management,* 48, 169–186.

Potter, C. and Lobley, M. (1992) Ageing and succession on family farms: the impact on decision-making and land use, *Sociologia Ruralis,* 32(2/3), 317–334.

Poudevigne, I., van Rooij, S., Morin, P. and Alard, D. (1997) Dynamics of rural landscapes and their main driving factors: a case study in the Seine Valley, Normandy, France, *Landscape and Urban Planning,* 38, 93–103.

Pretty, J. (1998) *The Living Land* (London, Earthscan).

Rackham, O. (1980) *Ancient Woodland: Its History, Vegetation and Uses in England* (London, Edward Arnold).

Ramsay, P. (1993) Landowners and conservation, in F. B. Goldsmith and A. Warren (eds) *Conservation in Progress* (London, Wiley).

Rannikko, P. (1999) Combining social and ecological sustainability in the Nordic forest periphery, *Sociologia Ruralis,* 39(3), 394–410.

Ratcliffe, P. R., Peterken, G. F. and Hampson, A. (1998) *A Forest Habitat Network for the Cairngorms* Survey and Monitoring Report No.114 (Edinburgh, Scottish Natural Heritage).

Reed, M. (1997) *The Landscape of Britain: From the Beginnings to 1914* (London, Routledge).

Ribe, R. (1999) Regeneration harvests versus clearcuts: public views of the acceptability and aesthetics of Northwest forest plan harvests, *Northwest Science,* 73, 102–117.

RSPB (1999) Land Care launch in Wales, *Field Fare,* 11 May.

Scott, A. J. (1998) The contribution of forums to rural sustainable development: a preliminary evaluation, *Journal of Environmental Management,* 54, 291–303.

Selby, J. A. and Petäjistö, L. (1995) Attitudinal aspects of the resistance to field afforestation in Finland, *Sociologia Ruralis,* 35(1), 67–92.

Selman, P. (1993) Landscape ecology and countryside planning: vision, theory and practice, *Journal of Rural Studies* 9(1), 1–21.

Selman, P. (1996) The potential for landscape ecological planning in Britain, in N. Curry and S. Owen (eds) *Changing Rural*

Policy in Britain: Planning, Administration, Agriculture and the Environment (Cheltenham, Countryside and Community Press).

Selman, P. (1997) The role of forestry in meeting planning objectives, *land use Policy*, 14(1), 55–73.

Sheail, J. (1997) The new National Forest: from idea to achievement, *Town Planning Review*, 68(3), 305–323.

Sheail, J. (1998) *Nature Conservation in Britain: The Formative Years* (London, The Stationery Office).

Shoard, M. (1980) *The Theft of the Countryside* (London, Temple Smith).

Short, J. R. (1991) *Imagined Country: Society, Culture and Environment* (London, Routledge).

Shucksmith, M. (1993) Farm household behaviour and the transition to post productivism, *Journal of Agricultural Economics*, 44(3), 466–478.

Simberloff, D. (1998) Flagships, umbrellas and keystones: is single species management passé in the landscape era? *Biological Conservation*, 83(3), 247–257.

Simpson, I., Parsisson, D., Hanley, N. and Bullock, C. H. (1997) Envisioning future landscapes in the Environmentally Sensitive Areas of Scotland, *Transactions of the Institute of British Geographers*, 22, 307–320.

Skerratt, S. and Dent, J. B. (1996) The challenge of agri-environmental subsidies: the case of Breadalbane ESA, Scotland, *Scottish Geographical Magazine*, 112(2), 92–100.

Stevens, T. H., Dennis, D., Kittredge, D. and Rickenbach, M. (1999) Attitudes and preferences toward co-operative agreements for management of private forestlands in the Northeastern United States, *Journal of Environmental Management*, 55, 81–90.

Thompson, P. B. (1995) *The Spirit of the Soil: Agriculture and Environmental Ethics* (London, Routledge).

Toogood, M. (1995) Representing ecology and Highland tradition, *Area* 27(2), 102–109.

Tsouvalis-Gerber, J. (1998) Making the visible invisible: ancient woodlands, British forest policy and the social construction of reality, in C. Watkins (ed.) *European Woods and Forests: Studies in Cultural History* (Wallingford, CAB International).

van Mansvelt, J. D., Stobbelaar, D. J. and Henricks, K. (1998) Comparison of landscape features in organic and conventional farming systems, *Landscape and Urban Planning*, 41, 209–227.

van Mansvelt, J. D. and van der Lubbe M. J. (1999) *Checklist for Sustainable Landscape Management. Final report of the EU concerted action AIR3-CT93–1210: The Landscape and Nature Production Capacity of Organic/Sustainable Types of Agriculture* (Amsterdam, Elsevier).

Vos, C. C. and Opdam, P. (1993) Preface, in C. C. Vos and P. Opdam (eds) *Landscape Ecology of a Stressed Environment* (London, Chapman & Hall).

Westmacott, R. (1997) *Agricultural Landscapes: A Third Look* (Cheltenham, Countryside Commission).

Whitby, M. and Lowe, P. (1994) The political and economic roots of environmental policy in agriculture, in M. Whitby (ed.) *Incentives for Countryside Management: The Case of ESAs* (Wallingford, CAB International).

Whitby, M. and Thomson, K. (1979) Against coordination, *Town and Country Planning*, 48, 51–52.

White, P. C. L. and Lovett, J. C. (1999) Public preferences and willingness-to-pay for nature conservation in the North York Moors National Park, UK, *Journal of Environmental Management*, 55, 1–13.

Wightman, A. (1997) *Who owns Scotland?* (Edinburgh, Canongate).

Wilson, G. A. (1996) Farmer environmental attitudes and ESA participation, *Geoforum*, 27(2), 115–131.

Wilson, G. A. (1997) Assessing the environmental impact of the Environmentally Sensitive Area Scheme: a case for using farmers' environmental knowledge?, *Landscape Research*, 22(3), 303–326.

Winter, M. (1996) *Rural Politics: Policies for Agriculture, Forestry and the Environment* (London, Routledge).

Winter, M., Gasson, R., Curry, N., Selman, P. and Short, C. (1996) *Socio-economic Evaluation of Free Conservation Advice Provided to Farmers in England by ADAS and FWAG* (Cheltenham, Countryside and Community Press).

WOAD/CCW (1999) *Tir Goval: An Agri-Environment Scheme for Wales* (Cardiff, Welsh Office Agriculture Department and Countryside Council for Wales).

9

LANDSCAPE PLANNING AND CITY FORM

Helen Armstrong, Helen Brown and Tom Turner

SUMMARY

This chapter reviews the principles of sustainable city planning in relation to landform, water, vegetation, eco-building and land use. It uses a number of examples to illustrate the view that although there is considerable public and political support for making cities more sustainable, surprisingly little has been done towards that end. In particular, the chapter discusses the case of the Greenwich Peninsula which is a large sector of London designed and partly built in the 1990s. Government departments, Greenwich Council and the design teams have boasted that development of this area was based on a new sustainable approach and this claim is reviewed and evaluated.

INTRODUCTION

Etymologically, to 'sustain' means to keep going. When a musical note is played, the meaning is unmistakable. With reference to environmental planning, it is totally unclear. On a geological time scale, mountains rise and fall, species evolve and become extinct. The ant has sustained its physical form and way of life for hundreds of millions of years. What would it mean for a human society to be sustainable? Terms such as 'Solubility', 'Affordability' and 'Sustainability' have meaning only in defined circumstances – for example, salt is soluble in water but not in oil; a house can be non-affordable for most of us but easily purchased from Bill Gates' petty cash and sustainability makes sense only as a comparative term. Labelling one city, or land use practice, 'sustainable' and another as 'non-sustainable' is meaningless. The concept of sustainability used in this chapter is based on the balance between inputs and outputs into the city system (Figure 9.1). A city with high inputs (of energy, food, water, etc.) and high outputs (of thermal pollution, sewage, vegetable waste, etc.) is viewed as less sustainable than a city of the same size but with lower levels of input and output. This usage accords with the circumstances in which the concept of sustainability was introduced, in the 1970s, when attention was drawn to the potential problems of resources running out. It also focused the attention of rich societies on pollution – a strong reason for making our cities more 'sustainable' in the defined sense. This concept of relative sustainability will be used in the chapter, with a consciousness of its weaknesses.

Landscape architecture can be defined with regard to its aims and methods. The aim is to 'make and conserve good outdoor space' with the word 'good' defined operationally. A good cricket bat is strong, supple, comfortable and well-balanced. A good landscape is useful, beautiful and sustainable. Inevitably, each of these epithets conflicts with the others. We must expect trade-offs between different landscape

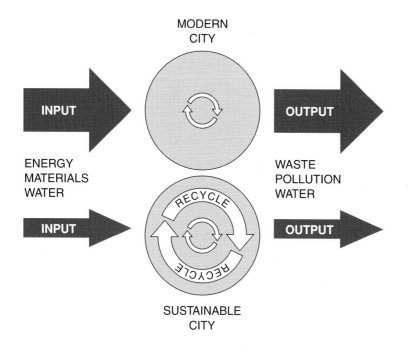

MODERN
CITY

INPUT

ENERGY
MATERIALS
WATER

WASTE
POLLUTION
WATER

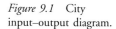

INPUT

RECYCLE

RECYCLE

SUSTAINABLE
CITY

Figure 9.1   City
input–output diagram.

goods as we do between community and privacy, work and leisure, safety and risk. The method of creating good landscape relates to the inter-relationship between people and the four primary components of the outdoor landscape: landform, water, vegetation and eco-building. This chapter will review methods of creating good city form through landscape planning for these four elements. Sections on each will be followed by a section on the choice of land for urbanization followed by the Greenwich Peninsula case study.

RELATIVE SUSTAINABILITY

Improving the relative sustainability of a city requires an evaluation of those features which affect its pattern of inputs and outputs. This is likely to include earth, water, vegetation, building types, transport systems and spatial organization. Once these are considered, it is then possible to assess the potential for change through landscape planning. This is a similar concept to the 'ecological footprint'

as defined by Rees (Rees, 1997; Wackernagel and Rees, 1995). Rees asks 'if cities are the nodes of consumption in a spreading human net, just how much productive land/water (ecosystem) area is required for the corresponding production?' (Rees, 1997, p. 305). A study by Rees (1997) in British Columbia calculated that to support the Vancouver-Lower Fraser valley community at its usual level of economic activity, consumption and disposal of waste, the land area required was at least 200 times the size of the city. This enlarged land area is thus the actual 'ecological footprint' of the city. The calculations can be varied according to which elements are taken into account, but Rees believes that this kind of result is typical of those which can be obtained by examining many cities including London. A sustainable strategy would attempt to reduce this 'footprint'.

In addition to such considerations, two major challenges are the attainment of sustainable landscape objectives in the densely built city core, which is often historic, and the need to engage communities in a desire for sustainable cities and the consequent

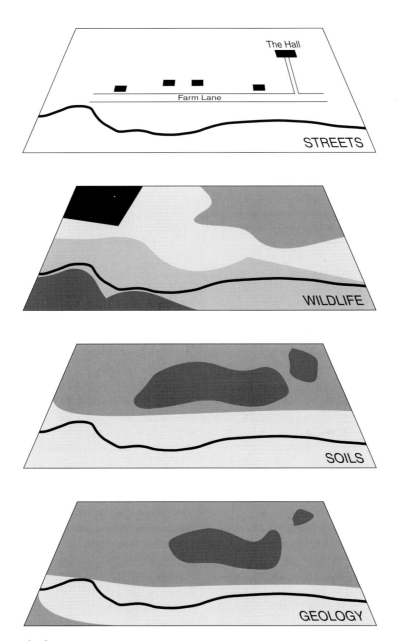

Figure 9.2 Layers of information.

changes that will ensue (see Chapter 4). The achievement of sustainability objectives, in existing cities which were built on less-sustainable principles, is a difficult process due to the complex web of social, physical and biological systems. Supporters of the 'compact city' solution to the issue of how to make a more sustainable city form argue for the creation of higher densities in existing cities (DETR, 1999). However, such 'town cramming' might lead to the further loss of existing vegetation and greenspace. Decentralization, on the other hand, might lead to an increased loss to development of agricultural land. Both would also have social impacts and it is not clear which solution is likely to be 'more' sustainable than the other. Some sections of the planning profession have focused on a concept of the 'Social City Region', based on Ebenezer Howard's garden-city principles, where the city is considered as part of a whole interdependent regional complex (Breheny and Rookwood, 1993). This identifies the need for changes in four main areas if sustainability objectives are to be achieved: natural resources, land use and transport, energy, pollution and waste . Whichever philosophy for change in cities is examined, all are in general agreement that the key to greater sustainability lies in a more integrated and strategic approach to tackling the urban question. Sustainability planners need to study, model and make proposals for the urban landscape at all scales and levels, in time and space, and beyond the usual span of three generations.

Urbanization conceals the original landscape character underlying a city and distorts its natural processes. The past is one of the many layers of complexity that contributes to our sense of a locations' place and time. A fuller understanding of the pre-urbanization landscape helps to explain a city's lost distinctive landscape character and natural legacy. Landscape and environmental planning requires a long-term view and a long-term information policy. The relative sustainability of a plan can only be assessed over time by monitoring and auditing.

The process of landscape planning to obtain a more sustainable city form requires the collation and manipulation of large amounts of information obtained over time. Government agencies, utility companies and the military create maps and plans and retain large amounts of survey information, primarily to reinforce and protect their own interests. Landscape planners need access to this kind of information and this is becoming possible through what Lawrence and Norton-Taylor (2000) describe as an explosion in digital mapping and easy access to it. From February 2000 customers will be able to type in a United Kingdom postcode or grid map reference into the Millennium Map web site (http://www.millennium-map.com) and for a payment of £17.50 receive, on-line, a digital map of their selected location at one to a million or one to a thousand scale. It is proposed that the Millennium Map will be completely reviewed every three years, which will also allow planners and environmentalists to monitor and identify changes in the landscape. Digital tools for manipulating such information will also make the landscape planner's job easier. In the near future the development of easy-to-use Geographical Information Systems (GIS) will allow cities to be represented as layered structures (Figure 9.2) and values may be given to each layer. These techniques and tools should improve our ability to collect and collate information, to integrate it and then to model a city's complexity.

LANDFORM PLANS

The topography of the city is constantly changing and is often buried by buildings and covered by pavements. Rivers are piped, hills are flattened, woods are felled, marshes are drained and valleys are filled. To understand these processes landscape planners require landform plans of city regions that should review the pre-urbanization relief, the alterations made through human use and the potential for change through the ongoing processes of cut and fill. Such plans might also be described as 'earth plans'. We need to protect existing positive landform features and identify the potential for the creation of new landscapes of green space, hill space, valley space, river space, quarry space, wild space, marsh space and beach space as well as respond to the geology, topography and soils in order to understand

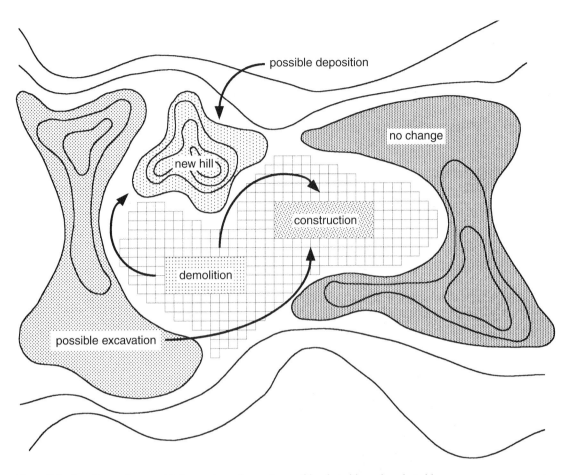

Figure 9.3 Landform plans could show where change is possible, desirable and undesirable.

the resources and hazards of an urban area. Too often, cities degrade or destroy the geological resources on which they depend (Figure 9.3).

The perpetual and accelerating cycle of demolition and construction in modern cities generates huge amounts of waste material. To reduce the need for new building materials, land fill requirements, material handling and transport inputs, waste needs to be reused where it is generated. Demolition materials should not be removed from building sites unless it can be shown that they will be put to good use elsewhere and wastes need temporary storage, sorting and dispersal. There is no lack of plots in our cities awaiting development that would be suit-

able for processing and stockpiling waste. Materials for recycling such as crushed concrete, road scalpings, inert fill, sand, gravel, clay, rock, timber, topsoil, green plant waste and composting facilities could provide neighbourhoods with construction materials as discussed in Chapter 10.

Winning and recycling construction materials provide opportunities to create new wetlands, to enhance rivers and waterways, to make new hills and viewpoints. To achieve these objectives it is necessary to take an overview of the urban landscape because significant opportunities rarely exist within individual construction projects but arise from synergy between projects. It therefore falls to municipal authorities to maintain plans which indicate areas for excavation, deposition and storage. The Greenwich Peninsula, as discussed below, provides an example of how this is or could be carried out. At Milton Keynes excavated material was used to create acoustic and visual barriers beside the grid roads (Turner, 1996, p. 368).

At present there is a paucity of survey information available, particularly details concerning the geology and soils in metropolitan areas. Landform plans, looking a century into the future, should identify and assess potential resources: flat land, stable ground, fertile soils, minerals, stone, sand, gravel, and existing scenic landform features. Hazards also need to be identified such as the potential for landslides, earthquakes, land shrinkage, ground collapse, clay swelling, heave, contaminated land, compacted land, erosion and flooding by river or sea. Landform plans should consider the factors which maintain and enhance stability. For example, in landslide-prone areas, stability can be increased by the regulation of land use, design, construction and maintenance (Spirn, 1984, p. 111). Ground subsidence is often a direct consequence of human activities, extracting coal, oil or ground water and building on unconsolidated landfill. The extraction of oil, gas and water decreases the pressure in the rocks beneath cities, causing them to subside. Inland, the damage is mainly to structural foundations and utility supply pipes. In coastal areas, subsidence can cause inundation at high tide or even lower the land to below sea level (Spirn, 1984, p. 99).

Geological hazards and problems associated with subsidence can be mitigated or prevented by the designation of suitable land uses. In unstable locations or areas of potential mineral extraction the land uses could include temporary areas for materials recycling, car parking, plant nurseries, golf courses or parks. In these potentially hazardous locations the land uses which should be discouraged are those that require significant built structures. Combining appropriate land uses, developing contour plans and employing construction guidelines for unstable land will create more sustainable city landforms. Sustainable land form plans should therefore do the following:

- exploit distinctive geological and topographical character;
- protect potential resources;
- provide opportunities for new integrated landform;
- plan for secondary and tertiary land uses.

WATER PLANS

Planning for sustainability in city regions requires the compilation of water plans that review urban water resources in relation to inputs and outputs. River and drainage authorities normally examine these issues on a catchment basis rather than within urban boundaries, where detailed decisions on paving and roofing and outdoor design have a cumulative impact on the overall water balance. Water plans have been pioneered in British, French and American new towns (Turner, 1996, p. 375) but they are also necessary for old towns.

Water contamination is an ever-increasing problem. In truly natural self-sustaining environments, such as the Bialowieska Forest in Poland, water quality is sustained by the ecological process. Untouched by humans for over 10,000 years, the water quality of this bison-inhabited forest survives because its many wetlands and drainage paths retain and filter the rainwater. The result is pure clear water rich in aquatic life. In the developed world where humans have transformed the landscape, protective vegetation has been removed and with the rapidly growing process of urbanization and mass road-building programmes, natural wetlands and waterways have been replaced by complex networks of drains designed to discharge rainwater and effluent into natural waterways. The result is a world where diffuse pollution is contaminating waterways, groundwater and seas and destroying natural ecosystems. An effective sustainable water strategy to redress this situation is to tackle the problem as near as possible to its source in order to attempt to re-capture the water quality found in Bialowieska.

Water recycling requires different treatment methods for different water types – referred to in this text as bluewater, blackwater and brownwater.

Bluewater (run-off from roofs and pedestrian pavements) can be allowed to infiltrate where it falls and techniques such as covering roofs with vegetation can help to detain and transpire bluewater. Blackwater (run-off from roads and vehicle parks) can be retained in detention ponds where the water can be filtered by reed beds to remove hydrocarbons. Brownwater or grey water (sewage water) can be treated in the city by using specialist technology and planting. Porous paving and sub soil drainage techniques can contribute to a reduction in the volume of run-off discharging into natural watercourses. Such methods have proved successful in the USA, Sweden and Germany over the last 20 years but in the UK, planning for sustainable water management has been a much more recent initiative (Gardiner, 1991). In order to produce more sustainable systems, urban areas need to provide plans for the accumulation and recycling of water. Three projects where this has been done are described below.

Dunfermline East expansion

Developers for this 1,250 acre regeneration site on the eastern edge of Dunfermline were presented with specific planning constraints. The urban expansion of the town could not proceed unless a water plan was devised which could prove that there would be no extra run-off from the proposed built-up area than was already discharging from the greenfield site. The river courses downstream were used to full capacity and the only way forward was to employ surface water management techniques to contain water within the new urban expansion zone. In 1998 Scotland's first integrated sustainable urban drainage project using source control techniques was implemented. It was a prerequisite for development. The surface water drainage plan for Dunfermline comprised the strategic location of source control elements:

- ponds and wetlands as permanent pools for storage and biological treatment (with reeds and emergent plants);
- attenuation basins to reduce potential flood risk downstream;

- detention basins and swales (ditches designed to infiltrate run-off) to restrict discharge rates.

As an alternative to the traditional 'end of pipe' method, Dunfermline's solution provides an environmentally efficient means of controlling water quantity and quality with both functional and aesthetic landscape benefits. Constraints on the way the Dunfermline site was developed, however, have resulted in a higher preponderance of ponds requiring greater land areas. The project is one of a number of key sites presently being monitored by CIRIA (2000) to demonstrate the effectiveness of sustainable landscape planning and practice (and see SEPA, 1996). Surface water management sites require full integration with patterns of landform, vegetation and human use.

Swedish sustainable water projects

In Malmö the existing city form has been greatly improved by sustainability-conscious planners working in collaboration with landscape design engineers. The 1815 maps were used to reveal the original water regime and then wetlands have been re-established to detain blue and grey water. After a decade's experience in recreating natural hydrological processes to control urban run-off, planners are today approaching landscape designers for advice in cost-effective techniques in water management. The trend in Malmö is to replace traditional planning procedures with a more integrated structure to city planning with water, green structure and waste plans being developed alongside the masterplan. Source control principles (infiltration and percolation), combined with detention/retention techniques (ponds and wetlands) form the basis of the approach at Malmö. Old watercourses have been re-instated as open drainage channels for surface water runoff and once-culverted streams have been replaced by a system of ponds and new wetland parks. The main objective was to control the quantity of urban run-off, but the resulting blue-green corridor of a naturalistic landscape also serves as an ecological base for a more sustainable city with new wildlife habitats.

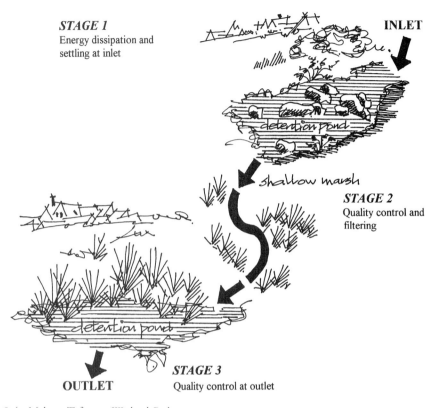

STAGE 1
Energy dissipation and
settling at inlet

INLET

shallow marsh

STAGE 2
Quality control and
filtering

detention pond

OUTLET   *STAGE 3*
Quality control at outlet

Figure 9.4   Malmö, Tofttanas Wetland Park.

The Toftanas Wetland Park (Figure 9.4) includes an attenuation facility for an area of Malmö where the existing outfall was unable to accommodate the increased run-off from a new residential development. Stormwater is controlled in three zones: (1) it passes through an inlet pond which serves as a sediment trap for heavier material; (2) water runs in a low flow channel meandering through a shallow marsh wetland within an excavated storage area. There is also a terraced dry pond which is flooded only during extreme wet weather; and (3) water is detained in a permanent pool at the outlet. Toftanas Wetland Park now provides good habitats for birds and wildlife which are protected by allowing public access only to the dry terraces. This system is an effective means of reducing peak flows and removing pollution. Measurements of water quality show a 40 per cent reduction in nitrogen and phosphorus.

The Sallerupsroad root zone (reed bed) facility in east Malmö was constructed to treat stormwater from a new 160-acre development site. From an inlet pond, which also serves to remove sediment, water runs in a meandering creek to the root-zone section (Figure 9.5). The root-zone is built of soil beds sited under a controlled groundwater level and planted with water plants (*Phragmites*, *Typha*, *Iridaceae*, *Phalaris*) which absorb nutrients and heavy metals in the stormwater. The pond and creek pre-treat the water as well as equalizing flow before it reaches the root zone.

The Earth Centre, Doncaster

The 'Living Machine' and wetland surface water treatment processes at the Earth Centre near Doncaster (Chapter 11) exemplify a fully integrated

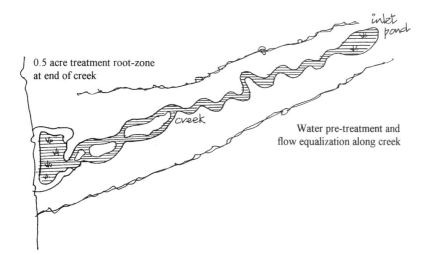

Figure 9.5   Malmö, Sallerupsroad root-zone (reed bed) facility.

approach. Waste water is recycled and purified in a series of tanks comprising a carefully sequenced network of micro-organisms and plants to break down harmful pollutants. In a simple greenhouse building the Living Machine replicates different aquatic ecosystems to treat waste from the Centre. Water is passed through a Bio Fence for final cleaning then stored for irrigation on site. The resulting water quality meets Environment Agency standards and ultimately water rejoins the natural water cycle through infiltration.

The above examples demonstrate the effectiveness of sustainable water planning in reducing the impact of urbanization and facilitating the recycling of a valuable resource. The creation of wetlands is a cost-effective and ecologically efficient method of meeting the environmental demands of tomorrow's cities. Source control can integrate water management with planning for recreation and planning incentives could significantly influence developers to release valuable development land for natural detention and filtering techniques. A wider strategy for water management to include brownwater purification would increase economic viability.

VEGETATION PLANS

In order that appropriate planting and management decisions can be taken with regard to sustainability objectives city regions need to develop vegetation plans (Figure 9.6). It is common practice for small-scale decisions to be taken concerning vegetation in cities without regard to the bigger picture.

Early cities had little non-productive vegetation. Urban land, often within city walls, was too scarce and valuable. As the technology of warfare changed and ruling elites consolidated their power, cities expanded beyond their protective walls. Physical expansion, together with lower building densities and relative peace, allowed gardens and parks to be created within the urban structure. These helped to raise land values. Horticultural design and management have a continuing influence on present-day city vegetation (Chapters 10 and 13). Typically we see 'amenity planting' or clear-stemmed trees placed individually in verdant close mown lawns with ornamental shrub and flower beds. This kind of gardenesque vegetation often lacks a functional role and does not respond to sustainability principles. To establish and maintain this vegetation requires heavy inputs of labour, machinery, fuel, chemicals and water often causing pollution of the air, water and soil, creating noise and destroying wildlife habitats.

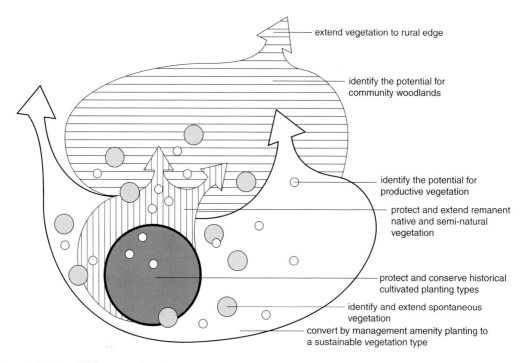

Figure 9.6 Potential for vegetation change.

Urbanization has overwhelmed natural and semi-natural vegetation, though fragments remain and can suggest plant palettes for particular locations. The sustainability objective of 'the most effective result for the least effort' should be tempered by practical and aesthetic considerations (Chapters 10 and 13). The main categories of vegetation now found in cities are the cultivated plant groups, remnant native and semi-natural plant communities and naturalized plant communities of robust and spontaneous exotic plants, often on abandoned land. However, urban sustainability could be enhanced by providing more productive landscapes in urban areas. These could include: city forests, bio-mass planting for fuel, community woodlands and orchards, nutteries and herb gardens, food-for-free hedgerows, allotments, fungi cellars and salad plots. Rees recommends that open-space planning should be integrated with other policies to increase 'local self-reliance in respect of food production, forest products, water supply, carbon sinks, etc.' (1997, p. 308). Areas of produc-

tive vegetation would thus improve the input–output balance of resources in cities, or in Rees' terms, reduce the ecological footprint. Such areas would also provide contact between communities, individuals and the land which is often abstract and remote for urban dwellers. The development of community gardens to grow food would help raise environmental awareness and self-reliance (Chapter 4) and many examples of this kind of initiative can be found in countries such as Germany and the Netherlands and increasingly in the UK. The New Towns had better vegetation plans than contemporary developments in other parts of the UK (Turner, 1996, p. 377).

Sustainable vegetation plans should therefore incorporate urban vegetation types which are native to the city region and will yield a planting character based on the city's ecological legacy (Spirn, 1984, p. 188). Species should be selected which are appropriate to the site conditions and are successional in the sense of having the capacity to maintain their structure and integrity over successive generations with the minimum of maintenance and resource inputs (Dunnett and Hitchmouth, 1996, p. 45). Multi-functional objectives should be integrated with vegetation plans to increase their relative sustainability, e.g. community participation through communal ownership and management; productive landscapes for food, timber and fuel; for wild life habitats (Rees, 1997), and to identify the potential for change in existing vegetation through sustainable management techniques (Chapter 13).

Sustainable vegetation plans should:

- moderate climatic extremes of city environments by cooling hot summer winds, by providing shelter and shade and by transpiration and trapping air-borne particles;
- aid surface water management by increasing soil porosity and water take-up through transpiration;

- choose vegetation types and management techniques for diversity, regeneration, and succession;
- utilize appropriate scales for vegetation communities in city regions, neighbourhoods and on individual sites (Dunnett, 1995, p. 28);
- provide for simplicity and robustness in the structure and composition of vegetation types;
- require low-energy inputs for soil preparation, planting stock production and plant establishment;
- require low inputs of non-renewable fuels, pesticides, herbicides, and treated piped water, and minimum maintenance operations.

Potentially the most effective and quickest route to more sustainable city vegetation is through the adoption of alternative management objectives and techniques for the conversion of less-sustainable vegetation types (Chapter 13). For example, on

Figure 9.7 Hundertwasser, Rolling Hills Hot Springs Village.

Blackheath in SE London the closely mown amenity grass areas not used for sports pitches were converted into herbaceous rich grasslands between 1995–99. Instead of mowing every two weeks, the meadow areas now have one cut in September and all arisings are removed. If this type of meadow were to be widely distributed with vegetated corridor links to the edge of the metropolitan region they could help provide new habitats for the song birds and insects that have been in decline in the country-side due to the intensification of agricultural produc-tion.

ECO-BUILDING PLANS

An area-wide strategy or plan for eco-building needs to be developed by city regions to define a frame-work which enables individual decisions on building designs to be taken with regard to sustainability objectives. Much twentieth-century planning has been widely criticized as providing a legacy of sick and sterile architecture. Hundertwasser, the radical Austrian artist, has proposed a new profession: 'the architecture doctor' (Hundertwasser, 1997) to coun-teract this problem. His philosophy is to mend the existing urban fabric by bringing nature back into the cities and repairing the landscape devastated by building (Restany, 1998) (Figure 9.7). This and other radical argument has spawned a wealth of information and advice on these issues; some is explored further in Chapter 10. The Green Building Digest (2000) is one example of a range of new web-based resources which are now available.

Some useful points can be extracted from the dis-cussion promoted by this kind of radical thinking which can help to justify the need for new architec-tural approaches based on eco-building. For example, greener cities have multiple benefits including more opportunities to sustain wildlife through the provi-sion of natural habitats and improving the value of amenity vegetation. The reasons for making vege-tated buildings are both ecological and economic. Vegetation enables cities to hold more water, take in more carbon dioxide and give out more oxygen. It also reduces glare, prevents reflections between build-

Figure 9.8 Hundertwasser, tree-covered roofscape.

ing surfaces, protects buildings from the elements and absorbs noise. Vegetation provides insulation: cooling in summer and conserving heat in winter thereby reducing energy costs. Greener streets and housing areas are more desirable to live in and often have higher monetary values.

Roofs provide the most significant opportunities in cities for eco-building (Figure 9.8). Advances in technology have overcome conventional barriers to vegetated roof construction and opened up possibil-ities from the smallest scale infill as at Sevenoaks Library (Figure 9.9) to the creation of new village communities in East Hanover (Figure 9.10). While the former provides visual appeal as well as a source of food and shelter for wildlife, the latter makes a wider environmental contribution by helping to cleanse the air. In Germany green roofs are recog-nized for the positive functions they fulfil, both tech-nical and environmental and in more than fifteen

Figure 9.9 Sevenoaks, library extension with green roof.

Figure 9.10 East Hanover, green roofing.

large cities vegetated roofs are now required by law and eligible for government subsidy. Studies on the performance statistics of roofs indicate that surface temperatures of traditional roofs can rise to over 80°C in summer while the green roof stays around 40°C, thus ameliorating the hot dry conditions of the city with a shady cover which can also increase the insulation value of a roof by as much as 10 per cent. In addition, green roofs act like a sponge storing between 50 per cent and 80 per cent of the natural rainfall, depending on the substrate. This is reflected in the servicing of some German cities where the charges for being connected to the sewer system are lower for green-roofed houses than for conventional dwellings.

The service life of a roofing membrane can be extended by a layer of planting. Scrivens' (1980–82) studies into roof gardens revealed that the roof membrane on the Kensington High Street building, originally Derry & Toms department store, was in 1980 discovered to be in excellent condition after half a century while exposed conventional flat roof surfaces have a 10–15-year life expectancy. Intensive vegetation (trees and shrubs) planting on roof gardens can filter out up to 80 per cent of suspended dust and air particles. By using a system of extensive greenery such as mosses and sedums the additional weight of vegetation can be minimized to 50–150 kg per square metre thus avoiding the need to reinforce existing roof structures. Such planting requires little care or watering thereby reducing roof maintenance costs. By 1989 there was an estimated one million square metres of such low maintenance grass roofs under construction in West Germany.

In his futuristic *City of Tomorrow* Le Corbusier instigated the trend by architects and planners towards raising imposing structures up into the sky without acknowledging the full human and social implications. In the new millennium designers will need to look at the city from ecological perspectives. They might become 'great mounds of vegetation' (Turner, 1996, p. 98) (Figure 9.11) with a network of green architectural zones transforming the skin of the city into a living landscape.

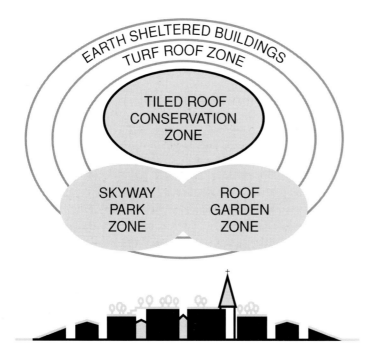

Figure 9.11 Eco-cities resembling green hills.

GREENING METHODS IN PRACTICE

Block 103, Kreuzberg, Berlin

This project is an example of a radical new approach to ecological renewal in an existing high density area. One green feature in particular, the vertical swamp, is highly innovative. Rows of swamp grasses in planters have been attached to the end façade on a building to provide a water cleansing facility. Measured amounts of water are released into the top planter and filter down through successive layers of grasses through a system of pipes and drains. At the end of the process, clean water is ready for reuse. This is one of a framework of pilot projects which includes roof planting, wall climbers, balcony and terrace planters and courtyard tree and shrub planting. New community gardens have been introduced that incorporate a 100-metre long wetland area to clean and filter water for recycling.

Wegsfeldhof, Hanover

The Wegsfeldhof district in east Hanover is an example of community planning using green architectural form. The new village comprises low-rise energy-efficient dwellings and is immediately distinguished from its more ordinary urban surroundings by its living green roofscape. Virtually all the dwellings, including the village school, are covered with a layer of grass which visually dominates the built environment in a variety of slopes and roof forms. It is the extent of green roofing throughout the entire village which is particularly impressive providing an immediate sense of unity and community to a new area of urban growth.

The greening of buildings is one aspect of an integrated approach to urbanization where enlightened architects, planners and developers work together with the community to produce a sustainable landscape strategy. Reviving the city with living roofs, walls and squares will be a significant step towards a healthier quality of city life (Johnston and Newton, 1993).

SUSTAINABLE LAND-USE PLANS

Consideration of sustainability in existing towns, urbanization projects and the selection of land for urbanization therefore gives rise to a number of questions: (1) Should the density of existing settlements be increased or should we build on agricultural land? (2) Should we expand existing settlements or start new settlements? (3) How should we choose between building on the most scenic land, the most agriculturally productive land and the land with the highest nature conservation value?

The sustainable development agenda has stimulated much thought and debate on these and other issues in relation to land use, development, transport and the statutory land use planning system (e.g. Breheny, 1992; Haughton and Hunter, 1994; Jackson and Roberts, 1997). The UK government requirement that all development plans should involve a system of strategic environmental assessment (Department of the Environment, 1993) and incorporate sustainable development objectives is symptomatic of the burgeoning activity in these areas, although careful analyses reveal that progress is slow and the barriers to progress are profound (e.g. Hales, 2000). Our concern in this section is with the methods sustainability-conscious landscape planners and designers should use, rather than with the final decisions. Our recommended method can be described as 'updated McHarg'.

The method Ian McHarg proposed in *Design with Nature* (1992, re-issue of original published in 1969) was based on mapping the resource value of land in as many ways as possible: aquifer recharge value, scenic value, wildlife value, agricultural value, etc. His initial idea was that each of these types of value could be hand-drawn onto overlay maps. Placing the layers on top of one another produced an X-ray-like composite (Chapter 14) in which the whitest zones had the least value and the darkest zones the highest value. The flaws in this approach were that each layer was accorded the same value and one could never be sure that the set of layers was representative. McHarg believed that computers would be able to solve both problems and his work gave a major boost to the development of what have become known as Geographical Information Systems (GIS).

Our proposed update of the McHargian approach is that it should be treated as a decision-support system rather than a decision-making procedure. A landscape planning database can improve the quality of land use decisions. Proposals which are sustainable from one point of view may be revealed as unsustainable from other points of view. For example, one could express the fact that it is financially cheaper to expand existing settlements, rather than initiate new towns, by describing the policy as financially sustainable. But if the expansion takes place on land of high ecological, scenic or agricultural value, the policy will be less-sustainable from these points of view.

A landscape planning database can be used to find the land which is best suited for urbanization. Often, as McHarg suggests, this will be the white land which comes through the overlay process as having the lowest aggregate landscape value. This method of choosing land for development would assist in sustaining landscape values. In the UK, the initiative for land development often comes from land owners who are thinking more about profit than the public good. Planning authorities accommodate some urbanization proposals in local plans and accede to other proposals from determined applicants supported by government guidance on the numbers of new homes to be built. This is a haphazard and short-term approach. The concept of landscape sustainability enjoins a longer-term view. We should hypothesize that the UK population will double, over an undefined period, and then consider in what order our land should be urbanized. If it does not happen, so much the better. If it does happen, as all history suggests it will, then expansion can be on the basis of a sustainable landscape strategy. A long-term urbanization plan might therefore include the following elements:

- Urbanization should take place on land which, in its existing use, has a relatively low capacity to yield public and private goods. As McHarg suggested in his Plan for the Valleys, this is likely to exclude land in river valleys and agriculturally productive land.
- Plans for urbanization should be fully integrated with landform plans (e.g. for winning minerals and disposing of excavation and demolition materials), with vegetation plans (e.g. for new habitats and new forests) and with water plans (e.g. for new lakes, streams and reservoirs).
- Settlements should be on land which takes advantage of environmental conditions (e.g. sheltered land rather than exposed land).
- Pedestrian and cycle routes should be integrated with public transport and should receive priority in transport planning.

These examples of sustainable land use strategies are intended to illustrate the long-term approach required by the concept of sustainability. A Landscape Planning Information System (a specialized GIS) where this information could be collated and manipulated could help provide more sustainable decision-making and bring about significant improvements in city form.

Case study: Greenwich Peninsula

The Millennium Dome at Greenwich opened on 31 December 1999. The building project has rarely been out of the news since the site was selected in February 1996 to host the UK's national Millennium celebrations (Irvine, 1999, p. 2). What is not so well known is the development of the eastern section of the peninsula which includes the Millennium Village, retail and leisure developments, new parks, wetlands and riverside walks.

The Greenwich Peninsula is a 300-acre site located east of the City of London, on the south bank of the River Thames. It is a useful case study because the Greenwich Council has had an Environment Strategy for a decade and because it is one of the largest development projects in London at the time of writing. This former industrial site is now owned by the UK government's urban regeneration agency English Partnerships. 'Greenwich Peninsula' is a 1990s' name associated with the urban regeneration project. The area used to be known as Greenwich Level or Greenwich Marsh. The Marsh can still be overlooked from the south by the higher land of the Blackheath-Shooters Hill ridge but much of the ancient ridge and marsh character has been dissipated.

In the 1820s Greenwich Marsh had wharves and associated riverside industry but was still the largest marsh area near the city (Mills, 1999, p. 13). But by the end of the nineteenth century it was heavily industrialized – a coal gas works which opened in 1880 and covered 140 acres was said to be the largest plant of its kind in Europe. These works and the adjacent Blackwell Point power station closed between 1970 and 1980. Half the peninsula was then abandoned and site clearance works began in 1990. As this was a brownfield site, the decision was sustainable from a land use point of view. When the Millennium development began in 1996, little was left of the old marshland character, though the ancient hydrological and geological conditions were

largely unchanged. The high public profile of the Dome project combined with the late commissioning of the building and the speed of the development programme has had a major effect on the planning and design process. It was conducted with good intentions but too little forethought. The changes to landform, water, vegetation and buildings are reviewed below.

Greenwich Peninsula: landform planning

Soil and subgrade contamination from the former industrial land use had to be treated before the new commercial and residential construction could begin. Specialist pollution consultants had been working on the site for twelve years before the site remediation began and the policy adopted was to deal with all pollutants on site excepting those which were too toxic. The two tar beds, a legacy from the coal gas production, had to be removed. These were excavated 100m diameter by 15m deep and the

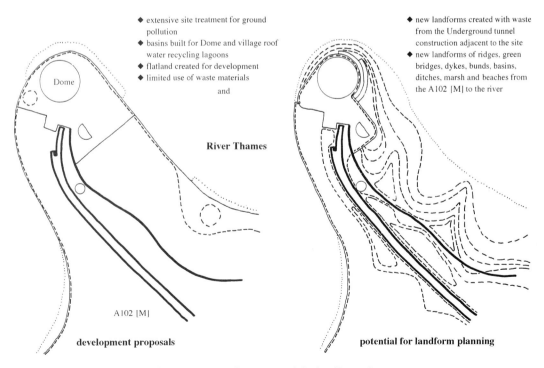

Figure 9.12 Greenwich: the development proposals – potential for landform planning.

contaminated spoil was transported off site, to authorized landfill sites. To clean the polluted ground, techniques employed on site were soil washing and vapour treatments. Several new water basins and earth bunds were made. The bunds were designed to screen individual plots from the arterial roads they have engineering profiles and were constructed from materials with low contamination excavated from the peninsula and capped with clean topsoil for planting. In spite of all this, the peninsula is being developed without an integrated landform plan or a clear vision. A long-term plan (Figure 9.12) could have done the following:

● ensured that the A102 [M] was contained within an ecological corridor;
● ensured that the bunds surrounding the road were treated as a projection of the Blackheath plateau;
● allowed for the creation of a new marshland between the bunds and the new development;

● allowed for the extension of the dykes from the bunds to the riverside embankment;
● provided the opportunity for the establishment of a greenway system for pedestrians and cyclists on top of the dykes and bunds.

Greenwich Peninsula: water planning

The volume of water run-off from development on a scale such as at Greenwich Peninsula creates a need and an opportunity to respond with a sustainable development strategy. To protect the ground water from potential site pollutants and to prevent any lateral movement of materials in the substrate, infiltration of surface water has had to be controlled. There are no infiltration basins on the site and all the new water bodies are separated from the substrate by an impermeable barrier. Run-off from the road system is collected into a piped network and is not treated on site. English Partnerships, the owners of the site, have agreed water plans and targets with

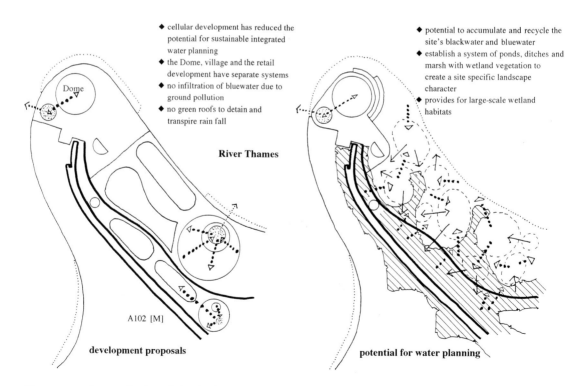

◆ cellular development has reduced the potential for sustainable integrated water planning
◆ the Dome, village and the retail development have separate systems
◆ no infiltration of bluewater due to ground pollution
◆ no green roofs to detain and transpire rain fall

River Thames

A102 [M]

development proposals

◆ potential to accumulate and recycle the site's blackwater and bluewater
◆ establish a system of ponds, ditches and marsh with wetland vegetation to create a site specific landscape character
◆ provides for large-scale wetland habitats

potential for water planning

Figure 9.13 Greenwich: the cellular development proposals – potential for integrated water planning.

each developer and will have independent monitoring of the results by the Building Research Establishment. Rainwater run-off from the Dome roof is to be recycled through reed beds and is used to service toilet facilities. A 30 per cent reduction in water demand is to be achieved in the Millennium Village with the aid of a bluewater recycling system and reed bed storage lagoons. In addition, stored and filtered roof water from the new retail store will be re-used in irrigation systems for new landscapes in the adjacent commercial zone.

The water plan objectives have been integrated into the open space planning of the two parks The Meridian Park to the north-west of the Dome includes reed beds which will provide a localized filtering system for roof run-off and a public wetland landscape linked to the ecological river terraces which are planned to form a habitat corridor along the river bank. The water from this wetland will be filtered and used in the Dome's toilet system. In the Southern Park the main water feature is the reed bed

storage lagoons which are used to polish roofwater before it is recycled within the village. This water body has two zones: one is a protected nature reserve with no public access, the other is a safe wetland park with public access. Flexibility is built into the design of the reed beds so that the water circulation can be altered and the total capacity increased.

The policy adopted at the Greenwich Peninsula treats water planning in a cellular way rather than as an integrated system. Each developer has planned buildings and landscapes to meet environmental targets, rather than forming part of an integrated water plan (Figures 9.13 and 9.14). The Greenwich Council planners see the Greenwich Peninsula development as having a 'snowballing effect of awareness' among developers in spite of the disadvantages highlighted here.

Greenwich Peninsula: vegetation planning

No overall sustainable vegetation strategy was prepared for the Greenwich Peninsula though individual

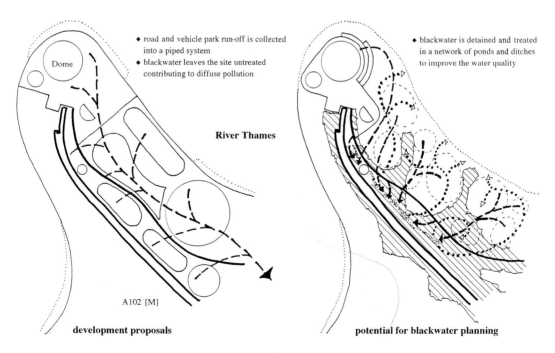

Figure 9.14   Greenwich: blackwater proposals – potential for blackwater planning.

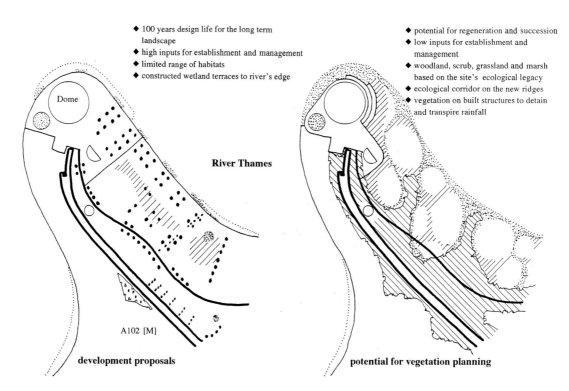

Figure 9.15   Greenwich: the development proposals – potential for vegetation planning.

development projects are being designed with the general intention of using native species and creating wetlands. For example, salt marsh terraces are being formed to provide strips of semi-natural habitat along the Thames river edge. These measures are welcome but a more comprehensive strategy (Figure 9.15) would provide for:

- animals as well as plants;
- a range of habitat types appropriate to the peninsula;
- a landscape ecological strategy for relationships between created habitats;
- a sustainable landscape management strategy for the new habitats;
- plans to maximize community involvement in landscape management and minimize the use of chemicals and fossil fuels;

- plans to derive sustainable food production (e.g. fruit, nuts, fungi and fish) from the created habitats.

Greenwich Peninsula: Planning for eco-building

Development of the peninsula includes a residential area (1,400 homes) known as the Millennium Village. The masterplan was conceived by Ralph Erskine and developed from his concept of community architecture, pioneered three decades ago at the Byker estate in Newcastle. The Millennium Village was planned with energy-efficient site planning and construction techniques. High density housing encircles the large Southern Park. The scale of the open spaces was related to community groupings to engender social cohesion so that each community of 300 dwellings has a communal open space and so-called 'gossip groups' of 30–50 units have smaller

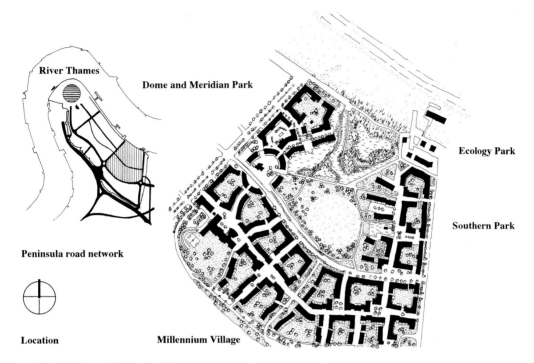

Figure 9.16 Greenwich: Millennium Village layout and the open space planning.

semi-private open spaces. These are connected to the wider landscape through a network of corridors and large green courts (*Building*, 1998, p. 25) (Figure 9.16).

This type of open space planning is common in Sweden, where Erskine has lived and worked. It was, however, severely criticized by Rasmussen (1948) when he praised the English tradition of providing private gardens instead of anonymous 'public open space'. England has no strong tradition of using communal open space in housing areas and, in places like New Ash Green in Kent, residents have resented the maintenance charges. From this point of view, local open space traditions have not been sustained. Nor are the supposedly ecological buildings being designed with green roofs to assist in surface water management and provide additional habitat space.

CONCLUSION

While it is true that provision has been made at Greenwich for public transport, that the buildings are less energy consumptive than some contemporaries, and that some landscape details have some claim to sustainability, the basic landscape planning harks back to the 1960s and adds little new thinking to the debate. It is of a lower standard than the New Towns (Turner, 1996, p. 358) and it neglects the principles of sustainable planning in relation to landform, water, vegetation, eco-building and land use which the authors believe are fundamental to the planning of more sustainable city form. This view concurs with others who believe that there is as yet little coherent vision of how sustainability would translate into practice in terms of city planning (e.g. Rees, 1997). However, an examination of the Greenwich Peninsula provides a useful way to review these topics and then consider how they could have been applied to this large and important area. Redevelopment of the Greenwich Peninsula is more sustainable than many contemporary developments in the UK but only in detail – and even the details lag behind the best of current practice (e.g. in Sweden, Germany). The development also falls short of the good landscape planning practice seen in the UK New Towns. There was no overall landform strategy, as there was at Hemel Hempsted and Harlow, nor a vegetation strategy, as there was at Runcorn and Warrington. Nor were the surface water management policies, such as those initiated at Welwyn and Milton Keynes, carried forward as they should have been. Perhaps worst of all the new landscape of Greenwich Marsh lacks vision. We seem to have learned little from the original thinking of innovative landscape planners such as McHarg (1992) and Lyle (1994) and the more comprehensive city greening strategies in other countries such as Germany. Certainly we do not appear to have moved forward to prevent the short-circuiting of natural cycles in urban areas, or to provide new thinking on how to create exciting designs built on a solid ecological foundation where the landscape is not only able to survive, but to thrive. Future projects of the Greenwich type should be accompanied by sustainable long-term plans: for landform, for water, for vegetation, for eco-building and for land use.

REFERENCES

Breheny, M. J. (ed.) (1992) *Sustainable Development and Urban Form* (London, Pion).

Breheny, M. J. and Rockwood, R. (1993) Planning the sustainable city region, in A. Blowers (ed.) *Planning for a Sustainable Environment*, (London, Earthscan), pp. 150–189.

Building (1998) Interview, Ralph Erskine, 24 April, pp. 22–25.

CIRIA (2000) *Sustainable Urban Drainage Systems: Design Manual for Scotland and Northern Ireland C52; Design Manual for England and Wales C522; Best practice C523.* Project RP555 (London, CIRIA).

Department of the Environment (1993) *Environmental Appraisal of Development Plans: A Good Practice Guide* (London, The Stationery Office).

DETR (Department of Environment, Transport and the Regions) (1999) *Towards an Urban Renaissance: Final Report of the Urban Task Force* (London, E and FN Spon).

Dunnett, N. (1995) Harnessing anarchy, *Landscape Design*, 245, November, 25–29.

Dunnett, N. and Hitchmouth, J. (1996) Excitement and energy, *Landscape Design*, 251, June, 43–46.

Gardiner, J. (1991) *River projects and conservation: a manual for holistic appraisal* (Chichester, Wiley).

Green Building Digest (2000) http://www.qub.ac.uk/tbe/arc/research/gbd/index.html, Accessed 9 February 2000.

Hales, R. (2000) Land use development planning and the notion of sustainable development: exploring constraint and facilitation within the English planning system, *Journal of Environmental Planning and Management*, 43(1), 99–121.

Haughton, G. and Hunter, C. (1994) *Sustainable Cities* (London, Jessica Kingsley/Regional Studies Association).

Hundertwasser, F. (1997) *For a More Human Architecture in Harmony with Nature* (Cologne, Benedikt Taschen Verlag GmbH).

Irvine, A. (1999) *The Battle for the Millennium Dome* (London, Irvine News Agency).

Jackson, T. and Roberts, P. (1997) Greening the Fife economy: ecological modernisation as a pathway for local economic development, *Journal of Environmental Planning and Management*, 40(5), 615–629.

Johnston, J. and Newton, J. (1993) *Building Green: A Guide to Using Plants on Roofs, Walls and Pavements* (London, Ecology Unit).

Lawrence, F. and Norton-Taylor, R. (2000) Lifting the lid on secret Britain, *The Guardian*, 27 January.

Lyle, J. T. (1994) *Regenerative Design for Sustainable Development* (New York, John Wiley).

McHarg, I. L. (1992) *Design with Nature* (New York, John Wiley).

Mills, M. (1999) *Greenwich Marsh: The 300 Years before the Dome* (London, M. Wright).

Rasmussen, I. E. (1948) *London: The Unique City* (London, Jonathan Cape).

Rees, W. E. (1997) Is 'sustainable city' an oxymoron?, *Local Environment*, 2(3), 304–310.

Restany, P. (1998) Hundertwasser: The Painter-King with the 5 Skins (Verlang GmbH, Cologne, Benedict Tascher).

Scrivens, S. (1980–82) Series of case studies of roof gardens, in *Architects Journal*. Derry & Toms, London, *AJ*, 15/10/80, pp. 759–766; Kantonsspital Basle, *AJ*, 17/02/82, pp. 65–70; Kingston Hospital, Kingston upon Thames, *AJ*, 24/02/82, p. 89; Design guide, *AJ*, 17/03/82, pp. 73–87.

SEPA (Scottish Environment Protection Agency) (1996) *Guide to Surface Water Best Management Practices* (Glasgow, SEPA).

Spirn, A.W. (1984) *The Granite Garden: Urban Nature and Human Design* (New York, Basic Books).

Turner, T. (1996) *City as Landscape: A Post-Modern View of Design and Planning* (London, E & FN Spon).

Wackernagel, M. and Rees, W. E. (1995) *Our Ecological Footprint: Reducing Human Impact on the Earth* (Gabriola Island, BC, New Society).

10

RESOURCES: THE RAW MATERIALS OF LANDSCAPE

Nigel Dunnett and Andy Clayden

SUMMARY

In this chapter we consider how the appropriate selection, use, manipulation and management of materials and resources, both organic and inorganic can aid the achievement of sustainable designed landscapes. Particular emphasis is placed on the environmental profiling of materials and schemes (at all stages of production and use). Plant selection and planting design are discussed at two levels. At the holistic level, vegetation can play a major role in achieving wider environmental sustainability objectives (for example, biodiversity and air and water quality). At the specific level, the actual operations of landscape planting must also be sustainable in terms of plant establishment and management, as well as at the plant production stage. The various current approaches to Life Cycle Assessment and Environmental Labelling of hard materials are introduced as the means for making informed choices in materials selection and guidelines for more sustainable design solutions, for both construction and planting are given.

INTRODUCTION

Appropriate selection, use, manipulation and management of materials and resources, both organic and inorganic, are central to the achievement of sustainable designed landscapes. In fact, it could be argued that deciding the nature and source of materials, and the way in which they are put together and interact on-site, can be the most fundamental and straightforward way in which designers can influence landscape sustainability. In terms of sustainable design it is impossible to separate materials selection, resource manipulation and subsequent management from the creative design process, all are dependent on each other.

Landscape professionals are perhaps better placed than all others involved in environmental design and management to embrace and fully promote the principles of sustainable design. Landscape architecture has a fundamental relationship with the environment, and landscape architects uniquely work with the full range of materials, both living and inert. Landscape architecture is often characterized as being firmly rooted in the uniqueness of 'place', yet opportunities to reinforce local and regional character and identity are often missed, at the expense of the continuing proliferation of the 'international style'. If the profession is to make its full contribution to the creation of sustainable environments, then, in addition to the up-front capital cost of materials, designers must be aware of the wider environmental cost of the materials they specify. In this chapter we discuss sustainable approaches to working with landscape vegetation and hard materials. In particular we discuss how materials selection and use can not only reduce wider environmental harm, but actually increase the environmental performance of any scheme.

For the purposes of this chapter, 'resources' will be defined as those components of a landscape that have potential to contribute to the functioning of that landscape. Physical resources (solid or liquid) will be referred to as 'materials'. They can, of course, be 'hard' (inorganic or non-living construction materials) or 'soft' (plants). Materials form the physical structure and form of landscape. They may be imported on to the site, already be present, or may be created *in situ*. Other resources are less tangible but are crucial to concepts of sustainability, such as energy, water and mineral nutrients. They are vital components of ecologically functioning systems. This range of materials, embracing both the living and non-living, organic and inorganic, upon which landscape professionals draw, sets them apart from others involved in the construction industries such as architects, engineers and urban designers.

The best way to consider the sustainable use of resources and materials within a designed landscape is to think of the site as a functioning system, with inputs and outputs of resources, and internal cycling (Figure 10.1). Unsustainable systems tend to be 'open', that is they require high resource input, minimize internal cycling, and release substantial waste and energy. Conversely, those involved in making and managing sustainable landscapes will aim to create systems that are 'closed', i.e. to reduce direct energy or energy-demanding resource inputs and maximize internal cycling of materials and resources.

It is important to realize that the closing of systems can be done at a range of scales. Individual sites cannot be seen in isolation. Cycles can be detected at site-specific to global scales. Sustainable resource management aims to close these cycles at the lowest possible point in this hierarchy.

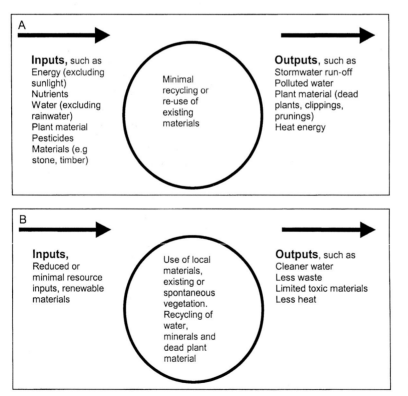

Figure 10.1 A systems approach to landscape. A: an open, unsustainable system. B: a more sustainable, closed system.

SUSTAINABLE LANDSCAPE PLANTING: HARNESSING NATURAL PROCESSES

The selection of plant material and the way that vegetation is used on site can have a profound influence on the sustainability of any designed or planned landscape. This influence is apparent at two levels:

1 At the holistic level vegetation can play a major role in achieving overall sustainability objectives. Plants and vegetation are crucial to ecological functioning and the promotion of natural processes and are therefore central to achieving environmental sustainability. Vegetation contributes, to a greater or lesser extent, to the main indicators of environmental sustainability: enhancement of air and water quality, biodiversity and soil resources. Vegetation also has a role to play in achieving social and economic sustainability.

2 At the specific level, the actual operations of landscape planting should also be sustainable: plant establishment and maintenance decisions must also be made about the practicalities of establishing and managing vegetation with the minimum inputs and outputs of resources necessary to achieve the objectives of that planting.

In this section we will first consider how the appropriate use of vegetation can contribute to overall sustainability, before going on to discuss details of planting design and specification. Vegetation management is dealt with in more detail in Chapter 13, however, it is impossible to separate management from considerations of planting design and vegetation establishment and therefore some aspects of management will also be touched upon in this chapter.

The contribution of vegetation to sustainable landscapes

Traditionally in landscape design, plant material has been selected for functional purposes (e.g. structure planting and screening) or aesthetic purposes (ornamental planting). There are, however, many other reasons to use plants, most of which can also fulfil functional and aesthetic objectives. It would be wrong to consider planting, vegetation and design strategies as a complete solution to these problems: in many cases they may ameliorate problems which require economic and political solutions.

1 *Pollution control and improvement in air quality* Vegetation, and in particular trees, may offer significant opportunities as buffers of pollution in cities (Lawson, 1996), although there is a research need to quantify many of the claims that are made. Plants can act as sinks for airborne pollution by either intercepting particulate or absorbing gaseous pollutants and heavy metals. Particulate pollution in particular has been blamed for exacerbating respiratory illnesses. Trees can act as biological filters, removing large numbers of airborne particles. The most effective control is achieved when trees are planted as close as possible to a pollution source, forming a buffer around it (e.g. street trees). Vegetation also reduces wind speeds, increasing the deposition of particles in their vicinity (Hodge, 1995). In a wide-ranging review of trees and urban air pollution, Beckett *et al.* (1998) recommend concentrating tree planting in pollution 'hotspots', promoting urban and suburban woodlands to reduce background concentrations of pollutants. Increased planting of conifers, which appear to show the greatest efficiency in reducing pollution, because of the large leaf-area index of conifers and the retention of foliage through the year was also recommended. This clearly presents problems in terms of promotion of biodiversity and seasonal change in landscapes, as well as the technical consideration that many conifers themselves may be more sensitive to air pollution.

2 *Climate amelioration* The concentration of buildings and paved areas in urban areas leads to the formation of a specific urban climate characterized by higher night temperatures, restriction of wind (and therefore of dispersal of pollutants) and increased run-off of precipitation. At the larger scale, vegetation can have a positive influence on climate: through evapo-transpiration humidity is increased and the heat required for evaporation can reduce air temperatures. Therefore urban greenspace can

produce cool air, although areas of less than 1ha have little effect individually (Von Stulpnagel *et al.*, 1990). However, vegetation within individual sites can be used to create favourable micro-climates for site-users.

3   *Energy balance* The energy-saving potential of trees and other landscape vegetation has been well documented (McPherson, 1994). The shading effect of trees around buildings offers a low-cost way to reduce air conditioning and cooling requirements, which in turn reduces carbon dioxide emissions from electricity generation (only deciduous species are of value in this respect – evergreens may actually increase energy needs in winter through shading). Greening of walls can also reduce heat losses in winter, by up to 50 per cent of that from exposed walls (Von Stulpnagel *et al.*, 1990). Green roofs can also have an important insulating function.

4   *Productive uses* While some landscapes are formally regarded as being productive, wider landscape planting also has potential. Urban woodlands can produce low-grade wood products such as mulch and bark chip, and fuel, and in some instances, high quality timber (Hodge, 1995). Short-rotation woody coppice crops for bioenergy have also been advocated as a productive interim land use for derelict urban land. There is also much greater scope for using fruiting and other edible plants as part of landscape structure plantings: for example, currants and apple trees are frequently encountered in Scandinavian housing schemes. Even if not consumed by humans, they will benefit wildlife. Increased food production near to the point of consumption has wider value in terms of reduced energy consumption in packaging and transport, healthier diets, and increased contact of people with natural processes, as discussed in Chapter 4.

5   *Noise reduction* Many claims are made about the value of vegetation in noise suppression, but there is little empirical evidence for these claims. Mixed shelter belts of deciduous and coniferous trees 25–50 m wide have been found to significantly reduce noise from railway lines, compared with open space covered with grass (Kragh, 1979). Other reports point to the value of dense evergreen belts at least 6 m wide. However, in most cases the effect is probably psychological: a combination of a minor change in the frequency spectrum caused by vegetation, and partly the visual effect of screening (Kragh, 1981).

6   *Waste water and storm water purification* Constructed wetlands, for purification both of waste water and storm-water run-off, take advantage of the highly productive nature of marsh habitats which promotes uptake of nitrates and phosphates by aquatic plants and the sedimentation of particulate matter (Hough, 1995). Such wetlands can be multi-functional, having significant wildlife, habitat and aesthetic value. Green roofs have a major role in reducing storm-water run-off (Johnston and Newton, 1995).

7   *Counteraction of carbon emissions* In addition to their value in reducing heating and cooling needs, vegetation, and again trees in particular, act as sinks for carbon dioxide, which is a major contributor to the greenhouse effect and global warming. In general terms, this represents only a temporary 'carbon neutral', steady state solution: if the wood is burnt or rots down, the carbon dioxide will be returned to the atmosphere. Large areas are necessary to achieve any effect: in the UK a hectare of new planting may only each year counteract the annual carbon emissions of a few cars. In this light, large blocks of multi-aged woodland can be thought of as long-term CO_2 stores (Kendle and Forbes, 1997). The only positive net contribution that can be made by vegetation is in those cases where the products are used to displace fossil fuels, such as may be achieved by bio-energy coppice crops.

8   *Habitat/biodiversity* Increasing the biological richness of an area and promoting ecological functioning is one of the goals of a sustainable approach to landscape design. Standard or traditional landscape planting usually has minimal habitat value and contributes little to biodiversity. This is partly a result of limited plant selection at the design stage, partly a result of the design approach itself (producing single-layered plantings or monocultures) and partly through management which aims to preserve a desired species mix and age-structure to the vegetation in perpetuity. By introducing a natural vegetation structure and dynamic management, a

'biotope' approach to planting (see below) can maintain functional and aesthetic roles while also increasing habitat value. However, simple species choices in more traditional landscape plantings can radically alter the attractiveness of that planting to, for example, feeding insects. Ecological planting need not be restricted to naturalistic zones within a scheme or habitat creation sites, neither need it involve just native species.

9 *Increasing local distinctiveness and sense of place* Sustainable landscapes have been described as those which are 'multi-functional, low maintenance, biologically diverse and expressive of "place"' (McPherson, 1994). Reflecting or enhancing local distinctiveness through planting can help maintain ecological integrity in any given area and counters the trend for specification of relatively small number of landscape plants nation-wide (Dunnett and Hitchmough, 1996). It also makes aesthetic sense. Locally distinctive planting will usually take common local native plant communities as its starting point, but can also reflect local cultural uses of plants in gardens or the wider landscape (Kendle and Rose, 1999).

Some well-known examples illustrate the point, at different scales:

- The vegetation strategy for Warrington New Town linked new residential, retail and industrial development with the existing semi-natural woodland vegetation (Tregay and Gustavsson, 1983) (Figure 10.2).
- In one of the most celebrated contemporary gardens, the late Derek Jarman brilliantly abstracted key elements of the distinctive flora of the shingle ridges at Dungeness, Kent, and mixed them with rescued beach debris to produce a landscape on the shingle that could only be of that place (Jarman, 1995) (Figure 10.3).

As well as contributing to environmental sustainability in the above ways, vegetation also contributes significantly to social sustainability, through the restorative, physical and mental well-being benefits of contact with nature and green surroundings (Dunnett and Qasim, 1999).

It is quite apparent that landscape planting, and greenspace in general, can and should be multi-functional, fulfilling utilitarian, recreational and aesthetic needs, but also contributing strongly to ecological cycles and environmental enhancement. Selection and use of plant materials should reflect this multi-functionality. So, if landscape planting can contribute to general environmental sustainability, what are the key aspects of sustainable landscape planting? How does sustainable planting differ from standard landscape planting?

Key principles of sustainable landscape planting

Current mainstream or standard landscape planting is characterized by the widespread use of large numbers of a relatively few species and cultivars. An international design style has emerged which works

Figure 10.2 Native woodland structure planting separating commercial development from informal recreational space. Oakwood, Warrington New Town.

Figure 10.3 The use of indigenous species and local artefacts roots the late Derek Jarman's garden firmly in its context.

with relatively simple compositions such as the common urban forms of shrub mass, with or without marginal ground covers or emergent trees, street trees with or without turf below, and mown amenity turf (Thoday *et al.*, 1995). Such plantings usually make little reference to local character and ecology, are maintained to produce a static effect, and may require considerable resource inputs in site preparation, plant establishment and long-term maintenance.

In contrast, sustainable landscape planting has been defined as that which *enables reductions in energy or physical resource inputs* at the stock production, plant establishment and vegetation management stages, is *locally appropriate*, and which *maintains wider ecological integrity* (Dunnett and Hitchmough, 1996). Sustainable plantings are often *dynamic* in that management does not aim to preserve the system in a steady state, but rather,

natural processes such as self-regeneration and nutrient cycling are encouraged. Sustainable plantings usually contribute to *local biodiversity*, but not necessarily through the total inclusion of native plant species. Diversity in vegetation is generally agreed to confer some resistance to environmental change and pests and diseases. The greater the number of plant species within a system, the more attractive it is for feeding and shelter to wildlife, and to predator species. Diversity also implies complexity and visual richness (Dunnett, 1995).

The basis of a sustainable approach to landscape planting must always be to choose species that are *suitable to the site*. This removes the need for expensive site manipulation, but also prevents long-term maintenance problems through specification of unsuitable plants. As a basis to sustainable planting design, therefore, the importance of thorough familiarity with site conditions cannot be over-emphasized.

Sound ecological principles are all very well, but for landscape planting to be truly sustainable it must also be *publicly acceptable* and *aesthetically pleasing*. Some landscape elements in certain contexts (such as traditional seasonal bedding) may fail to meet the above criteria but may be undesirable to remove for social or cultural reasons. A pragmatic approach is therefore desirable: provided the overall move is increasingly towards sustainability, a degree of flexibility can be built into the detail at any given site (Dunnett and Hitchmough, 1996).

One way of achieving acceptance of sustainable planting is through active community involvement at the design, implementation and management stages (Chapter 12). An inspiring example of this is the work of the charity Landlife in Liverpool, which creates very large-scale and beautiful flowering landscapes with native annuals on derelict inner city land, but also in vacant housing lots, school grounds and neighbourhood parks. Through their strong local links and outreach work they find the colourful effects encourage high community interaction with landscape.

Creating sustainable landscape planting: plant selection and planting

The creation of sustainable landscape vegetation involves what can seem like a complex array of considerations and decisions. Every stage of the process can be examined for its wider environmental implications. The major areas of decision, which are discussed below, include whether introduction of new plant material is necessary, the type of plant material to be used, establishment methods, the origin, provenance and source of material, and the methods involved in producing the material.

As discussed above, the starting point in the decision-making process is thorough site survey: site-responsive planting clearly evolves from knowledge of site conditions. An awareness of larger-scale vegetation patterns and structure in the immediate environment of the site and beyond is also extremely useful. The following three-stage protocol, although developed primarily for urban nature conservation, has much wider value:

1 Identify and plan for what already exists: a fundamental objective should be the enrichment of existing ecological capital.
2 Restore existing habitats which may be degraded.
3 Identify future potential. Create new habitats where land offers potential opportunities. Restore appropriate connections between habitats. These links can be within an individual site, or between a site and the surrounding area.

The value of this approach in a wider sense is that, first, it encourages the retention of vegetation capital, and, second, that ecological 'connectivity' is encouraged. Connectivity, or the linking of vegetation patches to enhance ecological functioning is a core principle of landscape ecology (Forman, 1995) and, if properly considered, ensures efficient movement of organisms, energy and nutrients within a site and between sites.

Manipulation of site conditions: traditional plantings versus sustainable plantings

This is perhaps an appropriate point to discuss site manipulation. Traditional, horticultural plantings have relied on relatively high fertility, organic matter and water availability for their success. Clearly, the continued satisfaction of these basic requirements goes against the principles of sustainable planting as outlined here. On many landscape sites, particularly urban sites, soils may be skeletal, nutrient poor, very free-draining, contaminated and subject to disturbance (Kendle and Forbes, 1997). Rather than trying to combat these problems by massive site manipulation (such as importation of topsoils, application of fertilizers and soil amendments), a more ecological approach is to work with these conditions. Adapting and learning from natural or spontaneous vegetation that grows under such conditions is the keystone of current ecological planting. In most instances, reduced fertility or other forms of environmental stress promote diversity and species-richness. An accessible introduction to creative adaptation of semi-natural vegetation to stressed substrates is given by Landlife (1997), and a detailed account by Kendle and Forbes (1997), while a brief introduction to mixed native–exotic systems is given later in this chapter.

VEGETATION STRATEGIES

The landscape designer is faced with an array of decisions, at all stages of the design process, which impinge on the sustainability of a scheme. These relate to issues of plant establishment techniques, site treatment, planting design and style and sourcing and specification of plant material.

There is no equivalent set of national guidelines to the BRE guidelines for building materials (see later in this chapter), that deals with the environmental profile of landscape planting. The major environmental impacts of landscape plantings are shown in Table 10.1 and discussed in more detail below.

Non-planting techniques

1   Retention of existing vegetation of value. A fundamental decision to be made is whether planting is necessary on all or part of the site. Surveys of existing site vegetation can give important clues about the nature of site conditions, and particularly soil characteristics. But there are other important reasons to be thoroughly familiar with existing vegetation. An important aspect of a sustainable approach to planting is to preserve and integrate vegetation already on site that may have ecological, structural or aesthetic value. Of course, retention of existing vegetation also gives a head start compared to starting afresh.

2   Natural regeneration. Encouraging natural regeneration as a means of vegetation establishment has advantages and disadvantages. Spontaneous natural vegetation will usually encourage species that are already plentiful in the area, and will ensure that the vegetation is directly suited to the site: competition will ensure that only those able to grow under the specific conditions of the site will survive. The same processes of competition may also encourage diversity of plant communities within a site as substrate and microclimate gradients select for different associations. Similarly an uneven-age structure may develop over time as successional processes take hold. Naturally regenerated systems are likely to be sustainable in that they will exhibit some of the characteristics of natural plant communities, such as nutrient cycling.

There are problems with this approach, however. The process is inherently unpredictable: there is no guarantee that the desired species will arrive, or even that the desired types of plant community or vegetation will develop. In fact in many instances, naturally regenerated communities may be species-poor. The vegetation that does arise may appear weedy, particularly in its early stages, and therefore is a problem with public acceptance in certain contexts.

Given these qualifications, natural regeneration can be very cost-effective as a means of producing site specific sustainable vegetation. An excellent example of this approach can be found at the

Table 10.1   Environmental impacts of landscape planting

Stage	Possible environmental issues
Plant production	Pollution, energy consumption, loss of finite resources and ecosystem function (e.g. horticultural peat), ecosystem depletion through habitat stripping
Distribution	Energy consumption, air and water pollution, use of finite resources in packaging
Site treatment	Energy consumption, ecosystem loss, hydrological effects, air, water and soil pollution
Plant establishment	Energy consumption (planting vs. succession/regeneration), air, water and soil pollution.
Design in use	Ecosystem disruption (native vs. non-native, local genotypes, habitat quality etc.), energy consumption, recycling of organic materials
Long-term functioning	Energy consumption, replacement needs (clearance and replanting, or dynamic succession)

Figure 10.4 At Duisberg Park North, part of the 1999 Emscher Park International Building Exhibition, spontaneous colonization of vegetation has been encouraged around giant industrial structures and formal planted tree grids.

Landscape Park Duisburg-Nord, part of the developments for the 1999 International Building Exhibition in the Ruhr, Germany (Figure 10.4). The re-use of existing materials and built structures lies at the heart of this project, and the same philosophy extends to the planting. In fact, one of the revolutionary aspects of this project was the decision not to plant – apart from some tree grids in the central area and some formal structural elements and horticultural gardens, the vast bulk of the site is becoming spontaneously vegetated. Much of the site is composed of post-industrial substrates and therefore the vegetation that does develop is specifically adapted to the site.

In this instance, a mix of planting and spontaneous vegetation (albeit with the emphasis strongly on the spontaneous) produces a sustainable result. And in most cases, mixing planting with natural regeneration is likely to be more satisfactory than relying on natural regeneration alone. Natural regeneration can be used in another way: as inspiration for more controlled planting mixes. For example, spontaneous vegetation that develops on disturbed or derelict urban sites can be composed of a mix of attractive native species and non-native garden or park escapes, particularly in its early stages: so-called urban common vegetation (Gilbert, 1992). It may, however, also appear relatively scruffy and weedy. Use of those species which succeed well on such sites over brick rubble and crushed concrete, and which also have attractive visual qualities can form the basis of planted schemes, or more cost-effectively, seed mixes (see below).

Specification of plant material

Seed

Like natural regeneration, seeding is a relatively under-used method of establishing landscape plants. Where appropriate, it is extremely cost-effective. The most common application is in grassland creation, either as traditional sports turf and amenity grasslands, or in habitat creation and restoration schemes through the creation of native wild-flower meadows. In this instance, mixes of forbs (flowering perennials) and grasses are sown onto cultivated soil. Again, as with natural regeneration, there is potential for a differentially structured vegetation to develop, as different species in the mix are favoured by microclimatic and structural gradients across the site, and again, natural selection produces a vegetation that is suited to the site. It is also attractive in that local material can be collected and used. Proper site preparation and management are crucial to the success of these ventures (Gilbert and Anderson, 1998). Seeding is now being considered as a viable option for the creation of more ornamental sustainable landscape vegetation (see below).

Direct seeding is sometimes advocated for woodland creation, however, this is generally less successful and more expensive than woodland planting

(Hodge, 1995), as a result partly of individual species' dormancy-breaking requirements, difficulties in weed control and partly through predation of seed in the seed bed. Certainly, trials in the UK have been disappointing (Stevens *et al.*, 1990) – even-aged stands of pioneer species such as birch can result. However, direct seeding of woody vegetation is widely used in North America, for example, and it may be that further research in the UK will widen its use (Gilbert and Anderson, 1998).

Plant material

A major factor which determines the overall energy budget of a planting, in terms of establishment and management inputs, and in terms of resource inputs into plant production at the nursery, is the size of plant material that is specified. Although for many non-native woody species there is little choice available in production methods, where alternative sizes are offered, it usually pays to plant smaller material: there is growing evidence to suggest that smaller material not only has higher establishment success but also higher growth rates, and will catch up with larger material if planted at the same time (Hitchmough, 1995). Large plant material involves considerable investment in energy and resources at the nursery, small material less so. Also, where choice is offered between bare-root and container-grown material, bare-root stock will invariably establish more satisfactorily, provided proper plant handling procedures are followed. There is clearly a time limitation on when bare-root material can be planted, but generally, autumn planted, bare-root woody plants will need minimal irrigation in the following growing season.

The use of bare-root material is to some extent restrictive, limiting selection to a narrower range than might be available in containers of deciduous species, and limiting planting time to the dormant months. However, there is little doubt that, in terms of sustainability, the great rise in container material at the expense of bare-root stock has involved much increased consumption of resources and energy, both in production and transport, site treatment, establishment costs and aftercare.

As mentioned above, there are no available standards for the production of environmentally sustainable nursery stock. The Horticultural Trades Association's *National Plant Specification* (HTA, 1997), which sets industry standards for landscape plants, contains no mention of sustainability or environmentally-friendly plant production.

Below is a list of factors to consider when sourcing plant material:

- Growing medium. It is now generally agreed that the use of peat, whether imported or from so-called non-conservation sites, is in the long term unsustainable. Plant material should be specified where possible as being grown in a peat-free medium.
- Source of material. The issues of native and local provenance are discussed below. However, there are other issues related to sourcing of material, that particularly relate to wild flowers and bulbous species. Many such plants are particularly prone to exploitation of wild stocks to fuel horticultural demand. Attention has been focused on bulbs from the Middle East, however, for example, some native UK woodlands have been stripped of bluebells to supply planting on landscape schemes. For wild flowers and species bulbs, cultivated sources must be specified.
- Resource inputs in plant production. Information is not available to allow quantification of energy and resource inputs into plant production at the nursery stage.
- Pollution outputs.
- Pest control. Does the nursery substitute, where possible, biological and cultural control methods for chemical pesticides (Jackson, 1995)?
- Packaging. Does the nursery use unnecessary packaging material or non-recyclable/biodegradable material? Does it have a recycling policy for pots and other horticultural sundries?

Native and exotic species selection

The question of whether to use exclusively native species or exotic (non-native) or mixtures of both in landscape plantings provokes much argument. In the

USA and Australia, for example, there are strong native plant organizations that promote the wider use of natives for landscape planting, and similar calls are being increasingly heard in the UK (Kendle and Rose, 1999). Although at first glance, a sustainable approach to landscape planting should advocate natives first and foremost, further consideration suggests that things are not so simple. It seems reasonable to propose that where a designer adopts a naturalistic planting strategy in rural, and many urban situations, then natives should be the first choice. Indeed, one of the greatest reason for the use of natives is that they enable the goals of increasing local distinctiveness and sense of place to be met, through emulating and connecting with spontaneous vegetation within and without a site. In this way the natural distribution pattern of plant species and the local ecology can be strengthened (South Yorkshire Forest, 1999). Planting of native species therefore contributes to local biodiversity directly, but also indirectly through provision of food sources to dependent fauna. Use of native species, particularly common woody species, is also cost-effective: small-sized material is available in quantity. The point about use of common species is one to be emphasized – unless there are specific nature conservation objectives, then only common native species, or species very typical of the immediate locality should be used.

It is often suggested that natives are better adapted to local climate and soil conditions and therefore will establish easily, will be disease-resistant and will require little maintenance. However, there is little logical basis to this proposition. Particularly where one is dealing with disturbed sites or sites heavily influenced by human activities then natives may not necessarily be at all suitable, and indeed, exotic species may be far better adapted. Where nature conservation or habitat creation goals are not paramount and where visual and aesthetic considerations allow, sustainable plant choices must be those that will best establish and succeed under given site conditions (Figure 10.5).

The best starting point for the specification of locally appropriate native plant communities (apart from personal observation) is the National Vegetation Classification (NVC) which indicates the species make-up of all the non-urban vegetation types of the UK. The most frequent application of the NVC is in woodland planting (Rodwell, 1992). Returning to the point made above about the use of common species, it is best to think of the NVC as providing a set of guidelines for specifying the dominant species in for example, locally appropriate woodlands, rather than providing a blueprint, or recipe, to be copied slavishly, particularly where less common species are involved. The NVC is based upon rural communities: there is no equivalent to

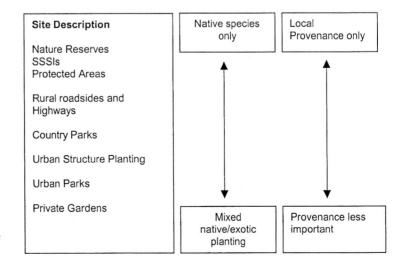

Figure 10.5 The context for native and local provenance planting. Principles do not need to be applied across the board, they are more important in some contexts than others.

the NVC for urban areas. In this case, regional and local distinctiveness is best met through reference to locally common plant assemblages. An excellent example of this is the planting strategy for the regeneration scheme for the Lower Don Valley in Sheffield, which took its inspiration from locally occurring spontaneous and cultural vegetation. Plant communities typical of cities were chosen and wherever possible, relating to local vegetation types. Planting mixes were strongly related to topography, with oak birch woodland on the higher acid ridges, ash-thorn mixes on the valley slopes and maple-dominated communities on the valley floor (adapted from local NVC vegetation types). Urban species typical of spontaneously vegetated vacant sites, such as buddleia, domestic apple, broom, bramble, birches and cotoneasters, were used liberally (Sheffield Development Corporation, 1994).

Genetically modified plants

It is too early to tell what the implications for landscape planting of genetic modification of organisms might be. For most people this is a personal ethical issue as much as an environmental concern. Currently the major debates occur within the agricultural context, and genetic modification to increase agricultural and horticultural production is likely to remain the major application of the technique. Landscape applications include the provision of plants adapted to stressful environments, able to utilize fertilizers and other resources effectively, with superior resistance to pests and diseases, and with an almost limitless choice of habit and colour (Dixon, 1999). How do GM plants fit within a sustainable view of landscape planting? In purely practical terms it could be argued that GM plants could be highly beneficial: genes for, say, pollution tolerance, disease resistance or drought tolerance could reduce or eliminate the need for costly resource inputs in plant establishment. However, as has been discussed previously in this section, a sustainable approach can reduce the need for intensive resource inputs in the first place. It is likely that genetic modification will allow the use of standard landscape planting techniques, and the specification of the bland 'municipal'

landscape style, in a wider range of contexts, thus reducing still further the expression of local identity. It is also likely that these plants will be more costly, and involve high resource use in production.

Provenance of plant material and local genetic diversity

Where native species are being specified, there is much current concern about the origin of plant material. In particular, should material, wherever possible, be of local provenance, i.e. collected from sites which experience the same or very similar environmental conditions to the site to be planted? It is suggested that local populations and ecotypes may have evolved specific genetic adaptations to that environment. Use of material from that gene pool, both aids conservation of local ecotypes, but also confers added fitness for survival to that material, if used in the same locality. It may also benefit invertebrates and other fauna that may be locally adapted to local plant ecotypes. Furthermore, introduction of native species from outside the local genetic area may disrupt local ecosystems, through breeding with local ecotypes and introduction of aggressive genes.

There is as yet little scientific evidence to prove that the genetic make-up of local populations of species is being altered by introduction of ecotypes from outside the area. And if it was, is this necessarily a bad thing, as is always proposed? The forecasts of climate and environmental change suggest that the concept of a locally adapted population is a rather irrelevant concept and that instead, a larger available gene pool may actually ensure local survival. A further problem with the specification of local provenance material is the definition of local. Does this mean that plants of a species should only be procured from sources within the breeding boundaries of local populations? A widely adopted rule is to specify material from within the same 'natural area', as classified by English Nature. Or should material be from the same region, or the same country? The more local one wishes to specify, the more difficult it is to obtain the right material. As a general rule, for most planting of native species, Native origin (i.e. from the UK) can be specified with confidence if no local origin material is available. There is a complicating factor here: currently, British Standards indicate that the country of origin is the country where the plant has been growing for the latter half of the most recent growing season (HTA, 1997). Clearly, clarification should be sought if there is any doubt about the original source of plant material.

Again, as with the use of native species, decisions should be based upon the context of the site. There is little point in adhering blindly to the principle of local provenance on, for example, disturbed urban sites with little nature conservation value. Conversely, in a sensitive rural site, specification of local provenance should be a standard consideration.

Local provenance or origin can be specified for individual species, or where plant communities are being created from direct sowing of a seed mix. This is particularly appropriate to meadow creation. It is becoming possible to obtain seed harvested from herbaceous plant communities for use in habitat restoration schemes within the same natural area. Although in this instance local origin is guaranteed, there is no guarantee that the resultant community will resemble that of the donor site because of differences between substrates on different sites and differential harvesting and representation of different species within the seed mix.

PLANTING DESIGN

While issues such as the type of plant material that is specified and sourced will go some way to determining the overall sustainability of a planting scheme, planting design and style will also be very important. The nature of the planting design will dictate the type and amount of maintenance that will be required, and it will also influence how effectively a scheme will achieve the different objectives of sustainable planting outlined in this chapter. In general, woodland is the most sustainable vegetation type over the long term, although maintenance requirements vary according to the age of the woodland and its stage of development (Jones, 1996). Designs which foster dynamic management, and working with or manipulating vegetation successions are clearly more sustainable than those which do not.

There are no hard and fast rules as to what comprises sustainable planting design. This partly depends upon precise definitions of sustainability. However, in most cases, naturalistic arrangements will tend to be more ecological in their functioning. This is not to say that sustainable design has to be relegated to those parts of a scheme designated as naturalistic or habitat – nature-like planting can be most effective when juxtaposed with, or contained by, very modern architectural forms.

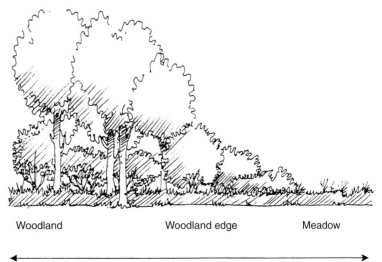

Figure 10.6 The shade-light continuum model for biotope planting.

Woodland   Woodland edge   Meadow

Shade   Light

Biotope planting is much used in continental Europe to produce vegetation types which are akin to the main wild plant community types (Figure 10.6). In the past this approach has concentrated on the use of native plant species (e.g. Tregay and Gustavsson, 1983). Ecological planting of this type can be low maintenance, but can also be visually dull in prominent areas and perhaps ignores social and aesthetic concerns (Forbes *et al.*, 1997). Nature-like design with high visual appeal, such as that often encountered in German and Dutch parks can be relatively maintenance-intensive.

Recently a rather different biotope-based approach has been developed (Hitchmough and Dunnett, 1997). This work aims to produce visually striking vegetations which share the visual appeal of continental European counterparts, but which are far more sustainable in terms of establishment and maintenance inputs. The following principles are employed:

- both native and exotic species are used;
- establishment is mainly by sowing *in situ*, with supplemental planting where appropriate;
- various forms of low-intensity site manipulation and management are used to restrict the development of undesirable species;
- they are inexpensive to create and manage, and consume low levels of energy.

In effect, these vegetations adapt techniques long-used by nature-conservationists to manage large areas of species-rich habitats at low intensity. Ecologically-functioning alternatives have been developed for the major landscape vegetation types. Meadows managed in a way analogous to old agricultural hay meadows, but composed of native wildflowers and grasses and naturalized exotic perennials provide colourful and exciting alternatives to traditional herbaceous plantings. Coppiced woodland-edge systems enable responsive woody plants to be mixed with colourful woodland-edge native and exotic perennials, grasses and bulbs to produce dynamic alternatives to shrub mass and structure planting. And native–exotic annual meadows bring energy and excitement back to public landscapes at relatively low cost. All these

systems once established are to some extent self-sustaining, requiring focused and limited management input and have the added advantage of appearing extremely attractive (Hitchmough and Dunnett, 1997; Dunnett, 1999)

HARD MATERIALS

It is perhaps not surprising that even in this chapter the hard materials play second fiddle to the more glamorous role of all things green. There is without doubt a closer affinity between the landscape designer and the plant nursery than between the designer and the builder's merchant. Landscape students at interview frequently talk of their concerns for the environment and of their passion for nature, and of how they want to protect, restore and improve our threatened landscape. The positive impacts that can be achieved through planting and habitat restoration can unfortunately be easily negated by a similar lack of rigour and sensitivity in detailing the built landscape. If we hope to create more sustainable environments, then, as designers we need to be more critical of the potential damage that we do with poor choice and use of materials, and less easily satisfied with the benefits that working with plants can so easily bring.

The landscape practitioner is today more than ever faced with a bewildering range of different materials. Choosing products that minimize the environmental impact of a development is only one aspect that the designer must consider when making their selection. Careful attention must also be given to other factors including; cost, fitness for purpose, future maintenance, and aesthetic qualities. In order that appropriate consideration can be given to the relative environmental implications of a material, the designer must be able to access reliable information that allows comparisons to be made across a range of products. Even for those with the best intentions of implementing environmentally sensitive solutions this information has not always been available to enable the designer to make an informed decision. There is, however, now a growing body of research and literature, which is beginning to address this issue. The aim of this section is to understand the

Table 10.2 Life cycle stage and possible environmental issues

Stage	Possible environmental issues
Raw materials extraction	ecosystem loss; finite resources loss; noise; dust; hydrological effects; transport infra-structure effects; air and water pollution; visual impact
Manufacture	energy consumption; finite resource depletion; air and water pollution; noise; dust; effects on ecosystems; global warming; acid gas emissions; ozone depletion.
Distribution	energy consumption; noise; dust; global warming; acid gas emissions; air and water pollution; effects on ecosystems.
Construction	noise; dust; air and water pollution; emission of hazardous substances; effects on ecosystems; packaging; waste minimization; good construction practice; ozone depletion.
Design in use	energy consumption; durability; maintenance requirements; replacement frequency; ease of replacement; global warming; acid gas emissions; waste water; soil contamination; ozone depletion.
Demolition and recycling	noise; dust; re-use; contamination of soil; energy consumption; global warming; acid gas emissions; ozone depletion.

Source: Amended to reflect landscape focus from Hobbs *et al.* (1996).

breadth of the problem, to identify what steps are being taken to inform designers in their choice of materials and finally to establish some general guidelines that aim to promote a more environmentally sensitive approach to selecting and working with materials.

Construction materials have an impact on their environment throughout their life cycle. Table 10.2 lists some of the more significant environmental issues which begin right from the extraction of raw materials and continue throughout the life of the product to its demolition or recycling. Some of the environmental consequences are at the local level and include loss of habitat, noise and dust pollution, while others work at the global scale and can result in ozone depletion and global warming. How, then, is the practitioner to decide the relative environmental profile of particular materials? There are a number of ongoing initiatives, which seek to address this issue, some of which are discussed below.

Life Cycle Assessment

Life Cycle Assessment (LCA) has become accepted as one of the more established approaches to environmental profiling, and forms the basis of more recent developments in environmental labelling. The principal aim behind LCA (also referred to as Life Cycle Analysis) is to gather information on all of the environmental impacts of a product from beginning to end. A full LCA would not only include all of the environmental issues listed in Table 10.2 but might also be extended to include social and economic impacts.

One of the most important components of LCA is the amount of energy that is used to produce a product. This is referred to as 'embodied energy' and is defined by the Building Research Establishment (BRE) as the 'total primary energy that has to be sequestered from a stock within the earth in order to produce a specific good or service'. The principal advantage of embodied energy as an indicator of environmental performance is that 'it is one of the few environmental factors for which absolute values can be calculated' (Hobbs *et al.*, 1996). Although the amount of embodied energy is a useful guide when comparing products, it is not the definitive statement of the environmental performance of a material. For example, one product may have a relatively low level of embodied energy but the LCA could record considerable environmental damage to an ecosystem as a result of the extraction of the raw material and pollution during processing. By conducting a complete LCA it should be possible to assess the extent to which a product causes environmental damage and to then identify and target possible solutions that would improve the environmental quality of the product.

LCA was originally developed to improve the efficiency of industrial processes (CIRIA, 1995). However, it was subsequently hoped that by applying the technique to individual products a scheme of environmental labelling could be developed which would enable consumers to compare products based on their LCA rating. This is not a straightforward task, mainly due to the incredibly complex and diverse range of information that must be gathered before an LCA can be completed. Before LCA can be used to make comparisons between products there needs to be a consistency of quantitative data, a definitive methodology for assessing the life cycle impact of materials, and finally a system of common quantitative units for comparing different environmental impacts (CIRIA, 1995). Comparisons between different environmental impacts present great difficulties, as do comparisons between processes occurring in different countries. For example, is the destruction of a local habitat due to the opening of a new quarry more, or less, environmentally damaging than the increase in road traffic which will result if the quarry is not opened? This example not only illustrates the complexity of comparing very different types of data but also the difficulties of balancing local and global impacts, a point developed further by Michael Herrmann and his colleagues in Chapter 11.

Environmental labelling

There are a number of ongoing initiatives that seek to provide a standardized method of assessing the environmental impacts of different products. One example is the system of environmental profiling which has been developed by the BRE in collaboration with industry and the DETR (Howard *et al.*, 1999). The product of this collaboration has been the development of a methodology that aims to establish common rules and guidelines for applying LCA to create environmental profiles for UK construction products. The environmental profiles are provided in two ways and look at raw inventory data for the following inputs and outputs:

- material use
- water use
- emissions to air
- emissions to water
- embodied energy
- emissions to land.

These factors are then characterized in terms of their contribution to environmental impacts under the following headings:

- climate change
- acid deposition
- water pollution: eutrophication
- water pollution: eco-toxicity
- ozone depletion
- minerals extraction
- fossil fuel depletion
- water extraction
- air pollution: human toxicity
- air pollution: low level ozone creation
- waste disposal
- transport pollution and congestion.

From this information, profiles have been calculated for building elements and building materials. Element profiles have been assessed on the quantities of different materials required to produce a 'functional unit' on a per square metre basis to enable comparison between comparable building elements. The element profiles are calculated for a lifetime from cradle to grave, which is set at 60 years in order that maintenance, replacement and disposal factors can be taken into account.

Environmental profiles have also been calculated for individual building materials, e.g. concrete, and are presented on a per tonne basis. These profiles take account of the environmental impacts from scratch to the factory gate. Provided that manufacturers are encouraged to undertake this assessment of their products, it has the potential to become an extremely useful tool in comparing the environmental performance of different products. This resource is currently available as an Internet subscription service from the BRE.

Table 10.3 Extract from *The Green Guide*

		Softwood (boards)			Chipboard (19mm)			Plywood (19mm)			MDF board (19mm)		
Toxicity	in manufacture	A	B	C	A	B	C	A	B	C	A	B	C
	in combustion	A	B	C	A	B	C	A	B	C	A	B	C
Primary energy		A	B	C	A	B	C	A	B	C	A	B	C
Wastes	generated	A	B	C	A	B	C	A	B	C	A	B	C
Recycling	% contained	A	B	C	A	B	C	A	B	C	A	B	C
	% capable of being	A	B	C	A	B	C	A	B	C	A	B	C
	% currently recycled in the UK	A	B	C	A	B	C	A	B	C	A	B	C
	energy required to	A	B	C	A	B	C	A	B	C	A	B	C
Summary rating		A	B	C	A	B	C	A	B	C	A	B	C
	cost range (£/m²)	9–11			5–6			18–20			15–17		
	replacement interval (yrs)	20			20			20			20		

Source: Reproduced by permission of the BRE.

Note: Table 10.3 shows only a selection of the available parameters for these materials and not the complete environmental profile.

Another important development from the BRE has been the production of *The Green Guide to Specification* (BRE, 1998) which aims to present the available data in a format that is easily accessible to relevant design professionals. In its current form it provides profiles for generic product types and not specific goods. The data have been presented for a range of different impacts on an ABC rating where A represents the best environmental performance (see Table 10.3).

The designer can compare the environmental performance of different building elements, and judge them on their relative strengths and weaknesses. Where it is felt that the parameters included do not reflect the full environmental impact, additional qualitative guidance is also provided. For example, for floor surfacing, the impact of cultivated forests on the landscape may have a bearing on the exact source of timber supplied. One of the principal advantages of this approach is that it allows the designer or organization to establish their own specific environmental parameters when selecting materials.

An alternative approach to *The Green Guide* is the Environmental Preference Method (EPM) which was originally developed in The Netherlands in 1991 by Woon/Energie. The Environmental Preference Method ranks products that are available on the market according to their environmental performance. Similar to the BRE method of environmental profiles, the Environmental Preference Method considers the full life cycle of the product and bases its assessment on the following issues:

- shortage of raw material
- ecological damage caused by the extraction of the raw materials
- energy consumption at all stages (including transport)
- water consumption
- noise and odour pollution
- harmful emissions such as those leading to ozone depletion
- global warming and acid rain
- health aspects
- risk of disasters
- reparability
- re-usability
- waste.

(From Anink *et al.*, 1998)

The analysis is presented in the *Handbook of Sustainable Building* (Anink *et al.*, 1998) which ranks materials in terms of their environmental performance. Each ranking is supported by a brief description of the environmental considerations that were

Table 10.4 Preference ratings for hard paving

Preference 1	Preference 2	Preference 3	Not recommended
Recycled concrete slabs	Concrete slabs, turf	Clay tiles, concrete blocks	Asphalt

Source: Anink *et al.* (1998)

taken into account, for example, under the section Hard Landscaping the preference ratings for hard paving are shown in Table 10.4.

In this example, recycled concrete slabs are the preferred choice for hard paving because they make use of secondary raw materials and have a lower embodied energy than clay tiles.

Both *The Green Guide* and the *Handbook for Sustainable Building* represent a significant step forward in raising awareness of the environmental consequences of selecting different materials and in assisting designers in their specification. In its current format *The Green Guide* is very much focused on buildings whereas the *Handbook on Sustainable Building* also provides information on a limited range of landscape components. However, the strength of *The Green Guide* is perhaps a more transparent approach to environmental labelling which enables the designer to make their selection based on their own environmental objectives. A new *Green Guide to Specification for Housing* is currently being developed and will contain information on landscape materials.

GUIDELINES TOWARDS MORE SUSTAINABLE DESIGN SOLUTIONS

Efficient use of materials

The most effective contribution that the designer can make towards developing sustainable design solutions is to keep to an absolute minimum the requirement to use new materials. This can be achieved by:

1 *Avoiding unnecessary replacement of existing onsite materials* By retaining and working with existing

materials the designer limits the environmental damage caused by demolition, disposal and replacement with new materials.

2 *Design gradients* This requires the designer to ensure that the design specification is functionally appropriate for the design context. For example, the extent of hard surfacing and materials used should support but not surpass the required level of use. Materials with high technical specifications tend to have a poor environmental performance and are therefore wasted in areas with low traffic.

3 *Design detailing* There is the potential when selecting materials and detailing a scheme to produce considerable wastage of both materials and resources because of a poor match between the design and the materials specified. For example, if the width of a new pavement does not correspond with the module size of the chosen paving there is an environmental cost due to increased transport of unused materials, onsite cutting and disposal of off-cuts. Efficient use of materials matches design with module size or combines different module sizes so that irregularities can be accommodated without unnecessary wastage or cutting (Figures 10.7a and b).

Wastage of materials is also caused by over-specification and poor detailing. A common example is the use of aggregates as hardcore in the formation of base material for pavement construction. By incorporating a geotextile between the formation and the base the quantity of hardcore can be reduced by up to a third which can make a considerable environmental saving on extraction and transport. The performance of a material may also be compromised because of inappropriate detailing. Wood is particularly vulnerable in this respect, a common fault are

Figures 10.7a and 10.7b Both illustrate the benefits of combining large and small paving modules in order to prevent unnecessary cutting.

posts encased in concrete footings which prevent free drainage and promote timber decay. This approach to detailing also impedes future re-use and inhibits future maintenance.

Designing for re-use (exit strategies)

The re-use and recycling of materials are potentially becoming ever more complex due to the development of new materials and new combinations of materials which make recovery difficult and consequently uneconomical (Nijkerk, 1996). The designer should look to implement design solutions, which will facilitate dismantling and re-use rather than the less sustainable option of recycling. For example, pavers that are laid onto mortar instead of sand may only be fit for recycling as hardcore rather than the more environmentally desirable option of re-use. By designing for re-use the designer is able to extend the lifespan of a product and thereby help close the cycle.

Selecting materials, which have the least environmental impact: re-use of materials

The re-use of materials is the most environmentally sustainable option especially where they already exist on site or can be obtained from a local source. Re-use should not be confused with recycling. A re-used material is retained in its original form although it may be used for a different function. A common example of re-use in the landscape industry is railway sleepers, which are used to construct a wide range of different structures such as retaining walls, and seats. By reclaiming materials we extend their lifespan and reduce the demand for landfill and new materials (Figure 10.8). Re-use may also assist in the support of local economies and the local vernacular by maintaining a demand for regional skills, crafts and materials.

The main environmental impact of selecting re-used materials is in the amount of embodied energy used in moving them from the point of supply to the site. For example, for a reclaimed brick to have the same embodied energy as a new brick on your doorstep it would have to travel 800 miles (1,280 km) (ACTAC, 1995). One could be fairly confident that in the UK, at least, a reclaimed brick would always appear to be the environmentally preferred choice when compared to new. Embodied energy levels will, however, be higher for denser materials such as reclaimed stone and imported goods which can, for example, include railway sleepers from as far away as Canada.

Another potential concern when selecting re-used materials is where the demand for the reclaimed material exceeds supply from natural demolition and reclamation. For example, reclaimed York stone became extremely fashionable in the late 1980s and

Figure 10.8   The use of reclaimed building rubble to fill gabions at a housing regeneration scheme in Berlin. By reclaiming this material onsite it reduces the environmental impacts of extracting new materials, transport and landfill.

early 1990s, especially in the London area. Because of the high price attached to the material, there were numerous cases of the theft of stone barn roofs in environmentally sensitive areas and the removal of mill floors.

Recycling of materials

Recycled materials are those which have been reclaimed and then processed to create a new raw material. Recycled materials can form a primary recycled product such as hardcore from building waste or may form secondary recycled raw material which in the case of aggregates could be used to produce concrete. Recycling helps to close the cycle by reducing the demand for non-renewable resources and the need for landfill.

When selecting recycled materials there is a need to consider what percentage of the new material, is recycled. There are also concerns regarding the amount of the pollution generated in the recycling of certain materials especially where the product is of low value. Instead of closing the life cycle this approach only extends the lifespan of the material (Anink *et al.*, 1998) This may result in the production of pollution through re-processing for only a limited return.

The UK produces an estimated 70 million tonnes of masonry and concrete waste each year, of which only 4 per cent is processed for use as secondary aggregate (Smith *et al.*, 1998) and 29 per cent for low level use on or near the site of origin. The landscape industry is potentially well placed to be more adventurous in its use of recycled materials. The technical/structural requirements of landscape structures are frequently less critical than other built forms and often the volumes required are large. By exploring the possibility of using a range of locally available, discarded materials a significant contribution could be made to the conservation of aggregate resources and landfill sites. This will, however, only take effect if there is suitable research and clear specification of where and how these materials might be used.

When specifying materials such as concrete it may be possible to require that in its production a propor-

tion be made from recycled secondary raw materials. For example, in the construction of the BRE new office development at Garston, Collins (1996) reported that crushed concrete was used 'as an aggregate in over 1,500m³ of concrete supplied for foundations, floor slabs, structural columns and waffle floors'. This was the first example of recycled aggregates being used in ready mixed concrete in the UK.

There is clearly a wide range of materials, which would be suitable for both re-use and recycling, but are frequently disposed of because of the difficulty in matching both supplier and user. This issue is now partly being addressed through the development of web-based material and waste exchanges. An example of one of these sites is that developed by the Department of the Environment Transport and the Regions (DETR) and hosted by the BRE. (http://www.connet.org/WEC/UK). This web site enables suppliers to advertise materials and users to search by material type and location. It also lists a wanted board and future demolition sites. The web clearly has a major role to play in promoting re-usable and recyclable materials but perhaps more importantly in informing potential users of the wide range of materials available and of their possible application.

Selection of new materials

In the absence of a comprehensive environmental labelling standard for all products, landscape professionals will need to base their selection on the existing material environmental profiles, green building guides and a good deal of common sense. There can be no hard and fast rules to material selection, as each situation will have its very own specific set of requirements, opportunities and solutions. The following notes are intended to provide some broad guidelines towards a more environmentally sensitive approach to selecting new materials:

1 *Maximize the use of renewable resources* Wood is potentially the most sustainable of all materials for the construction industry. Care must be taken in establishing origin of supply and management techniques, as this will affect the level of

embodied energy and degree of environmental damage. The use of local hardwoods and thoughtful design to minimize the necessity for chemical preservatives are preferable to imported hardwoods and treated softwoods. Timber-based products such as chipboard, plywood and MDF are less desirable due to increased levels of embodied energy and toxins contained in binding agents. These products also tend to be less suitable for re-use and recycling.

2 *Select locally available materials* Selecting local natural or manufactured materials will help to reduce the level of embodied energy and vehicle pollution due to the reduced transport requirements.

3 *Use natural stone and aggregates* If available locally, natural materials generally have a good environmental profile, they are low in embodied energy and can make an important contribution to the local economy, while also supporting local skills and helping to maintain regional character and identity. The main area of concern is at the point of extraction, especially where this takes place in environmentally sensitive areas.

4 *Minimize the use of materials with poor environmental performance* This includes many metal derivatives and synthetics, which typically have high levels of embodied energy and may emit harmful substances during processing.

The landscape industry tends to have relatively low demand for these materials, with the exception of bitumen for road and pavement surfacing. Although there are considerable potential environmental implications in the production of bitumen, which is a petroleum derivative, it is preferable to tar, which has a high content of polycyclic aromatic hydrocarbons, which are carcinogenic (Anink *et al.*, 1998). There is also the potential to use recycled road surfacing. Mackay and Emery (1996) have reported on a case study in Ontario, Canada, where reclaimed asphalt pavement is combined with new aggregates to produce recycled hot mix asphalt which is suitable for road and pavement surfacing.

If materials of poor environmental performance must be used, it is essential that the design makes suitable provision for ease of separation at demolition so that they can be effectively recycled. The contamination of synthetics results in a reduction in quality, making synthetic waste useless for high grade recycling (Anink *et al.*, 1998).

CONCLUSION

The development and implementation of a reliable method of environmental labelling for construction materials will play a major role in assisting landscape practitioners in producing less environmentally-damaging designs. There is a clear need for a similar protocol to enable informed plant materials choices. However, appropriate selection is only part of the solution. There is still considerable scope for designers to be more environmentally sensitive in the detailing of their schemes. In terms of landscape construction this may reduce unnecessary waste, extend the life of the scheme and enable reclamation of materials at the end. For landscape planting, this may result in reduced maintenance costs, wider ecological benefits and long-term environmental enhancement.

In the UK it is now possible to obtain a BREEAM (Building Research Establishment Environmental Assessment Method) certification for the environmental performance of a new building. The certificate provides a label for the building that allows the owners or occupants to gain recognition for the building's environmental performance (Baldwin *et al.*, 1998). At present these schemes are entirely voluntary and are restricted to new buildings and not landscape. We urgently need a similar procedure for new landscape developments (which potentially have much wider environmental impact than individual buildings). Material selection and use will be central to this environmental audit. As a consequence, practitioners will be forced to broaden their outlook beyond up-front cost and aesthetics.

REFERENCES

ACTAC (1995) Masonry materials, *Green Building Digest*, 1, January.

Anink, D., Boonstra, C. and Mak, J. (1998) *Handbook of Sustainable Building* (James and James (Science Publishers) Ltd).

Baldwin, R., Yates, A., Howard, N. and Rao, S. (1998) *BREAM 98 for Offices*. (London, BRE/CRC).

Beckett, K. P., Freer-Smith, P. H. and Taylor, G. (1998) Urban woodlands: their role in reducing the effects of particulate pollution, *Environmental Pollution*, 99, 347–360.

Building Research Establishment (BRE) (1998) *The Green Guide to Specification* (London, Building Research Establishment/ Construction Research Communications).

BRE (1999) Environmental Profiles of Construction Materials, Components and Buildings at: http://collaborate.bre.co. uk/envprofiles/background.html, accessed 15 August 2000.

CIRIA (1995) *Environmental Impact of Materials Volume A*, CIRIA Special publication 116 (London, CIRIA).

Collins, R. J. (1996) *Recycled Aggregates in Ready-Mixed Concrete*, proceedings of an international seminar, Building Research Establishment, edited by J. W. Llewellyn and H. Davies (London, BRE/CRC).

Dixon, G. (1999) GM origins and issues, *The Horticulturist*, 8(4), 2–7.

Dunnett, N. P. (1995) Harnessing anarchy, *Landscape Design*, November, pp. 25–29.

Dunnett, N. P. (1999) Annuals on the loose, *The Garden*, March, 168–171.

Dunnett, N. P. and Hitchmough, J. D. (1996) Excitement and energy: sustainable landscape planting, *Landscape Design*, June, 43–46.

Dunnett, N. P. and Qasim, M. (1999) Perceived Benefits to Human Well-Being of Urban Gardens, *Hort-Technology*, 10(1), 40–45.

Forbes, S., Cooper, D. and Kendle, A. D. (1997) The history and development of ecological landscape styles, in A. D. Kendle and S. Forbes (eds) *Urban Nature Conservation* (London, E & FN Spon).

Forman, R. T. (1995) *Land Mosaics: The Ecology of Landscapes and Regions* (Cambridge, Cambridge University Press).

Gilbert, O. (1992) *The Flowering of the Cities: The Natural Flora of Urban Commons* (Peterborough, English Nature).

Gilbert, O. and Anderson, P. (1998) *Habitat Creation and Repair* (Oxford, Oxford University Press).

Hitchmough, J. (1995) *Urban Landscape Management* (Melbourne, Inkata Press).

Hitchmough, J. and Dunnett, N. (1997) New public planting, *Landscape Design*, 264, 49–52.

Hitchmough, J. and Woudstra, J. (1999) The ecology of exotic herbaceous perennials grown in managed, native, grassy vegetation in urban landscapes, *Landscape and Urban Planning*, 45, 107–121.

Hobbs, S. J., Atkinson, C. J. and Edwards, S. H. (1996) *Sustainable Use of Construction Materials*, proceedings of an international seminar, Building Research Establishment, edited by J. W. Llewellyn and H. Davies (London, BRE/CRC).

Hodge, S. J. (1995) *Creating and Managing Woods around Towns* (London, HMSO).

Horticultural Trade Association (HTA) (1997) *National Plant Specification* (Reading, Horticultural Trades Association/Joint Council for Landscape Industries).

Hough, M. (1995) *Cities and Natural Processes* (London, Routledge).

Howard, N., Edwards, S. and Anderson, J. (1999) *BRE Methodology for Environmental Profiles of Construction Materials, Components and Buildings* (London, BRE/CRC).

Jackson, A. (1995) Biological control in ornamentals, *The Horticulturist*, 4, 25–29.

Jarman, D. (1995) *Derek Jarman's Garden* (London, Thames and Hudson).

Johnston, J. and Newton, J. (1995) *Building Green* (London, London Ecology Unit).

Jones, N. (1996) Woodland vs grassland, *Horticulture Week*, 29 August, 25–27.

Kendle, A. D. and Forbes, S. (1997) *Urban Nature Conservation* (London, E & FN Spon).

Kendle, T. and Rose, J. (1999) Native vs alien, *The Horticulturist*, 8(3), 6–9.

Kragh, J. (1979) A pilot study on railway noise attenuation by belts of trees, *Journal of Sound and Vibration*, 66, 407–415.

Kragh, J. (1981) Road traffic noise attenuation by belts of trees, *Journal of Sound and Vibration*, 74, 235–241.

Landlife (1997) *Wildflowers Work* (Liverpool, Landlife).

Lawson, M. (1996) Vegetation and sustainable cities, *Arboricultural Journal*, 20, 161–172.

MacKay, M. H. and Emery, J. J. (1996) *Mineral Aggregates Conservation – Reuse and Recycling*, proceedings of an international seminar, Building Research Establishment, edited by J. W. Llewellyn and H. Davies (London, BRE/CRC).

McPherson, E. (1994) Cooling urban heat islands with sustainable landscapes, in R. H. Platt, R. A. Rowntree and P. C. Muck (eds) *The Ecological City* (Amherst, MA, The University of Massachusetts Press).

Nijkerk, A. A. (1996) Recycling Techniques 'I am not old, I am recycled', proceedings of an international seminar, Building Research Establishment, edited by J. W. Llewellyn and H. Davies (London, BRE/CRC).

Rodwell, J. (1992) Classified information, *Landscape Design*, October, 14–16.

Sheffield Development Corporation (1994) *Landscape and Nature Conservation Strategy for the Lower Don Valley* (Sheffield, Sheffield Development Corporation).

Smith, M., Whitelegg, J. and Williams, N. (1998) *Greening the Built Environment* (London, Earthscan).

South Yorkshire Forest (1999) *Development for the Future: Sustainable Design Guide for Developers within the South Yorkshire Forest* (Sheffield, South Yorkshire Forest Partnership).

Stevens, F. R. W., Thompson, D. A. and Gosling, P. G. (1990) *Research Experience in Direct Sowing for Lowland Plantation Establishment*, Research Information Note 184. (Edinburgh, Forestry Commission).

Thoday, P., Kendle, T. and Hitchmough, J. (1995) Plants for landscape site, *The Horticulturist*, 4(3), 29–35.

Tregay, R. and Gustavsson, R. (1983) *Oakwood's New Landscape: Designing for Nature in the Residential Environment* (Sweden, Swedish University of Agricultural Sciences).

Von Stulpnagel, A., Horbert, M. and Sukopp, H. (1990) The importance of vegetation for urban climate, in H. Sukopp (ed.) *Urban Ecology* (The Hague, SPB Academic Publishing).

11

SUSTAINABLE LANDSCAPE DESIGN IN PRACTICE

Michael Herrmann, Chris Royffe and Andy Millard

SUMMARY

The actual experience of landscape architects in the delivery of sustainable landscape design is examined through the use of four case studies. The studies are chosen to highlight examples of good practice, as well as to indicate potential obstacles and complexities. The importance of nurturing good relationships through effective communication between all stakeholders is stressed, as is the need for a clear environmental strategy, accompanied by detailed design guidelines. The case studies illustrate the need for holistic, life cycle thinking throughout the design and management processes. Opportunities for raising awareness, and accessing information and tools are discussed, though the need for more detailed and specific design/assessment methods is highlighted. Finally, a checklist is presented to assist designers in the consideration of the wide spectrum of sustainability issues.

INTRODUCTION

Why is it that most landscape architects practising in the UK today do not fully address the sustainability agenda in their everyday work? Is it because it is felt to be a labyrinthine subject of intractable complexity, leading to unavoidably unsatisfactory results? Is it because neither they, nor their clients are terribly interested? Or is it because many practi-tioners inevitably care for the environment, and hold a strong sense of social justice, hence feeling that they are already 'defending the green battlements'? It seems likely that there is a grain of truth in all of these suggestions.

The effective delivery of sustainable landscape architecture depends on the successful integration of theory with practice, and the ability of practitioners to understand and prioritize the issues involved. While most landscape architects may feel that they are already considering certain aspects of the sustainability agenda, few take the time and energy needed for the consideration of sustainability in all its guises.

If practitioners are familiar with neither the possibilities, nor characteristics of a sustainable design process, expectations are inevitably low. Although motivation is not a topic covered here, there is a need to provide inspiration through examples of the experience in the delivery of sustainable schemes. Due to the wide scope of the landscape architecture profession, a range of new paradigms of sustainable design is necessary to serve as exemplars. In order to demonstrate the complexity of the issues involved, to illustrate the sustainable design process, and to extend the search for examples of best practice, a range of case studies is examined, conclusions drawn, and a checklist of sustainable design issues presented.

Due to the breadth of focus of sustainable design, it is unlikely that any single project can demonstrate best practice in all areas. The four studies presented are used to highlight areas of activity that demonstrate good practice, while acknowledging short-comings and obstacles encountered. Projects have also been selected in order to reflect the variety of scales and aspects of landscape design.

A study of the Earth Centre project, near Sheffield, examines some of the characteristic features of a large-scale project, holding as its primary aim, the exploration, demonstration, and communication of sustainability. The way in which issues were prioritized and balanced in the practical application of theory is examined in the concept development, the experience of selection and procurement of materials, and implementation. The Center Parcs leisure developments provide a demonstration of the benefits of the use of a conceptual environmental strategy, used to guide sustainable implementation and management processes. In London, a small-scale, community orientated scheme, Meanwhile Gardens, gives evidence of the potential for benefits of effec-tive liaison between the designer and user. Materials selection and community access policies are also con-sidered. Finally, a large-scale project in Holland, Oostvaardersplassen, is used to demonstrate the way in which issues of ecology and natural processes can be accommodated, managed, and reconciled with the interests of the large, local population.

CASE STUDY 1: THE EARTH CENTRE

The Earth Centre is an ambitious project that is being funded through public money, linked to private, matched funding. The financing comes through sponsors, including the European Commission, English Partnerships, and the English National Lottery Millennium Commission. Located on 160 hectares of urban fringe countryside in South Yorkshire, its aim is to combine pleasure with purpose; stimulating the public imagination with the ideas, ways and means for a sustainable future, while experiencing an exciting and memorable day out. The principal visitor attractions will include several galleries and pavilions, placing an emphasis on visitor involvement and 'edutainment', learning through fun. Features include global, forest, and drought tolerant gardens, interactive sculpture, creative and imaginative play features such as a sensory trail, and 'hands on' learning about ecology and natural systems. The design brief demanded the creation of a lively and original landscape setting for these features in the 10-hectare heart of the site. The first phase of the project opened to the public in April 1999.

During the concept stage a decision was made to locate the project on a brownfield site, capitalizing on the biodiversity that is often inherent on disused land, and thus highlighting the value of so-called wasteland. One hundred years of coal mining activ-ities had left a despoiled and scarred landscape in the Don Valley, as well as a community demoralized and impoverished by the loss of the principal industry. Located within easy reach of several million poten-tial visitors, the project hopes to demonstrate that a sustainable development can bring economic regen-eration, retraining and other tangible social and financial benefits to the local community.

Design philosophy and layout

Andrew Grant of Grant Associates, landscape architects to the scheme, explains that the landscape is conceived as a hard-working, carefully integrated ecosystem, incorporating nature conservation, food production, buildings, woodland management, archaeology, energy efficiency and water manage-ment; as well as play and recreation. Highlighting the extraordinary aspects of seemingly mundane land-scape features was an objective, demonstrating that working landscapes can have beauty and delight, alongside productivity and efficiency. The landscape architecture of the site aims to articulate messages regarding the issues that affect the management of land.

It will be a visual and ecological celebration of the restoration process. It will take time to mature, and will continue to evolve into the next century. The site landscape will be presented as an integrated system, in which aspects such as water conservation are shown alongside habitat and wildlife management. Novel structures and land management techniques are included to highlight the unique character of the site and to reinforce the message of sustainability.

(Andrew Grant, pers. comm., 1999)

The central area is described as a working model for future urban landscapes, demonstrating possibilities for urban regeneration schemes. Similarly, the wider site is conceived as a demonstration of how derelict rural landscapes can be transformed to support employment, enjoyment, enriched visual character, and biodiversity. The designers' primary objective was to introduce sustainable natural management systems, devised through the application of calculable rules and techniques. These systems then suggest the layout and structure of the landscape design. The first priority was given to the development of water management, including sewage and waste treatment. This was then complemented by the design of infrastructure, topography, and circulation (human and fauna). Topographic treatment and structure planting were also developed as a response to the site conditions, context and natural processes (Figure 11.1). A sustainable framework with a strong, integrated structure allows for the subsequent addition of elements and features, without disturbing the balance and function of natural systems and processes.

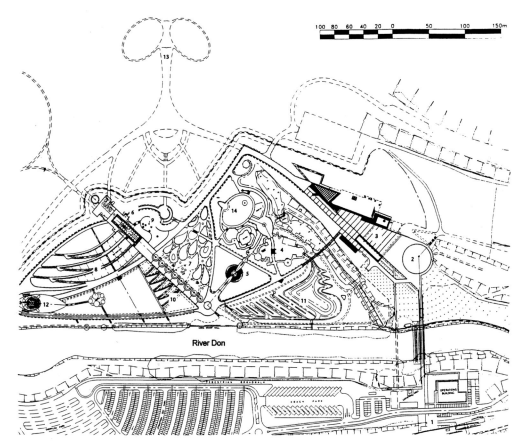

Site plan *1 railway station; 2 arrivals and Unwind Spiral; 3 Planet Earth galleries, restaurant and solar canopy; 4 NatureWorks; 5 EarthArena; 6 WaterWorks; 7 Forest Gardens with timber gridshell structures; 8 21st Century Terrace Gardens with cruck arches, 9 Dry Garden, 10 Bog Garden, 11 Devils's Ings Wetland; 12 FutureWorks; 13 The Ark building; 14 Children's Wilderness Play.*

Figure 11.1 The Earth Centre central area visitor attraction: a strong landscape structure, inspired by the study of natural processes. Source: Grant Associates

Within the central area of the site, a transition of spaces has been created as a response to varying conditions, from the wet, low south-east corner, to the drier north-west slopes. The planting specification responds to these differences, with bog and riverine vegetation nearer to the river, where a seasonally flooded wetland has been established, up to the series of south-facing terraces, where different planting schemes demonstrate drought tolerance and alternative agricultural crops and practices.

Part of the philosophy of the Earth Centre is that 'seeing is believing'. To this end they are confident that the creation of a large, high profile project is compatible with the aim of reaching a mass public audience. They anticipate the need for a series of 'satellite' centres at some point in the future, acting as 'outreach' posts to spread the principles and demonstration of sustainability far and wide. As well as a countrywide schools outreach programme, the Earth Centre web site and Internet communications channels are seen as a vital tool in the dissemination of information, as well as providing an excellent conduit and forum for the discussion of new ideas. The use of Information Technology and other multimedia applications to deliver some of the aims of the Earth Centre can meet the ecodesign ideal of 'dematerialization' (Fussler and James, 1996).

In anticipation of the opening of many new visitors attractions around the turn of the millennium, the Earth Centre is realizing that the forecasts for visitor numbers may have been optimistic. Partly as a response to this, and in the spirit of their plan to grow by stages, while remaining economically sustainable, future phases will be focused on the perceived niche market of sustainability and environmental education. In order to meet the needs of this audience, plans for the next phase include a conference centre, an educational visitors centre, as well as accommodation for research and study. In order to allow a consistency of approach, and continuity of care, Grant Associates are likely to continue to be involved with the project in future development stages. Consistency of professional contact is felt by the Earth Centre to be an important feature of a design process capable of delivering, refining and adapting sustainable solutions.

Access

Access issues are considered as a high priority, with links by rail, road, and boat. A long-distance bridleway crosses the site, as do several heritage and history trails. Although the central area is only accessible by entry payment, the wider site remains open to the local community, including access to the bollards that mark capped mine shafts; now an informal memorial to the miners who were buried alive in a pit disaster. The recognition of historical and emotional ties between people and the land should be seen as a important aspect of sustainable landscape design. Tuan coined the term 'topophilia' to define this 'affective bond between people and place or setting' (Tuan, 1974, p. 4) Robert Thayer refined the term to designate 'the range of positive human emotions relating to affection for land, earth, and nature' (Thayer, 1994, p. 5); and went on to stress its importance in the creation of sustainable landscapes. Sustainability issues have also been recognized in the pricing structure of the Earth Centre, with a discounted annual membership for locals, and reduced charges to visitors arriving by public transport, bicycle, or on foot.

Sustainability design brief

A sustainability design brief was developed (Earth Centre, 1997/8) to guide the designers and contractors in the delivery of sustainable solutions. The brief contains both generalized and specific considerations, setting out a series of checklists, which acknowledge the complexity of the issues involved. Within the design, construction and maintenance regimes, the aims and objectives include:

- Use the minimum quantity of resources possible to achieve the required construction.
- Specify re-used and recycled materials, wherever possible.
- Where it is necessary to use virgin materials, renewable materials from sustainable sources should be selected in preference to non-renewable materials.
- Materials should be selected with consideration given to their potential environmental and health

impacts during their life cycle; selected on a minimum impact basis, with consideration given to relative levels of embodied energy.

- Minimize the need for structural and other materials, avoid the 'over-design' of elements, particularly foundations, structure and cladding.
- Integrate recycling systems into the design and construction.
- The durability of materials.
- The potential for re-use and recycling after decommissioning.
- The health and safety issues associated with the manufacture and use of materials.
- Adverse social and political considerations associated with certain materials, resources, and companies supplying them.

Materials and resources

The sustainability design brief recognizes that 'In selecting materials a complex range of issues needs to be addressed, with trade-offs necessary to meet different objectives.' Re-used or recycled materials are substituted for virgin materials where desirable, the impact of their use being subject to scrutiny by the same rigorous criteria. As the brief points out:

> The potential complexity of the judgements to be made is illustrated by the fact that some recycled materials for instance steel, are, or can be over-subscribed, and The Earth Centre's use of these materials, therefore may cause someone else to use virgin steel.
>
> (Earth Centre, 1997/8)

Figure 11.2   The use of locally sourced materials such as limestone is a priority, though economic sustainability through the satisfaction of paying visitors, justifies the use of some exotic planting.

Complex life cycle analysis procedures were not generally used and instead reliance was on the perceived reputation of materials and processes, based on informed analyses.

The use of non-formaldehyde medium density fibre board (MDF), lead-free, water-based paints, and non-polyvinyl chloride (PVC) products, are all aims of the sustainable materials selection policy. Recyclable plastics are specified where possible. Due to the evidence condemning PVC in terms of the harmful effects associated with its manufacture and use (Thornton, 1997), the Earth Centre is prepared to spend more in order to specify medium density polyethylene (MDPE) pipes, rather than those made of PVC; fortunately, the supplier for these was local (Polypipe).

A sustainable materials policy will favour the use of local products and services. The Earth Centre design team selected a limited palette of locally available materials that can be applied in a wide variety of ways. Thus, local limestone is used for cladding, loose paving, and also as aggregate for concrete (Figure 11.2).

Figure 11.3 Innovative timber structures, used in lieu of extra heavy nursery stock, to give 'instant' height and form to the newly created landscape.

The planting specification for the central area demonstrates the wish to enrich the visitor experience through diversity. Attention to user needs is an aspect of sustainable design that requires careful consideration. Planting has not been restricted to low maintenance native species but instead employs a lively mixture of native and exotic species used in imaginative and original ways. The temptation to import large quantities of advanced nursery stock has been resisted, however, with a sense of height and structure instead provided through the imaginative use of a range of timber structures, and woven willow fences, tunnels and arches (Figures 11.3, 11.4, 11.5, 11.6). The tree planting for the site is predominantly of small whips. These are felt to be more appropriate than larger stock as they will better acclimatize to the site, and have fewer associated environmental costs (Chapter 10). The central area is managed organically, with non-chemical maintenance, although, due to the prohibitive cost of hand weeding on such a large scale, the non-residual herbicide, glyphosate, is being used on the wider site.

The sustainable application of modern technology and materials is explored, including the balancing and integration of these with traditional and ancient practices. An example of this symbiosis can be seen in the construction of the green oak, timber lattice structures which punctuate the heart of the site. Traditional hand tool techniques were used in their manufacture, but with stainless steel bolts and tensile cables to secure the laths to each other and to the sweet chestnut timber base. This illustrates the point that the use of modern materials can give social, economical, and environmental benefits that can sometimes outweigh use of more traditional alternatives. These structures, designed by Buro Happold, and known as 'gridshells', contain examples of 'forest gardens'. These are symbiotic, complementary, and productive planting arrangements, following the principles of permaculture (Figures 11.7, 11.8 and 11.9).

Procurement

The Earth Centre managed to source many of the sustainable products and materials that they wanted

Figure 11.4 Living and dead willow sculptural fencing provides quickly established visual interest.

Figure 11.5 Woven tunnels of growing willow enliven the visitor experience, adding an element of surprise and fun, while communicating a sympathetic relationship with nature.

to use, though by no means all. The team experienced difficulties sourcing steel, aluminium and plastic with significant proportions of recycled content. Proximity of supply was sometimes felt to outweigh concerns regarding the use of virgin raw materials, particularly as the greatest environmental costs are often associated with transportation, rather than with embodied energy (Chapter 10). In principle, the design team would have liked to use only recycled aggregate, however, in practice the use of virgin material was justified as a limestone quarry is located just a few hundred metres from the site. Although a non-renewable resource, it relates geologically, it provides local employment, and is quick, cheap and easy to transport to the construction site.

Flexibility was necessary in the development of soil amelioration strategies, capitalizing on the availability of suitable materials within a reasonable distance of the site. A wide variety of soil ameliorants are being used, including locally available spent mushroom compost, sewage sludge as well as animal and green manures. The project maintains that analysis can demonstrate that it may be preferable to ameliorate some areas through the use of surplus topsoil that is available just five miles away, rather than transporting sewage sludge from 30 miles away.

The design team made informed judgements regarding the evaluation of local procurement versus low impact materials. The social, economic, and community aspects of sustainability were given added weight due to awareness that European funding bodies hold the employment of local people, and stimulation of the regional economy, as a key measure of their support for the project.

The experience at the Earth Centre demonstrates that the required quantities of recycled materials

Figure 11.6   Timber structures evocative of natural forms, used to support climbing plants.

need to be sourced well in advance of the construction phase, taking full account of the relatively high environmental and financial costs of haulage. If stockpiling materials in advance of use, due consideration must also be given to storage issues. The client will ideally be sympathetic to the need to invest in additional contract management time; Dan Epstein, Director of Sustainability for the project points out, 'Somebody has to pay for the extra time it takes to procure sustainably'. If not monitored, the relative expense of the research, consultancy, and contractor management time can become a significant cost, outweighing potential savings. This is despite the fact that, given the rising cost of landfill, sustainable, perhaps locally sourced material, such as unwanted topsoil or recycled glass cullet, may cost less, or even be obtained free of charge.

Implementation

The Earth Centre's Sustainability Directorate produced specific guidelines regarding such issues as potential environmental and health impacts during implementation. Notably, it stressed the need for these matters to be considered at the design stage. Other factors considered include issues of re-use, health and safety, transportation, need for specialist labour and care not to over-specify materials.

Figure 11.7   Concept sketch for the 'gridshell' structures and 'forest gardens'.

Figure 11.8 Model of 'gridshell' oak and steel shelter, marrying ancient and modern technologies.

Figure 11.9 'Gridshell' structure, demonstrating traditional greenwood lath construction, and offering visual interest in the new landscape.

Maintenance issues were also considered by the designers, paying particular attention to the ease and cost of maintenance, the need for specialist contractors, the frequency of replacement of parts, and the health and safety issues associated with maintenance. As with management strategy, this is an area often overlooked in the conventional design process, despite being fundamental to the durability and longevity of a scheme, a point developed further in Chapter 13.

Life cycle thinking is at the heart of sustainable design (Brezet and van Hemel, 1997; Fussler and James, 1996). The Earth Centre demonstrates this through consideration, at the design stage, of after use and decommissioning. Issues such as the economic and practical viability of removal and re-use of building structures, foundations, cladding, fixtures and fittings are thus considered.

Conclusion

One of the clear aims of the project is to demonstrate a physical embodiment of sustainability at all levels, tackling a wide spectrum of sustainability issues and techniques. The visitor to the Earth Centre is presented with a landscape design that has been driven by ecological considerations. Natural processes and ergonomics have guided the design process throughout, thus allowing the buildings, plazas, paths, and gardens to become integral, symbiotic elements of the whole. By allowing natural systems to dictate the structure, the Earth Centre landscape demonstrates that a sustainably designed site can acquire a sense of integrity and permanence that grows directly from the designer's response to the environmental context and sense of place.

There is much published material that details the environmental costs and benefits of alternative materials. However, the experience at the Earth Centre demonstrates that it is the first-hand experience and incrementally acquired knowledge and understanding of the applications, contexts and systems, that prove instrumental in the successful delivery of sustainable design on such a scale. The ability of the project to call on a wide range of experts is a significant benefit of scale, as interdisciplinary working can allow synergy and potential idea and technology transfer. As sustainable design may require some unconventional practices, it is important that the rationale is discussed with the client and suppliers, and good channels of communication are maintained.

Had it not been the subject of a tight time-scale (detailed design began in April 1997, and construction started just six months later), the scheme might have developed differently, perhaps more organically. However, the skills of inspired, informed, and intuitive designers have allowed the delivery of sensitive and responsive solutions that provide a strong structure for the development of future phases. The site is 'deliberately planned to evolve and redefine its character well into the next century' (Grant and Bass, 1998, p. 33). While acknowledging that there are still many unresolved issues with the landscape at the Earth Centre, Dan Epstein is confident that they have come close to meeting their objective; 'We set out to create a case study in sustainable architecture and landscape architecture; what it is, and how it can be achieved. We've gone a long way towards this goal in many different ways.' He argues that it is the designer's approach, which is critical:

> To work sustainably requires a real paradigm shift in the way the world is seen. Many landscape architects use sustainable materials and techniques although the actual design is not inherently sustainable. It's very difficult to create something truly sustainable as an afterthought, you must have a feel for it, and therefore consider it from the outset.
>
> (pers. comm., 1999)

The creation of a large-scale physical presence is justified by the need to attract a mass audience of people who have not been exposed to sustainability issues. The project directors strongly felt that this could only be achieved by creating a centre that was big and exciting enough to generate national and international interest. As the largest integrated sustainable development of its kind in Europe, it is on a scale that allows best practice to be demonstrated in a context that can be applied to other large developments in towns and cities. The greatest claim that could be made for the project is the demonstration that, given the right approach, sustainable solutions can be accomplished within design interventions of all sizes, from suburban back gardens through to vast country parks or urban regeneration schemes.

With the aim of building a platform for sustainability, while still meeting the specific objectives of a large-scale project run to tight deadlines, the project provided a challenge to the landscape architects. In Andrew Grant's experience, one of the characteristic features of a sustainable design project on such a scale is the need for strong teamwork, with excellent communications between disciplines. This often breaks the mould of conventional practice and professional relationships, requiring the integration of different aspects of design work (pers. comm., 1999). Sustainable design, as found at the Earth Centre, is typified by its diversity, with the nature of spaces, land uses, and types of feature responding to variables such as microclimate, soil type, or aspect. Thus the design is enriched through a design process seeking to provide appropriate responses to what are sometimes subtle differences in context or circumstance.

Andrew Grant describes the work of a landscape architect concerned with sustainable design as requiring a 'huge amount of common sense, tempered by a good working knowledge of sustainability principles' (pers. comm., 1999). A pragmatic and flexible attitude is required whereby problems can be seen as opportunities, with constraints and 'wild cards' thus generating creative responses and often unconventional solutions; in other words, necessity is the mother of invention.

CASE STUDY 2: CENTER PARCS

The Center Parcs company was established in Holland in 1967, based on the concept of 'a villa in the forest' for short break holidays; giving the highly urbanized Dutch population the chance to escape the hustle and bustle of everyday life. It is an international organization, which sees a high quality, and sustainable environment as a fundamental part of its

Figure 11.10   The Center Parcs forest environment.

forest resorts, and which has put in place a range of processes to ensure that growth is appropriate, and that the landscape is developed with sensitivity (Figure 11.10).

Over the past thirty years the concept has continued to evolve. A number of forest resorts are now home to an extensive range of indoor and outdoor leisure facilities and accommodation, located in settings which provide access to nature; particularly the restful and restorative qualities of water and woodland. There are currently thirteen villages, located in five European countries, Holland, Germany, Belgium, France, and the UK. The first development in the UK was opened in 1987 at Rufford in the Sherwood Forest (Goodfellow, 1990).

From its inception, Center Parcs has been keen to establish its environmental credentials, in part because the promotion of sustainable living accords with the intended visitor experience, but also because

the company regards its long-term success as being dependent on sustainable practice. A regularly reviewed and updated corporate environmental strategy has existed since 1991, providing a broad framework for site development and operational management. The involvement of many environmental consultants with the developments has led to a particularly thorough and reflective approach to planning and design.

The principles of blending new villages harmoniously into the countryside, of taking into account water and energy demands in forward planning, of creating much needed local employment in rural areas, and of enhancing biodiversity within the village sites are some examples of the enlightened environmental practices of the organization. In sustainability terms, these concerns balance criticisms regarding development in greenfield locations, and the fact that most visitors arrive by car.

As a company demonstrating an awareness of environmental issues, and aiming to make continual improvements in performance, Center Parcs is closely aligned to the approaches identified in the Business Charter for Sustainable Development, established by the International Chamber of Commerce in 1991 (ICC, 1991). In partnership with English Nature, Center Parcs has developed a corporate Biodiversity Action Initiative, and in July 1999 achieved the ISO accreditation for effective environmental management systems (ISO 14001). This applics to all its sites.

Concept and design guidelines

The forest resorts are developed in accordance with an overall concept, which broadly reflects the philosophy of the first development at De Lommerbergen in Holland. This concept, promoting a number of planning principles and design guidelines, was established to guide all subsequent developments. As the company expanded, opening more resorts, this ensured comparable standards of visitor experience, through the application of good practice. Throughout the life of the company, the concept has evolved, with sustainable design and management practice taking on increasing significance.

In relation to landscape and site development the key aims are:

- to carefully integrate buildings and landscape, with minimal disturbance to significant existing site features and vegetation;
- to create a naturalistic setting with enclosure by trees, open glades, and views of water;
- to promote an informal visitor experience with opportunities for sport, recreation, and healthy living;

Figure 11.11 Villas in the forest.

Table 11.1 Summary of the impacts of the proposed Center Parcs holiday village at Aucombe Wood (Longleat)

Impacts of construction		Impacts of operation		
	Short-term		Short-term	Long-term
LAND		**LAND**		
Landscape	●	Landscape	○	○
Soil and geology		Soil and geology		
Emissions and deposits		Emissions and deposits		
Agriculture		Agriculture		
Forestry		Forestry		
Minerals (material assets)		Minerals (material assets)		
Waste disposal		Waste disposal		
WATER		**WATER**		
Surface water and drainage		Surface water and drainage		
Ground water		Ground water		
Water quality		Water quality		
AIR		**AIR**		
Air quality		Air quality		
Climate		Climate		
NOISE		**NOISE**		
VIBRATION		**VIBRATION**		
HEAT		**HEAT**		
LIGHT		**LIGHT**		
ECOLOGY		**ECOLOGY**		
Species	●	Species	○	○
Habitats		Habitats	○	○
CULTURAL HERITAGE		**CULTURAL HERITAGE**		
Archaeology		Archaeology		
Architectural heritage		Architectural heritage		
PEOPLE		**PEOPLE**		
Population		Population		
Local businesses	○	Local businesses	○	○
Employment	○	Employment	○	○
Traffic	●	Traffic	●	●
Infrastructure	○	Infrastructure	○	○
Recreation	○	Recreation	○	○
Pollution		Pollution		

Notes: ○ Significant positive impact
   ○ Minor positive impact
   ● Minor negative impact

- to enhance biodiversity within each of the village sites;
- to exclude cars from villages, with promotion of cycle and pedestrian traffic;
- to establish information and education programmes, focusing on conservation and landscape awareness.

This generic concept establishes a pattern, similar in idea to Christopher Alexander's *Pattern Language*, in which he specifies good practice guidelines for many aspects of urban design (Alexander *et al.*, 1977). In the case of Center Parcs, the pattern establishes an overall model for resort development, with factors such as layout relationships, size, and density specified. Design teams utilize the model in the development of site-specific plans, and must present a strong case if they propose to vary elements of the standard concept. This approach could be seen as excessively restrictive, inhibiting one of the tenets of ecological design, that solutions grow from place (Van der Ryn and Cowan, 1996, p. 57); however, it does ensure that the principles and standards set by Center Parcs are consistently achieved. The benefits of a modular approach with built in feedback and improvement mechanisms also result.

Development phase

Each development starts with the identification of the overall geographical catchment area. A thorough analysis of every area of forest within the catchment is undertaken, and features such as ancient woodland, nature reserves, archaeological sites, and areas of insufficient forest cover, are excluded from the potential development area. Typically a village site comprises 400 acres of coniferous forest of medium age. The coniferous woodland chosen for the

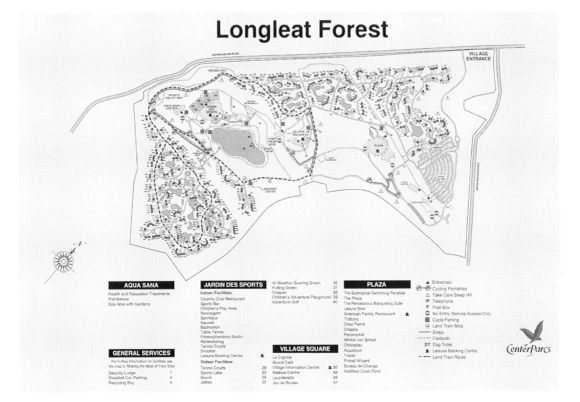

Figure 11.12 The Center Parcs' Longleat Forest Master Plan.

developments is always of low ecological value, though the forest setting is potentially attractive from within, and allows development to be visually absorbed by the surrounding landscape (Figure 11.11).

In the UK the most recent forest resort opened in 1994 at Longleat in Wiltshire. An environmental assessment was carried out in accordance with Department of Environment Guidelines (DoE, 1989), and in common with established practice, the assessment identified the extent of impacts of construction and operation related to the proposed resort, and also indicated mitigation measures (Table 11.1).

Ecological, visual and other site factors further influence detailed planning. Buildings and infrastructure are carefully located in accord with existing topography, and the development is screened through the retention of a wide band of mature trees around the site (Figure 11.12). Where appropriate, earth mounding is also used. As Managing Director

Peter Moore observes, 'The end result is a landscape where the buildings and infrastructure are subservient to the natural landscape' (pers. comm., 1999).

Typically, each forest resort is comprised of about 600 villas, a central plaza with a subtropical swimming pool, sporting and leisure facilities, and restaurants and shops. There is usually a main lake, with a series of connected water areas, and edge of site car parks, where guests must leave their cars. The layout of all sites follows the same pattern, with variations dictated by local factors and refinements aimed at enhancing the holiday experience. Some plans adopt a centralized approach to the location of facilities, while in others they are more dispersed. In general, the central facilities overlook the lake, with villas distributed around the site, and ancillary features, such as play areas, nature trails, and cycling facilities strategically dispersed within the enclosing woodland setting (Figure 11.13).

Figure 11.13 A cycle centre, a key feature of all forest resorts.

As construction is potentially the most damaging stage of development, problems of site disturbance and compaction are reduced through the designation of future lakes and waterway areas as storage compounds and construction routes. In recent developments, site impact has been minimized through the off-site manufacture of villas, which are then manoeuvred into position by crane.

The retention and protection of areas of ecological significance, the creation of lakes, streams and grasslands throughout the villages, and the introduction of certain species of plants and animals from local sources, all serve to enhance the overall aesthetic and ecological value of the forest locations. To ensure conservation of vulnerable features at the Longleat resort, protective fencing was erected prior to the arrival of contractors. Ecological monitoring was carried out during the construction phase, and did not highlight any loss of flora or fauna.

Biodiversity Action Initiative

'Action for Biodiversity', the recently published company mission statement (Center Parcs, 1999) is available to visitors and staff, illustrating a commitment to the notion of environmentally sustainable development. Objectives of the 'Action Plan' are:

- to avoid sites with high natural diversity; continuing instead to seek sites with low or damaged biodiversity, which can then be improved;
- to maintain and enhance the wildlife and habitats in the resorts, taking full account of the characteristic biodiversity of the local area;
- to ensure that operations do not conflict with other biodiversity action beyond the boundaries of a resort;
- to participate in local, national, and wider initiatives for biodiversity conservation and enhancement;
- to disseminate natural biodiversity conservation information to guests and public;
- to purchase materials from living sources such as wood, plants or composts, only when they have been shown to be harvested or grown in a sustainable manner;

- to monitor and review performance against developing local and national standards, updating actions as necessary.

This initiative has evolved from long-standing measures taken to enhance wildlife conservation on the forest resort sites. Center Parcs emphasizes the success of the approach, claiming in 1997:

> Some twenty-six locally or nationally scarce species of flora have been recorded amongst the 571 species recorded on UK villages to date. This includes over 182 species of nationally or locally scarce invertebrates, with twenty of these classified as red-data book species due to their rarity. Rare British breeding birds such as Crossbill are now breeding on all three villages and firecrest are breeding at Longleat village this year, for the first time. Fallow and roe deer are remaining on the villages since prior to construction and are breeding on site on an annual basis.
>
> (Center Parcs, 1997)

Describing the way in which such successes are achieved, they explain that:

> A typical example is the management of gorse to provide a habitat for linnet, a bird whose population has declined in the UK by fifty per cent for the past twenty-five years, with a mosaic of varying heights of gorse maintained to successfully attract nesting sites for this species.
>
> (Center Parcs, 1999)

The conservation measures are developed in line with recommendations contained within the Department of the Environment and UK Biodiversity Group's recommendations. (UK Biodiversity Group, 1994a, 1994b, 1998a, 1998b, 1999a, 1999b, 1999c, 1999d).

Continuing design and management

At the heart of the Center Parcs philosophy is the recognition that landscape is dynamic, requiring effective design and management on an ongoing basis. The landscape managers keep themselves informed through the use of annual site usage surveys, and ecological monitoring (Center Parcs, 1997). This work is undertaken by teams that include site managers, ecologists, and is headed in the UK by a chartered landscape architect, Mark Waller. Mark leads the Europe wide Center Parcs Head Office Development Landscape Group. With representation from each resort, this group meets regularly to address development and management issues, and review and refine policy.

Forest Management Plans are prepared by the Landscape Group to apply uniquely to each village (Figure 11.14). The aim of the plans is to ensure the continuing viability of the landscape, in accordance with the overall design principles; and to draw up financial schedules for the subsequent ten years. Biodiversity action targets are set to concur with the Biodiversity Action Initiative, and local authority environmental strategies. Detailed implementation is

achieved through forest resort 'Work Plans', and 'Standards of Performance'. These also feed into more general planning. Landscape types typically include: central area planting, outdoor recreational area planting, car park planting, villa areas, woodland and natural areas, ground services, utility areas, and waterways.

Management and design objectives will vary according to the intensity of use of an area type. The intended form for each landscape is identified, with consideration to requirements such as views, privacy, natural lighting, and specified planting characteristics. Management procedures are, in turn, identified for various plant types including; herbaceous, woodland edge, coniferous, and water and bank side vegetation. These procedures are very specific, covering such aspects as cultivation, planting, thinning, re-establishment and protection, as well as explaining the design intentions and costs.

Figure 11.14   The Center Parcs' Longleat Forest Management Plan.

Much of this work can be described as routine landscape maintenance, however, continuing design is a key feature in planning and management decisions, and sustainable design practice is high on the agenda. For example, instead of using concrete revetments to stabilize erosion of the lake edge at Sherwood Forest, living mats of vegetation were used. Ongoing landscape development can also involve working in conjunction with the local naturalist trust in the re-establishment of heathland, ancient woodland, and other habitat types. There is also a close working relationship with English Nature in relation to the national Species Recovery Programme (UK Biodiversity Group, 1994a, 1994b, 1998a, 1998b, 1999a, 1999b, 1999c, 1999d).

The absence of such a dynamic approach to landscape management undermines many potentially sustainable landscape designs, and highlights the uniqueness of the Center Parcs developments. This was recognized in the 1999 Landscape Institute Management Award given to Center Parcs. The jury commented that the 'landscape management plan is a fully co-ordinated, integrated, dynamic, enlightened and workable document' (*Landscape Design*, 1999).

Because of the forest locations, woodland rejuvenation is of particular significance. A detailed audit of woodland characteristics is made for each village, and felling cycles commence (with a 60-year cycle for conifers, 80 years for deciduous trees). Management methods take account of the sustainability and biodiversity of the forest, with large-scale clearance of trees avoided, maintaining continuous tree cover wherever possible. The diversity and regeneration of the woodland habitat are seen as a priority, achieved through management for natural regeneration, and complemented by the extensive planting of appropriate tree and shrub species. Forest products are used within the management cycle, where appropriate, including charcoal production for resale in local retail outlets, wood chippings for footpaths and ornamental planting, and first pole thinnings for fencing products.

In accordance with company policy, quarterly quality control meetings are held with ground services managers on each of the sites. Regular progress reports, with identified actions, are required. The Head Office Development Landscape Group vets any significant changes to the landscape, such as new buildings or facilities, in relation to the overall concept.

Conclusion

Center Parcs offers many examples of actions that are applicable in the pursuit of sustainable landscape design. These can be summarized as:

- clearly articulated company policy on environmental aspects;
- regular review and updating of overall planning and design concepts;
- tried and tested planning and design principles applied to all projects;
- the establishment of a corporate Biodiversity Action Initiative;
- annual ecological monitoring of sites to inform landscape management;
- ongoing landscape design, management, and quality control;
- regard for customer comment, and anticipation of customer demand;
- continuing investment in the environment, and in education of guests and staff.

The close adherence to a pattern of development initially planned as a response to the flat landscape of the Netherlands, maximizing proximity to water, has presented design difficulties on those sites, such as Longleat, with a more hilly terrain. Although these problems were largely overcome by discussion at the design stage, it suggests the need for Center Parcs to re-appraise the conceptual framework in relation to new developments that are geographically dispersed.

The use of cars is not allowed within the resorts, however, most visitors arrive and depart by car, due in large part to the rural locations of the developments. Ironically, the popularity and consistently high standards achieved by the organization seem to stimulate visitors to travel further in order to experience different forest resorts. While this makes commercial sense, it serves to illustrate the difficulty of planning for long-term sustainable solutions where circumstances are outside the direct control of an organization. Perhaps the most significant positive feature of the Center Parcs company is the willingness to continually review performance in relation to environmental good practice, and to take action accordingly.

CASE STUDY 3: MEANWHILE GARDENS

Located in Ladbroke Grove, West London, Meanwhile Gardens is a well-loved community open space. Established through the inspiration of the artist, Jamie McCullough in 1976, for a long time the site had a temporary nature and uncertain future. As a consequence, the park developed in a fragmented, piecemeal fashion, with trees, shrubs, furniture, and structural elements added over the years. In 1997, the Meanwhile Gardens Community Association applied for charitable funding in order to fund the rejuvenation of the park through redesign. Matched funding is being provided by several bodies, including the London Waterways Partnership. Following a competitive bidding procedure (including presentations to the Community Association), the client group appointed Planet Earth Chartered Landscape Architects as design consultants.

Concept development

Matt Davies, principal landscape architect of the practice, which specializes in sustainable design and community-orientated projects, describes the adopted approach as 'multiplicity within unity'. He describes this as an evolution from the traditional masterplanning route, whereby a single, comprehensive plan is finalized ahead of any groundworks, to a system of 'modular planning', employing a more flexible and adaptable approach. The aim is to create diversity of atmosphere and function within a unified whole, and to achieve this through the involvement of stakeholders in the design and implementation process. He is particularly concerned with the

involvement of interest and user groups, as well as of professionals. The degree and timing of this stakeholder participation vary according to the staging and available resourcing of the programme. The consultation and engagement process has enabled a more sensitive, site specific design development; one which can be fine-tuned and adapted over time, as appropriate (Matt Davies, pers. comm.).

As well as consulting the Association steering group, local opinion and ideas were actively sought during exhibitions of the proposals. These exhibitions were held at the local library, and at an on-site festival day. The fact that the response rate was not high can be interpreted either as the result of broad community support for the proposals (with no vehement objections), or as a result of apathy; or perhaps as a combination of both. This experience, developed further in Chapter 12, highlights a recurrent problem faced by designers seeking effective community engagement in community-based projects. Although in the case of Meanwhile Gardens the local Community Association has been closely consulted, such a group can prove to be representative of a vocal minority rather than of either the (silent) majority, or of other minority groups who may prove critical to the success or failure of a scheme. These minority groups can be diverse, possibly including; local teenagers, people with mobility problems, drug users, homeless people, or ethnic minorities.

Working with the fragmented nature of the linear park, the design team have embraced the different identities of the four distinct areas, seeking to enhance the diversity, as well as to enrich existing features, linking them through the use of unifying elements. The most overt example of this linkage is the meandering 'Golden Thread' path, which runs the length of the gardens (Figure 11.15):

Rather than imposing a grand plan, our proposal is to focus on the human-scale details of corners, edges, pockets, junctions and openings; to make subtle additions. A new sequence of fragments are threaded along a unifying spinal path . . . Elements will be composed of flexible systems and repeated motifs.

(Planet Earth, 1999)

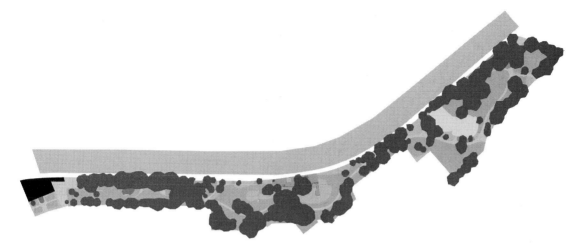

Figure 11.15   A composite plan of Meanwhile Gardens.

It is the intention of the designers to return to the site periodically after completion of their primary involvement, in order to monitor the efficacy of the redesign, and in order to suggest possible refinements and improvements.

Community involvement

The Community Association is encouraging the direct involvement of local users with the detailed design stage. Thus, one of the voluntary gardeners, who has worked for over ten years in the gardens, is providing planting proposals for a courtyard and pond area (Figure 11.16), and a skate-park designer is working with local skaters in the adaptation and refinement of an area of sculpted concrete landforms. The new design also allows space for the creation of a small Islamic garden by the local Moroccan community. Other parts of the site, such as the MIND Garden, function well and hence require only minor adjustment. The MIND Garden is the domain of a charity for people with learning difficulties (MIND), and has been gradually developed and improved over the years. It accommodates the gardening activities of members, as well as of local people undertaking community service duties.

Access

Meanwhile Gardens meets the sustainability criterion of accessibility at many levels. It is located close to a London Underground tube station, alongside bus stops, with boundaries defined by a road and a canal, thus allowing access by foot, train, car, bus, bike or boat. The London Waterways Partnership is co-operating in the removal of fencing along the Grand Union Canal, in order to make the gardens a part of the waterside environment. Links to other sites in the locality are provided along the towpath, for example, to the Peabody Trust and North Kensington Environmental Forum Site of Nature Conservation Importance (a former gasworks). The park is also located on the route of the annual Notting Hill Carnival Parade, and has large, inviting signs and route-marking at the two main entrances (Figure 11.17).

Unlike many urban 'pocket parks' and community spaces, the gardens are never closed. Twenty-four-hour access is a principle that the Community Association are keen to defend, preferring the vigilance of the gardeners and other local inhabitants and passers-by to the intrusive eyes of closed circuit television, or to the nightly closure of the community space. The Association also supports the maintenance and enhancement of the many points of

Figure 11.16 The pond area of Meanwhile Gardens is to be re-developed with the help of a local gardening enthusiast.

Figure 11.17 The gardens are the focus for community activities and events that encourage contact between the diverse social groups that use this inner city park.

access to the gardens, with the new design incorporating no fewer than fifteen points of entrance or exit, with a hierarchy of scale, type and signage, and paths or routes to match. The aim of providing so many points of entry and criss-crossing paths is to maximize the pedestrian permeability of the site. As a long, thin parcel of land, it is felt to be important to accommodate the needs and desires of users to pass through, into, and along the site.

As the gardens are long established, the design team has been able to benefit from surveys of usage. Thus pedestrian and cycle desire lines are being formalized, and paths and level changes are being upgraded to accommodate all users. The Community Association has specifically instructed the design team to incorporate features that allow shared access for pedestrian and wheeled users (including baby buggies, wheelchairs, skates and bicycles). Based on previous experience, they foresee no need for segregated paths, though as shown in Figure 11.18, the new path does enable a degree of separation. Motorcycle barriers have been incorporated along the canal towpath, but are designed to allow the passage of bicycles. The Association has, however, requested that the design incorporate lockable vehicle gates, in case of repeated incidents of fly tipping.

Materials

The Concept Statement for the (re)design of the gardens explains that 'Cheap, modern, and durable

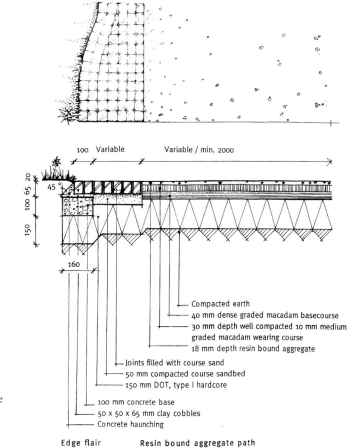

Figure 11.18 Construction details for the 'Golden Thread' path, and utilizing a previous path as a base course (drawn by S. Vercammen).

100 Variable   Variable / min. 2000

45°

150 100 65 20

160

Compacted earth
40 mm dense graded macadam basecourse
30 mm depth well compacted 10 mm medium graded macadam wearing course
18 mm depth resin bound aggregate

Joints filled with course sand
50 mm compacted course sandbed
150 mm DOT, type I hardcore

100 mm concrete base
50 x 50 x 65 mm clay cobbles
Concrete haunching

Edge flair   Resin bound aggregate path

materials will be introduced, and embellished with intricate detail' (Planet Earth, 1999). Matt Davies adds that other fundamental criteria in materials selection and specification are concerned more specifically with issues of sustainability. These include: reliability, durability, and low embodied energy. He points out that consideration of all the criteria gives rise to a matrix whereby the designer has to compromise, playing off positive features of one selection criterion against negative points of another. An example of the need for this pragmatic approach can be seen in the choices made by the design team in the selection of materials for the central path. In order to keep environmental and economic costs down, it was decided to utilize much of the existing tarmacadam path as the base for a new wearing course (Figure 11.18). This necessitated the use of resin to bind the surface layer of crushed stone and glass cullet. Although not an ideal solution from an ecological standpoint, this gives the natural, warm appearance preferred by the client, and does allow the use of crushed, re-cycled glass and re-claimed stone, or surplus quarry chippings. The meandering sides of this central spine of the path are constructed of *in situ*, coloured concrete. This provides an opportunity for the use of road scrapings or crushed brick/stone as aggregate. The edging to the path is of clay cobbles. Matt explains that these have a natural, warm and 'earthy' appearance, as preferred by the client; as well as having a low embodied energy content. Elsewhere, stone setts have been re-used from other areas of the site.

As far as possible, the material operation of Meanwhile Gardens is as a closed system. The two gardeners thus seek to use organic methods, with organic mulches and fertilizers, and on-site composting. Coppice wands can provide material for gardening, art, and craft use. The species selection and incorporation of organic matter within the soil reduces the need for watering, and it is intended that a solar-powered fountain will aerate the pond. The design incorporates basic principles of microclimate management, with windbreaks and shelterbelts, and the provision of shade trees.

Throughout the site consideration has been given to the selection of planting materials to foster habitat creation and biodiversity. Native species have been used, although not exclusively, as the wishes of the client group have been allowed to moderate purely environmental ideals. Wherever possible, imported plant materials are being sourced from organic nurseries as near to site as possible, and a low energy lighting system has been selected for evening and night-time use.

Conclusion

The redesign of Meanwhile Gardens seeks to address sustainability issues at many levels. It is a prime example of a functional inner city, community-orientated open space; a demonstration of landscape design which is flexible and holistic in approach, resolution and delivery. The layout and function of the site have been allowed to develop organically over the years, accommodating diverse activities and user groups, with the recent design adaptations proving necessarily sensitive and responsive, with built in mechanisms for refinement and adaptation.

CASE STUDY 4: OOSTVAARDERSPLASSEN

Prior to 1932 the land that now forms the Oostvaardersplassen nature reserve in the Netherlands was entirely beneath the Wadden Sea, an inlet of the North Sea. It now occupies some 56 square kilometres, a wide, flat landscape with open water, reed swamp, grassland, scrub, and woodland. The area conveys a strong sense of wilderness, and yet is virtually sandwiched between the fast-growing towns of Lelystad (population 60,000 to 80,000) and Almere (population currently around 200,000), about 35 kilometres north east of Amsterdam. Grazing herds of 'wild' cattle, horses, and deer further contribute to a feeling of being far from civilization, almost akin to the plains of the Serengeti. The reserve has considerable ecological interest, supporting a very impressive bird community, with 260 recorded species; ninety breeding, and thirty on the IUCN Red Data endangered list. The area is of international importance, supporting significant proportions of the population of several north-west European bird species, designated as a Ramsar Wetland Site, and Special Protection Area under the EU Birds Directive (Wigbels, 1997). The reserve currently attracts over 100,000 visitors annually.

History of development

The reserve has come about entirely as a result of human activity, although initially as an unforeseen consequence of a different project. In 1932 the construction of the Barrier Dam across the Wadden Sea created a large lake, Ijsselmeer, which became freshwater. Subsequently, parts of the lake were reclaimed by drainage to create four polders. The last of these, a 44,000-hectare polder called Southern Flevoland, was created in 1968 with the intention of using most of it for agriculture and new towns, but with 25 per cent zoned for forestry and nature reserves. The area to the west of Lelystad was intended for industrial development, but an economic

recession in the early 1970s prevented this from occurring. In addition, this part of the polder remained partially waterlogged because of rich clay deposits, and the marsh and open water that resulted succeeded in attracting increasing numbers of wetland birds.

In 1974, due to its developing ecological interest, a decision was taken by the Ministry of Traffic and Water Management (Ministerie van Verkeer en Waterstaat), responsible for the creation and development of polders, to designate the area as a nature reserve. Moreover, it was also decided that 'design and management' should be primarily by natural processes, and that human intervention should be minimal.

Hydrology

In 1974, an embankment was built around the 3,600 hectares of marshland and open water in order to maintain adequately high water levels while drainage

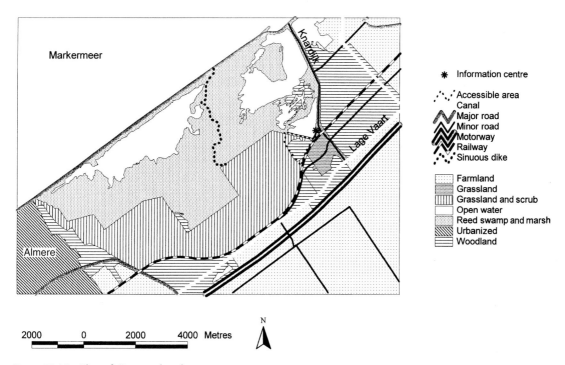

Figure 11.19 Plan of Oostvaardersplassen nature reserve.

of the surrounding area proceeded. At about the same time the latter was seeded in preparation for conversion to agriculture. However, by 1978 it was decided to add 2,000 hectares of this drier, partly cultivated land to the reserve, to improve the ecological integrity of the area (Figure 11.19). After some considerable discussion this was achieved through the realignment of the intended Almere to Lelystad railway, which would have gone immediately adjacent to the marshland. In 1997, this drier area supported ninety-two breeding bird species (Bijlsma, 1997). To help maintain the diversity of wetland habitat types, an additional sinuous dike was constructed across the marshland, separating the drier western part from the wetter eastern part (Figure 11.20). Nonetheless, over the succeeding years it was recognized that annual variations in climate, particularly the likelihood of excessively wet and dry years occurring once or twice every ten years, might themselves maintain habitat diversity, though

in a more dynamic and naturalistic way. Consequently, within the past three years, it has been decided to rely more upon climatic temporal variation, and the dike has now been breached in several places so that the eastern and western marshlands become a single system again.

Overall, the area experiences an imbalance between mean annual precipitation (860 mm) and evaporation (560 mm). Drainage from the marshland is necessary to prevent long-term progressive inundation. This is now being rationalized in the form of a single sluice in the north-west corner, designed to remove the excess water (300 mm annually), and thereby maintain the necessary temporal variation, irrespective of a particular year's climatic conditions. The hydrology of the 2,000 hectares of grassland is more carefully controlled, with the intention of approximately maintaining a ratio of 2:1, dry to wet grassland. Additional shallow pools are currently being excavated at the western end of the reserve.

Figure 11.20   View looking north across wetter, eastern part of Oostvaardersplassen.

These will attract birds and herbivores, thus allowing the people of Almere to view the wildlife from the perimeter of the reserve. The clay spoil from this operation is being sold for reinforcement of dikes damaged by recent floods, elsewhere in the Netherlands.

Grazing

Early in the reserve's history it was recognized that grazing herbivores would be a necessary component of the ecosystem, diversifying the habitat structure, and forestalling succession of most of the area to climax woodland. To further minimize the requirement for human intervention it was decided to select undomesticated herbivores that were effectively 'wild'. Between 1983 and 1985, thirty-five Heck cattle and twenty Konik horses were therefore introduced (Figure 11.21). The Konik horses came from Poland, and are close to the ancestral wild horse.

Heck cattle are a breed developed earlier this century in order to recreate something close to the extinct Auroch, the ancestor of modern cattle. The animals are allowed to roam freely across the reserve, setting up their own social groups, with no human interference. There are now approximately 470 cattle and 380 horses, all of which tend to stay in the drier areas.

In 1992, forty-five red deer were introduced (Figure 11.22). As a result of their successful breeding, about 360 individuals now play a significant part in grazing back the denser vegetation, which is not normally penetrated by the cattle or horses. The diversity of the reed beds is maintained through grazing by large flocks of migratory greylag geese (*Anser anser*).

Access

At present the majority of visitors arrive by car, the reserve being 10 kilometres from the nearest railway

Figure 11.21 A family group of Konik horses.

Figure 11.22   Red deer among the grassland and scrub of Oostvaardersplassen.

station in Lelystad. A significant minority visit by cycle, and a new cycle route that circumnavigates the entire reserve is almost complete. For most of its history, public access to the reserve has been restricted to the use of observation points around the site periphery, particularly along the Knardijk, on the eastern boundary. In 1996, however, the National Forestry Service (Staatsbosbeheer) took over the reserve, introducing a policy of greater public access and involvement than the previous managers, the Ministry of Traffic and Water Management. An information centre was established, together with marked trails leading to several observation points, across 75 hectares of the reserve. In addition, by prior agreement, guided excursions can now be taken around parts of the outer reserve, although in the case of bus trips these are restricted to two per day. There is no public access to the very sizeable core of the reserve.

Within the next two to three years it is intended to build a larger information centre with additional facilities. In addition, the triangle of land in the south-east corner, bounded by the railway line, Knardijk and Lage Vaart, will be developed for public access. A representative sample of habitats, complete with grazing herbivores, will be open to the public for no charge, thus reducing the anticipated growth in pressure on the main part of the reserve. Guided tours, booked in advance and charged for, will still be available around the peripheral regions of the main reserve.

Sustainable landscape design at Oostvaardersplassen

Biodiversity is a key indicator for any kind of sustainable development and the recent UK government publication on the subject (DETR, 1999) identifies populations of wild birds as one of fourteen key headline indicators. Since 1974 the principal aim of the Oostvaardersplassen project has been the conservation and enhancement of biodiversity, particularly for bird species, and in this respect Oostvaardersplassen has been very successful. Detailed, scientific monitoring of both vegetation and bird life has been undertaken since 1974. In addition to the growth in bird species' diversity, results for vegetation show marked increases in vascular plant diversity from just over fifty species in 1975, to over three hundred in 1995 (Jans and Drost, 1995). Vegetational structure has also improved considerably.

Another important component of sustainable landscape design is to work with natural processes, wherever possible. This has been the intention at Oostvaardersplassen, with the concept taken further than in many comparable schemes. The scale of the project allows for the co-existence of a diversity of habitat types and associated species, albeit in spatial configurations that change over time. Whitbread and Jenman (1995) argue the benefits of this approach, making the additional point that large areas, managed more by natural processes, are likely to have lower maintenance costs than small isolated nature reserves, requiring intensive management. However, Tubbs (1996) argues that minimizing human intervention may not produce the greatest benefits for biodiversity, and that extensive, traditional, low-intensity agricultural systems may be better. Also, despite the intentions at Oostvaardersplassen, there are clear practical limitations to the use of natural processes. There will always be a need to actively manage the hydrology, although attempts have been made to reduce the degree of intervention. In addition, continuing growth in the grazing herbivore populations could have serious consequences, both ecologically and politically. Computer models predict that the area could support twice the current number of grazing herbivores, but in so doing the mosaic of habitats is likely to suffer irreversible damage. As the carrying capacity of the area is reached, the starvation of herbivores could become a major issue. This has already occurred on a small scale during harsh climatic conditions. The alternative strategy of culling would also have serious public relations implications.

Although the main aim of the reserve is to enhance biodiversity, the sustainability of the project is heavily influenced by the relationships with other 'stakeholders', be they government bodies, birdwatchers or the local communities. Until the reserve passed to the National Forestry Service in 1996, biologists from government and other professional bodies had run the project almost exclusively. Local communities were not involved and, as indicated earlier, public access to the reserve was not provided. Recently, however, there have been discussions with the local authorities for Lelystad and Almere, and growing links with voluntary organizations such as the Almere birdwatching club with 200 members. There are also plans to allow the grazing herbivores into the Hollandse Hout recreational forest, on the outskirts of Lelystad. This will need extensive consultation with the community in Lelystad, as it would require the banning of certain activities, such as horse riding, and dog walking.

The close proximity of the railway line provides potential for a more sustainable means of reaching the reserve. The Dutch railway authorities are reluctant to open a new station close to the reserve at present, though may reconsider once a nearby housing area is completed. Alternatively, a park and ride scheme could operate from the new housing area.

Conclusion

The development of Oostvaardersplassen has not lent itself to major involvement by the landscape architects. Most of the significant decisions have been taken by ecologists and other scientists, although the landscape profession has been involved in the creation of the scrapes on the western side, as well as with some of the adjacent woodlands which may eventually be incorporated into the reserve. The intention has been to produce a particular type of wild, naturalistic landscape, which, as such, constitutes a form of landscape design, even though the final shapes and spatial configurations of the components cannot be exactly predicted. The degree of dependence on natural processes operating to both develop and maintain the landscape of a large site clearly contributes to the sustainability of the design approach.

Other, similar, ecologically suitable sites in lowland areas may not always be as amenable to the approach adopted at Oostvaardersplassen. For example, as Tubbs (1996) points out, it is likely to

Table 11.2 Checklist for sustainable landscape design

Category		Considerations
People (Design and Community)		
1	Concept development	Early and effective liaison with all stakeholders
		Early and effective liaison with other professionals
		De-materialize aspects of design (e.g. replacement of a feature with a service or leased object)
2	Optimization of design	Maximize use of existing/available features
		Vernacular styles adopted where appropriate
		Maximize utility and scope of design
		Versatile design
		Conflicts of interest considered
		Inclusive/universal design of all facilities
3	Access	Located within reach of target users
		Links to external routes/features/places/public and private transport
		Effective information and publicity systems in place
		Clearly signed, entrance and exit points, paths and routes, accessible by all ages, abilities, etc.
		Segregation of traffic where appropriate
		Inclusive/universal design of all facilities
4	Optimize initial lifetime	Reliability and durability considered
		Ease of maintenance and repair
		Adaptable/modular design and structural elements (allowing refinement and development)
		Aesthetically resolved/'classic' design
5	User stage	Productive landscape (e.g. food growing, art and craft materials etc.)
		Closed system where possible (e.g. composting scheme, harvesting of rainwater etc.)
		Monitoring mechanisms planned
		Responsive management systems established
		Follow up visits by designers
6	Community involvement	Consensus building/facilitated workshops with local people of all ages/cultures/sexes/interests
		Participation by local stakeholders in design process
		Support and supervision of workshops/activities
		Locals involved with supervision of site/security
		Safety features to at least minimum standard

(continued on next page)

be a lot more difficult to develop a project on the scale required if the site is in multiple, rather than government, ownership. Nevertheless, Oostvaarders-plassen does provide useful insights into some of the components of sustainable landscape design. A completely new landscape has been created from land that once lay beneath the North Sea; partly through the large-scale exploitation of natural processes. Even allowing for the necessary and continuous human intervention, the result is very impressive, achieving a high degree of biodiversity and wilderness quality, despite its location close to heavily populated areas. The importance of providing such a facility for urban populations is increasingly being recognized,

Table 11.2 (continued)

Category	Considerations
Planet (Environment)	
1 Biodiversity	Indigenous species given priority
	Local provenance of plant stock
	Disturbance minimized
	Pollution minimized
	Existing plants protected from damage
	Sensitive habitats/ecosystems protected during use
2 Natural processes	Thorough site survey and analysis
	Hydrology preserved or enhanced
	Existing soils restored or enhanced
	Best practice handling and storage of topsoil
	Best practice planting, handling and storage of plants
	Pollution mitigated
	Microclimates considered
3 Resources	Specification of materials and objects guided by ecodesign and life cycle thinking (Brezet and Hemel, 1997)
	Waste minimized
	Efficient working practices adopted
	Production steps minimized
	Renewable, local energy sources used where possible
	Recycle, re-use and repair where possible
	Separate and store waste for recycling
	Ergonomic layout
	Organic and low impact design and specification
Profit (Financial)	
1 Funding	Ethical financing
	Multiple sources
	Grants and sponsorships considered
	Self financing
	Viable in medium to long term
	Cash flow adequate for projected activities
	Adaptable to changing scenarios
	Worst case scenarios considered
	Exit strategy planned
2 Stakeholders	Community fundraising
	Community ownership/controlling interest
	Sponsorship by local businesses
	Favourable deal for locals for access charges
	Employment opportunities/experience for locals

and there is evidence that even some of those who would not visit such a site still value its existence (Millward and Mostyn, 1989). The landscape development has relied heavily upon detailed and well-planned monitoring throughout the project, a key requirement for sustainable landscape architecture. Allied to this, perhaps the most valuable contribution Oostvaardersplassen makes to the debate is that sustainable landscapes must be dynamic landscapes. They must be capable of responding to changes, not only in the physical environment but in the social, political and economic climate as well.

CONCLUDING DISCUSSION

The experience of designers at the Earth Centre and Oostvaardersplassen provides a good example of the way in which sustainable design responds to the context and specific conditions of the site. The detailed survey and analysis of ecology and natural processes thus inform the design process, from concept development, through to detailed design. The natural features and phenomena enliven the final scheme, with characteristics enhanced through exploration of the vernacular.

The case studies demonstrate the value of creating a sustainability brief to guide the client, designers, suppliers, and contractors. It should be seen as an 'unfinished work' allowing the addition or update of information as new materials arise, also allowing adaptation for projects with specific needs. The Earth Centre experience illustrates that though it can clearly sometimes cost more to procure sustainable materials, in many instances, costs of procurement, implementation, and maintenance will be reduced. This is certainly a language that the client will understand! At Center Parcs, the adoption of quality control certification in environmental management systems, and a clearly defined environmental policy, ensure that high standards are maintained.

A sustainability brief ought to incorporate the principles of life cycle thinking, with consideration of re-use or after use of the site, products, and materials (Chapter 10). Although several life cycle analysis packages are available, the case studies suggest that practising landscape architects rarely have the time or means to become familiar with their use. In lieu of such involved systems for the analysis of goods and materials, it is recommended that practitioners ensure that they familiarize themselves with the issues and available structures (e.g. embodied energy, renewable resources, the impacts of PVC, Forestry Stewardship Council certification, plastics clearly labelled and separable thus enabling recycling). If no member of the design team is familiar with the relative environmental performance of products and materials, access to the latest independent surveys, reports or 'green' building directories is essential; much of this is becoming available via the Internet. Strategic or specialist ecological advice is often available through local authority departments, as well as from national organizations and special interest groups (such as English Nature, Greenpeace, the British Trust for Conservation Volunteers or local naturalist groups).

The experience at the Earth Centre and at Oostvaardersplassen illustrates the benefits of accommodating complexity and diversity, thus allowing responsive solutions that are appropriate to the specific context. This in turn gives a richer user or visitor experience. This provision for complexity is another characteristic of ecological design (Van der Ryn and Cowan, 1996, p. 65).

Continuity of involvement, and the adoption of 'duty of care' commitments by the designers allow the adaptation and refinement of a design subsequent to implementation. By returning to a project, the designer is able to develop sensitive responses to changing conditions or unanticipated events and uses. The experience at Oostvaardersplassen and Center Parcs demonstrates the practical application of this approach. By encouraging feedback from the client and users, 'fine tuning' is possible, and the landscape architect can learn through reflections on the efficacy of the design.

A feature of many sustainable schemes seems to be the establishment of early and effective links with stakeholders. Designers need to explain and justify the ways and means of achieving a sustainable end result to clients, community groups, and potential users. This is particularly vital in relation to the implementation and continuing cost implications. With community-based projects, the creation of a sense of common ownership through early dialogue with user groups can prove to be critical to success. The apparent complexity of balancing the diverse aspects of sustainability makes the development of effective communication strategies crucial. The Meanwhile Gardens case study illustrates the importance of talking to clients, user groups, or other professionals with language that is understood by all, avoiding the use of acronyms and jargon.

Issues of accessibility are often fundamental to the sustainability of a scheme. For some projects, such as the Earth Centre and Meanwhile Gardens, economic viability and justification for existence depend on ease of access for visitors. Other projects, such as Oostvaardersplassen, have to carefully manage and limit the access of the public to sensitive habitats.

Another common feature of sustainable landscape design is the need for effective interdisciplinary and cross-disciplinary working, facilitated by good channels of communication between professions. The Earth Centre demonstrates that by maintaining good channels for the sharing and dissemination of information, a synergy can be achieved, and potential differences of opinion anticipated. The experience of landscape architects working both at the Earth Centre, and Center Parcs has been that they have experienced a gradual, incremental growth in their understanding of sustainable design. The means to accelerate the accumulation of knowledge, such as training courses and site visits, should be exploited.

Throughout the case studies, the need for consideration of sustainability issues in the design process has been stressed. Table 11.2 contains a checklist of sustainability issues to assist landscape architects in their work. In order to have a resonance with projects of a wide variety of scales and types, the categories presented are extensive, sometimes general, and sometimes very specific. Clearly the diverse nature of the profession means that not all of the categories will be relevant in every case. The list does not prioritize categories in relation to one another, according to their relative significance. For example, in some schemes community involvement may be of fundamental importance, while in others it may have little relevance. It is intended for use as a front-end design tool, though it could be adapted for use in appraisal, comparison, or reflection. The list is sub-divided into the three realms of consideration for sustainability, people, planet, and profit. Ethical issues are not listed, though they are considered to have a bearing on all three realms.

The quest for the wide-spread delivery of sustainable landscape design clearly requires practitioners to consider diverse issues. However, landscape architects have always needed to be skilled in the art of analysing and balancing diverse and often conflicting interests. The challenge then is to take these skills and harness them to incorporate the sustainability agenda into the routine pattern of day to day practice. If the landscape professions are to aspire to the rigorous standards to which the construction industry is proceeding (Building Research Establishment, 1991, 1993, 1995, 1998), consideration will need to be given to the creation and adoption of a more formal system for assessing and raising standards of environmental performance.

ACKNOWLEDGEMENTS

The authors gratefully acknowledge the assistance received during the gathering of material for the case studies; thanks in particular to Hans Breeveld, Frank de Rode and Adrie Stikvoort (all of the Dutch National Forestry Service).

REFERENCES

Alexander, C., Ishikawa, S. and Silverstein, M. (1977) *A Pattern Language* (Oxford, Oxford University Press).

Bijlsma, R. (1997) Broedvogels van de buitendijkse Oostvaardersplassen: Een Kartering in 1997, *A & W-rapport,* 180 (Veenwouden, Altenburg and Wymenga).

Brezet, H. and Hemel, C. van (1997) *EcoDesign* (New York, United Nations Publications).

Building Research Establishment (1991) Version 2/91, *An Environmental Assessment for New Superstores and Supermarkets* (Garston, HMSO).

Building Research Establishment (1993) Version 5/93, *New Industrial Units* (Garston, HMSO).

Building Research Establishment (1995) *Environmental Standard: Homes for a Greener World* (Garston, HMSO).

Building Research Establishment (1998) *BREEAM 98 for Offices* (London, CRC).

Center Parcs (1997) Sherwood Forest ecological monitoring 1996/97, unpublished report.

Center Parcs (1999) *Biodiversity Strategy,* pamphlet available at holiday villages.

Department of the Environment (1989) *Environmental Assessment: A Guide to the Procedures* (London, DoE).

Department of the Environment, Transport and the Regions (1999) *A Better Quality of Life: A Strategy for Sustainable Development in the United Kingdom* (London, DETR).

Earth Centre (1997/8) Sustainability directorate guidance document, unpublished report.

Fussler, C. and James, P. (1996) *Driving Eco Innovation* (London, Pitman).

Goodfellow, J. (1990) Village in the Forest, *Landscape Design,* 189, 51–53.

Grant, A. and Bass, G. (1998) Life on earth, *Landscape Design,* 270, 32–36.

International Chamber of Commerce (1991) *Business Charter for Sustainable Development* (http://www.iccwbo.org/soleharter/news_archives/2000/beacom.asp, accessed 27 July 2000).

Jans, L. and Drost, H. J. (1995) *De Oostvaardersplassen 25 jaar vegetatie-onderzoek*. Ministerie van Verkeer en Waterstaat, Rijkwaterstaat, directie ljsselmeergebied-Lelystad.

Landscape Design (1999) Center Parcs Village Management Plans: Center Parcs UK Ltd, *Landscape Design*, 285, A30–A33.

Millward, A. and Mostyn, B. (1989) People and nature in cities: the changing social aspects of planning and managing natural parks in urban areas, *Urban Wildlife Now*, 2 (Peterborough, Nature Conservancy Council).

Planet Earth (1999) Concept statement for Meanwhile Gardens, unpublished.

Thayer, R. (1994) *Gray World, Green Heart: Technology, Nature and the Sustainable Landscape* (London, John Wiley).

Thornton, J. (1997) *Dioxin from Cradle to Grave* (London, Greenpeace).

Tuan, Y. (1974) *Topophilia: A Study of Environmental Perception, Attitudes, and Values* (New York, Columbia University Press).

Tubbs, C. (1996) Wilderness or cultural landscapes: conflicting conservation philosophies?, *British Wildlife*, 7(5), 290–296.

UK Biodiversity Group (1994a) *The UK Biodiversity Action Plan* (London, HMSO).

UK Biodiversity Group (1994b) *A Summary of the UK Biodiversity Action Plan* (London, DoE).

UK Biodiversity Group (1998a) *Tranche Two Action Plans, Volume One: Vertebrates and Vascular Plants* (London, The Stationery Office).

UK Biodiversity Group (1998b) *Tranche Two Action Plans, Volume Two: Terrestrial and Freshwater Habitats* (London, The Stationery Office).

UK Biodiversity Group (1999a) *Tranche Two Action Plans, Volume Three: Plants and Fungi* (London, The Stationery Office).

UK Biodiversity Group (1999b) *Tranche Two Action Plans, Volume Four: Invertebrates* (London, The Stationery Office).

UK Biodiversity Group (1999c) *Tranche Two Action Plans, Volume Five: Maritime Species and Habitats* (London, The Stationery Office).

UK Biodiversity Group (1999d) *Tranche Two Action Plans, Volume Six: Terrestrial and Freshwater Species and Habitats* (London, The Stationery Office).

Van der Ryn, S. and Cowan, S. (1996) *Ecological Design* (London, Island Press).

Whitbread, A. and Jenman, W. (1995) A natural method of conserving biodiversity in Britain, *British Wildlife*, 7(2), 84–93.

Wigbels, V. (1997) *The Oostvaardersplassen*, pamphlet available from the Oostvaardersplassen Information Centre.

12

THE COMMUNITY AND THE LANDSCAPE PROFESSIONAL

Maggie H. Roe and Maisie Rowe

SUMMARY

Landscape professionals have been involved in community-based projects for some years. In doing so they have begun to experiment and adapt methods commonly used by other professions to encourage public participation. An examination of the experience of past and present projects which involve the community in a variety of ways and of research carried out concerning the success of participatory processes forms the basis for the discussion in this chapter. It is apparent from this that the nature of the professional–client relationship in many landscape projects is changing and the landscape professional is having to take on new roles and responsibilities. There is a great potential for practitioners to be at the forefront of these exciting developments within the profession, but professionals need to develop new areas of expertise and a toolbox of techniques in order to respond to the opportunities which are arising. Chapter 4 discussed the links between concepts of social sustainability and landscape projects. This chapter provides the next step in commenting on the problems and opportunities that arise from the practice of community landscape architecture.

INTRODUCTION

The imperative to create more sustainable landscapes has focused attention on the need to engage with social sustainability by addressing the relationships of people to each other, as well as the relationships of people to landscapes. Chapter 4 reviewed the main theoretical thinking behind this and in this chapter we aim to provide a view from the ground by reporting on new challenges for designers and practitioners and in particular what is meant by 'public participation' in relation to the practice of landscape professionals. In the discussion of design issues and techniques, problems and opportunities are identified for practitioners and for the profession using a variety of small- and large-scale examples of landscape projects.

PROCESSES FOR LANDSCAPE CHANGE – THE LANDSCAPE PROFESSIONAL AND COMMUNITY INPUT

Public participation can be defined as unpaid voluntary activity undertaken by citizens that influences government, policy-making and democratic accountability. Public participation in landscape projects is most commonly found used in conjunction with regeneration projects. Community involvement in such projects has been defined as 'the active partici-pation of local inhabitants in schemes to regenerate disadvantaged or declining areas' (European Commission, 1997, p. 9). In the UK participation generally occurs through consultation, through information dissemination and the incorporation of feedback from the public and stakeholders into the decision making process. The term 'stakeholder' is now commonly used to define individuals who represent groups, companies, etc. which have a particular interest in the existing state of the environment or in change which might occur. Landscape professionals have been involved in many ways in projects involving this kind of consultation of the general public by environmental planning and management bodies and this has for some time been standard procedure in the development plan process in the UK. The UK is quite unusual – even within Europe – in that public consultation is a requirement of the statutory planning system – such as in the development of Local and District Plans. Although the situation is by no means black and white, this discretionary, rather than zonal planning system, means that the public has greater potential for input into landscape development and planning decisions. In zoning systems it is generally more difficult for the public to influence decisions since the detailed agenda for discussion is largely already set by the developers and planners (Barlow, 1995). The semi-judicial process of public inquiry in the UK is another long-standing method by which the general community can object to proposals to change the environment although in some cases, such as in Simplified Planning Zones, this process has become optional (see Barlow, 1995). Chapter 4 discusses other ways in which public participation occurs or public opinion may be voiced in landscape issues through environmental activism, such as social movements, specific issue groups and direct action.

In addition to public participation in the smaller landscape projects – often collectively described as *community projects* – there has more recently been a growth in the recommendations to include the public in larger scale non-statutory decision making such as Estuary Management Plans, Landscape Strategies, Character Mapping, etc. Community projects on a smaller scale are often based on changing single sites e.g. school grounds, housing estates, parks, streets and small areas of greenspace. In addition to participation now being included more often in larger projects, the actual character of participation is changing. A distinction can now be made more clearly between our tradition of public participation (the citizen's right) and what is happening more recently, which is that people are being asked to be more active (the citizen's duty). The landscape is taking on new meanings and is part of a new agenda as a result of the emergence of a regeneration industry concerned with the built environment, which has encouraged new avenues of investment. New areas of work are opening up to landscape professionals and this means that landscape professionals are finding themselves in new roles, being expected to be fluent in new areas of expertise, able to develop and use a new 'toolbox' of techniques. These are described and discussed in the first part of the chapter. This changing professional environment has the potential to stimulate and refresh a profession that is not always seen to be at the cutting edge in policy or practice issues. Naturally, these changes raise a number of challenges for practice and practitioners and these are discussed in the concluding parts of the chapter.

NEW ROLES

Design and management decisions concerning the majority of public landscapes are taken 'on behalf' of communities by local councils, environmental agencies and non-governmental organizations (NGOs) who employ professionals to carry out the work. In a number of professions the traditional relationship between client and professional is now being questioned, particularly by a public which is increasingly suspicious of 'professionals'. New types of professional relationship are being formed with community groups as the 'client' for example. In his book *The Reflective Practitioner,* Schön (1983) developed the idea of 'a vision of professionals as agents of society's reflective conversation with its situation, agents who engage in co-operative inquiry within a framework of institutionalized contention'. Rather than being 'locked into a view of themselves as technical experts' (ibid., p. 69) professionals need to develop a process of 'reflection-in-action' or the ability to think about what, why and how a particular action is being taken and the ability to criticize, restructure and reassess the process. Schön believes this will improve the professional's ability to deal well with 'situations of uncertainly, instability, uniqueness, and value conflict' (ibid., p. 50). This ability is particularly important for those taking on the new roles that are now demanded by the changing public expectations and social agendas emerging to a large extent from the institutional context now evolving (see Chapter 4). Landscape professionals have the potential to work in a multitude of ways. However, commentators such as Turner (1998) believe that many landscape professionals do not have the skills to be able to take up new opportunities. Certainly the existing Landscape Institute professional recognition system fails to recognize or accommodate many of these different roles, thus weakening its and its members' flexibility to respond to new situations and thereby reducing its credibility and influence with its own members, with other professionals and with the public.

A great variety of project structures are now emerging as a result of work which does not conform to the norms of a single client and the growing demand for longer-term thinking from a number of sectors – particularly that of landscape management. Many conventional landscape projects are dictated by clients whose briefs are based on short-lived capital initiatives and which exacerbate the well-known problems which plague landscape projects such as the separation of executive and management responsibility and the lack of revenue budgets. This means that the growing and changing nature of landscape and the creative role of landscape management are not adequately recognized or supported in the planning and funding of many projects (see Chapters 4 and 13). In community work the emphasis on these issues is fundamentally different because the client is often more concerned with problems linked to the management and maintenance of the landscape than with short-term project investment.

However, features of modern life such as the apparent need for instant gratification seem to affect all kinds of projects and encourage the belief by clients *and* the public that an instant fix is possible and that solutions can be bought rather than built. This view commonly changes when communities become involved in landscape projects where the difficulties of implementation and management become apparent. If more attention is paid to the consideration of longer-term landscape design, management and maintenance through a greater emphasis on community participation, then the nature of the structure and funding of projects as well as the type of projects themselves may change.

The roots of community landscape work lie in the imperative to find new ways to regenerate inner city environments, particularly residential areas (tower blocks, housing estates), parks and open spaces, streets and town centres. A number of organizations now exist where projects based on landscape and landscape issues and on public participation are central to their work (see Box 12.1) and which are helping to change the face of professional landscape work in this country.

Those landscape professionals who are already involved in this kind of community-based work, particularly those working mostly at the smaller scale, are often young and idealistic and as a result tend to get 'burnt out' by the stresses of the job. As inexperienced practitioners they are often thrown in at the deep end with no senior to guide them or technical staff to back them up. However, many display enthusiasm and dedication in spite of (often) poor pay and heavy responsibilities. Other professional characteristics appear to be important – such as the need to be generally optimistic, recognize the change in the expert role with the community as client, not assume you know best, recognize you may make a difference (but not always), be a good listener and motivator, have good presentation and publicity skills and a 'community vocabulary'. When asked 'why do it?' one young landscape architect replied 'Why do it any other way?' Twelvetrees (1996) found that even where salaries are good, organizations working with communities find it difficult to recruit and keep staff.

Box 12.1

Three examples of organizations which work extensively in the Community Landscape Sector

BTCV formerly known as the British Trust for Conservation Volunteers

The British Trust for Conservation Volunteers (BTCV) began in 1959 and has now become the biggest practical conservation charity in Britain with 85,000 people volunteering annually to help work on environmental projects. These include active protection and enhancement of the landscape and wildlife while improving access into the countryside. Activities include tree planting, hedge-laying, footpath construction and pond creation. The organization filled a gap in landscape construction and management guidance by the production of useful down-to-earth publications illustrating techniques to carry out these kinds of operations. Workshops and training sessions are also run by the Trust. BTCV often works in partnership with other similar organisations on community landscape and environmental improvement projects.

Common Ground

Common Ground states that it links nature with culture and focuses on the 'positive investment people can make in their own localities'. It 'champions popular democratic involvement and inspires celebration as a starting point for action to improve the quality of everyday places'. Much of the emphasis is on developing a more participative and flexible society. The organization produces a number of publications and arranges special events such as Apple Days and Field Days. The focus on locality and place has led to the development of the concept of Parish Maps and Community orchards, and a campaign for local distinctiveness.

Parish Maps: these are based on the 'smallest theatre of democracy' – the ecclesiastical parish. Communities are helped to examine and map their community spaces in pictures words and events. It is regarded as a catalyst in helping to bring existing communities together to express values and improve community involvement and by so doing change passive acceptance of existing conditions to active engagement in changing situations which can be changed.

Community orchards: this is a campaign to save vulnerable old orchards and identify opportunities to plan new ones to act as a community resource – for quiet enjoyment, a wildlife refuge, a food resource and a reservoir of local fruit varieties.

Groundwork Trust

The Groundwork Trust was established in 1981 to respond to the need to regenerate areas that most local authorities, developers and the governments would not consider. It is one of the biggest employers of landscape architects in the country and now provides work through 43 individual trusts. Although Groundwork is now well known as a major facilitator of community-based initiatives, and indeed in some areas community landscape projects have been almost totally devolved to the local Groundwork Trust, the organization experiences problems in its relationships with the rest of the landscape profession and with funding bodies. Groundwork grew as the result of partnerships between private sponsors and government. However, core funding from government is now being withdrawn from the older trusts and this is likely to change the nature of the work (see Davies, 1999 for further information).

Although landscape architects in other sectors also take on various roles that appear remote from their original training, the community landscape architect's role is a particularly good example of the diverse nature of the profession. This job is often predominantly one of the social worker-cum-social scientist and it is clear that designers are now involved in trying to solve the wider problems of the perceived social, economic and environmental crisis as described in Chapter 4. Working with the community is not an easy task, not least because outside consultants are often regarded as intruders into communities. But the potential for linking social learning and landscape projects has now been recognized by policy-makers and the increasing attention to community issues and public participation will undoubtedly increase the potential and diversity of work for landscape professionals in this field. This means that a number of landscape architects are finding themselves questioning their traditional capacities and relationships because they are finding themselves in new roles as facilitators, trainers and community builders (Figure 12.1).

Consultants as 'community builders'

Although it is understood that the objectives of public participation are not simply to provide an improved physical environment, there is often an assumption that community projects are more likely to achieve this. However, local communities are often sceptical about environmental improvements

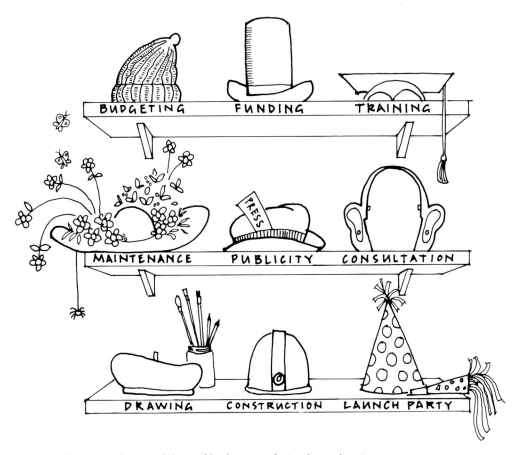

Figure 12.1 The roles and responsibilities of landscape professionals are changing.

and do not share the premise of would-be 'improvers' that environmental improvement is always a 'good thing'. At a basic level, discussion injects realism into projects and allows for a better understanding of popular opinion by professionals and policy-makers. It is therefore essential in order to ascertain whether particular landscape management polices and strategies are likely to succeed. A more inclusive process helps to create a sense of 'ownership' of the project which promotes the feeling that the community has control over the decisions that may be made and that being involved means being able to make real improvements. This sense strengthens individual commitment as well as providing the opportunity for individuals to understand differing viewpoints and develop consensus.

Conflict resolution through consensus building is central to the participatory process. This can be realized through commonly practised techniques but also through a more subtle understanding by professionals of the importance of people as a resource in the landscape. This perhaps should not need to be said, but the climate of large regeneration projects sometimes breeds a feeling among decision makers that community consultation is an expensive and time-wasting exercise. Contrary to this view, local people can be a major source of local information and knowledge (Clifford, 1994; Davis, 1996; O'Riordan and Ward, 1997) that might be difficult or expensive to obtain in other ways. For example, in O'Riordan and Ward's analysis of public participation in the North Norfolk Coast Shoreline Management Plan one of the participants clearly felt that locals had not been considered a useful or reliable source of information concerning changes in the coastal environment and that instead of consulting locals 'expensive professionals' had been used to ascertain the same information. As a result 'local people lost heart [in the project] because their valuable knowledge was not being tapped' (ibid., p. 272). However, liberating information from local sources can be difficult. It is by no means easy to plan for community participation because it is notoriously difficult to obtain any kind of consensus view when dealing with a wide variety of groups and individuals. This makes the process unpredictable. Even if an agreement is reached at the planning stage, conflict often appears at the implementation stage. There is a large amount of anecdotal evidence from professionals in the field of community work which concurs with the summary provided by Twelvetrees (1996) that community-based organizations 'are beset by infighting and are incompetently and narrowly led by people with no vision who exclude those who they do not like, often the most deprived'. However a number of approaches have now been developed both in practice and theory (e.g. see Margerum and Born, 1995; Petts, 1995) to alleviate some of the problems. These involve the designer in the role as the facilitator of projects working in partnership with other professionals, funding bodies and community groups. Within this role the landscape professional is likely to face the challenges of solving problems of communication between the groups in order to build consensus, rather than solving design problems. Communities need to be provided with the momentum and support that help them achieve consensus. This requires new expertise in a number of professional areas.

NEW EXPERTISE

In considering the need for landscape professionals to develop new expertise, understanding the context of decision making is particularly relevant. The actual extent of participation in environmental projects has a wide spectrum of inclusion from projects which are instigated and run by the local community – often the small single-site projects – through those where the general public is consulted at various stages, to those where stakeholders and public are simply asked to comment on projects which are in the final stages of completion. There is still much debate about whether the process of environmental planning and management based on an even more 'citizen-controlled system' (Arnstein, 1969) would provide greater real benefits in comparison to the consultation system commonly used (see Chapter 4). However, there appears to be little doubt that there are moves being made towards a restructuring of the existing decision making structure.

Government and quasi-governmental bodies are increasingly recommending or requiring that partnership and public consultation are carried out as part of the establishment and management of landscape projects as exemplified in the New Deal for Communities initiative. This is providing £20–£50 million in each case to selected stressed neighbourhoods in certain urban areas of England (see Schlesinger, 1999). Mechanisms for the design and implementation of landscape projects have also changed, largely under the Local Agenda 21 initiative. In working on such projects the professional is now required to have the ability to provide access to a wide range of information concerning funding bodies and grant application procedures and also to be able to interpret complex official information in terms which are relevant to local communities. Professionals are also required to act as enablers, to ensure that community energy is channelled in appropriate directions and that a clear path is found through the maze of official documents and regulations. Therefore, in addition to expertise which allows professionals to work with people at the community level, the professional must also have a working knowledge of the system by which such projects are run and be able to keep a grasp on the long term 'bigger picture' (Figure 12.2).

The expertise of landscape professionals in small-scale community projects has been developing over a number of years, as already described in Chapter 4. The development of a more inclusive process generally means that the public can now be involved in the processes for landscape change in various different ways (see Table 12.1) which can involve a number of agencies (see Table 12.2).

Professionals are becoming involved in a number of large-scale landscape assessment, planning and management projects that include involving the community at a variety of stages. Sometimes the client may be a consortium of organizations which forms a Steering Committee consisting of representatives from the major stakeholders, local and national environmental and governmental regulatory groups. In simple projects the role of consultants is to gather survey material that includes information from the local community or communities, provide

Figure 12.2 Landscape professionals need to keep an eye on the 'bigger picture'.

an analysis and put forward recommendations. Another type of participatory process can be seen in the strategy developed for the National Forest in the English Midlands. A complex network of links, partnerships and participatory action has been used to help achieve landscape transformation in a degraded non-urban area. The aim of participation and partnership is to build upon and implement the specific goals as *already defined* by the Strategy, particularly to develop enthusiasm to encourage practical involvement in the forest's development. This is done through fairly formal links with organizations, agencies and volunteers (Bell and Evans, 1998). In other large-scale projects there may be a specific brief to consult with the community prior to the

Table 12.1 Public participation/community action in projects for landscape change

Example of type of participation/community action	Example of type of project	Example of organizations involved
Direct voluntary (physical) work as an individual	Restoration or repair of particular landscape features e.g. footpaths, hedge-laying	BTCV, National Trust (NT)
Involvement in local group: meetings, discussion, workshops etc.	Action on particular subject/interest areas or sectional groups to improve the quality of life e.g. lobbying local council for disabled access in urban areas	Women's groups, disabled groups, youth councils
Involvement in local group: meetings, lobbying, creative projects/ workshops, physical improvements	Change or manage a particular site	Tenants' groups, residents' associations, tenant–management co-operatives, school playground improvement group, Millennium Green committee, Home Zone initiative etc.
Involvement in strategic planning initiatives: meetings as individuals or groups, focus groups, consultation by direct and indirect means (letters, posters, exhibitions etc.)	Planning or management strategy for a large-scale landscape, designated area or region	Management Strategy for the Area of Outstanding Natural Beauty (AONB) (e.g. Kent Downs Jigsaw Project); Estuary Management Plans; recreation strategies
Involvement in decisions covering a single issue: citizens' panels, citizens' juries, focus groups, public meeting and other consultation methods	Change a particular site/site development proposals; part of environmental assessment process	Private company, local authority
Involvement as a business partner/sponsor	Urban development/restoration projects, educational projects. Site-based projects, reward schemes.	Private companies, large multinationals (e.g. Shell, BP); Charitable organization (e.g. WWF)
Membership of a local or regional group. Some active participation.	Promotion of a particular aspect of landscape conservation or management	Wildlife Trusts, 'Friends of' particular landscapes
Membership of a large and influential national or international group: little active participation except through special events or campaigns	The individual tacitly agrees with the aims of the organization and representation is via a paid employee of that association (often in a stakeholder capacity)	Royal Society for the Protection of Birds (RSPB), National Trust (NT), political parties
Membership of a particular sectoral action group	Promotion or cause groups concerned with changing policy	Friends of the Earth, Greenpeace
Direct (risk) protest action as individual or group: occupation of sites	Siting of controversial infrastructure in the landscape e.g. roads (Twyford Down), railways (Channel Tunnel), power stations, etc. Preventative action e.g. anti-tree removal, anti-nuclear, anti-genetic engineering.	Individuals e.g. 'Swampy'. Groups e.g. Friends of the Earth (FOE), Greenpeace

Table 12.2 Agencies

Community	Business	Public authorities and utilities	Cross-sectoral
Community centres/groups	Chambers of commerce	Local authorities	School, colleges, universities
Tenants' and residents' committees/associations	Chambers of trade	Parish councils	Community health councils
	Industrial organizations	Health authorities	Political parties
Councils for voluntary service; voluntary support organizations	Individual industries/businesses	Service utilities (energy, water etc.)	Trades unions
			Housing associations
Urban wildlife/ environmental groups	Business-environment clubs	Local training and enterprise councils/organizations	Campaigning organizations
	Lottery organizations		Charitable organizations and trusts
Religious groups		Transport interests	
Artists and artists' groups		Regulatory bodies	Healthy environment groups and organizations
Sports and leisure recreation groups			Transport consultative committees
Minority groups bodies: women, ethnic minorities			Urban development agencies and trusts/regeneration initiatives
Work clubs			Local Agenda 21 groups
			Facilitating bodies/trusts/ agencies

Source: Adapted from Freeman *et al.* (1995)

development of a full project brief. Consultation then becomes the main basis for the analysis and recommendations relating to the project – as is commonly now found in community projects at the small site scale.

NEW TECHNIQUES: THE TOOLBOX

There are a number of techniques that have been tried and tested by other professions that the landscape professional can call upon in order to fulfil new roles. However, many of them require a new interpretation and as much of the expertise has been developed within other areas of professional work, so landscape professionals are now experimenting with and adapting various techniques.

To be able to connect with groups, manage problems and understand the community's relationship to landscape processes the professional needs to develop a problem-solving approach that is somewhat different from the traditional approach. This is all about helping others to find their own solutions rather than solving problems for them. This skill is particularly relevant when helping communities to develop a project brief. It will be up to the professional to manage the group's expectations as there tends to be a gap between a community's *expectations* of what is possible and what is *actually possible* in projects. For example, communities should be made aware of the significance of regulations and policies (Petts, 1995) because some decisions made concerning the environment such as those taken at European Union level cannot be controlled or influenced by the immediate community but they may affect the outcome of projects at the local level. In order to retain commitment, the community needs to feel that they can influence the process and the result of the project by being able to discuss their standpoint rather than simply listen to information, or the views of others. The professional acts as interpreter and facilitator in this process.

It is important for the professional to consider how to meet the consultation needs as part of pre-project planning. Issues such as the timing of consultation and providing a number of different opportunities for participation should be considered. Full and effective consultation cannot be hurried (Grabrovaz, 1995). This can be a problem if the project has a very limited budget or a tight timescale. It is also makes it difficult for estimating project costs. Budgeting problems can be overcome by proper resourcing which is built in from the beginning so that adequate fund-raising can be carried out. It is important that adequate time for discussion is allowed before a decision is required and this should include time for analysis of project progress. In many cases, further studies may be required where the community, the committee or the consultants feel that there is inadequate knowledge to make a decision.

At the early stages of projects, the production of a vision statement (or 'action plan') which all members of the community or stakeholders can sign up to has been found to be useful (Kidd, 1995; Rowe and Wales, 1999). This helps in the development of a shared vision – but it is important to avoid unrealistic expectations which cannot be met and which can cause disillusionment in the project (Freeman *et al.*, 1996). The New Economics Foundation (NEF) has been developing various visioning techniques

including the IMAGINE approach and 'Appreciative Inquiry' where community groups identify what is working well, the things they feel good about the area, the achievements they have made and the reasons why the good things could happen. NEF believe that by allowing community groups to talk about the good things in both the past and present creates an enormous positive energy which can then be harnessed. Their approaches also aim to produce dialogue between generations, provide young people direct access to decision makers, and root the discussion within institutions that can act (Walker, 1998; NEF, 2000). In many community projects local people will commonly have an idea that they want to 'do something' with a piece of land, but little conception of what to do or how to do it. In fact it sometimes can create more difficulties if communities have a well-developed idea which may be totally unrealistic. Difficulties arise because issues deemed 'real' by the community may seem insignificant to professionals and management authorities (Smith, 1994). The brief should therefore help define what the *real* problems are, identify who should be involved as well as a range of solutions. Identification of the key elements on which to focus attention makes the development of plans for complex projects more manageable for the community. The briefing or initial meetings between the community, stakeholders and the facilitator or consultant team should set the agenda for the project and ensure that all parties taking part are in an equal position with common goals. The identification of potential funding is also crucial at this stage if it has not already been found. Much time may be needed to plan funding provision and initial meetings or events as undertaken in the 'Canterbury Vision 21' project set up by Kent Property Services' Landscape with Canterbury City Council. In this project participating schools were provided with information and a date was set for the workshop a year in advance so that it could be included in their financial planning and curriculum timetable (Bartlett, 1999).

The traditional survey-analysis-design (SAD) approach, which is all about a series of questions that are answered in certain ways, is likely to be inappropriate in working with communities. The emphasis in community landscape work is much more about developing process-based approaches to design – an emphasis on *how* it is done, as well as *what* is done. Thus a more flexible approach is needed which creates space for partnership-working and collaboration with other professionals, such as architects, engineers, horticulturists, artists and students in addition to local councils, agencies and voluntary sector bodies. Bringing artists together with communities has produced some particularly creative and interesting results for all concerned. The Quaking Houses 'Seen and Unseen' project in a semi-rural former coal mining area of County Durham in the North of England is an example of this (see Figure 12.3). Here various groups, technical experts and sponsors came together with the com-

munity to combat minewater pollution of the Stanley Burn by creating a small wetland using innovative techniques. Artist Helen Smith fulfilled the role as community facilitator. She designed walkways and paths through the site, carried out broadcasts publicizing the projects and trained young people to present research on water quality and 'sound pictures' of country life through a listening post within the wetland (Miles, 1998). Although the project suffered a number of difficulties (see Kemp and Griffiths, 1999), it illustrates how a broad range of people within a community can come together to achieve physical improvement of the landscape and at the same time obtain a number of social benefits for that community in the process. Such collaboration not only provides investment for communities

Figure 12.3 Quaking Houses 'Seen and Unseen' wetland project was a collaborative solution to the problems caused by water pollution in the landscape.

in their landscapes and cultural resources but helps redefine professional roles. In this case, the emphasis of the artistic involvement was on issues rather than site. The integration of culture, biodiversity and economic development concerns helped to draw new forms of sponsorship and support into an area of landscape regeneration where funding is often difficult to obtain.

An increased acceptance of the necessity for participation is evidenced by a growing emphasis in landscape regeneration and urban policy on work that is based on public consultation and the development of partnerships. This produces multiple benefits gained from being able to draw on different areas of expertise and the creation of a more stable funding base.

The professional needs to have the sensitivity and skills to be able to communicate with different client types and project partners working on very diverse projects, but also help build a more integrated approach to tackling landscape problems. For example, in large-scale projects particular complex problems may need resolution. Large-scale landscapes in particular often suffer from a malaise referred to as the 'tragedy of the commons'. This is a concept based on an analysis by Garrett Hardin (1968, 1993) of community behaviour and the destruction of land as a result of many small actions or a 'tyranny of small decisions'; carried out in the interests of the individual, but not of the community. In the UK, this can be a problem where there is a complex mosaic of land ownership and management responsibilities and numerous interest groups and individuals. As Common Ground (see Box 12.1) has identified, this may not simply be decisions directly concerned with the landscape:

> Hundreds of small acts of clairvoyance may precede decisions to pull the hedge out, to build on the allotments, to shut down the factory, to culvert the stream, to cease running the festival, but they are achieved in separate pigeonholes, and their effect each upon the other is hardly ever considered. Rarely is their cumulative impact upon us discussed either.
>
> (Clifford, 2000)

In another project, the Verde River Corridor Study in the USA, it was found that involvement in the process of visual assessment helped the community to develop greater visual awareness and to understand the effects on the landscape of incremental, individual actions which cumulatively created major impacts (Whitmore *et al.*, 1995). In response to such findings, landscape professionals can build practical frameworks for integrated working by turning to concepts such as ecosystem-based management (e.g. see Hartig *et al.*, 1998), partnership forum frameworks (see Venter and Breen, 1998) and those put forward under Integrated Environmental Management (IEM) approaches which promote a collaborative, interactive process with the holistic approach necessary for success in the long-term management of environmental projects (see Margerum and Born, 1995; Selman, 1992). An important part of the integrated thinking on which IEM is based includes empowerment through community participation – a concept discussed more fully in Chapter 4. This aims to help prevent the problems caused by the adverse effects of many small decisions by, amongst other things, raising community awareness and understanding of landscape processes. However, the characteristics of integrated and partnership approaches make projects based on them particularly susceptible to failure, as well as to criticism – an important consideration for landscape consultants who may act as catalysts or enablers in the process.

In addition to forming integrated frameworks for action, it is often the combination of many minor tools that help to build a co-operative atmosphere. For example, although it is sometimes easier to have a constant meeting place, arranging meetings at different places within the community may help to enforce feelings of involvement in the project. In larger projects it may be important to review membership of any stakeholder or topic groups to ensure that they are truly representative. Early and continuous targeted consultation is recommended so that the community can help shape the project or policies as far as possible rather than merely commenting on draft proposals produced by someone else.

Experience has shown that one of the most useful tools for the practitioner is to plan to use a variety of consultative methods based on the fact that individuals in the community are exposed to information in different ways (Petts, 1995). This approach helps to address the problem of lack of skills available in the community that may affect people's ability or willingness to participate. In the early stages of the project it is important to reach as many people as possible and publicity methods including posters, letters, press campaigns, public meetings, exhibitions, newsletters, etc. can be used to invite individuals and groups to register interest in the project. There are numerous communication methods for information gathering and dissemination, and providing feedback opportunities, but recent practice favours the more interactive and creative approaches.

A visual rather than a verbal approach was used in a visioning process for the Kent Downs Jigsaw Project (Bartlett, 1999). A 'jigsaw' or photomontage of photographs taken by members of different parishes was put together during community workshop sessions. These helped people to focus on issues and helped people to overcome the difficulty which is common to many local projects – that of understanding and analysing the 'special' nature of a familiar landscape (Hough, 1990). Model-making is another useful hands-on approach. Such events can also help build an understanding between the different participants of alternative viewpoints (e.g. Bartlett, 1999; Roe, 2000) which is regarded as one of the difficulties commonly found in the participatory process.

The rise in the use of computer-based technologies and the development of specialized software for landscape and social science applications has led to the experimental use of information technology (IT) as a tool for public participation (see, for example, Al-Kodmany, 1999; Ervin, 1999). Geographic Information Systems (GIS) can be used to map key community assets and environmental conditions (Kellogg, 1999). GIS and Computer-aided Design (CAD) models may be used as part of a visioning process or to explore the implications of the environmental impacts of various management techniques or policies. Virtual landscapes and simulated views based on aerial photos have been found to be a powerful way of illustrating landscape change and human impacts (Jones, 1999). However, as with more conventional visioning methods, it must be emphasized that the images produced are representative and confusion should be avoided between 'virtual' and real landscapes. Careful use of such tools may stimulate the interest of often excluded sectors of the community such as teenagers, but it is important to assess whether such tools will be used fairly and competently and whether they will improve the likelihood of achieving the aims of public participation (Webler *et al.*, 1995) or simply be used because they are a 'new technology'. Using IT requires certain prerequisites relating to technical and organizational conditions and personal skills (Kellogg, 1999). A lack of these can prove a formidable obstacle to IT use by community-based organizations and practitioners.

The Internet is being used in a number of ways from voluntary survey via questionnaires on the Worldwide Web to email for more informal communication. Local authorities have established interactive websites and booths with video questionnaires have been set up in busy shopping streets to canvas opinion. Other computer-based tools such as multimedia and CD-ROM have been used. For example, the Cybestuaries multi-media project guidelines on CD-ROM was commissioned by the ESTURIALES Network which is a partnership of European local government authorities with an interest in the sustainable management of some of the major estuaries in Europe. It was set up under the Life Action programme of the European Union (City of Sunderland, 1998). The project provides a model for estuary management based on information from various estuary projects around Europe (not only the five partner estuaries from the ESTURIALES Network). Although it is not yet clear who this CD-ROM is aimed at and how it will be distributed, it appears that the procedure of compiling the enormous amount of information and developing the model has been of great value to the partner organizations as part of a communication and learning process.

People can participate at all stages of projects depending on whether participation is aimed at the instigation of a project or simply commenting on a completed design. Research on other types of environmental management projects suggests that engaging the community in collaborative information-gathering or survey work helps to establish the public alongside the government agencies in the role of decision maker (Finney and Polk, 1995). One of the problems with this approach can be the difficulty people may have in understanding the technical nature of some information. However, it has been suggested that sometimes people's ability to handle complex and technical information is underestimated (Petts, 1995). So a balance needs to be found between making technical information accessible to ordinary people and not patronizing the community by over-simplification. In addition to formal contact, informal contact such as site visits, discussions and fact-finding outings can help to break down the barriers and provide open access for the public to decision makers. It helps communication and comprehension simply by allowing people to connect issues discussed with problems on the ground (Webler et al., 1995). Activities such as locality mapping, walkabouts, visits, measuring, working with children and spending time simply talking with individuals are examples of how both the process and the product is important (Rowe and Wales, 1999) (Figure 12.4).

At the design stage, people can be involved in Planning for Real exercises. This technique, which has been developed by the Neighbourhood Initiatives Foundation, provides an opportunity for people to work with drawings, collages and models. It may include structured and unstructured debate and activities such as drama, art and music. A number of such exercises were used in the development of a

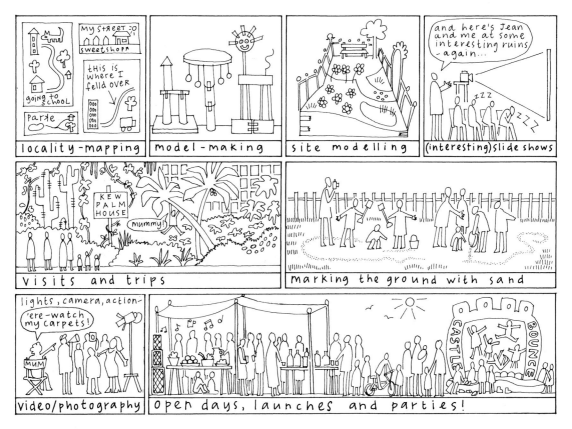

Figure 12.4 Innovative techniques: process is as important as product in community landscape projects.

Box 12.2

Snapshot of a project: The development of a community garden at Warburton and Darcy Housing Estate, Hackney, London

Warburton and Darcy Estate consists of high rise housing blocks built during the inter-war years in Hackney, East London. The Tenants and Residents Association (TRA) of Warburton and Darcy Estate approached Groundwork Hackney for help with improving the estate in 1996. Refurbishments were carried out to the housing blocks funded by the local authority. In addition, Groundwork were able to offer funding from a scheme called Cities for Children which allowed for environmental improvements to be carried out in partnership with pupils of a local school. This led to collaboration between

pupils of the school with a local artist to produce steel shapes that were fixed to the railings of the green space within the housing estate. The shapes were of sheep and a shepherd and were designed to indicate that the site was on a former route to market.

The tenants and residents then expressed an interest in developing the green space into a community garden. Designs were drawn up by Groundwork's landscape architect and, following a vote to select the preferred option, the community helped implement the scheme during a Planting Day organized by Groundwork and the TRA. A long-standing idea to create a mural for a wall in the community garden was also implemented. In collaboration with the landscape architect, the community developed the idea of a ceramic mural using the technique of firing crushed bottle glass into clay reliefs to create strongly coloured plaques.

Figure 12.5 Activities such as planting projects and visiting other community gardens can help to raise confidence and communication within a community. *Source*: By permission of Jon Rigby. *Continued on next page*

Box 12.2 continued

By this time, the TRA had successfully campaigned to obtain a community flat in which to hold meetings and events, which had been beautifully refurbished by members of the TRA committee. Now there was space for an artist in residence to run community workshops so that the community could create the plaques themselves. These workshops proved extremely popular with all members of the community. The finished plaques included a picture of a giraffe, the Michelin Man on a bicycle, the design of a carpet and a picture of somebody's father in his garden.

In spite of the apparent success of these various events, tenants and residents expressed their dissatisfaction with the garden. They wished the garden to be different, but lacked the skills and confidence to change it. Groundwork raised money for a pilot Gardening Club to act in a training and confidence-building capacity. It

involved planting projects, visiting another community garden and building contacts with other community gardeners.

This example demonstrates some important points that are of relevance to the character of community projects and the development of more sustainable environments:

- projects often lead from one to another and overlap to create a jigsaw of improvements;
- as skills and experience develops, levels of participation can increase and the process can become more meaningful for more members of the community;
- professional skills can be developed in response to the needs of the project and the community;
- you can consult people at length, but they will not always be prepared to say what they want – or know what they want.

---

local park at Isledon Road in North London facilitated by Community Land and Workspace Services (CLAWS), a non-profit-making technical aid centre providing a range of design and planning services (Stamp, 1996). A sense of involvement in the decision making process was developed through general discussion, a 'hands-on' approach and in simple techniques such as voting on preferred solutions. Other approaches include more practical aspects such as gardening, making art, growing plants, painting, creating murals and mosaics, setting out and constructing the landscape elements (see Box 12.2 and Figure 12.5).

Hands-on approaches may be used to help build a sense of commitment to a project and as a serious part of training and capacity building to increase the skills base within the community. Equally important can be the development of community relationship skills such as negotiation, contract procedure, management of groups, working with agencies and the development of an understanding of how large organizations and government bodies function – particularly local authorities – in order to develop

strategies for 'getting more out of them'. An atmosphere of flexibility, a willingness to learn and even alter opinions where necessary will help in building consensus. In larger projects it may help to ask stakeholders to set out their objectives (Statement of Interest) early in the process. This identifies guiding legislation, the primary roles and activities of stakeholders relating to the landscape, their top priorities and main internal data sources (Grabrovaz, 1995) and provides an objective way of identifying issues. If people can see that the process will help them to meet their own objectives, they are more likely to be willing to participate in it.

Although some local government organizations tend to like the idea of open public meetings as a good forum for public consultation, such meetings can often get out of control and may be taken over by particularly vociferous groups or by individuals pursing egoistic aims before collective ones. It is particularly stressful for facilitators dealing with this tendency. In particularly contentious projects, such conflict may increase the feeling of alienation and mistrust between parties. Workshops organized around a particular problem or small topic groups have been found to be more effective than large meetings (Webler *et al.*, 1995). Using citizens' panels and juries (see Chapter 4) or opinion polling instead of a public meeting have been seen as a way for policy-makers to reduce the opportunity to 'generate a bandwagon of opposition to pet projects and provides time to spin results to favour the establishment' (Burall, 1999). However, the public meeting may have the advantages of exposing local authority members to the 'real life' of communities precisely because it can be an indicator of strength of feeling. If professionals are able to recognize the difficulties inherent in certain approaches such as these, they are more likely to be able to develop methods to deal with the difficult issues of understanding and managing group dynamics in the participatory process.

Although it is possible to develop a 'toolbox' of techniques in public participation projects, each project must be assessed for appropriate methods on an independent basis. For example, it is clear that the relationships that rural communities have with their landscape and each other will be very different from that of urban communities. Projects based in rural locations often cover much larger areas with much less dense populations than the 'neighbourhood scale' of urban areas, so a transferral of techniques must be carried out with care. As a result of studies based on the larger scale, Jones (1999) recommends an examination of two main sets of issues – contextual and process-orientated – in order to determine the nature and type of participatory process to use (see Table 12.3).

Table 12.3 Determining suitable participatory methods for community landscape projects

Contextual issues	Process orientated issues
Social	*Process and power*
What is the nature of the land use patterns, land ownership patterns and impact of humans and land use patterns on the ecosystem?	Whose idea was the project? Who identified the need? (top down, bottom up or middle out)
	What information will participants need in order to participate in a meaningful way? What methodology should be used?
Ecological	
What is the nature of ecological systems and processes within the landscape?	What is the scope of involvement? How many should be involved given the nature of the problem and the constraints? If a limited number, then who?
Communal	Who is unlikely or unable to participate, given the choice of process and the nature of the problems? Will non-participation by some present problems in the future in terms of project acceptance and implementation?
What is the nature of the community structure (political, economic and social) within the landscape?	
What is the nature of the relationships between participants in the project?	*Goals and outcomes*
Has there been a change in the social fabric of the community over time?	What is the desired outcome of the process? Can this process succeed in realizing the desired outcome, given the resources (time, information professional and communal) that exist or that will exist?
Who wields power, how much power and over whom?	Who decides? Who implements? Who controls/maintains? Who evaluates performance?

Source: Adapted from Jones (1999)

THE PRACTITIONER AND THE COMMUNITY

The growing emphasis on community liaison and community-based initiatives has led to large amounts of money now being injected specifically into community-level action to change the environment (e.g. Single Regeneration Budget (SRB), private sector sponsorship, charitable funding and New Deal for Communities) and these are accompanied by the delegation of budgets and decision making to local level. However, new problems are emerging from the new opportunities and these are discussed below.

Issues for the practitioner

The question of landscape quality has been at the forefront in the debate about what really is achieved in designing with the community. It could be argued that the process of community design results in the dilution of 'pure design' or a 'dumbing-down' of landscape quality. In beginning to emphasize the importance of process over outcome, participation can be given more importance than other areas i.e. function, and aesthetics. The problem with this is that what is being achieved may be the lowest common denominator with the basic needs of the community placed before design considerations. For example, the Byker Wall estate community in Newcastle upon Tyne (see Figure 12.6), famous for its design based on community consultation in the 1970s is now calling for the demolition of part of the estate including forty energy-efficient houses designed by Ralph Erskine in order to provide a car park. The question is, can great art or design ever result from community-based initiatives when the stated aim is to create appropriate and meaningful landscapes and does this matter? Richard Haag clearly shows his thinking concerning these issues at the time he designed the Gas Works Park in Seattle. He describes the public consultation process that included lengthy debate in the local press and radio talk shows. However, when describing the community process involved in the Gas Works Park he states firmly that there 'was no public participation in the *design*' and that 'just because people had a lot of

Figure 12.6   Byker housing estate: now a contested landscape.

enthusiasm and love for those towers didn't mean they knew anything about designing a park. How can you expect a solution to come from somebody who's never really thought about space and how hard it is to create pure space in a park?' (Jory, 1991, p. 201). On the other hand, examples of community spaces, such as two well-known small parks in London – the William Curtis Ecological Park near Tower Bridge (1978–85) and Camley Street Ecological Park near King's Cross – seem to contradict this theory. Both have been used by professionals as examples of good practice. Both produced well-used, well-loved and surprising oases in the heart of the city providing aesthetic pleasure in a number of ways. Indeed, Dee Stamp, a practitioner who has worked on a considerable number of community-based landscape projects, suggests that sometimes through community participation 'a landscape of complex textures emerges – the produce of many imaginations and the tenacity of the people who want to be involved in their local environment' (Stamp, 1996, p. 37). Professionals need to be wary of assuming that pleasure or success is inevitably linked to the quality of the design or the process. Projects may take considerable time to show any measurable benefit and each project should be assessed on its own merits.

In relation to the sustainability debate, an important question for the professional engaged in this type of work is: if the community is designing it, what is the point of the professional? Part of the sustainability debate represents a crisis of faith in technology and the technological fix – or in designed solutions. The rejection of the over-arching views or 'meta-narratives' that characterized the postmodernist viewpoint has eroded faith in the professional and in expertise as being fundamentally *good*. The question that emerges is: why do we need a professional if the community knows best? Rebuilding

faith in professionals, designers and experts as well as dealing with the crisis of faith in policy-makers can be an implicit part of working with the community. Although Schön's (1983) description of the crisis of confidence in professional knowledge was based in America, a similar crisis is now affecting the professions in the UK. Blowers' concise summary of the problem shows that it is one which is not restricted to landscape professionals:

> Experts hold enormous power. decision makers cannot act with expert advice and the feats of citizens or the claims of environmental movements are thereby excluded. Moreover, the experts themselves are frequently acting as an interest group on behalf of major industries or of governments who depend on such industries for economic performance. This condition leads to an authoritarianism that denies democratic participation. However, uncertainty itself breeds dissent. Experts may come not to be trusted or their advice may be contested. Increasingly, counter-expertise is developed to challenge the conventional wisdom.
>
> (Blowers, 1997, p. 160)

Figure 12.7 Communities may have unrealistic expectations of professionals and what can be achieved by community landscape projects.

Although many of the techniques used by professionals are aimed at encouraging a creative response from the community, such methods can raise expectations beyond what is feasible in terms of financing or other project constraints as already mentioned. Providing opportunities for involvement in determining environmental change can also increase feelings of impotence rather than vice versa, and more involvement can make decisions and solutions more not less difficult to reach. Such problems or 'mechanisms of in-built failure' put the professional into a paradoxical position of raising people's expectations only to show them why they cannot be met (Figure 12.7).

The professional is further challenged by the assumption that individuals have the latent ability to come together and act as a 'community'. In some cases this is true, such as the 'triangle estate', in North Tyneside, where the community came together to develop basic principles for improving the environment of a mixed private and rented residential area in order to encourage people to settle more permanently (J. Wilson, pers. comm.) Here, awareness of the problems and the potential was high and there was good communication with those outside the community. However, in many communities, it is difficult to find people who are good community leaders and willing to volunteer to take on the necessary responsibilities for establishing and running such projects. Obtaining a broad cross-section of representation is also very difficult. The most enthusiastic participants are often those who have time on their hands, do not have to organize childcare and are not involved in shift work – often older women. Even if men attend meetings, it is notoriously difficult to get them to express their opinion.

Consultation, participation or community involvement are sometimes restricted because of the nature of localized democratic structures. The professional might find that in many cases it is necessary to first 'restore' a community in order for it to have the ability to take action. This is a tremendously complex undertaking, based on a range of assumptions such as: 'restoration' is desirable/beneficial; the community *can* be restored; and policy-makers and professionals are the people to do the restoration. It

tends to be easier for the professional to work through an existing community establishment such as a school where there are already good links into the community and existing organizational structures, e.g. parents' groups, which can be tapped into more easily and more successfully than trying to navigate local democratic structures.

All this indicates that the character of work in the community sector is changing. The participatory process appears to be moving into a new stage where partnerships of organizations such as tenants and residents' groups are involved in their own 'wheeling and dealing' and are now in conflict or competition for the same resources as the more established community agencies and groups. Further complexities have arisen because of the number of participatory projects around. Bell and Evans (1998) describe the conflict between Local Agenda 21 initiatives and the Community Forest initiatives in the English Midlands as a result of different objectives articulated by both for a forest vision.

The idea of landscape as morally regenerative is not a new one, but the concept of environmental regeneration is now closely linked in the eyes of policy-makers with the moral regeneration of communities and on community capacity-building through training and skills-building. Characteristics of this include the provision of new facilities such as community spaces and halls, the development of training programmes and indicators of success such as citizenship awards. Practitioners may find themselves involved in projects aimed at the regeneration of cultural as well as the physical landscape. This is because there is a blurring of cultural, moral and physical regeneration and professionals need to be more aware that the establishment of landscape projects may have much broader significance to a community and encompass much wider and often politically motivated aims of policy-makers (see Chapter 4) than simply the physical improvement of an area.

Issues for communities: problems from within

Communities are facing a number of problems that restrict their ability to participate in projects. New

Box 12.3

Snapshot of a project: Shrubland Road Estate, Hackney, London

Shrubland Road Estate is a low-rise housing estate in East London. The Tenants and Residents Association (TRA) approached Groundwork Hackney in 1996 to help them solve the problems associated with a disused car park on the estate. The use of the area was compromising the security of the surrounding ground floor flats because young people playing football in the space were causing noise nuisance and vandalizing the surrounding wooden fences. Community fears over this were compounded by a rumour which said that a child had been assaulted in the space.

With the agreement of the TRA the space was closed with fencing and apportioned as garden extensions and new garden areas for the adjacent residents. The majority of the community generally seemed to be delighted with the scheme and several carried out elaborate improvements to their new gardens. However, a small number of tenants felt they had not had the opportunity to obtain garden space – they had been asked, but had turned down the chance and had not attended the relevant meetings. The aggrieved individuals created feelings of acrimony within the community.

On another part of the estate conflict arose over a larger space with similar problems. The Chair of the TRA was keen to see provision made for young people here and proposals were formulated to instal football or basketball facilities. Antagonized

Figure 12.8   Garden extensions created from disused car park areas on the Shrubland Road Estate encouraged some residents to carry out elaborate improvements to their gardens.   *Source*: By permission of Jon Rigby

Continued on next page

Box 12.3 continued

by the behaviour of young people playing football in the space until late at night the tenants and residents opposed the scheme. Debate raged for eighteen months and the process became so acrimonious that Groundwork moved attention to another area of the estate. In yet another disused car park further garden extension areas were proposed for adjacent residents, but a small number of tenants and residents vociferously opposed the scheme that was favoured by the majority.

After nearly three years difficulties arose because although the funding which was provided on an annual basis had been held over, it was likely to be lost if it was not now spent. Attention returned to the larger space and an agreement was gained to turn this into private garden areas. Planning permission and contracts were drawn up for this work. However, problems erupted again. In despair, the Chair of the TRA resigned and a new committee formed. Their vision, now formally approved, was to divide the space into communal gardens, accessible to named keyholders, rather than provide

extensions to the gardens of ground floor flats. The new committee is implementing this scheme.

The ex-Chair of the TRA, freed from her responsibilities, has begun a new life as a karaoke singer. The re-formed committee is embarking on new projects. This example demonstrates some important points:

- the degree of antipathy towards young people that can be unleashed at the community level may be so strong as to amount to hatred and mistrust;
- even if the whole community is consulted someone will always claim not to have been asked;
- annual funding of projects can cause problems because it can take communities a long time to reach a decision on how to spend money;
- if a committee or a project depends too much on the vision of a single person this may not be sustainable because it places unacceptable pressure on that one person;
- consensus building takes a long time.

---

opportunities are opening up for communities to participate in regeneration processes, yet communities are circumscribed by their access to skills, time and resources. The tension between opportunities and limits creates pressures for communities. The emphasis on community action also denotes a retreat from the strategic planning system and an erosion of the common purpose that this system was supposed to represent. At its worst it can even herald a retreat into a mentality of petty local rivalries, as, for example, when housing estates refuse to share scarce resources – such as a community hall – as a common good with other estates. A characteristic of the difficulties in landscape projects which arise within community groups is that landscapes become contested (see Box 12.3).

Other problems may arise within community groups, for example the more powerful members may direct attention away from difficult topics, particularly by statutory policy-makers where they are involved in

the proceedings. Professionals should ensure that all of the options, including the ones not favoured by some of the parties are discussed. The initiation of projects sometimes opens up a can of worms in the community which no one knew existed or could predict would be revealed. Such problems can fragment a community into factions and unleash self-interest and prejudices such as racist attitudes or antipathy to young people. This is entirely contradictory to any sense of common purpose or community spirit. It also raises a sinister picture of a future fragmentation of urban areas into micro-communities, competing with each other for scarce resources, rather than working together towards a common vision.

One of the major problems with participation in environmental decisions is that it is very difficult for communities to focus on the broader implications of what is decided, and concerns are expressed in local terms (Selman and Parker, 1997). The effects of regional, national and global environmental problems are often simply too impossibly large to apply to everyday life whereas immediate concerns, such as litter and dog mess, feature highly in many studies carried out to ascertain people's concerns about the environment (e.g. Hull *et al.*, 1997; Selman and Parker, 1997; Smith, 1994). It is also difficult for communities (as well as funding bodies) to grasp the time-scale required for projects – particularly certain groups such as children. People involved often want to see an immediate benefit to themselves as well as the community as a whole.

The focus of certain funding bodies and environmental organizations has been not only on communities as a whole, but on the provision of help for specific groups and specific landscapes within communities. Children have been particularly in focus for reasons already described. The Learning through Landscapes Trust (LTL) was established as a charity in 1990 to improve school grounds and persuade local government and the teaching profession to take the potential of school grounds for teaching purposes seriously. LTL has gained funding for research to assess the quality of school grounds and their impact on educational life. The organization is also developing ways in which teachers and children can participate in the design process and is developing partnerships with landscape professionals and artists (Lucas, 1993). LTL has recognized the importance of providing better landscapes for children in the form of more interesting and useful school grounds and also that encouraging the participation of both children and teachers in the determination of the shaping of new school grounds has relevance for social learning and sustainability.

Most landscape architecture schools in the UK now have some community landscape component although this is variable and has not so far been regarded by the professional accreditation body (the Landscape Institute) as an essential part of students' education. Final year undergraduate degree students on the Landscape Architecture course at Leeds Metropolitan University have been working with community groups since the late 1970s and have now helped communities with over eighty projects within the Leeds and West Yorkshire area. Much of this work is based on renovating school grounds or playgrounds. This programme has developed to such an extent that a separate Landscape Design and Community Unit has been established within the School to respond to the demand for help by community groups (see Royffe and Taylor, 1987; Thwaites, 1995). Second year and graduate students are now also involved in the process. This programme has experienced a number of difficulties, not least those posed by Health and Safety Regulations which restrict the physical involvement of students because of legal implications. However, there appears to be a growing interest in the UK and the USA in the potential of community outreach projects for research and teaching purposes.

It can be difficult for community groups to obtain funding for landscape projects, hence the interest shown by many community groups in involving students in the process rather than in employing design professionals. There are now at least some opportunities to obtain funding for community projects, particularly if they are linked to community capacity building in some way or if there is an existing initiative. However, funding limitations often exist because communities lack access to the necessary sources of skills and experience in order to capture the funding available. There are still relatively few potential funding bodies aside from those directly or indirectly connected with government but funding now can be obtained through sponsorship from organizations involved in the partnership process and from charities. An example of such a charitable organization is PACE (Positive Action for Community Environments) which now provides money for wages and capital projects such as school grounds improvements. Multinational companies also now provide potential funds through a variety of environmental schemes. Shell Better Britain Campaign (BBC) is an example of this. Through the Shell BBC network community groups can gain free information and case study examples of community projects. Examining the general aims of such bodies helps to define the kind of project likely to be successful in obtaining funding.

Some organizations now form partnerships to provide awards to help inspire community groups.

The Urban Oasis Project at Apple Tree Court, Salford, Manchester in the north west of England (Nicholson Lord, 1996; Paxton, 1997), is a well-known example of a scheme that won such an award in 1999. In this case the British Telecom/WWF Partnership award was given for the transformation of a wasteland around a 1960s' residential tower block into a 'tropical oasis' community garden. The area had been part of a scheme where low-rise redevelopment was gradually replacing tower blocks. But existing tenants objected to this and in 1988 formed a partnership with an environmental charity and local organizations that had an alternative proposition culminating in the creation of organic allotments, orchard, duck pond, woodland, wild-flower meadow, seating area, Japanese garden and community café. Physical and financial help was obtained from the government, the Civic Trust, local schools, the probation service, unemployed youngsters and people with disabilities. After ten years the project achieved greater autonomy through the tenants' group obtaining Tenancy Management Company (TMC) status (achieved 1996) thereby taking over responsibility for the estate's finances and maintenance. It is an example of how 'techniques of sustainable, permanent household agriculture' (Tony Milroy, quoted in Nicholson Lord, 1996, p. 69) can be applied to the inner city. This project also counteracts the commonly held view that the only answer to the problems of such landscapes is to demolish the tower blocks and build low-rise housing.

Although some community groups seem to exist simply on the energy of particular participants, it is not generally sustainable to rely on individuals to hold up an organization, as can be seen in the example in Box 12.3. The community organization needs a sustainable broad base of support with the community to achieve the results of Apple Tree Court. Lack of long-term planning as a result of lack of long-term financing seems to be a perennial problem of community groups. Those groups which do manage to achieve financial stability are often those which have property, land or some other 'asset base' which can be rented out commercially or used to provide collateral in order to fund the community's activities. However, such capital assets can also become a burden because they are subject to market values.

Issues for communities: problems from outside

If communities are limited in their access to skills, time and resources, this is equally true at the level of policy-makers. Obtaining resources, particularly financial resources in the form of core funding, is a major source of difficulty for communities and community organizations, as can be seen by the demise of the community-based Architecture Workshop in Newcastle upon Tyne. Resources are rarely sufficient to meet the raised expectations of a participative community. If resources are accessible, time is generally limited and subject to the restrictions of funding timescales. The process of community regeneration is also limited by the expertise available. Thirty years of initiatives – from the Housing Action Areas of 1969 to the New Deal for Communities of 1999 – have seen many lessons learnt and unlearned and thus policy and good practice is still evolving. Moreover, there is still much that is done badly or half-heartedly, with much consultation poorly thought through or as a token response to perceived problems.

Efficacy of present methods: assessment and measurement

It is notoriously difficult to assess the success of projects. Each party involved will have different criteria for success and therefore different indicators and so no one set of indicators or methods of measurement is appropriate. One of the problems with the evaluation of social projects is that qualitative techniques are not well developed and so quantitative methods are often used which may be inappropriate (Twelvetrees, 1996). Webler *et al.* describe a method to assess the success of public participation which includes an assessment of competence, fairness and 'social learning' (1995, p. 444). Measurement of *competence* (or whether a satisfactory solution was found to the problem) was carried out through a series of on-going reviews by expert and community members; *fairness* of the process was evaluated by experts in discussion with participants; *social learning* (which is described as the benefits which people derive from 'working out a mutually acceptable solution to a project or problem that affects their community and their personal lives') (ibid., p. 444) was evaluated by consideration of a number of criteria including:

- cognitive enhancement – understanding the nature of the problem and the issues;
- moral development or problem-solving and ability to work together as a group;
- development of a group identity;
- participation in activities such as site visits and working groups;
- expressions of satisfaction with process;
- positive change of views, e.g. evidence of trust in facilitators;
- evidence of greater self-confidence in individuals and the group as the project progressed.

While indicators such as the one suggested by Smith (1994) – of counting the numbers of volunteer work days per annum – are tangible and quantifiable, many are much less so. Perhaps a more useful method is to construct questions which individuals, the participants or the facilitator can ask in order to provide an indication of success (see Freeman *et al.*, 1996; Grabrovaz, 1995; Hartig *et al.*, 1998). Examples of these are:

- How many people attend events? Has this number altered or been sustained over the course of the project?
- What is the cross-section of groups in the project? Does this reflect the cross-section of the community?
- Have common goals been identified?
- Has there been a commitment to work together and an agreed work programme?
- Is understanding of the issues increasing as the project progresses, e.g. is less time spent on basic explanation?
- Is there a feeling of shared 'ownership' of the project? Do the outcomes portray a shared vision and shared ownership of all aspects of the vision?

- Have the community contributed, and feel they have contributed, to a change in policy of decision makers as a result of the project?
- Has a sense of local community developed during the project process?
- Has there been early, continuous and targeted consultation?
- Have partnerships been created for implementation and funding?
- Has the project achieved its aims on the ground?

In many cases the success of the participatory process will not be reflected in anything which can be measured in landscape terms or in terms which might be considered 'good design' by conventional design assessment criteria. The gain in terms of social capital building may have increased while change in the landscape may not have been achieved because of problems such as lack of funding, or because stakeholders renege at the implementation stage on earlier agreements. This highlights the problem inherent with many non-statutory agreements – there is no statutory compulsion for stakeholders to honour their commitments. However, having said this, commitments made publicly by stakeholders can provide the basis for evaluative criteria since such undertakings openly made are more difficult to ignore than those made in private meetings. As with other aspects of community-based landscape projects, the identification and development of useful indicators are difficult, the information is disparate and very variable and has not yet been well tested or researched.

CONCLUSION

As discussed in Chapter 4, issues of social sustainability and the practice of community landscape architecture are affected by the conflation of moral and social regeneration, the ambiguity about who is expecting what and the contradictions inherent in the sustainability agenda, such as questions of local democracy and justice.

One of the major problems is determining the success of community projects and whether the involvement of landscape architects in such projects is effective. Intermediary organizations often promote self-help through a variety of methods and this is where the community landscape architect can perhaps be of most help to communities. The partnership approach can provide benefits of both private and public sector working and can be seen as the establishment of an 'intermediary partnership'. Twelvetrees (1996) regards the intermediary sector (not public, not private) as the key to promoting and organizing successful neighbourhood development in deprived areas. However there may be difficulties in ascertaining accountability in this sector. Schön (1983) supports the view that the practitioner should 'play an intermediary role' and although the conflicts inherent in that role cannot be avoided, the practitioner 'has considerable freedom to choose the role frame he will adopt and theory of action according to which he will behave' (ibid., p. 235). Parker sees 'the only block to the development of [better public participation] methods may well be a prevalent "professional" attitude' (1996, p. 27) but it is clear from the discussion in this chapter that the situation is much more complex than this and many of the limitations lie within communities themselves as well as a result of the larger issues reviewed in Chapter 4 such as the nature of the decision making structures existing in this country.

Funding for community projects is an obvious problem and is perhaps simply a part of the overall difficulties caused by lack of funding for the design and management of all public spaces as identified by Tony Kendle and his colleagues in Chapter 13. Such areas cannot respond simply to 'market forces'. We include in our public landscapes values which should be more enduring than those which respond simply to economic restrictions and conditions. Of course, sensible forms of funding are essential and society must ensure that the right priorities are provided for, such as the funding of public participation in landscape projects if we are to provide happier communities, connected to their localities.

Although it can be argued that community participation 'dumbs down' landscape design, we also have to ask whether 'expert' design has created public landscapes which are any 'better' and what the assessment criteria for good landscape design might be. Can we harness some of the vivacity found in our communities into the structure of degraded landscapes by making the spaces more user specific and 'owned' by particular groups? Marcus et al. argue that 'claim to a particular territory, however informal, may be necessary for [people] to maintain a sense of group cohesion and identity' (1990, p. 74). Landscape professionals can only develop a better understanding and an intuitive feeling for the use, association and meaning of particular landscapes by working with or for the community in a much more integrated way. Community landscapes can be positive statements of community values and provide vibrant living environments as is illustrated by the success of numerous projects such as the one exemplified by Apple Tree Court, Salford.

In landscape projects, engaging people to provide views on what should be done is often not difficult. However, there are many difficulties in actually getting people to take action or become involved in the management of that action; this may be partly because the majority of people believe that the responsibility for environmental analysis and problem-solving lies squarely with central and local government (Selman, 1996). However, evidence suggests that existing democratic structures do not necessarily respond to the desire to create more sustainable landscapes. There may be a number of ways to address these broader problems (see Chapter 4), but for example, two issues central to the concept of sustainability can be tackled through good participatory techniques: (a) that it is particularly difficult to develop an understanding and acceptance of the time-scales of landscape change; and (b) the role of appropriate maintenance.

Community involvement in landscape projects has been found to provide a significant difference to the success of projects and particularly in the creation of a forum for good communications, building partnerships and building a positive local attachment to the space (e.g. Woolley and Lai, 1999). Professionals can help foresee the changes required in the landscape and make landscape projects more sustainable through the examination of social trends and through facilitating the involvement of often excluded groups, such as older people and multicultural groups. Tony Kendle and his colleagues in Chapter 13 also write that the involvement of people in management of landscape counteracts the often pessimistic anti-humanitarian view that the world would be better off without people and can show that positive change is possible.

In the 1980s there was much controversy over the statements made by environmental determinists such as Oscar Newman (1972) and Alice Coleman (1985, 1986) concerning the ability of design professionals to 'design out crime'. This helped landscape professionals to re-examine the interaction of landscape design with the social environment. However, the discussion has moved forward and it is accepted that social ills cannot be healed and human nature cannot be changed simply through a change in the physical landscape. The focus is now on how to remove the social injustice, which breeds crime. However, we can identify that professionals can use the potential of landscape change as a means to foster more positive community relationships. Patterns of landscape use can be changed, links to the landscape rebuilt and meaning given to local environments. Practitioners working with communities have reported that the sustainability agenda has brought about changed expectations and that participants often feel a part of something moving forward which engenders an optimism that the status quo does not necessarily have to be maintained – or sustained (Figure 12.9).

Landscape practitioners have an opportunity to be at the forefront of new ways of thinking about and managing landscape change. Working with the community may be one way in which people can create landscapes which are not only more responsive to local needs and culture but to local environmental conditions. Successful landscape regeneration is heavily connected to the regeneration of the communities that inhabit them so that the landscape is used, reclaimed and considered as an integral part of that community. New investment possibilities being channelled into this type of community-based work and new thinking concerning the development of practice based on a partnership approach is likely to expand opportunities in landscape projects for professionals. Developing the expertise to respond to this and the more integrated environmental thinking

Figure 12.9 Landscape improvements cannot solve all the problems found in communities, but can help to build more positive community relationships.

demanded and instigated by the sustainability agenda is a new and exciting challenge for landscape practitioners and academics.

ACKNOWLEDGEMENTS

Particular thanks to Rebecca Cushnaghan and Joan Wilson of the Northern Environmental Workshop Ltd, Newcastle for discussions concerning their work on community landscape projects, and Kevin Thwaites from Leeds Metropolitan University for clarifying information concerning the LMU Design and Community Project. Many thanks also to the Shrubland Road and Warburton and Darcy Tenants' and Residents' Associations.

REFERENCES

Al-Kodmany, K. (1999) Using visualization techniques for enhancing public participation in planning and design: process, implementation and evaluation, *Landscape and Urban Planning*, 45, 37–45.

Arnstein, S. R. (1969) A ladder of citizen participation, *Journal of the American Institute of Planners*, July, 216–224.

Barlow, J. (1995) *Public Participation in Urban Development: The European Experience* (London, Policy Studies Institute).

Bartlett, D. (1999) Kent Downs Jigsaw Project, *Landscape Design*, 277, February, 44.

Bell, M. and Evans, D. (1998) The National Forest and Local Agenda 21: an experiment in integrated landscape planning, *Journal of Environmental Planning and Management*, 41(2), 237–251.

Blowers, A. (1997) Sustainability: the context of change for planning, in A. Blowers and R. Evans (eds), *Town Planning in the 21st Century*, p. 71 (London, Routledge).

Burall, P. (1999) *Going public*, Town and Country Planning, March.

City of Sunderland (1998) Cybestuaries Information Pack, Esturiales Life Project, LIFE95/UK/A41/EU/834 (Sunderland, City of Sunderland).

Clifford, S. (1994) Agenda 21 in Little Gidding, *Landscape Design*, April, 36–37.

Clifford, S. (2000) *Places, People and Parish Maps* (Common Ground http://www.commonground.org.uk).

Coleman, A. (1985) *Utopia on Trial: Vision and Reality in Planned Housing* (London, Hilary Shipman).

Coleman, A. (1986) Dangerous dreams, *Landscape Design*, 163, 29–31.

Davies, K. (1999) Groundworking for people, *Landlines*, 105(11), 3–6.

Davis, C. (1996) The process is as important as the product: an examination of the role of public participation in estuary management plan development in the UK, Conference paper, July (Seattle, Coastal Society).

Ervin, S. (1999) The Internet advantage: how can landscape architects best use the Internet? *Landscape Architecture*, June, 36–42.

European Commission (1997) *Community Involvement in Urban Regeneration: Added Value and Changing Values* (Luxembourg, European Commission).

Finney, C. and Polk, R. E. (1995) Developing stakeholder understanding, technical capability and responsibility: the New Bedford Harbour Superfund Forum, *Environmental Impact Assessment Review*, 15, 517–541.

Freeman. C., Littlewood, S. and Whitney, D. (1996) Local government and emerging models of participation in the Local Agenda 21 process, *Journal of Environmental Planning and Management*, 39(1), 65–78.

Grabrovaz, M. (1995) *Review of Estuary Projects*, Report (Peterborough, English Nature).

Hardin, G. (1968) The Tragedy of the Common, *Science*, 162, 12432–12448.

Hardin, G. (1993) *Living Within Limits: Ecology, Economics, and Population Taboos* (Oxford, Oxford University Press).

Hartig, J. H., Zarull, M. A., Heidtke, T. M. and Shah, H. (1998) Implementing ecosystem-based management: lessons from the Great Lakes, *Journal of Environmental Planning and Management*, 41(1), 45–76.

Hough, M. (1990) Formed by natural process: defining the sustainable city, *Landscape Architectural Review*, October, 8–11.

Hull, A., Roe, M. H. and Norwood, T. (1997) *State of the borough: the environment (towards a state of the Environment Report)*, Review and Research Report for Sedgefield Borough Council, County Durham (Newcastle upon Tyne, University of Newcastle).

Jones, S. (1999) Participation and community at the landscape scale, *Landscape Journal*, 18(1), Spring, 65–78.

Jory, J. (1991) *Modern Landscape Architecture: Redefining the Garden* (New York, Abbeville Press).

Kellogg, W. (1999) Community-based organizations and neighbourhood environmental problem solving: a framework for adoption of information technologies, *Journal of Environmental Planning and Management*, 42(4), 445–469.

Kemp, P. and Griffiths, J. (1999) *Quaking Houses: Art Science and the Community: A Collaborative Approach to Water Pollution* (Charlbury, Jon Carpenter).

Kidd, S. (1995) Planning for estuary resources: the Mersey Estuary Management Plan, *Journal of Environmental Planning and Management*, 38(3), 435–442.

Lucas, W. (1993) Unlocking the landscape, *Landscape Design*, 221, 11–17.

Marcus, C. Cooper, Watsky, C. M., Insley, E. and Francis, C. (1990) Neighborhood parks, in C. Cooper Marcus and C. Francis (eds), *People Places: Design Guidelines for Urban Open Space* (New York, Van Nostrand Reinhold).

Margerum, R. D. and Born, S. M. (1995) Integrated environmental management – moving from theory to practice. *Journal of Environmental Planning and Management*, 38(3), 371–392.

Miles, M. (1998) A green and pleasant land: ecological art in the UK, *Public Arts Review*, Fall/Winter, 26–29.

New Economics Foundation (NEF) (2000) httrp://www.new economics.org/

Newman, O. (1972) *Defensible Space* (New York, Macmillan).

Nicholson Lord, D. (1996) Making a difference, *BBC Wildlife*, December, 68.

O'Riordan, T. and Ward, R. (1997) Building trust in shoreline management: creating participatory consultation in shoreline management plans, *Land Use Policy*, 14(4), 257–276.

Parker, A. (1996) A view from the inside? *Landscape Design,* February, 247, 26–27.

Paxton, A. (1997) Farming in the city, *Landscape Design,* September, 53–55.

Petts, J. (1995) Waste management strategy development: a case study of community involvement and consensus-building in Hampshire, *Journal of Environmental Planning and Management,* 38(4) 519–536.

Roe, M. H. (2000) Landscape Planning for Sustainability: Community Participation in Estuary Management Plans, *Landscape Research*, 25(2), 157–181.

Royffe, C. and Taylor, A. (1987) Design and the community, *Landscape Design*, 165, 20–23.

Rowe, A. M. and Wales, A. (1999) *Changing Estates: A Facilitator's Guide to Making Community Environment Projects Work* (London, Groundwork Hackney).

Schlesinger, A. (1999) New deal for communities – one year on, *Town and Country Planning,* 68(11), 345–347.

Schön, D. A. (1983) *The Reflective Practitioner: How Professionals Think in Action* (New York, Basic Books).

Selman, P. (1992) *Environmental Planning: The Conservation and Development of Biophysical Resources* (London, Paul Chapman).

Selman, P. (1996) *Local Sustainability: Managing and Planning Ecologically Sound Places* (London, Chapman).

Selman, P. and Parker, J. (1997) Citizenship, civicness and social capital in Local Agenda 21, *Local Environment*, 2(2), 171–184.

Smith, B. J. (1994) The Medway River Project: an example of community participation in integrated river management, in C. Kirby and W. R. White (eds) *Integrated River Basin Development* (Chichester, Wiley).

Stamp, D. (1996) Parks are us, *Landscape Design*, 254, October, 34–37.

Thwaites, K. (1995) Down on the farm, *Landscape Design*, 245, 42–45.

Turner, T. (1998) Twelve alternatives, *Landscape Design*, 267, 42–45.

Twelvetrees, A. C. (1996) *Organizing for Neighbourhood Development: A Comparative Study of Community Based Development Organizations* (Aldershot, Avebury).

Venter, A. K. and Breen, C. M. (1998) Partnership Forum Framework: Participative Framework for Protected Area Outreach, *Environmental Management*, 22(6), 803–815.

Walker, P. (1998) Participation works! *Local Environment*, 3(3), 349–353.

Webler, T., Kastenholz, H. and Renn, O. (1995) Public participation in impact assessment: a social learning perspective, *Environmental Impact Assessment Review*, 5, 443–463.

Whitmore, W., Cook, E. and Steiner, F. (1995) Public involvement in visual assessment: the Verde River Corridor Study, *Landscape Journal,* Spring, 14(1), 27–45.

Woolley, H. and Lai, Ming-chia (1999) The people's parks? *Landscape Design*, 278, March, 37–38.

13

SUSTAINABLE LANDSCAPE MANAGEMENT

Tony Kendle, Juliet E. Rose and Junko Oikawa

SUMMARY

Sustainable landscape management can be approached from two different perspectives. The first explores the environmental impacts of inputs and activities. The scope for reducing impacts is comparatively limited, as many impacts are already small or changes require trade-offs between different impacts. Significant gains come from functional changes in the landscape that may not be acceptable. To be able to evaluate the acceptability of even small inputs we need a better understanding of outputs and values of landscapes and of the management process.

There are situations where more rather than less management is needed. The common drive to minimize or even avoid management sometimes comes from a perception that this comprises dull and routine tasks with the primary objective of maintaining stasis. In some cases the presence of people, and management inputs, into natural systems is seen as automatically degrading. The role of management as a means of dealing with, rather than denying, environmental change needs to be explored. The concept that people can be a positive force for environmental improvement also needs to be fostered. This will be the best way to meet the requirements of sustainable development, which is based on the principle of positive human action for environmental care rather than inaction.

INTRODUCTION – THE RELATIONSHIP OF LANDSCAPE MANAGEMENT TO DESIGN

Like many things, landscape management is not difficult to grasp, but is difficult to define. Landscape managers work in public and private sectors, in rural or urban contexts. They look after natural and man-made landscapes. They can be responsible for areas primarily intended for recreation (passive and active) and sport, for nature conservation, for scenic enjoyment, for ecosystem function or for multiple benefits. They normally do not have primary responsibility for 'productive' cropping of land through farming or forestry (Chapter 8). Certainly, in this text issues related to sustainable crop production will not be directly addressed except where comparative data are useful or to illustrate how crop-focused land use can differ from landscape management. Green (1986) emphasized how significant the differences in approach and priorities can be when he wrote:

> if the amenity land manager is ever in doubt as to his best course of action, he has merely to think of what a modern farmer or forester would do, and do the opposite. His objective is to make one blade of grass grow where two grew before.

This is perhaps too glib a statement as there are times when an amenity land manager needs to produce very productive vegetation, for example, to withstand heavy wear, but Green's point memorably underlines how the objectives can be more complex than those of contemporary agriculture.

Data do not exist to quantify the different types of landscapes that may be managed by the profession. This is partly because their work extends beyond the responsibility of any one monitoring body and includes a mix of public and private land, and partly because the management responsibility of different professions is normally determined by objectives rather than land type. For example, a woodland used primarily for recreation may be managed by different people to one managed primarily for timber output, but they are not distinguished in land survey. A nature reserve may be 'farmed' to preserve ancient semi-natural habitats such as heathland, but the primary objective is conservation and not food production.

Even where it would be reasonable to expect the most basic statistics to exist, they do not. For example, the number of local authority managed parks in the UK cannot be quantified. Estimates of the number of urban parks in the UK range from 5,000–30,000 (Environment, Transport and Regional Affairs Committee, 1999). Perhaps the most coherent estimate of any component of the landscape estate ever attempted in the UK was by NERC (1977). Amenity grass, defined as all areas with recreational, functional or aesthetic value and of which agricultural productivity is not the primary aim, made up perhaps one-fifth of total grassland cover. The Forestry Research Co-ordination Committee (1988) estimated that the area beneath amenity trees in the urban UK was in the region of 500,000 hectares, roughly 25 per cent of the size of the total British forest cover, but equivalent to the area under broadleaved woodland at the time. Amenity land is therefore a sizeable proportion of the total land cover of the UK.

Sustainability and landscape management

In addressing the issue of sustainability in relation to landscape management a key distinction should be made between *creating and managing landscapes in sustainable ways* and the development of *sustainable landscapes*. The former is an approach focused on making sure that inputs and practices carry the lowest environmental cost, protect resources, reduce wastes etc. However, the very lowest environmental costs would be if the activity did not happen at all. The term sustainable *development* is balanced to reflect an awareness of the need for initiatives that improve quality of life and the environment (UNEP/FAO, 1997). Reducing impacts is the more obvious and also the easier issue to tackle. It also sets an important standard for our own credibility, but if that is the only move we make we have undersold the purpose of our professions. Landscape designers and managers, as the most explicitly creative of the land professions, have to debate how to favour those outputs that leave the best legacy for the future, how what we choose to do is justified by its influence on the broader picture of social attitudes, living environment etc. If it is possible to achieve these benefits, our environmental costs are justified.

In this context, the landscape designer's contribution to environmental change, often involving a specific creative and constructive act, can be easier to identify and review than the work of the landscape manager, where goals are frequently less explicit. Similarly, the undesirable impacts of a landscape design and creation process are usually acute and obvious, those of landscape management often chronic and subtle. A designer may be responsible for between 20–50 per cent of the lifetime costs of a park, invested over just 2 per cent of its life (Environment, Transport and Regional Affairs Committee, 1999). A landscape architect may be involved in a construction project that allows development to completely destroy and denature soil structure and quality (Kendle, 1996); a landscape manager is more likely to be concerned with subtler long-term degradation processes such as soil degradation from repeated user pressure.

While there is always an interaction between design and management in new landscapes, because processes of management must begin to be addressed as soon as landscape components are specified, there is not always the same interaction between management and design because not all managed landscapes have been designed. A landscape manager's objective is sometimes to bring a designer's vision to fruition, and then to maintain stasis or cyclic renewal but this model only fits a fraction of the work. The actual relationships are more complex and can be divided into:

- *Management for design* – as described above, but even here changing circumstances, internal or external to the site, frequently mean an adjustment to plans.
- *Management by design* – where the landscape design embodies a consideration of the costs of the management process and options for minimizing maintenance overheads. For example, this could be by designing a landscape that can be maintained with fewer energy inputs or labour inputs, such as a closed ground-cover.
- *Design by management* – in the majority of cases landscapes have had no formalized design, they are shaped and formed by the accumulation of a series of management decisions. This is particularly the case with rural landscapes such as nature reserves and National Parks. In rare cases the ability of the management process to be creative is explicitly recognized, but in many situations, particularly in the case of nature reserves, it can be seen as important for the integrity, sense of continuity, and above all for the sense of naturalness of the site, that the management is regarded as preserving an inherited landscape rather than forming a new one. Here there are the greatest challenges in resolving multiple land uses and the woven legacies of past attitudes and presumptions about the site.
- *Design for management* – where the landscape design embodies a consideration of the opportunities presented by the management process. Designers may produce landscapes where the management process itself is not seen as a chore but becomes one of the positive outputs of the process, for example if it maximizes opportunities for participation and community involvement (Adams and Ingham, 1998).

The landscape manager's opportunity and options for exploring sustainable approaches will differ in each of these cases. In principle, landscape design and management should not really be isolated, and sustainable approaches in particular require that the long-term implications of design choices are considered. Nevertheless many sites are also in the care of managers for vastly longer periods than is the case with designers and they may need to be continually re-designed, even re-invented, by management through a series of gradual transitions and in response to evolving circumstances. A core concept for managers to address is therefore change and the response to change, but the tendency to inherit legacies and presumptions about how things should be done is also greater for managers who have to work harder to see sites with fresh eyes. The standard management plan sequence widely adopted is based on the premise that aims and objectives are made explicit before determining and monitoring operations (Leay *et al.*, 1986). Nevertheless many organizations maintain land without explicit objectives, and even where objectives are identified they are typically superficial and self-referential and fail to identify, or certainly question, the fundamental purpose of the site or the management activity. The range of possible land use and social changes approaching in coming decades require that the managers also learn to constantly review their activities in ways that many are not accustomed to.

MANAGING LANDSCAPES SUSTAINABLY

This section reviews some of the issues that arise when we try to change methods and techniques to make them sustainable. To date this has probably been the primary focus of discussion for landscape managers. It is of course vital that a profession addresses its own standards of work and daily impacts, but it is a secondary issue that must not be allowed to confuse the primary goals of the work. At their worst the issues debated in the name of sustainability are *ad hoc* and overly influenced by

Box 13.1

Is peat renewable?

Bragg (1990) reviews figures for peat coverage in Finland of between 10 and 10.4 million hectares. With average formation rates taken as a conservative 0.5 mm a year, the national annual accretion is therefore likely to be 52 million m³. Bragg gives a conversion of weight to volume of peat of approximately 1 tonne to 2.5 m³. The annual increment of Finnish peat is therefore approximately 20 million tonnes. Extraction for horticulture in Finland is given as 220,000 tonnes per annum, and that for fuel production as at 1,500,000 tonnes. In 1990 the UK used 2.7 million m³ per annum total (calculated as 0.0025

of world reserves) and imported about one half of this. The calculation is not completely simple, as not all peat reserves are suitable for harvest and not all have the same conservation value, but the orders of magnitude difference between demand and accretion suggest that peat can be seen as a renewable resource, and that the real issue is one of sensitivity of source rather than of use of the material *per se*. Of course, there are issues related to the energy demands of peat transport, and whether it actually functions as an optimum material for plant growth (Kendle, 1990), but it could be argued that the blanket condemnation of the material has obscured such issues and forced a focus onto alternatives such as coir which have even greater associated transport costs.

specific campaigns – use of chemicals, recycling, avoiding peat, etc. – without a coherent overview. Some of the approaches adopted are therefore of marginal benefit or even have an air of cliché about them; others are complex and subtle issues that get reduced to simplistic concepts.

Working in the public sector creates particular challenges (see Chapter 12). The public, and politicians, can legitimately demand and enforce changes based upon their beliefs, without any need to make reference to the 'truth' of such beliefs. For example, many people believe that man-made chemicals are more harmful to them than 'natural' chemicals but this is difficult for scientists to accept as it is a flawed premise. Ames and Gold (1998) show that 99.99 per cent of the pesticides we eat are natural plant compounds, usually secondary metabolites developed to protect the plants against insect attack. Of these approximately 50 per cent can cause cancer in tests on rodents if applied at the same rates as used for testing man-made chemicals. Plant-derived insecticides can also be persistent and toxic to humans and non-target organisms such as fish or beneficial insects (Widdowson, 1987). Nevertheless the organic farming movement has demonstrated that 'alternative' producers and consumers can develop a supply and consumer system that fully embodies the belief

that man-made chemicals are not as safe, and cares nothing for the scientists' protests.

Environmental lobbies present issues to the public in ways designed to foster the necessary strength of opinion. For example, opposition to the use of peat in horticulture specifically avoids any discussion of different sources and their relative environmental costs. Scarce and fragile habitats of international importance, such as the lowland raised bogs of the UK that need to be protected, are not distinguished from vast and accreting resources of what is, in many cases, a renewable resource in other countries (see Box 13.1).

So how do we respond to issues driven by public opinion? At the end of the day, farmers have to worry about balance sheets and the customers' ethical aspirations are tempered by the realities of production. Things are much more difficult for the landscape professions, where the outputs are not clearly quantified. Landscape is a thing of the mind as much as a physical reality (Sack, 1998); it cannot be separated from the perceptions of the people who use it. It may therefore not be relevant if the 'truths' people quote are not real. If they want the landscape to feel 'natural', and a defining concept of this naturalness is the avoidance of man-made chemicals, then this position is hard to overrule.

Of course, there are times when concrete outputs are identifiable and a debate can be attempted. When developing new woodland environments for Warrington New Town, Moffatt (1986) tells of how he originally tried to work without chemicals, but learnt how short-term application of herbicide could increase the area of tree cover established within the budget. This approach was also found to be true at the Earth Centre, discussed in Chapter 11. Real opportunity costs, in terms of lost woodland cover, would arise without herbicide.

However, for many managers the difficulty of reconciling public opinion with their own assessment of the necessity to use herbicides has led to the development of a secret management culture whereby certain operations are deliberately obscured. Conservation agencies and organizations faced with the need to control vigorous invasive weeds such as *Reynoutria japonica* find that they are impossible, or at least extremely costly, to control by any means other than using chemicals (e.g. Garnett *et al.*, 1992) but do not like to publicize this. Parallel situations exist with the control of damaging animals such as muntjac deer (*Muntiacus reevesi*). Animal rights activists, unable to distinguish between the rights of individual animals relative to the rights of all animals represented by an intact ecosystem, have made it necessary for activities such as shooting or baiting to become covert (Jackson, pers. comm.). It is hard to see how the professional contribution to the evolution of a sustainable society can really be delivered in the longer term when the reality of the choices to be made are kept hidden.

Inputs, outputs and protection of resources

To manage sustainably we aim for reduction in unnecessary inputs, reduction or elimination of undesirable outputs and wastes and protection of the core resources. In one of the first guides in the field applied to landscape management Sibley (undated) identified the following specific issues:

- Energy
  - energy saving
  - renewable energy supplies

- Water
  - reducing waste
  - plant selection
  - collection and re-use
- Chemicals
  - reducing or avoiding pesticides
  - reducing or avoiding fertilizers
- Soil
  - avoiding compaction
  - organic waste recycling
  - avoiding peat

Some of these issues span both management and design and many are reviewed in Chapters 10 and 11. Others are discussed below:

Agrochemicals

Agrochemicals are largely labour-saving tools that have parallels with mechanization. They allow the achievement of jobs that would take a great deal of repetitive and persistent effort to complete by hand: sometimes they allow the achievement of results that would not have been possible otherwise. Although they require significant amounts of fossil energy in manufacture and application and this is sometimes raised as an issue (Pimentel, 1980), the saving in human energy is normally of more significance to us (see discussion on machinery and labour below). Agrochemicals sometimes allow the treatment of problems that simply could not be tackled by effort, such as disease infestation in an important tree. They also bring some unique difficulties in terms of environmental risk assessment.

To understand the issue of risk it is important to understand the precautionary principle. This is based on the idea that when the environmental consequences of an action are unpredictable but could be severe, then that action should be avoided. It is particularly pertinent for situations where scientific data are absent or conflicting or when it is likely that the full range of possible consequences of an action cannot be identified by scientific research.

This latter situation is actually common, and this is not surprising when the full complexity of the world's biological systems is considered. The use of man-made pesticides or the introduction of new species or genetically manipulated organisms are examples where environmentalists would argue that we can never really know that a problem would not result despite any amount of scientific testing because of the huge complexity of ecological connections on earth. Since these organisms or chemicals have never before existed in that ecosystem, we do not have the weight of empirical evidence to suggest that they are safe.

Agrochemical manufacturers and researchers aim to produce new chemicals that will be more efficient at hitting the target organisms, have reduced human toxicity or other desirable characteristics. Nevertheless, organic farmers, for example, would rather use a pesticide of natural origin even if it were known to be toxic to the user and to have a broad spectrum effect on a variety of organisms. Despite their disadvantages, such natural chemicals are believed not to pose a major risk to the ecosystem because they have already been present in the biosphere and a long-term empirical trial has already taken place. The optimum for an organic farmer is of course a pesticide of natural origin that is also very safe for people to use. Nevertheless where such an ideal does not emerge, the ideological preference is to place ecosystem safety above immediate personal health on the grounds that in the long term no one can be healthy in a damaged world.

This argument, focused on hidden and complex impacts of novel materials, is effectively irrefutable – it cannot be countered with 'evidence' or research, since there are always possibilities that may be missed. Sceptics can regard many such environmental arguments as 'unscientific'. In some ways they are and always will be – they arise from a deep sense of holistic inter-relationships that are essentially 'unknowable' rather than a focus on reductionism and cause and effect.

The problem with the precautionary principle is, however, that precaution can grow to fill all of the available space, presenting intractable problems in terms of achieving primary objectives. An interesting parallel exists with regard to the risks of introduction of invasive organisms. It has been convincingly

demonstrated that despite many research programmes, attempts to predict which species will become invasive are unsuccessful (Williamson, 1996). Australia has therefore adopted a precautionary approach whereby imports of all novel species are restricted unless their safety can be demonstrated (Environment Australia, 1997). It is a fine example of environmentally sensitive thinking, but is likely to be eventually challenged by the World Trade Organization as unnecessarily restrictive.

Most professional landscape managers aim to strike a middle ground – precaution but with limits. They select pesticides that have low toxicity and low environmental persistence and are prepared to consider man-made chemicals if these show advantages. However, not all government-approved chemicals may be trusted. Residual herbicides are often avoided on precautionary grounds as they are designed to have a prolonged activity and therefore may persist (Robinson, 1980; Marrs, 1984).

The ideal is to avoid pesticide use completely, but difficulties should not be underestimated. Actually the landscape profession already only uses small amounts of insecticides and fungicides. There are exceptions such as high quality sports turf, but for most landscape work any plant that shows itself to be susceptible to problems quickly falls from favour and is replaced by something more robust. Most professionals (and most amateurs probably) do not see the value in fighting to keep ailing plants alive when many alternatives exist (Thoday and Wilson, 1996). In Reading Parks pesticides are 'almost never used except for sports turf, for spot treatment of *Reynoutria japonica* or other unacceptable weeds' (Yates, Reading Borough Council, pers. comm.) and in Bushy Park in London 'they are never used except where wasps nests are a hazard' (Swann, Bushy Park, pers. comm.).

Avoiding herbicides is not always possible. Weed problems cannot be avoided in many systems and alternative control methods are not always effective. The common adage 'a weed is a plant in the wrong place' misrepresents the situation badly. A weed is a plant that is difficult to control and in the wrong place. In landscape planting the problem species are those perennials that can compete in planted areas,

Box 13.2

Rates of pesticide use in landscape management

Data on herbicide use on amenity land are hard to obtain, not least because of the sense of caution shown by management in publicizing this issue – quantification of herbicide use by conservationists are particularly difficult to find.

Some figures are available from forestry that are of interest. Each year the area of the productive forest estate that was treated with herbicide was about 1 per cent of the total (Dewar and Charles, 1992). Over 70 per cent of this treatment on an area basis was with glyphosate, chosen because of its benign reputation and low mammalian toxicity. Glyphosate is not usually blanket applied around existing trees and shrubs, a localized spot treatment is more common. Assuming spot treatment gives a land coverage of 40 per cent and that glyphosate is applied at 0.54 kg/ha of active ingredient (Willoughby, 1996) and that one application per annum is normally applied, the application rate per hectare treated is 0.22 kg/ha/annum and the application mean for all forested land could be less than 0.003 kg/ha/annum. The figures are estimates and the real application could be, say, double this, but the order of magnitude is likely to be correct. That compares with an average of 4.0 kg/ha/annum herbicide application for arable and horticultural crops in the UK (Oskam *et al.*, 1992).

Total pesticide use figures are available for Holland (Oskam et al., 1992) where from 1984–88 pesticide use in public parks and gardens was 0.6 per cent of the national total. The mean parks application rate was 0.17 kg/ha active ingredient compared to 19 kg/ha for arable farming and 106 kg/ha for vegetables under glass. It is impossible to judge the relative area of 'parks and gardens' compared to all other types of landscapes managed by our profession, but on the assumption that high-pesticide use areas such as sports or rosebeds are concentrated in parks and gardens rather than in the wider landscape, the use per hectare within the total landscape may be an order of magnitude lower.

and that proliferate from root or rhizome regeneration under cultivation. While most herbicides could, in theory, be replaced by hand labour, this is only at a phenomenal cost in time and effort. The regenerating organs can never be removed from existing plant roots, and chopping the plants out (at the frequency that is affordable in professional maintenance rather than that shown by a determined amateur) propagates rather than controls the problem. Loose mulches such as bark are effective against annual weed but not established perennials. Sheet mulches can control established perennials but limit the growth forms of the desirable plants that can be introduced (Hitchmough, 1994). Some problem species such as *Convolvulus arvensis* or *Agropyron repens* spread beneath sheet mulches until they escape through a planting hole. Heat or flame treatments are again not effective against established perennials. Where the wrong weed does arise, there are some combinations of plants and even planting style that simply cannot be made to work without herbicide. Even recognizing these constraints, the total use of herbicides in most landscape work is again low (see Box 13.2).

However, often problem weeds could be instantly controlled by a change in the landscape design. Convert a *Convolvulus*-infested ground cover to a grassland and the weed is gone. Allow a rough grassland infested with ragwort (*Senecio jacobaea*) to scrub up or mow it more intensively and the weed is gone.

This, then, is one key to effective weed control without herbicides – if weeds are plants out of place, and the plants will not move, then redefine the place and the weeds disappear. Design style is also important in the effect it has on weed thresholds. A formal rose bed is visually disrupted by one weed – the tolerance of weed infestation in some landscape features is therefore vastly lower than would be the case with any productive crop. In Germany there has been a subtle programme of public education in some cities that has redefined weeds as 'spontaneous vegetation', beautiful in their own right. There is perhaps a metaphor for some aspects of the move to landscape sustainability – some unreachable goals are best addressed by changing what we want.

Machinery, energy, labour and costs

These factors are related. Mechanization uses external energy to substitute for labour, in theory freeing us to do other tasks and usually reducing cost at the same time. However, the paradox of mechanization is perhaps most clearly seen in agriculture – almost every innovation that has been introduced as a benefit for farmers has 'benefited' them by driving many of them out of employment and has led to fewer farmers (Bayliss-Smith, 1982). The agricultural revolution is often quantified in terms of yield per hectare, but the real change has been in yield per person involved. A question that is worth review is whether it is always desirable to have fewer people. This perspective makes sense if management is seen purely as a chore, but where it is seen as a desirable opportunity for development of the people doing the work (Lewis, 1992) then mechanization needs to be applied carefully.

Energy, labour and time in landscape management

Comparative assessment of energy use in agriculture has been attempted much earlier than for landscape management. A seminal review of UK agriculture was produced by Tatchall (1976). His calculated figures are of course dated and energy efficiency gains are likely to have been achieved since then, but it seems a reasonable assumption that such improvements will operate across the board and that his comparative evaluations still provide valuable insights. He quotes primary energy consumption in the sector as:

Solid fuel	2 per cent
Oil	34 per cent
Electricity	13.5 per cent
Fertilizers	29 per cent
Agrochemicals	0.5 per cent
Machinery	21 per cent

Of striking impact is the energy cost of fertilizer use, most of which is associated with nitrogen fertilizers, needed in greatest amounts and requiring much more processing than other macronutrient fertilizers. On the basis of yield response curves, the incremental returns from the use of fertilizers can be evaluated. Tatchall (1976) uses this as a measure to compare with the energy investment required to cultivate additional land for arable farming, assuming land supply is not limiting. In other words, he explores the energy savings if we grew less food per area, but over a wider land base. He finds that by such extensification there can be some direct energy savings of approximately 30 per cent if yield alone is considered. If indirect energy costs are taken into account, given increased transport, machinery wear and other infrastructure investment costs, he sees insufficient evidence to justify such a strategy. Barbour (1992) quotes figures that show that a 30 per cent reduction in nitrogen fertilizer on cereal could reduce yields by 22 per cent but reduce profits by 112 per cent because of consequent losses in efficiency, and that removing all nitrogen fertilizers would increase the land requirement for arable farming beyond the total lowland agricultural area of the UK.

Of course fossil energy sources are finite – we will probably need farming systems in the future that have fewer total energy requirements. New approaches are emerging (Pimentel, 1993) but they can require fundamental changes in methodology and systems rather than simple reduction of inputs. Tatchall's (1976) analysis at least shows that the trade-offs are not simple and that high-profile high-energy inputs such as fertilizers may still be efficient. This is particularly well illustrated by the use of pesticides. Tatchall's figures suggest that these represent a minor input (0.5 per cent) into agricultural energy use. Unlike fertilizers, the incremental 'return' from pesticide use is difficult to calculate in energy terms as sometimes applications are precautionary and they often have to be applied at a set dose to be effective, but there are clearly instances where yield collapse from pest and disease attack would be acute rather than chronic if the chemicals were not used.

In the case of herbicides, figures relating to the value of weed control vary widely from crop to crop and are dependent on which weeds are present, but 60 per cent reductions in fruit tree growth without weed control are quoted by Davison, Jones and Lawson (1982), a crop that perhaps has most in common with landscape plantings. An increase in crop growth of this scale, compared to a 0.5 per cent energy input, shows that on energy budget grounds pesticides are almost certainly defensible.

Herbicides are of course more 'replaceable' than many pesticides, in that their function can often be substituted by other means including mechanical cultivation or hand labour. However the real revolution in agricultural output as a result of energy inputs is not to do with maximizing food output, or even optimizing the use of land area, but rather to do with increasing output per person working. Bayliss-Smith (1982) illustrates how the net energy yield of an industrialized farm in Wiltshire in 1972 had increased sixfold over 150 years, but the energy output per person employed on the farm had increased sixtyfold. Each worker on the farm produced one thousand times more food energy output than they and their family consumed.

Tatchall (1976) only considers external energy inputs and, on this basis, energy conversion efficiencies are calculated, that show that cereal production yields approximately 3 times the amount of food energy relative to the energy input. In contrast beef production yields a ratio of only 0.15–0.2. The 'inefficiency' of energy conversion in animal farming is widely recognized (Odum, 1993) and is often used as an argument for a change in agricultural focus, but Tatchall points out that energy conversions of this kind need careful interpretation. Not all forms of energy are equally useful to us or equally usable by us. Certainly animal farming allows us to process and live from vegetation that we cannot directly digest, grasses and heathers for example, and to exploit land types that are unsuitable for crop production, such as upland Britain. It is also important to recognize that once such a production system

has been established over a long timescale, as in the UK, it would be devastating for biodiversity conservation if activities such as managed grazing of grass and heathlands were abandoned (Green, 1990).

How many of these principles are relevant to landscape work? The issue is not simple. We do of course have a concern to increase the 'output' per person, all other things being equal, and mechanization and agrochemicals can be used to do this. Thoday (1980), Robinson (1980) and Moffatt (1986) all emphasize the extra environmental gains that judicious use of herbicides offer since they allow otherwise labour-intensive tasks to be achieved despite limited budgets. However, in some cases we may also be specifically concerned with maintaining 'low labour efficiency' ecosystems, such as where nature reserves are managed in ways that echo traditional agricultural practice to sustain semi-natural plant and animal communities.

The 'energy' expenditure of human labour is rarely evaluated in landscape work and we use measures of time instead, or of cost which is closely correlated (Hitchmough, 1994). These costs are usually empirical figures representing an amalgam of labour fees × time plus sometimes consumable items, with issues such as depreciation of equipment poorly highlighted. Tables of comparative costs for maintenance of different features or situations do exist (see Table 13.1) as do more sophisticated models of life-cycle costs for different features (see Figure 13.1). We can therefore evaluate the superficial costs of different landscape elements but also of different methodologies. For example, Percy (1982) shows that the costs of establishing 'low maintenance' ground cover shrubs can rise by up to nearly three-fold when herbicides are substituted by manual cultivation, dependent on the level of weed infestation and the quality standards employed.

These figures allow financial planning if the status quo remains, but they provide no insights into the component environmental costs of operations. They therefore do not allow planning for alternative scenarios, such as if energy costs rise, and are not as helpful as they could be as aids for the move towards sustainability. To move beyond such a simple cost evaluation we have a data gap that needs to be filled

Table 13.1 Approximate labour costs of various grass types

Vegetation type	Typical annual maintenance in hours/100m²		Cost of maintenance relative to lowest cost vegetation type	
	Small units	Large units	Small units	Large units
Gang mown general recreational turf (5 unit gang mower 24 cuts per annum)	0.24	0.14	2	1
Recreational turf and widely spaced trees (as above)	1.5	0.9	10.7	6.4
Rough grass (flail mown 4 times/year)	0.20	0.17	1.4	1.2
Intermediate mown turf on steep banks (rotary cut, 500 mm, 12 cuts per annum)	8.0	5.0	57.1	35.7

Source: Adapted from Hitchmough (1994)

by research. The first step must be a vastly improved articulation of what the components of maintenance costs are. The vacuum caused by the data gap has of course been filled by speculation and assumption.

A full and detailed assessment of the environmental costs of different systems is challenging, as there are always trade-offs, and some of these are site-specific. Fixed costs are much easier to identify than variable site costs. For example, the energy associated with manufacture of low-bulk inorganic fertilizers is widely identified, but the transport, spreading and incorporation costs of bulky manures are rarely quantified. Neither Tatchall (1976) or Pimentel (1980) address energy costs of manures, but it is worth noting that a fertilizer dressing of 100 kg of ammonium nitrate supplies as much readily available nitrogen as 25 tonnes of farmyard manure (Cooke, 1982). Pimentel (1993) does describe a farming system that is energy-efficient based on manures, but this relies on local manure production. Similarly, the relative costs of maintaining long and short grass are finely weighed in many cases, and therefore the best solution will be determined by

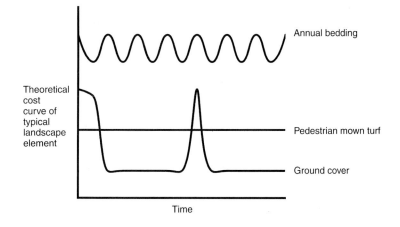

Figure 13.1 Simplified life cycle models for different landscape elements.

Source: Adapted from Hitchmough (1994)

Box 13.3

Bushy Park

Bushy Park is one of the less well known of London's Royal Parks, run by the Royal Parks Agency. It receives a lower proportion of tourist and international visitors than the other Royal Parks, but there is a strong sense of local ownership and involvement.

An active group of volunteers is involved in the park. They do not carry out any maintenance work, and do not save money, but add value to the site at a level equivalent to several full-time staff. They run an environmental education centre and carry out outreach and interpretation work with local schools based on activities such as a nature trail walks and pond dipping. The park also hosts riding and cycling and horticultural activities for disabled people, most of which rely on volunteer support (Figure 13.2).

Bushy's origins are complex, as it is an amalgam of what were once three different parks and contains many elements added over centuries, as well as reflecting modifications by a succession of managers. There are formal avenues and woodland gardens, but much of the park has a naturalistic feel and planting in these areas concentrates on natives.

Large areas of the estate were used as a hunting reserve, and there are still populations of deer that add to the atmosphere and sense of history. Culled deer are sold, but the direct income does not usually cover costs of the gamekeeper, although they are easier to look after than sheep because of fewer veterinary problems.

Indirect costs include the damage done to trees, and the expenditure needed on tree guards. The deer do not graze on most of the grasslands, preferring to eat the areas that are already mown, but they do browse tree and shrub seedlings. As a result, most of the grassland at Bushy does not get mown, because the deer control successional scrub invasion. About 15 hectares are also managed as a productive hay meadow that provides winter feed. The economics and energy investments involved in managing Bushy are therefore not easy to unravel, but it is clear that a system has evolved that gives great value to the park and its users.

issues such as whether new machinery needs to be purchased and particularly the distances that long grass wastes need to be transported before they can be disposed of.

Sometimes innovative approaches completely redefine the range of options and costs, for example a few urban grasslands are managed by grazing (see Box 13.3) or by contract cutting of hay by a farmer such as on Reading University campus, but these also represent not just methodology changes but also shifts in the quality or nature of what can be produced. Sports pitches are certain to be more energy demanding than rough grazed grasslands, but the conversion of the energy is necessary if we want to be able to do sports.

In such cases when trying to decide whether an energy input is worthwhile, we are confounded by an inability to quantify the output, the environmental gains, in equivalent quantified terms. 'Energy output' as is used in agricultural evaluation by Tatchall (1976) certainly seems inappropriate. On energy terms, landscape managers are thus able to account 'the cost of everything and the value of nothing'.

Another important dimension in sustainable systems is ethics with regard to labour. In the UK systems to support workers' rights and working conditions are well evolved in a bureaucratic way, but in parallel we have been stripping many jobs of their day-to-day rewards. Workers in environmental disciplines are poorly paid, and organizations exploit the fact that it is comparatively easy to find people who want to work in this area for other rewards. However, when drives for greater 'efficiency' mean that people lose interesting tasks, or the chance to develop skills and training and to become better at their work, or lose any sense of responsibility, then a collapse in morale is inevitable and eventually manifests as recruitment problems.

Figure 13.2   Assistant Manager of Bushy Park, Bill Swann, guides an educational visit.

We have seen that landscape managers have traditionally used 'cost' as the surrogate indicator for how hard or easy a landscape will be to maintain, and that this approach is often unsatisfactory. There is also a human dimension that needs consideration in this debate. We take the attitude that one hour of a worker's time costs the same whether that person is doing a pleasant task or having to sweat. Certainly if we are interested in encouraging greater involvement by communities in management, we need to begin to assess tasks in terms of human factors such as effort required, skill levels required or risk involved. We also need to identify when tasks are time critical, or have some degree of flexibility, and the frequency and duration of the jobs.

Water

The misuse of water in landscape management in the UK has risen as an issue in a very rapid period of time,

and is an exemplar of the way in which a profession can be distracted by issues that, while not irrelevant, should be low on the agenda. Although the situation is different in countries with extreme seasonal droughts where low-water use landscape design is an important issue (Hitchmough, 1994) the vast majority of contemporary landscape designs in the UK do not use irrigation water in the maintenance phase (see Box 13.5). Water is used for plant establishment, for certain high profile features such as bedding plants, containers and roof gardens, and high quality sports turf – the extent of such elements is small. Assuming that all flower borders, roses and pedestrian mown grass in Figure 13.3 were irrigated, the total is between 1.5–2.5 per cent of the total estate.

With regard to annuals and other high-impact colour there have been two contrasting trends that make it difficult to judge what changes in water use there have been – the total area of these plantings has declined (see Box 13.5), but they are now positioned

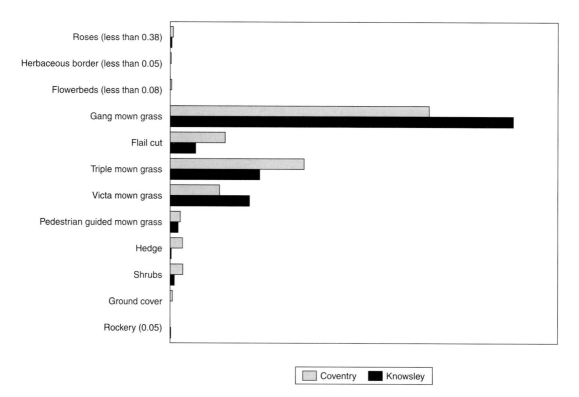

Figure 13.3 A survey of landscape elements by percentage area in Coventry and Knowsley.
Source: Handley and Bulmer (1987)

in key locations. To maximize impact there has been a growth in use of hanging baskets and containers (Southern Water, 1999) that have almost no water-holding capacity. The net result is a smaller area of planting needing more frequent watering.

Water companies in the UK are promoting plant selection for drought tolerance, recommending species from dry summer climates such as the Mediterranean (e.g. Southern Water, 1999). There are two errors commonly made in these lists that represent a lack of understanding of plant ecological strategies for dry conditions. First, some plants of dry regions are actually drought avoiders, capable of harvesting water through deep or extensive root systems. Although these plants may not need 'watering', some are water spenders and can utilize lots of water and make soils dryer for other plants around. Examples include some *Fraxinus* and *Quercus* species, although there has not been sufficient focused research on

water-efficient landscapes to allow these subtleties of plant performance to be highlighted in more than a few taxa (Hitchmough, 1994).

Second and more significantly, the drought avoidance mechanisms of many plants are affected by containerization. Turn off the irrigation mid-summer in any container nursery and the most drought tolerant species will be those that have physiological or leaf adaptations rather than root adaptations. Those which are most resistant to drought could not be predicted by simple analysis of habitat origins (see Figure 13.4).

Experimental trials were carried out in 1998–99 at the University of Reading to explore the relative survival of reported 'drought tolerant' and other species of ornamental plants when watering was stopped while they were still containerized. Reportedly drought tolerant taxa such as *Cistus* died more quickly than species not claimed to be drought tolerant. The plant that survived to the end of the trial and maintained

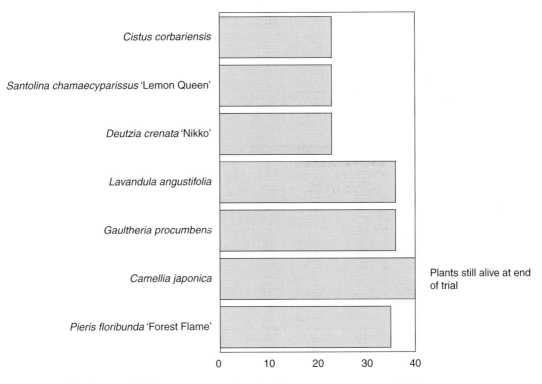

Figure 13.4 The tolerance of different species to drought when root systems are restricted.

high aesthetic quality was *Camellia japonica* which is almost never listed as drought tolerant by water authorities and other advisers (Donyavi, unpublished data). Very few landscape plants withstand drought before they have established a root system, and yet in temperate countries very few need irrigation once establishment has happened. A potentially more important issue to address will be how we respond to the risk of fundamentally changing weather patterns – discussed below.

Water companies do not have an innate interest in garden design styles *per se*, their justification for passing comment on plant selection arises from a concern to reduce water use. However, figures for national UK water use are revealing (Latham, 1994). Of all water produced for consumption by water companics, 3 per cent is taken by agriculture. Of this 3 per cent, a further 3 per cent is used for crop irrigation, i.e. 0.09 per cent of total production. Data for non-agricultural greenspace are not available, but

'Miscellaneous Uses' are 1 per cent of the total, and within this are included swimming pools, building construction, building restoration, street cleaning, fire fighting and also parks. This suggests that the latter use may represent perhaps in the region of 0.25 per cent to 0.5 per cent of total production. Domestic use of water is 40 per cent of the total. Of this figure 3 per cent is used for car and garden maintenance, giving something in the region of perhaps 0.6 per cent of total production used on domestic gardens. In contrast 14 per cent of total production is used for flushing toilets, and 27 per cent of total production is 'lost'. A 90 per cent reduction of water use in domestic and public gardens would save less than a 5 per cent cut in water loss.

Of course, problems can arise from peaks in demand as well as from absolute totals, but seasonal summer increases in water demand are of the order of 10–30 per cent, compared to the diurnal peak of cooking and washing in the morning which can be

150 per cent greater than mean hourly demand (Latham, 1994) – irrigation avoiding these peaks would put no excessive demand on the supply infrastructure. Water shortages when they do occur in the UK reflect problems in capturing and storing adequate reserves during abundant high rainfall periods rather than an absolute shortage of the resource (ibid.). One significant factor is the degree to which urbanization prevents soil recharge and leads to excessive run-off that puts pressure on drainage systems. Water harvesting is now addressed in urban planning (Haughton and Hunter, 1994) and studies on the effectiveness of different planting styles and species for water trapping and infiltration to restore aquifers may be more important in urbanized temperate countries than issues of water use.

Waste management

Attention to the generation and disposal of wastes is one of the more tangible outputs of greater environmental awareness. Local governments in the UK now typically have some form of recycling systems in place, frequently including 'green wastes'.

A more fundamental issue still awaits research – the way that different landscapes and landscape management patterns generate wastes. The components of this can be quite subtle. Wastes, especially organic wastes, are usually materials that can be valuable but are out of place. Closed or healthy ecological systems are seen as those where wastes are not generated, and all material is cycled and used (Odum, 1993). Systems exploited by people often become leaky or cycles are broken such that wastes accumulate. For example, one of the major causes of rural pollution arises from animal wastes, caused by the separation of animal and crop production in contemporary farming. Crop soils lack organic inputs, but the cycle cannot be closed because of the energy and transport costs associated with shifting bulky organics (Cooke, 1982). Waste generation can therefore be a factor of land use and pattern. These are aspects that the landscape professions are skilled at addressing, but they cannot be addressed without consideration of political, social and economic land use contexts.

Management of generated wastes in urban landscapes is similarly a question of context and of land use patterns. For example, leaf collection and disposal in urban parks are influenced by the patterning of grass and woody plants, species selection and user expectations. The typical 'parkland' pattern of large trees in grass generates a leaf disposal problem in autumn as the leaves cannot be left where they lie without damaging turf quality. A woodland area would not generate 'waste' in the same way even though leaf production could be higher.

A slight change in the density of the trees therefore gives different outputs but also a different biotope and very different utility. Composting the leaf litter reduces it to a lower volume, and a much more stable material, but does not remove the disposal problem. The organic material can be used in woodlands, beneath shrubs or in open cultivated land but not at its point of origin.

There is clearly scope for the waste, and all associated management activity, to be removed by a redefinition of the landscape structure, a case of Management by Design, but at a cost in terms of the function. More research is needed concerning the waste generation or absorption potential for different landscape types.

However, of perhaps greater importance is the question of user-generated wastes. Different landscape styles vary in their ability to 'absorb' litter (shrub beds hide things that lawns cannot) but it is debatable if this is good or not. Different styles may also affect the likelihood of littering – anecdotal evidence suggests that fly-tipping is more likely in naturalistic areas, but more evidence is needed. It is also important to consider the efficacy of different landscape styles for trapping, absorbing or filtering materials from air and water, contributing to integrity of the urban ecosystem (Bolund and Hunhammar, 1999).

Soils and soil additives

Soil protection and the prevention of degradation are one of the most important issues of resource protection associated with land-based industries. In landscape work the most significant and acute destruction of soil quality occurs during new development (Craul, 1992). The landscape professions have sometimes stood by ineffectively while soil quality destruction occurs on a massive scale. Changes would require a re-evaluation of contract systems and arrangements that are heavily entrenched within the construction industry.

Proven cases of soil degradation as a result of landscape management are rare, certainly in the UK. This is because in most cases permanent vegetation cover is maintained. For example, the landscape survey reported by Handley and Bulmer (1987) (Figure 13.3) showed that regularly cultivated land made up less than 0.5 per cent of the total estate. Opportunities for erosion or organic matter loss are therefore few. However, again soil degradation can occur as the result of user pressure, such as footpath erosion on popular recreation sites or sports pitches (Canaway, 1980). Various techniques exist for repairing or reducing such impacts (Hitchmough, 1994) but the root cause must be accepted if the sites are to perform their function.

How much management does a landscape need?

We have seen that attempts to reduce the 'environmental footprint' of landscape management by addressing some of the techniques and components of the work are to date limited. This is partly because of a lack of information, and partly because the existing environmental impacts are often already low even where it is commonly assumed that they are not. More significant gains seem to be possible through fundamental changes in landscape components and design – Management by Design. Achieving low maintenance landscapes has become a widely accepted goal (DoE, 1996) and one that is rarely questioned, but is it *always* desirable? Ensuring a landscape fulfills its purpose by the most effective and efficient means possible is clearly important. However, the presumption that this justifies a drive to reduce inputs *per se* is driven at least in part by a perception that the process of management is basi-

cally a chore that absorbs costs, energy and resources that are better redeployed elsewhere. However, there are times when management of the land is a positive process that needs to be actively pursued and expanded, and where denial of the management threatens the entire exercise.

One example is in relation to nature conservation. In Europe the majority of extant high-value biodiversity areas are semi-natural habitats that exist in balance with certain human interventions. To abandon such lands 'to nature' would be almost as undesirable as intensively farming them (Green, 1990). Management itself is inseparable from the nature of these sites as a dancer is from the dance. The approach to nature conservation of most semi-natural areas in Europe is therefore to try and mimic the traditional low intensity farming systems that created the habitats in the first place. In some cases this involves maintaining practices on marginal land that most farmers have long since abandoned because they are inefficient. Perhaps the clearest example is lowland heathland which must be managed to limit tree invasion – its 'natural' state would be secondary woodland, which is of limited biodiversity value and certainly not a priority for conservation since new secondary woods can be had any time we want them (Marrs, 1984). Despite the over-riding need for this management, it is striking that the core strategy for biodiversity protection in the UK, the designation of Sites of Special Scientific Interest, is founded on the principle that nature is protected only by preventing active damage. The threat to these sites if necessary management is not sustained is barely addressed by the legislation (Kendle and Forbes, 1997).

For conservation organizations to spend their resources trying to farm lands that farmers do not want is undermined by factors such as poor economies of scale, and resolution will only come if biodiversity protection is fully integrated into wider countryside policies (Kendle and Forbes, 1997, and Chapter 8). In the meantime, European nature conservation is in a management crisis. The failure to resource the inputs needed for all but a selection of sites is one of the greatest threats to biodiversity in the UK, probably much more serious than road building or urban development, but rarely made explicit or quantified.

More management rather than less is also needed when the presence of people on site is desirable. For example, urban park safety is an issue that is dominated by unrealistic risk perception by the public, but a vicious circle can easily set in whereby those who feel unsafe stop visiting, making the site feel bleaker and more dangerous for others (see Chapter 4, for more on risk). Burgess (1994) reports that the incidence of crime in parks, commons and urban wastelands is far less than in other public or private spaces such as housing estates, but there is a high level of fear of crime and a sense of 'being most vulnerable in public spaces, especially parks, commons and woodlands'. Some responses to the problem are defensive and reactive in nature, such as removing shrubs and trees that could be settings for crime, even though this crime is already rare, and run the risk that the landscapes become bleaker and lose their value. The alternative approach is to encourage and inspire activity and intensity of use (Burgess, 1994) and one important component of this approach is investing in site-based staff, which

had tended to decline as a result of the move to 'more efficient' contract maintenance (Environment, Transport and Regional Affairs Committee, 1999). This will cost more, and require more management, but is the option that will allow open spaces to fulfil their purpose.

Management can also be seen as a process that offers ongoing benefits to the people involved. The improved design of school grounds has received a great deal of attention in recent years (Lucas, 1994) and it is clear that the greatest benefits come when the children are involved in a constant and ongoing process of landscape evolution that is far removed from formal design (Adams and Ingham, 1998) (see Box 13.4, and Chapter 12). Management as a process of 'care' for the environment also has a major role in acting as a vehicle to foster stewardship and develop skills. This is discussed below.

The concept of management as a drain on resources, and one that has no end in sight, may go some way to explain the abhorrence of revenue or recurrent costs rather than capital costs seen so often in government financial systems. Such an approach has at best favoured sites focused on Management by Design and at worst has produced

Table 13.2 Estimated costs for managing amenity and wild flower grasslands

	Number of cuts/yr	Machinery	Estimated costs	
			£/cut	£/ha/yr
Small areas (<0.2 ha)				
Amenity med quality	16	Ped. rotary	187.5	3000
Amenity low quality	3	Ped. flail	350	2800
Wild flower grassland	3	Ped. flail + hand rake	666.7	2000
Medium areas (0.2– 0.8 ha)				
Amenity med quality	16	Triple	39.4	630
Amenity low quality	8	Compact flail	100.0	800
Wild flower grassland	3	Compact flail + sweeper	400.0	1200
Wild flower grassland	3	Amenity forage harvester	200.0	600
Large areas (>0.8 ha)				
Amenity med quality	16	5 unit gang	21.9	350
Amenity low quality	8	Compact flail	55.0	440
Wild flower grassland	3	Compact flail + sweeper	116.7	350
Wild flower grassland	3	Amenity forage harvester	100.0	300

Source: From Ash *et al.* (1992)

Box 13.4

Coombes County Junior School, Arborfield, Reading

When Susan Humphries arrived as headteacher at the Coombes County School in the 1970s it was set in a featureless expanse of grass. Since that time she has followed a vision of developing a woodland setting for the buildings, starting by introducing woodland leaf litter and tree seed. The evolution of the grounds has been gradual but far-reaching, resulting in one of the most complex and inspiring school estates to be seen anywhere in Europe. The grounds provide areas for wildlife, games and story-telling, sheltered refuges as well as open areas for play and productive plants such as apples used for harvests.

Nearly all of the work has been carried out by the school community, and a growing network of friends and contacts inspired by the achievement. All phases of the landscape development involve the participation of the pupils. The school serves a large army community and many of the pupils do not have gardens to play in. The school therefore gives them a chance to develop an understanding of what the landscape means to people, and how people can improve and protect the quality of their environment (Figure 13.5).

Figure 13.5 A high quality learning environment has evolved at Coombes School through a process of pupil involvement.

sites crippled by a lack of maintenance (Bradley, 1985).

The most cost-effective landscapes to maintain have traditionally been large flat expanses of gang-mown grass (Hitchmough, 1994), but the disadvantages are obvious. Are there more rewarding and functional landscape styles that will also be as efficient and cheap to maintain? Certainly this is frequently a 'selling point' used by advocates of ecological approaches to design and management (e.g. Brooker and Corder, 1986) but evidence is limited (Kendle and Forbes, 1997). The expectation of reduced costs can be based on a misapplied collec-tion of semi-ecological concepts. The promise of savings will backfire if they cannot be delivered.

Do ecological styles of landscape require less inputs?

The presumption that naturalistic approaches are inevitably low maintenance is widely expressed (DoE, 1996; Handley and Bulmer, 1987; Brooker and Corder, 1986) but real supporting data are hard to find. Where data do exist related to specific oper-ations, they do not convincingly prove the case (Table 13.2). For example it is widely believed that long grass must be cheaper and use less energy to maintain than short grass, based it seems on an assumption that reducing frequency of operation automatically reduces inputs (e.g. Brooker and Corder, 1986; Handley and Bulmer, 1987).

In practice not only frequency but also duration and effort need to be taken into account. When long grass is cut, the operation can be slow and require more work per cut. Superficially costs are at best slightly cheaper. However, long grass also generates waste problems and disposal costs may outweigh cutting costs (unless these can be used as hay) (Oland, 1986). All grass management costs are weather dependent, but Oland (1986) argues that the increase in costs of managing long grass in wet weather is more significant than for short grass.

In practice, management costs are frequently most strongly driven by issues such as efficiencies of scale, determined by the complexity of the landscape, and work needed to meet user needs and to repair user impacts. In the data above, the choice of landscape style and mowing machinery at any scale modifies costs by at most 2 times, in contrast the transition from large machine to pedestrian mowing increases costs by over 8 fold (in Table 13.1 the impact of scale and topography was shown to increase costs as much as 35 fold). A naturalistic landscape that is designed to have a complex mosaic of different landscape types and that receives high visitor pressure will be more expensive to maintain than if the area were converted to uniform but high frequency gang mowing.

Large simple spaces are basically cheap and small complex spaces are expensive, but the latter probably also have a higher visitor capacity per area and maybe even popularity. A comparison of some London parks perhaps clarifies the point. Bushy Park covers approximately 445 hectares, the majority of which is in a 'historic' naturalistic style dominated by native species. In 1997–98 it had a budget of approximately £380,000 that also covered work on the Longford River. Costs within the park are therefore significantly less than £850 per hectare. Greenwich Park is 74 hectares with intensive ornamental horticultural features. In 1998–99 it had a budget of £630,000. Costs are therefore nearer £8,500 per hectare (Royal Parks Agency, 1999). Greenwich visitor numbers are estimated at over twice that for Bushy (Swann, pers. comm.), giving a price per visit that is closely comparable between the two. Camley Street Nature Park is 0.9 hectares. In 1988–89 it had no 'maintenance staff' but revenue costs including managers who co-ordinate volunteers were £65,000 (Johnston, 1990). Camley Street derives maximum value from less than a hectare, with a constant demand for school visits, but the fixed costs mean that the per hectare budget is significantly higher than that for Greenwich.

Extensification, rather than style, is thus the key to maintenance cost reductions, but it is not a goal that will necessarily maximize use. Wittkugel (1988) argues that labour-saving mechanization, while cost-efficient, creates an undifferentiated, extensive, landscape that is ecologically monotonous, and that what

Table 13.3 The costs of establishing and maintaining three types of open space (£ ha⁻¹)

Type of scheme	Capital cost		Establishment cost (0–5 yrs)		Maintenance cost (5–10 years)	
	Mean	Range	M	R	M	R
Native	4,482	609– 9,854	1,767	519– 3,870	640	303– 2,160
Naturalistic	36,166	6,734–57,091	10,600	2,560–15,718	3,578	1738– 5,950
Amenity	20,679	4,952–56,000	7,488	1,450–20,942	5,513	1450–17,592

Source: From Groundwork Trust (1986)

Notes:
Native: derelict areas that have colonized adequately to allow minimal reclamation thus retaining the colonized vegetation
Naturalistic: derelict areas that have been treated so that they simulate natural habitats
Amenity: derelict areas that have had traditional reclamation to grassland with or without trees and shrubs.

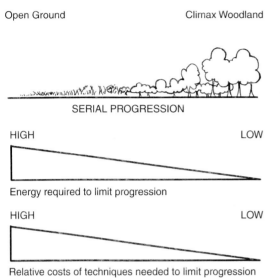

Figure 13.6 The theoretical relationship between successional stage and management inputs.

Source: Adapted from Brooker and Corder (1986)

is needed is a mosaic with some areas of high-maintenance intensive care in balance with extensive treatments.

There are data that support the idea that landscapes that are managed with minimal intervention are cheaper than those where the management interventions are high (Table 13.3) – it is a truism and would inevitably be the case. These figures are difficult to interpret as they do not address the question of the functional utility of what the management achieves on a given site. Even so, abandonment of sites to natural patterns and processes has been suggested as a possible approach for parks management. Balmori (1993) argues to 'abandon the old model's emphasis on the connection between use and programme' and 'adjust usage to plant-life cycles and evolutionary change'. In other words, if we allow sites to evolve as they will, and fit whatever use we can into the process, they will not be expensive to maintain.

An extrapolation sometimes made from this latter concept is the idea that ecosystems near to their climax successional state, or 'natural equilibrium'

(Handley and Bulmer, 1987) by definition need less management input than ones that approximate to early successional stages (see Figure 13.6).

This idea can be challenged on several grounds:

- *It presents a simplistic model of succession that many ecologists would no longer recognize.* Ecosystems probably have multiple possible equilibria, with the capacity for transition between them (Westoby *et al.*, 1989). Where new but stable states have developed and are undesirable, considerable management intervention may be needed to reverse the change (Puigdefabregas, 1999). Moss (1989) describes how nutrient pollution in the Norfolk Broads triggers a switch to an algae-dominated system that cannot be reversed just by removing the nutrients.

- *It assumes that the 'natural state' is acceptable – when it is not, management cannot be avoided.* Biotopes, even when in a natural state, are usually dynamic and fluctuate around a median in both structure and composition. Some fluctuations are extreme (Dale *et al.*, 1998), such as in coastal or river systems where natural changes may include complete vegetation destruction. Such fluctuations may go past acceptable limits and management intervention may be required to prevent or repair the extremes.

  Plant communities may be vulnerable to invasion by exotic components which are seen as undesirable and management may be necessary to maintain quality (Usher, 1988). Managers are increasingly faced with the dilemma of 'managing natural areas' to maintain their perceived integrity, or leaving them open to natural processes that will involve changes seen as degradation.

- *The correlation between successional stage and the energy required to maintain plagioclimax is not plausible.* The energy requirement of some management operations may be very limited, but can still maintain a system far from its climax stage. An example is the effect of deer grazing in arresting succession in Bushy Park (see Box 13.3).

- *It does not accurately represent the management requirements of all 'artificial' landscapes.* Careful plant selection and design can produce exotic and ornamental plant communities that are regarded as very low maintenance over their life cycle such as the ecologically sophisticated but non-native planting systems pioneered by Hansen and Stahl (1993).

Cost savings

Cost savings may even backfire if they *are* delivered. The gradual decline of park quality in the UK during the twentieth century has many contributing causes (Ward-Thompson, 1998), but one of the primary driving factors was a search for cost savings that gradually removed the features of interest from the parks (see Box 13.5). These savings also removed many of the incentives for visitors to go (Elliott, 1988). If people do not support spaces, political support also disappears and other functional outputs such as water trapping or pollution amelioration may be lost.

Perhaps the most vivid example of how such a spiral of decline was reversed is in Central Park in New York where a commitment to unusually long-term management financing was linked with restoration (Environment, Transport and Regional Affairs Committee, 1999). Mechanisms for securing adequate financial commitment to site management do exist, ranging from the Central Park example, where the key step was a revision of government perspectives on the capital/recurrent cost divide, through to public/private sector finance initiatives, income generation systems such as 'view taxes' (Ward-Thompson, 1998), management bonds or trust funds associated with development schemes, the greater use of volunteers or complex partnerships and combinations between many of these (DoE, 1996). Some of these approaches have spin-off benefits such as greater community involvement and other gains that can come from partnership, but as purely financial solutions they are primarily systems that redistribute the costs of investment in landscape in novel ways. They embody sometimes a presumption that the benefits of green space are local and need to be paid for locally, an issue worthy of greater debate. Above all, they are 'solutions' when existing

---

Box 13.5

Loss of features from urban parks

Table 13.4 shows some of the landscape features lost from two parks in Knowsley Borough from 1974–86 (from Handley and Bulmer, 1987). Of particular note is that these were post-war parks, and date from a time that did not represent a period of particular obsession with horticulture, in contrast to some of the parks described by Elliott (1988). Features for active as well as passive use were lost. Some changes of course represent changing fashions and declining popularity, but the net effect is clear.

In 1998/9 £538 million was spent on parks in the UK, a fall of 16 per cent in real terms over just 8 years (Environment, Transport and Regional Affairs Committee, 1999), yet this was long after the decline documented above, or discussed by Elliott (1988). Parks were no longer just rationalizing, they had fallen off the political agenda.

Table 13.4 Landscape features lost

Feature lost	Webster Park	Wignall Park
Ornamental flower beds	17	28
Rose gardens	–	1
Pergola	1	–
Peat garden	–	1
Rockery	1	–
Garden for the visually impaired	–	1
Sand pit	1	–
Paddling pool	1	1
Tennis courts	4	8
Crown bowling greens	2	2
Putting greens	1	–

budget mechanisms are politically unpopular, and when costs need to be massaged out of the most evident public taxation purses – the costs do not go away. The real issue of concern is one of commitment and recognition of the value of what is done. Finance, by whatever route, is only sustained when the value of what is being done is well understood.

While making the best of resources is necessary, there is absolutely no reason why there should be a constant aspiration to reduce management, especially if it is recognized as a positive process of landscape stewardship and evolution rather than just a depressingly predictable cycle aimed at protecting the status quo. Managers have become so accustomed to the rhetoric of cost cutting that there is a risk that even they will lose sight of the value of civic investment. 'If ways cannot be found to measure and then improve the value of the product, the landscape manager will be forced to fall back on cost reduction in the search for greater effectiveness' (Handley and Bulmer, 1987). What is certainly clear is that under-funding can maintain a spiral of decline that completely wastes the money that is invested (Environment, Transport and Regional Affairs Committee, 1999).

An important aspect of sustainable development is the promotion of green economics systems allowing intangible benefits to be quantified to balance against costs, outputs against inputs. The potential importance to the landscape professions is clear and applies to design as well as management. These issues are therefore raised throughout this book but gain particular focus in Chapter 3. There are few clear examples of practical outcomes yet applied to landscape management, an early exception being the widely used Arboricultural Association methodology for valuing amenity trees (Coombes, 1994). The benefits of a well-treed city could manifest as pollution reduction or climate amelioration (Bolund and Hunhammar, 1999), more tourists or greater attraction for living and working which could lead to greater regional investment. When the real 'incomes' from the landscape are not accounted properly, management sometimes gets seduced into trying to produce revenue from items such as timber sales (Hibbard, 1989), requiring that trees are grown and

harvested in ways that can compromise other returns such as nature conservation or amenity (Kendle and Forbes, 1997).

In conclusion, issues related to the adjustment of techniques of landscape management to reduce environmental impacts are complex and involve many trade-offs (e.g. we save on chemicals by using more energy). Significant effects are often only feasible with fundamental adjustment of the landscape structure or function, but even then the 'savings' may not be to society's best advantage. To decide which modifications to practice are acceptable we need to think about what type of landscapes we really need, and why.

MANAGING SUSTAINABLE LANDSCAPES

We have seen above that in many cases the negative environmental impact of the landscape management profession is often limited, but even small impacts can only be justified if the outputs have value. The 'value' of landscape is a broad and complex issue, addressed throughout this book and in many others. In this chapter there needs to be a particular discussion on whether landscape *management* offers unique contributions to achieving sustainability, and how.

Attempts to instigate greater environmental awareness and better practice in society have a long history, but the promotion of Sustainable Development was a deliberate and focused attempt to break the mould of traditional environmental debates and confrontations that were largely failing to achieve the desired goals (UNEP/FAO, 1997). To make a contribution to this movement, we need to consider how the new philosophy differs from traditional environmental positions.

The traditional environmental perspective embodies certain ideas and principles that are increasingly seen as unworkable or even at times naïve. One is the fundamental idea that a feature of nature is homeostasis, a natural balance (Turner, 1993). For example, this is seen almost everywhere that nature reserve policy has attempted to create protected sites that have no mechanism for reacting to changing landscape dynamics such as natural (or even unnatural but unstoppable) erosion (see Box 13.6) (Sheail *et al.*, 1997). Another is the presumption that people are the root of all negative impacts on nature, and that effective nature conservation means just keeping people out or avoiding impact. The concept of sustainability embodies different philosophies (UNEP/FAO, 1997) including:

- that we will best conserve what we use and value, and that links between nature and people must be fostered not broken;
- that the right sort of 'development' provides a key to successful environmental protection;
- that biodiversity conservation needs to be addressed throughout society, not just in reserves;
- that environmental care is a responsibility for everyone, and that developing capacity for that to happen is an important task.

These concepts throw out challenges to all of the landscape profession, the question of developing the capacity and will to act to manage and protect the environment is a core concern of landscape managers.

We have seen that a landscape manager's association with a site is normally much longer than that of a landscape designer, and management plans need to allow for and integrate evolutions in use and site character. A second over-riding issue for landscape managers to address is therefore change. These two issues are reviewed below.

Enhancing the role of people in landscape management

Consensus and democracy in decision making are critical elements in the development of a sustainable society (UNEP/FAO, 1997) and the application of this concept to landscape architecture is addressed in more detail in Chapters 4 and 12. As well as decision making, participation in management *activities* can also be important. There are budgetary dimensions to the use of volunteers and community workers (Chapter 4), but the greatest value is as a means of development of the people doing the work. For example, in the USA public involvement in

management of urban gardens has proved to be an effective method of community development (Lewis, 1992) and involvement in management of natural areas has fostered environmental care (Packard, 1990).

Why should these benefits arise? Obviously pride, responsibility, the development of skills are all important dimensions but a key seems to lie in the fundamental issue of what place people have in the landscape (Jordan, 1994). The traditional environmental perspective is that people are the root problem in ecosystem degradation, and solving this degradation is taken to mean removing people from the equation (e.g. McKibben, 1989). Not surprisingly the public cannot respond to the message 'you are a problem, the earth would be better if you were not here' (see also Stott, 1998). Involvement in landscape management allows people to learn that positive change is possible and above all that they have a role to play. Perhaps for the first time ever in their lives they can finish the day thinking 'today the world is better thanks to me, not worse' (Packard, 1990).

Viewed from this perspective, landscape management is not seen as a chore, but as an opportunity for environmental care, which is seen as an output in its own right. It also raises the issue of who should be given the right to manage, and what the objectives should be. Many organizations run volunteers and friends groups where some level of community participation is encouraged, but these are often targeted on meeting the objectives of the management of the site – they are product-oriented. Not enough organizations make the development of the people doing the volunteer work a primary objective, a process-oriented approach to landscape management. In the UK, notable exceptions are the British Trust for Conservation Volunteers and many Urban Wildlife Groups (Bradley, 1985). Of course, not everyone will be involved, and of course some inputs will need to be provided by professionals, but the scope and value of the approach increases the value of the landscape.

Despite citing some positive examples of participation in management, Bradley (1985) argues that it is the capital phase of landscape development that

Box 13.6

Titchwell Marsh Nature Reserve

The Royal Society for the Protection of Birds' reserve at Titchwell is one of several nationally and internationally important sites on the North Norfolk Coast threatened by coastal change and inundation (Figure 13.7). The paradox is that the development of richness on these reserves is the result of very dynamic processes that now threaten their survival. From a broader landscape perspective the coastal dynamism should allow the development of new areas of equivalent value somewhere else along the coast. The problem is that the reserves have become 'institutions', with regular visitors, a complex infrastructure, and defined policies and plans.

The RSPB is open with visitors about the prospects for change at Titchwell. Plans are developed for the purchase and creation of new reserves. The existing reserve has been so heavily managed and optimized since its inception, that the concept of making a new reserve does not cause any concern about compromising 'naturalness'.

Figure 13.7   The RSPB reserve of Titchwell Marsh, threatened by coastal change.

best suits community involvement. She argues that volunteers need motivation and look for benefits or rewards from what they do. The capital stage is the time of 'maximum change, and also fun and excitement' whereas after-care is 'less exciting, regular and carefully timed activities' or even 'mundane and repetitive and can rapidly become a chore'. Here her focus on maintenance is based on a vision of Management for Design, maintaining the status quo after the creative phase has ended, but if community groups are given a sense of ownership and responsibility for the land, and if they are in a position to instigate and direct change, Design by Management, then the situation is very different and there is evidence that positive inputs can be sustained (Lewis, 1992; Packard, 1990). The motivations in these examples are easy to see – people believe that they are doing something important, and that they are making a difference. These are the beliefs that need to be fostered.

The first step to achieve this is to emphasize that the people on the land have a positive role and contribution to make, and this is where a conflict with traditional environmental ideology arises. It is not uncommon to find the perspectives, policies and practices of conservation biology hinged on the idea that human action or even presence must be a degradation, that nature needs people to be absent. Even the fundamental hierarchy of habitat classification into natural, semi-natural and artificial is based on degree and nature of human impact (Green, 1990; Ratcliffe, 1977), while the concept that people and nature cannot co-exist is woven into policies such as the National Parks strategy of the USA (Budiansky, 1995), but is being revised in international debates (Chapter 5).

However, the belief in the separation of man and nature is increasingly under attack on grounds that range from the most pragmatic through to a post-structuralist re-assessment of the philosophical bias of Western societies (Peterken, 1996; Jordan, 1994, and Chapter 2). On functional grounds human influence is not only becoming globally pervasive, but is increasingly recognized as having been so throughout history. Many 'pristine natural' habitats have in fact been significantly modified by indigenous humans, but in ways that were overlooked by the developed world or colonizing Europeans (e.g. see Ellenberg, 1979; Budiansky, 1995). As Callicott (1991) states, European immigrants to North America 'in fact found a man-made landscape, but they thought it was a wilderness because it didn't look like the man-made landscapes that they had left behind'.

The perception that human agency can only be opposed to nature, and indeed to be human is to be the very embodiment of what is not nature, lies at the root of our current environmental crisis, an ultimately sterile distinction that is not valid but that effectively undermines the goal of fostering positive human influence by denying us a place in a sustainable world (Jordan, 1994; Brown, 1997). Perhaps most significantly, it is a position that has no future since the only way that we are likely to preserve ecosystems that we want in the future is to get involved in their management – even systems that were never managed before will change in perhaps undesirable ways unless we provide inputs (Usher, 1988).

Traditional environmental philosophies (Chapter 2) seem to allow full scope for people to have negative impacts on the world, but deny all chances for positive change. We need new philosophies that empower people to undertake the management that will be necessary in the future. One of the most significant developments in this regard is the concept of Biosphere Reserves, conservation designations that can only be awarded if people are involved with the land rather than if they are not (IUCN, 1998 and Chapter 5).

Management in a changing world

Traditional environmental perspectives hold a model of nature that is based on the idea of optimum states that are degraded by change. However, the landscape does not always behave according to the value judgements that people try to apply – change is an unavoidable reality. This requires that we are flexible and creative about landscape management, and above all avoid the temptation to demand stability and stasis in the name of sustainability (Stott, 1998).

In all sectors of landscape work, from urban amenities to rural nature conservation sites, goals and directions are evolving at amazing speed. Sustainability challenges us to consider how environment, society and the economy are all integrated, but none of these components are currently stable.

Societies are changing, becoming more ethnically mixed but also ageing, developing in sophistication in some areas and remaining frustratingly naïve in others. Will we continue to become more urban, or will there be a new age of migration back to attractive countryside areas? Economic activities such as agriculture (Chapter 8) are facing revolutions, for example the introduction of GMOs, that could fundamentally change the structure of the landscape. Will production localize or globalize, intensify or extensify? The environment itself is in a state of flux. Will climate change undermine our entire strategy for the identification and protection of 'key' nature reserves, or will it cause fundamental problems of food supply? Will biological invasions threaten the integrity of local ecosystems? Some changes to the world we live in will be undesirable, and should be prevented if possible, others will provide opportunities as well as costs, and many will be inevitable.

We know therefore change is certain, but the nature of the change is uncertain. Climate change is inevitable, but there are broad disagreements about the nature of the effects we will see. The UK may get warmer or colder, wetter or drier or may change in a wide range of more subtle parameters such as precipitation patterns or frequency of storms that have completely unpredictable effects on plants and animals. Anodyne comments about landscape responses to these issues, such as the widespread assumption that we should be moving towards greater use of drought resistant plants or warmer-climate species, need to be replaced by a much more sophisticated debate on how to manage a landscape in flux. To do this we need to develop analytical tools to better describe landscape changes and help to articulate which of these are acceptable and which are not. We also need to avoid developing policies and philosophies that will constrain our ability to respond flexibly or that generate unresolvable conflicts.

Important lessons come from those ecologists studying impacts and changes in natural systems. Concepts of ecosystem stability and equilibria, once seen as fundamental to ecology theory, are now recognized as unrepresentative of many systems (Stone et al., 1996). We are learning that non-equilibrium states are not only common in nature but also important in many cases for maintaining diversity and landscape richness. Sometimes this fluctuation is regular, small scale and easy to inte-

grate. However, responses to large, infrequent, disturbances that may also be integral to biotope dynamics are normally poorly addressed in management plans (Dale et al., 1998).

However, if change progresses far enough we will then see systems in transition between fundamentally different states (Westoby et al., 1989). Again, it is often low-recurrence events that push landscapes beyond their limits of resilience, and can lead to unpredictable new states (Puigdefabregas, 1999). This shift in state is frequently assumed to be degradation but may also present opportunities. Often the norms in land use systems are based on terminology and concepts that derive from agronomy and are not always applicable to the times when the landscape managers goal is 'to grow one blade of grass instead of two'. Agricultural systems are degraded if they are stressed, reduce in productivity or lose consistency and predictability (Johnson and Lewis, 1995) but these are the very factors that may allow the development of diverse or otherwise valuable natural plant and animal communities (Kendle and Forbes, 1997). We need to learn more about which disturbance events maintain biotopes (no matter how devastating they may appear), which cause a shift to new states, and how to identify whether such new states are unacceptable or just different.

Evaluation of landscape 'quality' is therefore important but we have to apply appropriate measures of value. The coming decades may bring extensive environmental degradation that will require enormous efforts to resolve. These challenges need to be carefully prioritized, and we need to identify when changes have significant functional consequences compared to changes that simply differ from our presumptions of how things should be.

An example of how we deny change relates to current concerns over the movement of 'invasive' species. Species distributions will change if climate changes, and they will have to change if the species are to survive. Demanding that they stay in place will not make it so. Nevertheless, conservation yardsticks are based on 'snapshots' of plant and animal distribution, and community composition, that do not allow much room for dynamism in the landscape. The very concept of 'native' status is based on one such, highly selective, snapshot. In the UK 'a native plant is one that has arrived before neolithic times, or has arrived since without human agency' (Webb, 1985).

Luken (1994) argues that, given that the movement of non-native plants into a region is inevitable, the problem of dealing with invasive species is being aggravated by the definition of impossible boundaries, conceptual as well as physical, to species movement. We need to distinguish between the arrival of species that will have a clear and undesirable impact on ecosystem function, from those that simply represent flux. The former represent genuine problems (Usher, 1988); the latter may be neutral (Lugo, 1997) or even be important to maintain ecosystem stability as previously established species become less viable (Williams, 1997). The terminology used by researchers and policy-makers do not distinguish between these (Pyšek, 1995), and large sums of money may be spent trying to control 'invasions' when the root cause is environmental change which makes it impossible for previously established plant communities to survive (Anderson and Barrows, 1998).

Actually Webb's (1985) definition does allow for species distribution changes, as long as post-neolithic humans are not involved. This is because Webb argues that it was during this time that humans 'ceased to be in any ordinary sense a part of nature'. Since the identification of 'invasion' arises from the concept of 'native', we once again see a technical problem that is clouded by the philosophical presumption that humans are separate from nature and degradative. 'The unwillingness – or inability – of ecologists to successfully incorporate the human species in ecological theory has by default devalued ecological processes associated with human activity' (Luken, 1994).

The distinction between 'human-influenced' and 'natural events' is already generating tension. The paradox of how conservationists increasingly pour resources and management effort into sites to keep them 'natural' is explored by various authors (Duffey, 1974; Peterken, 1996) – sites without management may change in ways that differ from our expectations of 'nature' (for example non-native species may

arrive), but sites that are managed are no longer 'natural'. If we want to maintain previously 'natural' conditions while the world is changing, then we will even need to introduce inputs into systems that have never needed inputs before or to repair problems such as fragmentation (Whitmore, 1998). In some ways, management of the landscape we live in is not avoidable – even the decision to do nothing is a management strategy that will shape the environment in certain ways.

Conservation biologists, planners and managers have begun to evolve the techniques for dealing with such situations, such as species translocation programmes, but this was only possible as the result of a gradual and often painful shift in attitudes and perception that allowed for conservation to be based on creative acts rather than just preservation (Sheail *et al.*, 1997). Landscape managers have much to contribute to the issue of how we can positively manage environmental change, but this is only possible once it is accepted that we *should* positively manage change.

CONCLUSION

Concerned both with humanity and culture and also environment and ecology, landscape professionals could be expected to be leading the debates about sustainability. However, to date contributions have been reactive rather than proactive. Issues of vanishingly small importance have tended to dominate the agenda, distracting attention from real points of significance.

The methodology and techniques of landscape management do need review to ensure that impacts are minimized, but the likelihood is high that changes in practice will give small environmental gains. Much more important is the need to address how to protect, and clearly justify the protection of, those landscapes we have received in trust, how to make good degradation and deficiency in that landscape infrastructure and how to help foster people capable of looking after that resource. These are not easy tasks. The challenges facing the landscape professions are huge.

The environmental movement has failed to properly address the role of people in the natural world, and has therefore failed to counter an accountant mentality that sees inputs as costs and chores to be minimized. In practice we cannot remove people from the world and we cannot avoid many of the negative impacts, what it seems we can achieve is to deny scope for positive intervention and opportunities. One result is a countryside that is in a management crisis.

Management is in part also to do with responding to change. Environmentalists have not always shown a clear understanding of change when evolving policies, but we seem to be entering an even more sinister stage where we are writing policies that demand that change will not occur just at the time when change may be accelerating.

Management of the land is the very expression of our relation to that land. If we are not prepared to imagine how that relationship will change, for better as well as worse, and how despite negative change we can have a positive role to play in the stewardship of our own environment then sustainable development will be a hollow dream.

ACKNOWLEDGEMENTS

The authors would like to thank Andrew Jackson, Kew, Hossein Donyavi, and Kate Lloyd-Bostock of Reading University, Mark Yates, Reading Borough Council, the RSPB, and particularly Bill Swann of Bushy Park and Susan Humphries of Coombes School, all of who have helped us to learn something of what a positive approach to sustainable management can mean.

REFERENCES

Adams, E. and Ingham, S. (1998) *Changing Places: Children's Participation in Environmental Planning* (London, The Children's Society).

Ames, B. N. and Gold, L. S. (1998) The causes and prevention of cancer: the role of environment, *Biotherapy*, 11(2–3), 205–220.

Anderson, B. and Barrows, C. (1998) The debate over Tamarisk, *Restoration and Management Notes*, 16(2), 129–139.

Ash, H. J., Bennett, R. and Scott, R. (1992) *Flowers in the Grass* (Peterborough, English Nature).

Balmori, D. (1993) Park redefinitions, in H. Muschamp, S. B. Warner, P. Phillips, E. Ball and D. Balmori (eds), *The Once and Future Park* (New York, Princeton Architectural Press).

Barbour, D. (1992) Land use and management: a discussion, in Vegetation Management in Forestry, Amenity and Conservation Areas, *Aspects of Applied Biology* 29, 5–16. (Wellesbourne, Association of Applied Biologists).

Bayliss-Smith, T. P. (1982) *The Ecology of Agricultural Systems* (Cambridge, Cambridge University Press).

Bolund, P. and Hunhammar, S. (1999) Ecosystem services in urban areas, *Ecological Economics,* 29(2), 293–301.

Bradley, C. (1985*) Community Involvement in Greening Projects* (Bolton, Groundwork Foundation).

Bragg, N. C. (1990) *A Review of Peat Reserves and Peat Usage in Horticulture and Alternative Materials* (Petersfield, Horticultural Development Council).

Brooker, R. and Corder, M. (eds) (1986) *Environmental Economy* (London, E & FN Spon).

Brown, N. (1997) Re-defining native woodland, *Forestry* 70(3), 191–198.

Budiansky, S. (1995) *Nature's Keepers* (London, Weidenfeld and Nicolson).

Burgess, J. (1994) *The Politics of Trust: Reducing Fear of Crime in Urban Parks. The Future of Parks and Open Spaces* Working Paper 8 (Stroud, Comedia/Demos).

Callicott, J. B. (1991) The wilderness idea revisited: the sustainable development alternative, *Environmental Professional,* 13, 236–245.

Canaway, P. M. (1980) Wear, in I. H. Rorison and R. Hunt (eds) *Amenity Grassland: An Ecological Perspective*, (Chichester, John Wiley).

Cooke, G. W. (1982) *Fertilizing for Maximum Yield*, 3rd edition (London, Granada).

Coombes, S. A. (1994) Amenity evaluation: the Helliwell system revised, *Arboricultural Journal* ,18(2), 137–148.

Craul, P. J. (1992) *Urban Soil in Landscape Design* (New York, John Wiley).

Dale, V. H., Lugo, A. E., MacMahon, J. A. and Pickett, S. T. A. (1998) Ecosystem management in the context of large, infrequent disturbances, *Ecosystems*, 1(6), 546–557.

Davison, J. G., Jones, A. G. and Lawson, H. M. (1982) Weed control in perennial crops, in H. A. Roberts (ed.) *Weed Control Handbook: Principles*, 7th edition (Oxford, Blackwell Scientific Publications).

Dewar, J. and Charles, J. N. (1992) The role of herbicides in forest management in Britain: current practice and possible developments, in: Vegetation Management in Forestry, Amenity and Conservation Areas, *Aspects of Applied Biology*, 29, 125–130, (Wellesbourne, Association of Applied Biologists).

DoE (1996) *Greening the City: A Guide to Good Practice* (London, The Stationery Office).

Duffey, E. (1974) *Nature Reserves and Wildlife* (London, Heinemann Educational Books).

Ellenberg, H. (1979) Man's influence on tropical mountain ecosystems in South America, *Journal of Ecology*, 65, 401–416.

Elliott, B. (1988) From people's parks to green deserts, *Landscape Design*, 171(1), pp. 13–15.

Environment Australia (1997) *National Weeds Strategy*, Community Information Unit (Canberra, Environment Australia).

Environment, Transport and Regional Affairs Committee (1999) *Twentieth Report: Town and Country Parks*. Report and Proceedings of the Committee (3 volumes), House of Commons Session 1998–99 (London, The Stationery Office).

Forestry Research Co-ordination Committee (1988) Arboricultural research: report of the review group on research on arboriculture, *Arboricultural Journal*, 12(4), 307–360.

Garnett, R. P., Hirons, G., Evans, C. and O'Connor, D. (1992) The control of *Spartina* (cord grass) using glyphosate, in Vegetation Management in Forestry, Amenity and Conservation Areas. *Aspects of Applied Biology*, 29, 359–364 (Wellesbourne, Association of Applied Biologists).

Green, B. H. (1986) Controlling ecosystems for amenity, in A. D. Bradshaw, D. A. Goode and E. Thorp (eds) *Ecology and Design in Landscape: The 24th Symposium of the British Ecological Society*, (Oxford, Blackwell).

Green, B. H. (1990) *Countryside Conservation*, 2nd edition (London, Allen and Unwin).

Groundwork Trust (1986) *Report Of The Working Party on the After-Care of Reclaimed Land in St Helens and Knowsley* (St Helens, Groundwork Trust).

Handley, J. F. and Bulmer, P. (1987) The design and management of cost effective landscapes, in B. Rigby (ed.) *Report of the 27th Askham Bryan Amenity Technical Course* (York, Askham Bryan College of Agriculture and Horticulture).

Hansen, R. and Stahl, F. (1993) *Perennials and their Garden Habitats*, 4th edition (Cambridge, Cambridge University Press).

Haughton, G. and Hunter, C. (1994) *Sustainable Cities* (London, Jessica Kingsley).

Hibbard, B. G. (1989) *Urban Forestry Practice*, Forestry Commission Handbook 5 (London, HMSO).

Hitchmough, J. D. (1994) *Urban Landscape Management* (Sydney, Sydney Inkata Press).

IUCN (1998) *Biosphere Reserve – Myth or Reality?* Proceedings of the Workshop on Biosphere Reserves, World Conservation Congress, Montreal, Canada, 1996 (Gland/Cambridge, IUCN).

Johnson, D. L. and Lewis, L. A. (1995) *Land Degradation: Creation and Destruction* (Oxford, Blackwell).

Johnston, J. D. (1990) *Nature Areas for City People*, Ecology Handbook 14 (London, London Ecology Unit).

Jordan, W. R. (1994) Sunflower Forest: ecological restoration as the basis for a new environmental paradigm, in A. D. Baldwin, J. De Luce and C. Pletsch (eds) *Beyond Preservation – Restoring and Inventing Landscapes* (Minneapolis, University of Minnesota Press).

Kendle, A. D. (1990) Soil ameliorants 1, *Plant User*, 3, 3–5.

Kendle, A. D. (1996) Soil conditions on landscape sites and the implications for plant selection, in P. Thoday and J. St. J. Wilson (eds) *Plants for Landscape Sites* (London, Institute of Horticulture).

Kendle, A. D. and Forbes, S. (1997) *Urban Nature Conservation* (London, E & FN Spon).

Kessler, J. J. (1994) Usefulness of the human carrying-capacity concept in assessing ecological sustainability of land use in semiarid regions, *Agriculture, Ecosystems and Environment*, 48(3), pp. 273–284.

Latham, B. (1994) *An Introduction to Water Supply in the UK*, IWEM Booklet 4 (London, Institute of Water and Environmental Management).

Leay, M. J., Rose, J. and Young, J. D. (1986) *Management Plans: A Guide to their Preparation and Use* (Cheltenham, Countryside Commission).

Lewis, C. A. (1992) Effects of plants and gardening in creating interpersonal and community well-being, in D. Relf (ed.) *The Role of Horticulture in Human Well-Being and Social Development* (Oregon, Timber Press).

Lucas, B. (1994) The power of school grounds, in P. Blatchfold and S. Sharp (eds) *Breaktime and the School* (London, Routledge).

Lugo, A. E. (1997) Maintaining an open mind on exotic species, in G. K. Meffe and C. R. Carroll (eds) *Principles of Conservation Biology* (Sunderland, MA, Sinauer Asociates).

Luken, J. O. (1994) Valuing plants in natural areas, *Natural Areas Journal*, 14, 295–299.

Marrs, R. H. (1984) The use of herbicides for nature conservation, in Weed Control and Vegetation Management in Forests and Amenity Areas, *Aspects of Applied Biology 5*, pp. 265–274 (Wellesbourne, Association of Applied Biologists).

McKibben, B. (1989) *The End of Nature* (New York, Random House).

Moffatt, D. (1986) The natural approach to open space, in R. Brooker and M. Corder (eds) *Environmental Economy* (London, E & FN Spon).

Moss, B. (1989) Water pollution and the management of ecosystems: a case study of science and scientist, in P. J. Grubb and J. B. Whittaker (eds) *Toward a More Exact Ecology* (Oxford, Blackwell Scientific Publications).

NERC (1977) *Amenity Grasslands: The Need for Research*, Publications Series C, 19 (London, Natural Environment Research Council).

Odum, E. P. (1993) *Ecology and Our Endangered Life-Support System* (2nd edition) (Sunderland, MA, Sinauer).

Oland, L. (1986) The management of amenity grasslands and woodlands, in R. Brooker and M. Corder (eds) *Environmental Economy* (London, E & FN Spon).

Oskam, A. J., van Zeijts, H., Thijssen, G. J., Wossink, G. A. A. and Vijftigschild, R. (1992) Pesticide use and pesticide policy in the Netherlands, *Wageningen Economic Studies*, 26 (Wageningen Agricultural University, Wageningen, Holland).

Packard, S. (1990) No end to nature, *Restoration and Management Notes*, 8(2), 72.

Percy, D. (1982) Cover design, *GC & HTJ*, 193, 17.

Peterken, G. (1996) *Natural Woodlands* (Cambridge, Cambridge University Press).

Pimentel, D. (ed.) (1980) *Handbook of Energy Utilisation in Agriculture* (Florida, CRC Press).

Pimentel, D. (1993) Environmental and economic benefits of sustainable agriculture, in M. G. Paoletti, T. Napier, O. Ferro, B. R. Stinner and D. Stinner (eds) *Socio-Economic and Policy Issues for Sustainable Farming Systems* (Padova, Cooperative Amicizia S.r.l).

Puigdefabregas, J. (1999) Ecological impacts of global change on drylands and their implications for desertification, *Land Degradation and Development*, 9(5), 393–406.

Pyšek, P. (1995) On the terminology used in plant invasion studies, in P. Pyšek, K. Prach, M. Rejmanek and M. Wade (eds) *Plant Invasions: General Aspects and Special Problems* (Amsterdam, SPB Academic Publishing).

Ratcliffe, D. (1977) *A Nature Conservation Review,* 1 (Cambridge, Cambridge University Press).

Robinson, D. W. (1980) The present and future role of herbicides in amenity land management, in R. J. Stephens and P. R. Thoday (eds) *Weed Control in Amenity Plantings* (Bath, University of Bath).

Royal Parks Agency (1999) *The Royal Parks Agency Annual Report and Accounts 1998/99* (London, The Stationery Office).

Sack, R. (1998) *Homo Geographicus* (Madison, WI, University of Wisconsin Press).

Sheail, J., Treweek, J. R. and Mountford, J. O. (1997) The UK transition from nature preservation to 'creative conservation', *Environmental Conservation,* 24(3), 224–235.

Sibley, P. (undated) *The Sustainable Management of Greenspace* (Reading, Institute of Leisure and Amenity Managers).

Southern Water (1999) *Water-Wise Recommendations.* http://www.southernwater.co.uk/.

Stone, L., Gabric, A. and Berman, T. (1996) Ecosystem resilience, stability and productivity: seeking a relationship, *American Naturalist,* 148(5), 892–902.

Stott, P. (1998) Biogeography and ecology in crisis: the urgent need for a new metalanguage, *Journal of Biogeography,* 25, 1–2.

Tatchall, J. A. (1976) Crops and fertilizers: overall energy budgets. *Conservation of Resources, Special Publication,* 27, 119–136 (London, The Chemical Society).

Thoday, P. R. (1980) The weed problem in amenity plantings, in R. J. Stephens and P. R. Thoday (eds) *Weed Control in Amenity Plantings* (Bath, University of Bath).

Thoday, P. R. and Wilson, J. St. J. (eds) (1996) *Plants for Landscape Sites* (London, Institute of Horticulture).

Turner, F. (1993) The invented landscape, in A. D. Baldwin, J. De Luce and C. Pletsch (eds) *Beyond Preservation: Restoring and Inventing Landscapes* (Minneapolis, University of Minnesota Press).

UNEP/FAO (1997) *Negotiating a Sustainable Future for Land: Structural and Institutional Guidelines for Land Resources Management in the 21st Century* (Nairobi, UNEP/Rome, FAO).

Usher, M. B. (1988) Biological invasions of nature reserves: a search for generalizations, *Biological Conservation,* 44, 119–135.

Ward-Thompson, C. (1998) Historic American parks and contemporary needs, *Landscape Journal,* 17(1), 1–25.

Webb, D. A. (1985) What are the criteria for presuming native status?, *Watsonia,* 15, 231–236.

Westoby, M., Walker, B. H. and Noy-Meir, I. (1989) Range management on the basis of a model that does not seek to establish equilibrium, *Journal of Arid Environments,* 17, 235–239.

Whitmore, T. C. (1998) Potential impact of climatic change on tropical rain forest seedlings and forest regeneration, *Climatic Change,* 39(2–3), 429–438.

Widdowson, R. W. (1987) *Towards Holistic Agriculture* (London, Pergamon Press).

Williams, C. E. (1997) Potential valuable ecological functions of non-indigenous plants, in J. O. Luken and J. W. Thieret (eds) *Assessment and Management of Plant Invasions* (New York, Springer).

Williamson, M. (1996) *Biological Invasions* (London, Chapman & Hall).

Willoughby, I. (1996) Dormant season application of broad spectrum herbicides in forestry, in Vegetation Management in Forestry, Amenity and Conservation Areas, *Aspects of Applied Biology* 44, pp. 55–62 (Wellesbourne, Association of Applied Biologists).

Wittkugel, U. (1988) Urban park management in Berlin, *Landscape Design,* 171(1), 23–26.

14

VISIONS OF SUSTAINABILITY

Kristina Hill

SUMMARY

Worcester, Massachusetts, is a blue-collar city of 180,000 in the northeastern United States. Its economy has been in decline since the late nineteenth century. The residents, however, are well known in that region for loyalty to their city. This loyalty is expressed through an ironic sense of humor and a tradition of storytelling that reminds the current residents of Worcester that it was once a prominent regional centre of American politics and culture. Residents under 40 refer to the city as Wormtown, in bittersweet recognition that the city is no youthful American utopia. The decomposition and detritus of what is rumored to have been a grander past are the raw materials for life in the city's present. The stories told there today are frequently about that past. They provide intimate gossip about past residents, like anarchist Emma Goldman or poet Elizabeth Bishop, or celebrate hometown inventions ranging from barbed wire to the typewriter to the birth control pill. 'Firsts' are a prominent part of the stories: Worcester claims America's first public park and the printing of its first newspaper and novel. 'Seconds' are also on the list, like the Second National Women's Congress, a major national suffrage event held in Worcester in the late nineteenth century. Unique events also make for some wry storytelling, like the story of the East Coast's only buffalo hunt, an event initiated when some 50 head of buffalo escaped a Barnum and Bailey circus enclosure and had to be hunted across the entire County (Farnsworth and O'Flynn, 1934).

My family is a part of this grassroots Rumpelstiltskin-like network of local storytellers who spin trivia into pride. Raised among those stories of place, inventions, and politics, these humorists' approach to civics has persuaded me that sustainability is not an issue of technology, planning or policy alone. First and foremost, sustainability derives from cultural resilience and adaptability. These qualities are rooted in the knowledge of place and human behavior that is encoded in stories. Stories affect our decision making to the extent that we have come to identify with the characters and situations described in these stories, and to the extent that we suspend our disbelief long enough to believe we live in the world those stories describe.

INTRODUCTION

The concept of sustainability, as I understand it, contains three major arguments: an argument for efficiency that still allows for new growth, an argument for conservation of resources, and a third for the restoration of human health and environmental quality. The three arguments must be woven together, because alone they are politically and practically inadequate. In this chapter, I am interested in

Figure 14.1 'Ralph's Chadwick Square Diner,' one of Wormtown's post-industrial social institutions.

exploring the conceptual aspects of sustainability, as an idea that could be implemented at the landscape scale. I am curious about how will we know what to do, and what to value, in order to achieve it – aside from pursuing greater efficiency in our use of resources. In short, what visions will we pursue, and where will they come from? How will we develop those visions for particular landscapes?

My answers to these questions are heavily influenced by my belief that we need visions that can become popular culture, through a new tradition of stories and community events in which people want to participate. To develop this kind of compelling vision that can have broad and lasting effects on human behavior, we must first be able to think in new ways. Stories and language can help us do that – and always have. Stories can also be the basis for a new popular culture – of entertaining characters, events, and ideas that teach new insights

and encourage the development of shared values and new choices for action.

In this chapter, I present some of the relationships between language, stories, and mental models that I believe are critical to conceiving and realizing visions of sustainability. I say that they are 'critical' because without the unique tools available in language, stories, and mental models, we cannot build a shared sense that more sustainable ways of dwelling in our landscapes truly *do* exist. Evolving a shared vision takes more than a few good stories, of course. It requires a culture of storytelling, and whole cycles of stories that deliver related messages. But those elements have historically worked to provide a shared sense of possibility in particular cultures and places (Radner, 1993). That shared sense of possibility is the fertile soil we need to cultivate if our visions of a more sustainable future are to grow from seeds to fruit. And frankly, stories are one of the most entertaining forms of persuasion. It's going to be a lot more fun to advocate for sustainability if we can entertain ourselves with good stories about our inventions, our landscapes, and the occasional bumbling hunt for metaphorical buffalo along the way.

THEORY AND STORIES IN THE AGE OF THE POSTMODERN NARRATIVE

Writing as a postmodern theorist, Jean-François Lyotard has made a distinction between two kinds of narratives that he calls the *grand* or meta-narrative and the *petit* or small narrative (Lyotard, 1984). Theories of science would qualify as grand narratives, because they purport to hold true in any time or place. The laws of physics are not expected to vary for phenomena that occur in Paris versus New York, for example, and they would lead us to expect that rocks fell to earth with the same acceleration rate from the roofs of medieval cathedrals as they would from the roof of a shopping mall. Small narratives, on the other hand, are taken as truth locally, in time and space, and only because the teller of the narrative performs her tale persuasively. Lyotard argues that the postmodern age is one in which more thinkers are questioning both the search for grand narratives and the extension of these narratives to our understanding of what it is to be human. He and others have argued for the variety, beauty and value of small narratives that cannot be reduced to parsimonious universal truths, on the basis of their ability to allow us to express the richness of human experience in a world of multiple cultural dimensions.

In fact, sociologists and historians of science have demonstrated that scientific theories are constructed in a social and cultural context that influences the theories that develop (Rose and Rose, 1976; Crawford *et al.*, 1993; Harding, 1998). Individual scientists promote their theories through arguments advanced in person and in print, and these theories are evaluated not only on their truthfulness but also on the basis of the performance, prestige and collegial associations of their authors. These analyses from the sociology of science allow us to see theory-building as a process of persuasion that involves the use of personal performances and small narratives that are winnowed over time into defensible meta-narratives. But taken together, a sociological analysis of the practices of scientists and Lyotard's presentation of the differences between storytelling and theory-building open a window on the world of knowledge that is important to sustainability. This window allows us to see that influential preconceptions exist in the form of shared mental models, and that these mental models influence our ability to reason about our world. It also allows us to see the small narrative as something that mediates between experience, knowledge, and action, instead of dismissing the collective wisdom of stories as a smokescreen that keeps us from seeing the 'truth.'

While I do not wish to argue that theories should be discarded in favor of local storytelling, I would like to point out that many aspects of ecological theory, theories of design in architecture and engineering, cultural theory, and economic theory are untested. Even the theories that have been tested have rarely been subjected to confirmatory tests by independent investigators in other parts of the world. The robustness of physical and mechanical laws is often touted as evidence that scientific theories are the basis for the successful development of new technologies. But in our efforts to achieve sustainability, we should acknowledge that the sciences of ecology and conservation biology, economics, and public health have not achieved that level of predictive ability. I think that our definition of rigorous, reliable thinking for the development and testing of visions of sustainability must rely instead on more time-tested strategies and on the practices of storytelling to build a collective confidence that greater sustainability is a goal we can achieve. We do not need theory or predictive models to confirm, for example, that human communities that use toxic substances will, as an unavoidable consequence, from time to time spill them into the environment; or that as the influences of urbanization expand on every continent of the globe, one of the major reasons for unsustainable resource use is that we have simply developed too much of our land base.

As the news media continue to misuse scientific debate to present many land use arguments as polarized cases of pro and con, we clearly need a richer and more compelling vehicle for sharing the knowledge and visions that can lead us to recognize unsustainable policies and practices. The question is, what can that vehicle be, and how can we continue to learn while we drive it? My argument here is that the vehicle we need is a body of folklore that can more complexly represent what sustainability is, what it is not, and how we can steer in its direction. Visions of sustainability can be coded into these stories to create new mental models of what is possible, how issues are connected, and how we will need to act to sustain ourselves both individually and collectively in a changing world. I would call this intentional coding of visions into stories the Lyotard Principle, if it didn't automatically conjure an image of the whole world wearing body suits and tights. Maybe we can just leave it as the Narrative Principle, and move on to some more specific examples before worse puns come to mind.

CODING VISIONS INTO STORIES

I have imagined that there are three pre-eminent messages that must be included in a set of stories that supports a vision of sustainability. These messages are (1) that we need to cultivate our insight into the challenges we face; (2) avoid the human tendency towards ideological and technological hubris; and (3) perceive the patterns in our landscapes that have implications for ecological processes and human health. In the three sections below, I'll present a core story and some related stories for each of those three messages, in order to demonstrate how messages can be coded into narratives.

Sight and insight

Scholars of folklore know that complex cultural information can be transmitted through story cycles, in which individual stories build into epics (in the case of hero tales) or, to borrow a metaphor from the Irish writer Angela Bourke, individual stories can weave a net of belief across a landscape that is pegged down in specific places by local details (Bourke, 1996). In this 'net' or epic series, certain stories become more popular or contain information that is critical to understanding the others. I'll take the risk of referring to these stories as 'core stories' in a body of folklore, because I would like to propose several stories that I think would be good core stories for a folklore that supports sustainability. The first of these comes from the body of stories that comprises Norse mythology:

Odin and the Oracle of the Well

Long ago, there was a time when a race of giants attacked the villages of Odin's people. The villagers begged their hero, Odin, king of the gods, to rescue them from this overwhelming invader. Recognizing the extraordinary difficulty that his people faced, Odin traveled to a sacred place to seek the advice of the Oracle of the Well. When he arrived at the cave that contained the Well, he approached it and asked the Oracle how to help his people save themselves from their attackers.

'The price of the answer to your question is one eye', replied the Oracle, from deep within the Well.

Odin agreed to make the sacrifice, and at the cost of great pain, tore out one of his own eyes and dropped it into the well. He waited for the Oracle's answer. Finally, it said, 'If you wish to know the answer to your question, you must look with both eyes'.

Other Norse stories that referred to Odin as a one-eyed hero-god relied on the audience's knowledge of this particular story to provide significance to Odin's lack of an eye, and to connect that physical blindness to the wisdom that provided him with superhuman insight. The story of Odin's encounter with the oracle in the well makes this connection in a way that can be interpreted as tragedy, or ironic humor, or symbolic wisdom. A traditional storyteller would provide additional detail to make the story longer and more suspenseful for an audience, and to create a tone that encouraged the audience to interpret Odin's actions as tragic, comic, or wise.

This story is an important one in the story cycle I imagine as a vehicle for conveying a vision of sustainability. Although it is simple and brief, it offers ample opportunity for complex, multi-layered interpretations. Mine is that, first, we often do not realize what alternative senses or forms of 'vision' are available to us as ways of gaining insight when we confront situations that we have defined as problems. And second, that multiple perspectives are fundamentally necessary for insight, even when bringing them to bear may seem to involve extra pain and extraordinary effort.

There are many related stories that could help strengthen and enrich our interpretation of this one, as should be the case with what I have called 'core stories'. For example, I remember reading an analogy made in a science fiction novel that could be developed as a supporting story on this theme. The analogy was that the act of defining a problem is like slicing an apple; there are many options for how to slice it, but if you ask someone to draw a sliced apple for you, they almost always draw a slice through the middle, made from top to bottom. But a drawing of four irregular-sized ellipses spaced close together also represents a slice of an apple (at least of the Red Delicious variety), if you were to slice it horizontally, close to its base (see Figure 14.2). We could think of a worm in an apple as analogous to the kind of surprise that proves some human actions unsustain-able, like the connection Rachel Carson (1962) wrote of between DDT exposure and thinner song-bird eggshells. If we wanted to find all possible evidence of worms in an apple, we'd have to slice it in an infinite variety of ways. The degree of risk we associate with finding the worm would influence the number of ways we tried to slice the apple. Each slice represents a different perspective, a different opportunity for insight. But the effort to gain this insight comes at greater cost than the effort it would take to slice the apple only once. This story implies that (1) we often limit our representations of a situation unnecessarily, in ways that can be misleading to us, and (2) we must weigh the effort of gaining additional insight against our sense of the magnitude of risks associated with the problem.

And, as it should, that spin-off story reminds me of another. Peter Jacobs, a landscape architect who teaches and practices in Montreal, Canada, tells a story of his work with the Innuit people, a Native culture in northern Canada. As I recall it, he tells of the engineers who came to persuade the Innuit that there was only a minuscule risk associated with accepting the passage of an oil pipeline through their landscape. The engineers offered really small numbers like 0.00001 to describe the probability of a catastrophic leak from the pipeline. This, to the engineers, was evidence of a very low 'risk' (which really meant 'probability of disaster'). But the Innuit replied that the real risk they would have to accept was that, if they allowed this new pipeline to go across their land, they

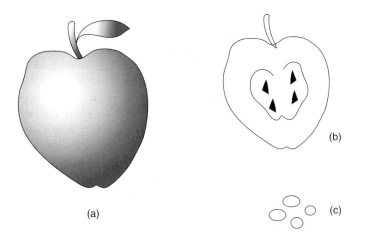

(a)

(b)

(c)

Figure 14.2   Slicing an apple: (a) the whole apple (of the Red Delicious variety), (b) the slice most people would draw if you asked them to show you a cross-section of an apple, and (c) a very particular cross-section, drawn horizontally near the very bottom of the apple.

faced a new risk of losing everything they valued and depended on in their landscape, in the case of a catastrophic leak. No matter what the probability of this leak, why should they accept a risk that could destroy everything they valued about their land? What compensation could ever be sufficient for that?

This story highlights the very common and significant misapplication of probability theory in our thinking about sustainability and risk (Schrader-Frechette and McCoy, 1993). The idea that risk is low because the estimated probability of an event is low is a logical fallacy. One of the basic strategies of sustainability must be to avoid the risk of irreversible losses of our sustainable resources. This is an area in which the rigor of scientific reasoning about statistical significance has often been misapplied, and in which intelligence and wisdom would guide us otherwise if we had the right story to remind us.

Hubris and anthropocentrism

The second 'core story' I would like to propose also comes from the tradition of Native storytelling in the Americas. This tradition is one of such breadth, beauty, and relevance to landscape that I wish the colonial Europeans who settled North America had paid more attention to collecting and learning from these stories. The use of local resources that we have inherited from them would probably be more sustainable if they had. In fact, sometimes I am so struck by the wisdom of the stories told by American indigenous peoples that I wonder whether the most effective vision of sustainability wouldn't be to put their contemporary descendants in charge, by giving the land back to them and just leasing it – conditional on some kind of joint approval of land use decisions. I realize full well that this comment leaves me open to charges that I am idealizing an indigenous culture. But I can't help thinking that future generations will look back at us and wonder why we didn't put more effort into involving the people who lived here before us in managing our common landscapes, no matter how unacceptable that idea is in contemporary politics.

The story is a creation story. I heard it from Charlotte Black Elk, a lawyer and microbiologist who lives and works on the Pineridge Lakota (Sioux) Reservation in South Dakota, USA. I am retelling it here from memory, and apologize for any details I may have gotten wrong as an outsider to that culture.

The Great Flood

In the beginning, the Creator made a wonderful two-legged creature. The four-legged creatures came later. Many years later, a great flood came. This flood threatened to wash all of the creatures away that the Creator had placed on the earth. When the waters receded, the Creator saw that all but one of the animals that had been created had perished. The one surviving animal was the first two-legged the Creator had made. This is the animal that was the most wonderful of all that had been placed on the earth, and the Creator was pleased to see that it had survived. From it, the Creator would make all the other animals.

And that is how it happened that we are all descended from the bear.

Again, our preconceptions are what allow us to appreciate the ironic humor in the ending of this story. The Lakota category of 'two-legged' creatures includes humans, but it also includes bears.

This story has something in common with the old joke heard in the 1970s that told about a doctor who treats two car crash victims, a father and son, and exclaims upon seeing the boy, 'That's my son!' The storyteller then asks the audience, who's the doctor? (Answer: the boy's mother.) It's hard to believe now that this joke was ever a brainteaser, but at the time it helped listeners acknowledge and laugh at their own sexism, which was the reason why they couldn't figure out that the doctor must be the boy's mother – a woman.

Just as that story helped us recognize and laugh at our own sexism, the Lakota story can help us laugh at the anthropocentrism we often display in our concerns for sustainability. Is sustainability only about sustaining human societies, or does it include an argument for sustaining other life forms? If so, which other life forms, and why? Are we really so terrific that it's important to sustain our predominant contemporary culture? Why? What aspects of it are worth keeping? What would be so bad if that way of life ran its course and didn't go on forever as it is now?

This story brings up a whole area of reasoning that we must address if we wish our human cultures to become more adaptable and resilient, as I argue we must if we are to move towards sustainability. People from diverse fields have begun to ask new kinds of questions about the way human beings construct and use categories in language and reasoning. Psychologist Ellen Langer uses the term 'mindfulness' to refer to reasoning that pays explicit attention to the formation and use of categories (Langer, 1989). Her research offers a wide range of examples from different settings, related to everything from data analysis to bidding at an art auction. Similarly, in *Women, Fire and Dangerous Things:*

What Categories Reveal about the Mind, linguist George Lakoff has written about the way that categories connect language to reasoning (Lakoff, 1987), citing work by ethnobotanists (Berlin *et al.*, 1974) and cognitive psychologists as evidence that we create linguistic and mental categories as a result of our embodied experiences in the world. We then use those categories in stories and in all other forms of reasoning, making the manner in which they are defined and constructed quite influential in our ability to understand the world and our role in it.

Engineers and scientists have also begun to seriously question the role of preconceived categories, both in the development of theory and in technological applications. Lotfi Zadeh has developed a field of research into what he called 'fuzzy sets' (see Figure 14.3). Fuzzy sets which are categories in which elements can have graded degrees of membership (Zadeh, 1965). This theory is a generalization of classical set theory, and differs from classical

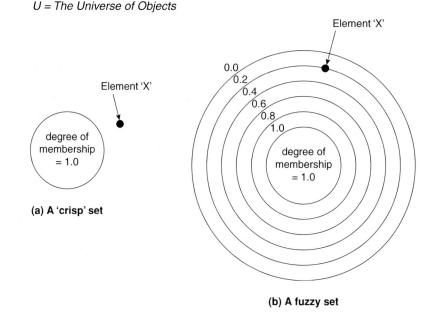

Figure 14.3 A fuzzy set vs. a crisp set. The classic theory of sets requires an element to either belong to the set completely, or not at all (using the Law of the Excluded Middle). Fuzzy set theory relaxes this rule, and allows elements to belong to a set to some degree. The degree of membership is represented using a coefficient that ranges from 0.0 to 1.0.

theory mostly in that it relaxes what mathematicians call the Law of the Excluded Middle (Ross, 1995). This is the axiom that states that an element either belongs to a set or it doesn't, leaving no middle ground in defining membership. It was critical to the methods Aristotle used to develop the classification systems that later became models for scientific classifications during the Age of Enlightenment. Scientist and historian Evelyn Fox Keller has noted that this Law is an example of how widespread the human tendency is to reduce relationships that exist across a gradient to dichotomous concepts (Keller, pers. comm.). She has suggested that this may be related to the fact that anatomically our bodies have bilateral symmetry, and that our species has two sexes; but her point is that this tendency to form dichotomies introduces oppositions into our theories and language that are not defensible on the basis of observed phenomena. Once again, these are preconceptions that should be challenged if we want to move towards greater adaptability and, as a result, greater sustainability.

Categories play significant roles in many complex expressions of ideas, including the predictive models planners and researchers use to decide which land may be developed and which land should be conserved. If we construct our categories of 'development' and 'conservation' in ways that are too simplistic, we will be unable to gain new insights about what has already happened to the land and what we might wish it to be like in the future. As our technologies for mapping the landscape have changed, so have some of our methods for constructing categories and our ability to perceive patterns and recommend spatial strategies for conservation and development. The work of landscape architect Ian McHarg makes an interesting case in point, since the methods and categories he described in his 1969 book, *Design with Nature*, appear to have been influenced significantly by an earlier technological advance in a different field – and have subsequently influenced the use of other new technologies in the world of digital geographic information systems (McHarg, 1969).

In order to explain what I mean, I'd like to provide a little background information for my story.

Design with Nature became a widely read book among people who plan and design landscapes, particularly in the years between its publication in 1969 and the early 1980s. I was re-reading the book in 1991 before showing it to students in my classes, and at the same time happened to be reading a book by Susan Sontag called *Illness as Metaphor* (Sontag, 1990). In reading the two books at once, I came across a connection that suggests the origins of McHarg's particularly compelling use of multiple grayscale overlays in mapping.

In the introduction to *Design with Nature*, McHarg describes his experiences as a tuberculosis patient in first a Scottish and then a Swiss sanitarium. It's significant to his book because he says his attitude towards landscape planning was inspired by the open-air setting and philosophy of the Swiss sanitarium, after his experiences with the cramped, untidy and depressing surroundings of the Scottish sanitarium. He also writes that he spent his time reconsidering all that he'd learned in his graduate education, trying to sort and make sense of it all while confined to bed. Sontag describes the life of a tuberculosis patient in her book, and notes the amount of time patients spent comparing their lung X-rays (see Figure 14.4), since those images revealed their state of health and were the main tools doctors consulted in providing a prognosis for recovery. She writes that patients often carried copies of these X-ray images around, folded up in the pockets of their pajamas and bathrobes. McHarg mentions that when he moved from Scotland to Switzerland for a new phase of his recovery, all he brought with him in the move was a small number of personal belongings and a file of X-rays (*Design with Nature*, p. 4).

X-rays use grayscale images to reveal the health of the body. McHarg modified existing overlay mapping techniques by introducing the use of multiple grayscale layers (see Figure 14.5). In his method, dark areas meant that many factors combined to rule out new development, while light areas indicated that a particular form of development might be possible without disturbing the health of the land. It's plausible to infer that the technology of medical imaging provided the model for this persuasive technique. It may have seemed compelling

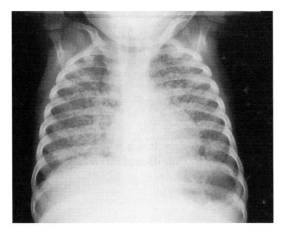

Figure 14.4 An X-ray image of tuberculous human lungs: perhaps the technology of medical imaging provided the model for McHarg's overlay mapping technique.

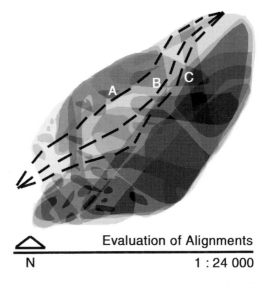

Evaluation of Alignments

N   1 : 24 000

Figure 14.5 McHarg's mapping technique used overlapping layers, each of which represented a particular theme using shades of gray. The final map, made by assembling all of the thematic layers, allowed a planner to see if there were any suitable sites left at the end of the analysis for the intended land use change. These potentially suitable sites would appear as relatively light areas in the final map.

to McHarg himself because of his personal experience reading X-rays, those grayscale images that were very significant to understanding his personal state of health and prognosis for recovery. The story of his own sickness and recovery was clearly important to McHarg; so much so that he used it as the introduction to that now-famous book on his philosophy and method, *Design with Nature*. My point is that a combination of stories, personal experiences, mental categories, and the representations we use to make use of those categories exerts an extraordinary influence on both the visions we develop and the power of their expression.

Perceiving significant patterns

Landscape ecologists like Richard Forman have written about the changing patterns of landscape using the analogy of a shifting mosaic (Forman, 1995). In relation to sustainability, Forman proposed that it may be possible to optimize the spatial patterns of this mosaic using a knowledge of the ways that spatial patterns influence ecological processes as diverse as the movement of animals, seeds, and fire (Forman, 1990). We might try to harvest trees in forested landscapes to preserve the largest possible contiguous patches of trees, for example, and control those cuts

so that we maintain corridors among those woods that animals can travel through to get from patch to patch. The idea of the shifting mosaic is that people can alter landscapes over time, as long as they protect the critical 'skeleton' of large patches and movement corridors needed to preserve the diversity and habitat quality of all life. Woods can regenerate, wetlands can disappear and re-appear, grasslands can be tilled and re-planted – as long as at any given moment in time, the dimensions of the mosaic pattern allow critical ecological processes to occur.

There are several risks to sustainability in this idea, although it may turn out to be the only politically acceptable option we have for conserving the landscape. The major risk is the possibility that we will miss some critical process or dimension in our 'optimal plan' for a particular landscape, and as a result, we may lose what we had wanted to keep. The kind of large-scale experiment that this idea proposes may be most appropriate in landscapes that are already disturbed, like agricultural landscapes, second-growth forested areas, and suburban regions. But the experiment will be quite difficult in areas where there are lots of resident humans – in suburbia, for example, or in densely-populated agricultural landscapes. It will be difficult there in part because contemporary people have very few stories that reinforce the sacredness of the backyard woodlands and greenbelts that would form the skeleton of such an optimal landscape structure.

In the storytelling tradition of one densely populated agricultural landscape, nineteenth-century Ireland, there are some very good examples of stories that helped human communities preserve a sense of sacredness in their common landscapes. One of the interesting things about this tradition of stories is that it accomplished some of the goals of biodiversity conservation without trying to convince humans that small animals or insects are worth saving. Instead, it starts from a very different angle.

These stories rely on a belief in the existence of anthropomorphic creatures that live in a parallel world to the human world; a world occupied by territorial creatures that will fight back with power and intelligence when their world is infringed upon. In many of the Irish stories, these creatures (known in English as the Fairies) are human-sized, recognizable as non-human only because they wear blue clothing from head to foot, have bright red hair, and often play tricks on humans using exceptional powers. The Fairies are said to live under hills and large rocky outcrops and under water, but to travel surface roads and pathways at night, or in the daytime at particular times of the year. I heard a number of these stories from Angela Bourke, a professor of Irish at University College in Dublin, whom I met while she was a visiting professor at Harvard University in 1994. She emphasized the cultural function of this story tradition, in that warnings about dangerous Fairies occupying certain areas of the landscape served to create off-limits zones in a densely populated world. These zones served social purposes as no-man's land between disputed properties, and perhaps as places where unsanctioned activities could take place. But they also created small 'islands' and 'corridors' of potential habitat where human disturbances were infrequent.

My core story from this complex tradition of stories comes from Canada's maritime landscape, and was collected by Barbara Rieti (1991). Rieti provides an extensive social context and recounting of Fairy stories from Newfoundland's Avalon Peninsula in her book, *Strange Terrain*. The story below is actually three stories from that book, joined together here to provide an example that has more breadth, and conveys a more complete sense of the extent to which fairy stories were embedded in that region's landscape by its people.

The Fairy Path
(in the words of Barbara Rieti's informants)

This story recounts what happened to a man who moved his house to a woodland full of old footpaths:

> It seems that he had built his house on a fairies' path. One night when Jack was at a dance, his mother heard a young child walking back and forth along the front of the house crying. The child stayed there crying all night, and when Jack got home she told him. Later Jack heard the crying himself while in the stable. He eventually moved his house again and had no more trouble from the fairies.
>
> (Rieti, 1991, p. 55)

Another story tells of a family that moved from their house, after losing all but one of eleven children to suspicious illnesses, and finally losing the mother as well. The husband (Mr Butler) finally built a new house across town, having decided that the old one must be on a fairy path (and therefore unlucky), remarried, and had six healthy children. The couple who bought the old house subsequently had two children who could neither walk nor talk. When they relocated the house to the yard next door, they had a third, healthy child.

This story tells of the goings-on that continued to affect Mr Butler's former neighbors near the fairy path:

> Behind the house is a large cliff and on the other side of this mountain is believed to be the home

of the fairies. On certain days goats can be seen running – or could be seen, in those days – down from the mountain as if being chased by the fairies. This occurrence was usually followed by a heavy wind or rainstorm. This was attributed to the fairies who were upset. Several other families moved across the road so they would not be affected by the evil of the fairies. Sometimes during the summer rocks would fall down the side of the mountain for no reason whatsoever. This, according to Bill, was the fairies driving people away from their home. Today in Butlerville the foundations of the houses can be seen. The remaining houses in the area have been boarded up and have not been lived in since. Many of the people in the community are familiar with the story and believe in the power of the fairies and do nothing to get them upset.

(Rieti, 1991, p. 57)

Another couple lived peacefully in the community of Avondale until one night they were disturbed by a huge racket, and went downstairs to discover their door swinging open. They called in the priest to help them figure out what to do:

The pastor told him to check old paths to the bog behind his house. He found an old path and sure enough when neighbors had put up their new picket fence it crossed the path and the fence joined on to his, which went to the corner of the house, thus blocking off the passageway of the path to the house. Immediately Bill took down the obstruction. This solved the mystery of the racket and the swinging door.

(Rieti, 1991, p. 58)

It would be difficult to over-estimate the complexity of the relationship between stories like these and people's behavior. The storytellers themselves have varying degrees of belief in the stories, as do their audiences. But the lesson they offer is that there are places in the landscape where one should not put a house. This very simple statement has turned out to be one of the most difficult issues for American planners to address as we seek realizable forms of sustainability: where are the appropriate limits to suburbanization, and how can landowners be persuaded to accept them without generating legal conflicts over the limits of government authority? What beliefs and observations can we use as a basis for such limits? What stories, maps, and studies will persuade contemporary people that the concerns are valid, with sufficient persuasive power to bring about the permanent protection of a sustainable network of habitat patches, corridors, lakes and waterways?

Both maps in Figure 14.6 represent a hypothetical farmhouse and its surrounding landscape, for the sake of example. The left-hand map shows (a) two suspected 'fairy paths', and (b) an area that was suspected of having frequent fairy activity (in which they had been seen dancing in the wet meadow, or encountered on the ridge or in the woodlot). The right-hand map shows zones identified for a landscape pattern analysis: (A) the road and farmstead; (B) wooded patches; (C) a wetland patch; (D) two riparian corridors; and (E) a ridgeline corridor. Fairy activity was often described in areas formed by the edge of two different ecosystems (a forest and meadow, or a wet area within a mesic field) and where a stream or ridgeline formed a pathway through a landscape. My point here is that, in this example, conserving areas associated with fairy legends could serve the added purpose of conserving areas important to ecological functions.

Two excellent and recent examples of this link between human self-interest and biodiversity come from the growing literature on the connections between human health and the environment. Sandra Steingraber, an ecologist and poet, has written of the influence environmental contamination has on the development of cancer in humans and other animals (Steingraber, 1997). She has traced the spatial patterns of contaminated soils, air, and water, and demonstrated that each of us has a history of specific exposures that she calls our 'ecological roots', that can be defined by knowing where we have lived at different phases in the development of our bodies, the food we have consumed, and the activities in which we have been engaged.

One of her most compelling stories is of her trip back home to her native landscape of central Illinois, an agricultural region that is the source of much of the corn syrup produced for use in the American food industry. In that trip, she recognizes that the tall grass prairies that covered the state for several millennia are now only present as the soil itself; in the molecules of deep, black soil are the molecules of the grasses and forbs that grew in that landscape. Next she calls on her American reader to recognize that, even if they have never been to Illinois, if they walked that soil they would, in a sense, be walking on familiar ground – because as the grasses became soil, and the soil became corn, and the corn became corn syrup, we have consumed that soil. In a literal sense, with no mythical transmutation required, those soils have become a part of us all. We *are* central Illinois. The recognition of that simple fact could utterly change a person's sense

of the limits to their self-interest, and increase the political will to practice a more sustainable form of agriculture.

In an equally compelling set of essays, the book *Biodiversity and Human Health* (Grifo and Rosenthal, 1997) presents the connection between the spread of pathogens and the global destruction and degradation of the habitats of non-human species. In examples ranging from the Asian flu to Lyme Disease and the fish-borne pathogen, *Pfiesteria*, the authors detail situations in which human degradation of habitat has allowed pathogens to flourish in stressed non-human populations. These pathogens, in a limited but significant number of cases, can cross hosts to seriously affect human health as well. Other chapters argue that global emissions that have thinned the ozone layer allow

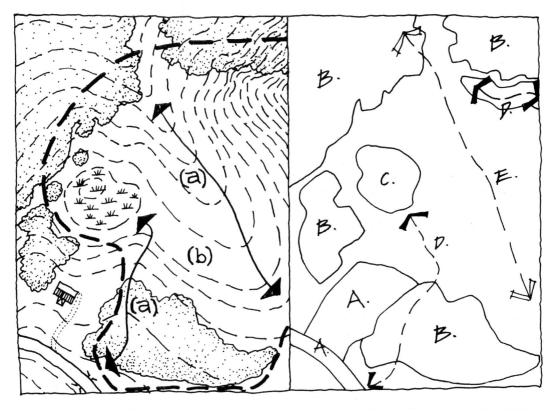

Figure 14.6 A hypothetical farmhouse and its surrounding landscape showing 'fairy paths', and zones identified for a landscape pattern analysis.

harmful radiation that suppresses the immune response of humans and other animals, creating a biological environment ripe for epidemic disease events.

These stories, rich in detail and scientific support, teaches us that humans are not isolated at the top of the food chain; rather, we are holding the end of the chain of cumulative impacts that determine health and wholeness. Perhaps this would be a good era in which to return to the metaphor of a 'Great Chain of Being' promoted by Anne Conway and other vitalist philosophers of the late seventeenth century (Conway, 1982). A vision of sustainability that is based only on the mainstream philosophical heritage of modern science cannot provide us with enough tested theory to prescribe courses of action in a world of complex, cumulative impacts. While fairy stories are surely unlikely to be the alternative, some form of philosophy and 'new tradition' of storytelling that allows us to see ourselves, our interests, and our actions in a larger historical and biological context is absolutely necessary to a successful vision of sustainability. From my own perspective in the academy, I think that we are at the threshold of a new age of natural philosophy that will draw our attention to alternative ways of ordering the complexity of our world and of our experiences as human beings.

I argue that it is precisely this re-ordering of our mental models that is the most critical step we can make towards achieving greater sustainability. That's the role that our visions can play – offering alternative sets of values, priorities, and roles that can be implemented and reinforced by the practices of individual people, small groups, and larger cultural communities. It can begin with a set of core stories that promote insight, help us to avoid hubris, and allow us to perceive hidden patterns in the landscapes we live in.

Each of the core stories I've presented carries a message – coded in the experiences, behavior and attitudes of its protagonists. Those three messages are that we must:

- develop insight into the nature of our current challenges;
- avoid the human tendency towards ideological and technological hubris;
- perceive patterns in our landscapes in new ways, but particularly as they affect ecological processes and our own biological 'wholeness'.

Taken together, these three messages are the supporting framework of a vision of sustainability. The stories I've included here are the beginning of what could become a story cycle, that evolves to present and re-present those messages with different protagonists, different settings. These multiple stories could subsequently be performed (and metamorphosed by those performances) in countless ways, and in countless local places, as the 'small narratives' preferred by Lyotard's post-modern philosophy. That evolution of stories and story cycles would be a rich medium in which to cultivate a lasting, shared vision of sustainability.

LANGUAGE AS INFRA-STRUCTURE, LANDSCAPE AS INFRASTRUCTURE

As the building material of stories, language is an essential component of visions and terminology bears the fingerprints of ideas. The concepts we craft or harness in a vision are coded into stories by our use of terminology, in association with our underlying mental categories. When we consider crafting a vision of sustainability for urbanized landscapes, for example, we come up against a historical division in our language and mental categories that provides us with the terms 'city' and 'countryside'. These terms are absolutely inadequate to describe the sprawling patterns of urbanization that have occurred in most parts of the world over the last century. Likewise, the terms 'urban' and 'rural' have lost most of their meaning in these sub-urban regions – whether they consist of the villas of the middle class or the informal settlements of landless people. Many authors have argued that re-shaping these urbanizing regions is the geographical key to landscape sustainability. But what word could we use for these relatively new settlements that would convey their future potential as part of a different vision, one that can move them toward greater sustainability?

If we want to build stories that convey a vision of sustainability, we will need to come up with terminology that challenges our preconceptions at the same time as it acknowledges them. These terms are the basis for new visions and new stories. But like good poetry, the terms we use should combine multiple meanings in interesting ways. Designers and inventors have used this linguistic strategy for centuries – perhaps forever. Ebenezer Howard's advocacy of something called a 'Garden City' relied on a term that is practically an oxymoron (Howard, 1902). It combines two very different mental categories into a challenging new term that represents a challenging concept, particularly for a pre-suburban era. Even the modern term 'sustainable development' grew from initial status as an oxymoron – reflecting a conceptual dissonance we have all but forgotten in our current familiarity with the term. Gro Harlem Brundtland, leading author of the UN report that promoted this term in 1987, has herself commented on the choice of this term as an explicit exercise in what she called 'constructive ambiguity' (Brundtland, 1989). By putting apparently opposite terms side-by-side, the UN Commission on Environment and Development hoped to bring groups together that had been polarized (WCED, 1987).

What terms could we use to re-conceive the nature and future potential of urbanizing landscapes, a key problem in the sustainability of many regions? Since I consider the term 'suburban' too general to allow us to imagine the actual and potential nature of these places, I present a list of options below as examples of both the problem and the opportunity offered by terminology. The main issue here is whether we can come up with a language that supports perception of the significant patterns of landscape that comprise the ecological infrastructure of sustainability.

As I see it, this language is the infrastructure of our stories and mental models. Terminology, when it

challenges our preconceptions and is based on new concepts, offers the building blocks of a shared vision that is something other than business-as-usual. The terms below each suggest different goals for the functionality and symbolic meaning of new urban settlements. Several of them incorporate language from the vocabulary of landscape ecology, which may be critical to combining a knowledge of natural processes and functions with human goals. Other terms are clearly laden with past cultural meanings, like 'wilderness', and for that reason function more as 'constructive oxymorons' when combined with the term 'city'.

Terms for new urban regions:

Habitat city	Boat city
Metro patch	Underground city
City field	Walled city
Network city	Parkland city
Wilderness city	Gradient city
Metro mosaic	Restoration city
Bridge city	

These are not all new terms; the 'walled city' idea, for example, has been around for millennia. But if we use it to mean we wish to wall out contaminated groundwater, for example, rather than human attackers – or to wall *in* the impacts of human activities – an old form takes on new possibilities. Some combination of the vocabularies of cultural history and landscape ecology must, I believe, offer significant potential for us to re-invent our understanding of those rapidly-expanding landscapes of human settlement that surround older city cores. In this larger metropolitan landscape, we must create and maintain habitat areas and wildlife corridors, allow for clean water to travel at the surface in streams, lakes and wetlands, disperse polluted air, and conserve and improve the fertility of soil. Yet we have such a paucity of terms for this territory, in part because it is relatively new and in part because outdated assumptions, linked to unquestioned and outdated mental categories, cloud our perception of these landscapes.

A different strategy would be to start from the component parts and work upwards, by re-inventing our terms for the constituent elements that drive the development of infrastructure networks within these extensive sub-urban patterns – the house, the street, and the pipe (or ditch). Few people realize, for instance, that surface streets are 'streambeds' for stormwater run-off. Even fewer recognize that, in addition to the rivers and lakes we see at the surface of the landscape, there are other rivers and lakes underground.

Urban historian Sam Bass Warner, Jr., has named three urban rivers – the river of surface and groundwater, the river of stormwater travelling in sub-surface pipes, and the river of drinking water that becomes wastewater, also flowing underground (Warner, 1994). Figure 14.7 represents Warner's 'three rivers' metaphor for urban hydrology. It shows a central city on a river, and an outlying residential district. The white arrow (a) represents the first of Warner's 'rivers' – the river of surface water and groundwater. Smaller arrows on the right side (also labelled 'a') show the link between the two, as surface water infiltrates the soil to become groundwater. The second metaphorical river is the river of stormwater (b), that falls as rain or snow and runs off city streets and rooftops into an underground network of storm drains. The third 'river' is the river of water taken from a water supply source (a reservoir or aquifer) that passes through our homes and our bodies before it becomes wastewater. This river also travels through a network of underground pipes, that are under positive pressure when the water is clean but are no longer under pressure when they convey wastewater. Similarly, our concept of the watershed as a meaningful unit of landscape breaks down into a wholly different three-dimensional network of shapes in landscapes that have been developed with roads and underground drainage systems. There, the watersheds are tiny, fragmented areas overlying sprawling spider-webs of pipes that often siphon off groundwater as well as surface water, or leak sewage into the surrounding groundwater, or allow vapors to seep upwards into buildings from groundwater that, in a landscape of cars and trucks and gas stations, is often contaminated with volatile organic chemicals.

The language we use to convey the definition and significance of these elements of spatial pattern forms the conceptual infrastructure for our visions of sustainability. Meanwhile, stories provide us with aids for navigating that conceptual infrastructure, for choosing our direction and for checking our course, since through the example of a protagonist the audience can be provided with a link between knowledge and action.

This attention to language is not just a way to enhance the rhetoric of sustainability. Evelyn Fox Keller and others have written of the importance of metaphor and analogy in scientific research, where ideas are formed and tested to build theory (Keller, 1995). In my own current research, I am trying to identify spatial patterns that would allow urban designers to map the geographical distribution of the impacts of urbanization on ecological processes. The difficulty is that it's hard to know which spatial patterns might be worth examining, and what new ones can be defined that could have a measurable impact on specific processes. In addition, the categories used to classify the landscape exert a fundamental influence on the patterns that can be defined. The connection between the land classification used in this type of mapping and the underlying mental categories of the researcher is undeniable, and is something worth studying in and of itself. Choices of language in research can reveal these underlying categories. A new vocabulary of re-conceived landscape elements would help to create a theory of ecological infrastructure for both urban designers and urban ecologists.

The ecological infrastructure of a landscape forms its physical and biological skeleton. But we are often unable to perceive the patterns that are of new significance to the processes that we wish to sustain, because we lack both the mental categories and the terms that could provide labels for those patterns. Visions can lead the way for both research and design, to the extent that they help conceptualize new patterns or elements in a re-invented, sustaining infrastructure – an infrastructure we have not used recently in urban design. I've generated a brief list of possible terms below as examples. It's a throw-away list at this point. Making these terms meaningful would require specific examples of their use in urban design, and stories that reinforce the most viable ones through repeated use. But I include

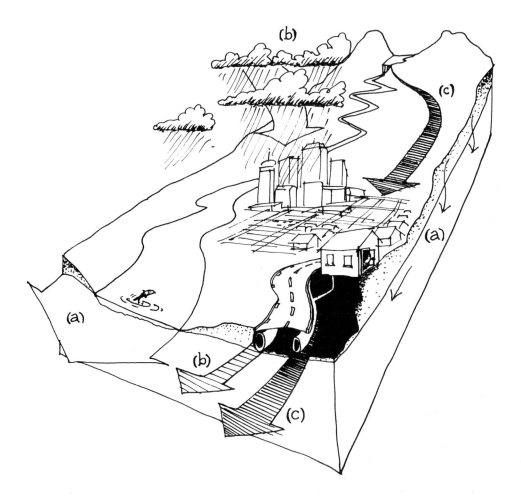

Figure 14.7   Warner's 'three rivers' metaphor of urban hydrology.

them here because they show the challenge of combining terms related to landscape ecological functions, terms related to human health and human bodies, and terms related to urban form. That is the kind of powerful mix we will need, in order to communicate compelling visions of sustainability for particular landscapes.

Terms for the critical elements of an ecological infrastructure

Park bridge
Park shoulder
Metro vein
Arterial stream

Buffer park
Park spine
Park wall
Corridor belt
Metro edge
Urb-belt
Metro-bosque
City vein

Heart stream
Green lung
Rain fields
Shrublawns
Urbfields
Mall meadows
Water eyes
(for wetlands, from a Spanish term for springs)

I present these terms without definition because I hope that readers will imagine their own possibilities for meaning. Language and meaning are constantly evolving, and do so differently in different places. This cultural dynamic seems to provide the primary motivation for several academic conferences each year, as various disciplines attempt to standardize the relationships among terms and ideas. But the meta-stable nature of language and terminology is a good thing, in that it indicates change and offers opportunities for insight into how our ideas and experiences are themselves metamorphosing over time.

As a specific example, it seems to me that the development of new adjectives and adverbs often precedes the development of new nouns (or new meanings for old nouns). 'Green', for example, is now applied to other nouns to produce a new meaning that refers to reduced environmental impacts. 'Fish-friendly' (or 'salmon-friendly') is a favorite new adjective here in the Pacific Northwest, where American government agencies are trying hard to re-frame their activities as helpful to the salmon species that are now listed as threatened by their federal government. We now refer to 'fish-friendly' dams, 'fish-friendly' culverts under roads, and say that our approach to resource planning is a 'fish-first' approach. Although writers like George Orwell have satirized this tendency for government agencies to promote the evolution of official oxymorons (Orwell, 1961), I am more optimistic. Changes in language can indicate changes in practices and goals. I am optimistic about these changes in language if, and I must stress 'if', the underlying ideas we employ in planning and designing landscapes are also changing, and the implementation of these plans and designs results in measurable improvements in environmental quality and human understanding.

LANGUAGE, VISION, AND STORIES – A CONCLUSION AND A BEGINNING

I am not arguing that we can or should create a vision of sustainability based on fairy stories, or Native American belief systems, or Norse myths. But I do think we need to find stories that can provide people with an immediate connection between their environment and their self-interest. As long as sustainability is discussed as something one 'should' do or want, rather than something that it is in our own best interest to seek, it is not likely to be widely implemented. It will remain solely the domain of its orthodox members, who wag their fingers at the rest of us from a position of what they see as moral superiority. I suspect that there can be no real sustainability if it is only a moral 'elite' that practices it. The trick to increasing our chances of achieving greater sustainability is to find a way to influence the political will of our larger communities. If there's one thing we've learned from landscape ecology, global climate change studies, and epidemiology, it's that no place is truly separate from the larger influences of human action. That's a story we must share with a very wide audience indeed.

It is impossible for any one person, or group of persons, to develop the entire infrastructure of stories and language we need to support international visions of sustainability. But it is certainly possible to develop the small narratives Lyotard recommends for a local landscape context. It is also likely that sharing these stories, language, and visions will allow powerful examples to migrate from place to place, germinating and evolving as they go. That's my hope. My intent in writing this piece is to encourage a more explicit embrace of both storytelling and the use of new language as two strong posts supporting visions of the future.

But two posts cannot support a vision with as much stability as three. The third post, as I see it, is simply having the courage, idealism, and imagination to describe and share visions of a reality that doesn't exist yet. Some visions (and their creators) will be vilified, others implemented, others ignored. Our visions reveal our values and priorities, and leave their creators open to broad criticism. But without these visions, sustainability is nothing but a covert, revisionist philosophy, and will be unlikely to engage the wide audience it needs in order to succeed and, in succeeding, become a part of a shared global culture (with unique local expressions!).

My own very local vision, as I sit here in Seattle, is that I'd like to live long enough to see some radical changes in this region's continuously urbanizing landscape. I'd like to live long enough to be on a crew of volunteers that breaks up freeway concrete and hauls it away. And on another crew that celebrates and helps to maintain the region's lowland prairies by going on 'burn walks' (another invented term). I'd like to be part of an effort to plant sword ferns in wooded cemeteries as nest sites for songbirds, and check the progress of future old growth forests nearby. I'd like to ride an elevated rail line from San Francisco to Seattle, and watch eagles fish for salmon from off of an abandoned highway bridge.

When I look with both eyes, I can almost see it.

REFERENCES

Berlin, B., Breedlove, D. E. and Raven, P. H. (1974) *Principles of Tzeltal Plant Classification; An Introduction to the Botanical Ethnography of a Mayan-Speaking People of Highland Chiapas* (New York, Academic Press).

Bourke, A. (1996) The virtual reality of Irish fairy legend, *Eire-Ireland* 31 (1/2), 7–25.

Brundtland, G. H. (1989) Plenary Lecture in Proceedings of the Forum on Global Change and Our Common Future, held on 2–3 May, at the National Theatre in Washington, DC, and organized by the National Research Council's Committee on Global Change.

Carson, R. (1962) *Silent Spring* (Boston, Houghton-Mifflin).

Conway, A. (1982) *The Principles of the Most Ancient and Modern Philosophy* (First printing, 1690, Amsterdam) P. Loptson and M. A. Hingham (eds) (Boston, Kluwer).

Crawford, E., Shinn, T. and Sörlin, S.(eds) (1993) *Denationalizing Science: the Context of International Scientific Practice* (Dordrecht and Boston, Kluwer Academic Publishers).

Farnsworth, A. and O'Flynn, G. B. (1934) *The Story of Worcester, Massachusetts* (Worcester, MA, The Davis Press, Inc.).

Forman, R. T. T. (1990) Environmental sustainability: the role of spatial configuration, in I. S. Zonneveld, and R. T. T. Forman (eds) *Changing Landscapes: An Ecological Perspective* (New York, Springer-Verlag).

Forman, R. T. T. (1995) *Land Mosaics: The Ecology of Landscapes and Regions* (New York, Cambridge University Press).

Grifo, F. and Rosenthal, J. (eds) (1997) *Biodiversity and Human Health* (Washington, DC, Island Press).

Harding, S. (1998) *Is Science Multicultural?* (Bloomington, IN, Indiana University Press).

Howard, E. (1902) *Garden Cities of Tomorrow* (London, Swan Sonnenschein and Co., Ltd).

Keller, E. F. personal communication.

Keller, E. F. (1995) *Refiguring Life: Metaphors of Twentieth-Century Biology* (New York, Columbia University Press).

Lakoff, G. (1987) *Women, Fire, and Dangerous Things: What Categories Reveal about the Mind* (Chicago, University of Chicago Press).

Langer, E. J. (1989) *Mindfulness* (Reading, MA, Addison-Wesley).

Lyotard, J.-F. (1984) *The Postmodern Condition: A Report on Knowledge* (Minneapolis, University of Minnesota Press).

McHarg, I. (1969) *Design with Nature* (Garden City, NY, Natural History Museum Press).

Orwell, G. (1961) *1984: A Novel* (New York, New American Library).

Radner, J. (ed.) (1993) *Feminist Messages: Coding in Women's Folk Culture* (Urbana, IL, University of Illinois Press).

Rieti, B. (1991) *Strange Terrain: The Fairy World in Newfoundland* (St John's, Newfoundland, Institute of Social and Economic Research, Memorial University of Newfoundland).

Rose, H. and Rose, S. (1976) *The Political Economy of Science: Ideology of / in the Natural Sciences* (London, Macmillan).

Ross, T. (1995) *Fuzzy Logic with Engineering Applications* (New York, McGraw-Hill).

Schrader-Frechette, K. and McCoy, E. (1993) *Method in Ecology: Strategies for Conservation* (Cambridge and New York, Cambridge University Press).

Sontag, S. (1990) *Illness as Metaphor and AIDS and its Metaphors* (New York, Doubleday).

Steingraber, S. (1997) *Living Downstream: An Ecologist Looks at Cancer and the Environment* (Reading, MA, Addison-Wesley).

Warner, S. B. Jr. (1994) A manifesto for the Charles [River], and for you and me, a manuscript prepared for a talk at the Harvard University Graduate School of Design, Cambridge, Massachusetts, 12 February, 1994.

World Commission on Environment and Development (1987) *Our Common Future* (Oxford and New York, Oxford University Press).

Zadeh, L. (1965) Fuzzy sets, *Information Control*, 8, 338–353.

INDEX